ELIZABETHAN AND JACOBEAN JOURNALS 1591–1610

ELIZABETHAN AND JACOBEAN JOURNALS 1591–1610

G. B. Harrison

VOLUME I
An Elizabethan Journal
being a record of those things most talked of during the years 1591–1594

VOLUME II
A Second Elizabethan Journal
being a record of those things most talked of during the years 1595–1598

VOLUME III
A Last Elizabethan Journal
being a record of those things most talked of during the years 1599–1603

VOLUME IV
A Jacobean Journal
being a record of those things most talked of during the years 1603–1606

VOLUME V
A Second Jacobean Journal
being a record of those things most talked of during the years 1607–1610

ELIZABETHAN AND JACOBEAN JOURNALS 1591–1610

Volume I

An Elizabethan Journal

G. B. Harrison

London and New York

First published 1928 by Constable & Co. Ltd

Reprinted by Routledge 1999, 2002, 2004
2 Park Square, Milton Park,
Abingdon, Oxon, OX14 4RN

Simultaneously published in the USA and Canada
by Routledge
270 Madison Ave, New York NY 10016

First issued in paperback 2010

Routledge is an imprint of the Taylor & Francis Group

Publisher's note
The publisher has gone to great lengths to ensure the quality of this reprint but points out that some imperfections in the original book may be apparent.

British Library Cataloguing in Publication Data
A CIP record of this set is available from the British Library

Library of Congress Cataloging in Publication Data
A catalogue record for this book has been requested

ISBN 978-0-415-22144-3 (hbk) (Volume 1)
ISBN 978-0-415-60593-9 (pbk) (Volume 1)
5 Volumes: ISBN 978-0-415-22143-6 (Set)

AN ELIZABETHAN JOURNAL

AN ELIZABETHAN JOURNAL

BEING A RECORD
OF THOSE THINGS MOST TALKED OF
DURING THE YEARS
1591—1594

G. B. Harrison

ROUTLEDGE
London and Boston

First published in 1928
by Constable & Co. Ltd
Reissued, bound in one
volume with
A second Elizabethan Journal
and A third Elizabethan Journal
by George Routledge
& Sons Ltd in 1938
Reprinted in 1950
Reprinted in three volumes in 1974
by Routledge
2 Park Square, Milton Park,
Abingdon, Oxon, OX14 4RN
270 Madison Ave,
New York NY 10016

ISBN 0 7100 7881 1

CONTENTS

" The hand of the Lord was upon me, and carried me out in the Spirit of the Lord, and set me down in the midst of the valley, which was full of bones, and caused me to pass by them round about: and, behold, there were very many in the open valley: and, lo, they were very dry.

" And He said unto me, ' Son of man, can these bones live? '

" And I answered, ' O Lord God, Thou knowest.' "

PREFACE

THIS work originated in the summer of 1921. I was preparing an edition of Will Kemp's *Nine Days' Wonder*, the record of his adventures during his famous dance to Norwich in the spring of 1600,[1] which caused great excitement at the time, and was discussed for years. In that summer Mr. Charles Chaplin had visited England, where he was received most royally. His triumphant progress was a prime item of news in every popular paper, though other events—the first implementing of the Versailles Treaty, for instance—were of greater historical importance. It was likely that though historians and politicians of the future would have much to say about the Versailles Treaty, they would not notice Mr. Chaplin's visit to England as one of the most-discussed events of the summer of 1921. Neither he nor Will Kemp came within their horizon; yet both had a larger place in the hearts of their contemporaries than those more august personages who are usually regarded as historic. It seemed, therefore, that to understand the interests of Englishmen during the age of Shakespeare a new kind of history book was necessary, a record of those things most talked of when Shakespeare, Marlowe, Jonson, Bacon, Donne, and the rest were writing and first being read.

It was not easy at first to decide the form of such a book It should be something more coherent and intimate than a Source Book, less personal and individual than a private diary. At the same time chronology, as exact as posible, was essential, for English literature developed so rapidly during the last decade of the sixteenth century and the first of the seventeenth that the difference of even a few weeks sometimes altered the whole conception of its growth. It seemed therefore that the

[1] See iii, *Eliz. Journal*, pp. 68–79.

book should be a Journal, and as far as possible a day by day record.

There were difficulties in this arrangement. Many records can only be dated approximately ; and even with those which bear a date there is abundant chance for mistakes, especially in the first quarter of each year, because in the 1590's there were three methods of reckoning the beginning of the year. The regnal year, dating from the completed years of the Queen's reign, began on 17th November ; the year of the Christian era began with the feast of the Annunciation—25th March ; but the reckoning of the Julian Calendar, which started the year on the 1st January, was coming into use. Hence a document dated 1st February, 1590, may belong either to 1590 or to 1591. This practice has caused much confusion, particularly in the dating of books, for unless there is some means of checking, either by an entry in the *Stationers' Register* or a dated preface, it is often impossible to tell in which of two years a book first appeared.

With a few exceptions each entry in the *Journals* was based on a contemporary source, which is recorded in the Notes ; but I used my sources freely, at one time borrowing phrases, sentences, and even whole pages, at another condensing or paraphrasing as suited my purpose. I did this deliberately, believing that if the book was to have any artistic unity all the events should be seen in the same perspective, for it was my hope that the *Elizabethan Journals* should be readable and not merely a work of reference.

To preserve the unity of tone, and especially as I was as often trying to convey a mood as to state a fact, it was necessary to preserve a contemporary style of writing. There was, as I well realized, a danger that the whole might smack of 'Ye Olde Village Inne' ; but the problem of how a historical work should be written is considerable, and especially when the author is trying to convey something more than information ; and I agree entirely with Anatole France's observations in his *Life of Joan of Arc* :—

"I believe that unless it possesses a certain unity of language a book is unreadable, and I want to be read. It is neither affectation of style nor artistic taste that has led me to adhere as far as possible to the tone of the period and to prefer archaic forms of language whenever I thought they would be intelligible, it is because ideas are changed when words are changed and because one cannot substitute modern for ancient expressions without altering sentiments and characters."[1]

Each entry was therefore recorded as it might have been noted down by a contemporary in his journal; and as gossip varies from place to place I imagined the diarist to be such a man as Edward Knowell, senior, before he began to take his family responsibilities too seriously; one who was more interested in events than in their historical significance, and who regarded authors, dramatists, and players as not less important members of the State than generals, politicians, and clergymen. It was essentially, and by intention, a Londoner's Journal.

At the same time I did not keep too rigidly to the idea of a personal diary. It would be a criticism too captious and pedantic that no single man could have known everything here recorded. Gossip at all times is elusive, and in attempting to chronicle the gossip of a past age the difficulty is not so much to find news as to discover how far any particular event was generally known or generally discussed, and in what mood. From the years 1591 to 1594 few private letters survive by which general news can be checked, but from 1595 onwards, when the letters of John Chamberlain and his friends, or of Rowland Whyte to Sir Robert Sidney, become available, and when the Satirists begin to comment on immediate events, it is possible to estimate how far news, confidential or otherwise, was generally circulated.

The Elizabethan gentleman had an excellent nose for news of any kind. Far more was discussed than was ever committed

[1] *Life of Joan of Arc* by Anatole France, translated by Winifred Stephens, 1925, vol. i, lxv.

directly to writing. Moreover, my own experience between the years 1914 and 1919 of conditions of life not wholly dissimilar, showed that those on foreign service in small forces, whether as political officers or soldiers, occupied about a fifth of their leisure time in jests of the kind that I afterwards found in *The C. Merry Tales*, another fifth in planning the agenda of their return to London, and the remainder in prying (and usually with some success) into the affairs of their superiors. More things were bandied about a mess tent than were ever recorded in an official *communiqué*. However, with much that is preserved in manuscript sources, one could only guess whether it was or was not a matter for talk. When there is no check, the chronicler must follow his own instinct whether any particular item was likely to be generally known or discussed. If I occasionally erred on the side of generosity, let it be forgiven.

Actually, however, I was at some pains to verify the publicity of my news items; and in the *Second* and *Last Journals* I have from time to time noted evidence of confidential matters being publicly discussed. It is clear that even the private letters which passed between the Earl of Essex and his enemies at Court were widely known and discussed.

As the Journal progressed, the problems changed. In the *First Journal* there were months when it was difficult to find any news at all. I had therefore recorded, from Henslowe's *Diary*, the performance of plays at the Rose Theatre week by week. In the *Second Journal* there was no room for these weekly lists; for, as the years went on, the records were multiplied fivefold. In the *Salisbury Papers*, to mention but one instance, the Calendar for the four years 1591–4 occupies 622 pages; over 4,000 pages are required for the years 1595–1602. Moreover the Sidney papers, Chamberlain's letters, and the State Papers, Ireland, all began to yield new sources of information. So much material remains that for some months during the last eight years of Queen Elizabeth's reign it would be possible to compile a daily newspaper.

The method of compilation may interest students. First a detailed calendar of the years was constructed, either on cards or in notebooks. The main source for this calendar were such works as Stow's *Annals*, Camden's *Elizabeth*, the various Calendars of State Papers and Historical Manuscripts, the *Acts of the Privy Council*, Birch's *Memoirs*, Collins's *Sidney Papers*, Strype's *Annals of the Reformation*, Chamberlain's *Letters*, Dyson's *Proclamations*, and D'Ewes's *Journals*.

Stow and Camden were particularly valuable as general guides. John Stow's *Annals of England from the first inhabitation* was first published in 1592, re-issued and brought up to date in 1600, 1601, and 1605, and continued by others after his death. Stow kept some sort of diary, and as he had no sense of proportion but a curious interest in the unusual he was frequently more useful than a better historian. William Camden's *The True and Royal History of Elizabeth, Queen of England* (first published in Latin in 1615, in English in 1625–6) is a very different book, and an excellent piece of historical writing. Camden had a large understanding ; he knew how to use his sources, both contemporary pamphlets and original documents, and he had been an eye-witness of many of the events which he described. He was therefore a useful source and often gave some additional detail or valuable comment ; but he wrote when James of Scotland had succeeded Elizabeth, and in retrospect he saw the importance of events in Scotland in the history of England. He gave therefore about the same space to Scotland as to France in his history : if the *Stationers' Register* is any guide publishers sold twenty books on French affairs to one on Scottish.

Then the *Stationers' Register* and the *Short Title Catalogue* were consulted and a list of every book and pamphlet which seemed of any significance was compiled. As the *Journals* were originally intended to be a background to literature I paid particular attention to books printed, and those interested in the Elizabethan book trade will find details in two papers in the *Library*, 1591–4,[1] *Books and Readers*, 1591–4, and *Books and Readers*, 1599–1603, of which the first is summarized in Appendixes 1 and 2 of the *First Journal*. Of over 2,000 entries in the three *Journals*, about a fifth are concerned with books of various kinds. About one in five of contemporary books originally read yielded an entry. Particular attention was paid to news-pamphlets, and to private letters. When this structure had been erected, I began to write the *Journal*.

The first *Elizabethan Journal* appeared in 1928, the *Second* in 1931, and the *Last* in 1933, ending a work planned eleven and begun seven years before. In this volume I noted in the preface : " My purpose in the *Elizabethan Journals* was not to compile a book of reference but to write a journal of those things which most occupied the minds of Englishmen during the years 1591–1603. Such a book, collected from sources so diverse and considerable, cannot be made by any mechanic rule or rigid principle : it must be as much a work of art as of scholarship. Others, doubtless, might have shown themselves more learned scholars or better artists, had they but tried ; but, since no one had hitherto endeavoured to re-create this background to Shakespeare, and many have erred through ignorance of it, I undertook it myself. If the common reader, who is the ultimate judge of all books, has found that the *Elizabethan Journals* have brought a freshness and colour to his reading of Shakespeare and his contemporaries, the work has fulfilled its intention ; and if, further, he has taken some pleasure in the *Journals* themselves, the pains of the author have been well rewarded."

I wish to repeat my grateful acknowledgment to those who in various ways helped me, by advice, guidance, criticism, or proof reading, and particularly to Dr. S. H. Atkins, Mr. R. L. Atkinson, the late Mr. A. L. Attwater (whose memory will not fade in those who knew him), Professor Geoffrey Callender Miss Molly Chamberlain, Dr. D. C. Collins, Professor J. E. Neale, Miss G. Puddifoot, Mr. S. C. Ratcliff, Miss Doris

[1] 4th series, vol. viii, no. 3, vol. xiv. no. 1.

Rosling, Professor C. J. Sisson, the late Sir Emery Walker, Professor J. Dover Wilson. And, most of all, to Professor A. W. Pollard for encouragement when it was most needed and for allowing me access to material which saved me much labour; and to the late Sir Israel Gollancz, who stimulated me to undertake this work and to whose interest and help many scholars, particularly of the younger generation, owed much, and I not least; and to Miss Helen Waddell, whose inspiration, particularly in the earlier volumes, can now publicly yet inadequately be recorded.

G. B. Harrison.
24th August, 1938.

PUBLISHER'S NOTE

For ease of handling and binding we have reverted to the old three volume format for the 1974 impression.

R.K.P.

A BRIEF SURVEY OF THE YEAR 1590

In the beginning of spring, the Queen, lest she should be taken unawares by the Spaniard, made levies of men in England and the south part of Ireland, fortifying Duncannon in the mouth of the river and also Milford Haven in Wales; and for the safeguard of the Navy assigning £8970 yearly. She was at great charges in lending money for the Army in Germany; and for the pay of the garrisons in Flushing and Brille she paid every two months 125,000 florins, and to the 3000 horse and foot serving in the Netherlands 260,000 more. She was also at great charges against the attempts of the Pope and the Spaniard in Scotland.

Nevertheless she repaid beyond expectation the money borrowed not long since of her subjects, so that many wondered whence this money came, seeing she was in no man's debt. But the truth was that, being providently frugal, she scarcely spent anything but for the maintenance of her royal honour, the defence of the Kingdom or the relieving of her neighbours; and Burleigh, the Lord Treasurer, looked narrowly into those that had the charge of customs and imports, by whose avarice much was underhand embezzled, and through negligence much not exacted. Not long before this the Queen being informed by one Carmarden of the mysteries of her farmers of Customs had caused Sir Thomas Smith, the customer, as he was called, who farmed the Customs for £14,000 a year, to pay from thenceforth £42,000 and afterwards £50,000.

Abroad the Zealanders were reconciled with the Hollanders. The ships of the Venetians and Florentines taken by the English were restored and strict proclamation made that no violence should be offered to the Italians, Venetians, French, Danes, Netherlanders or those of the Hanse Towns. Yet the Spaniards were grievously afflicted, many prizes being taken near the Azores, and the castle in the isle of Faiall razed to the ground by the Earl of Cumberland.

Between the Turks and Moldavia peace was established and the Poles saved from the threat of a difficult war.

In Scotland, to confirm amity with the Scottish King, the Earl of Worcester was sent to congratulate him on his marriage and safe return from Denmark, and to signify to him that he and the French King had been chosen Knights of the Garter, and withal to put him in mind to suppress in time the Popish faction growing strong in Scotland. The King received him very graciously, and to show his amity to England sent Colonel Stewart into Germany that some course might be taken with the King of Denmark and the Ambassadors of the Princes for renewing the peace between England, Spain and France.

In France, the rebellion of the Leaguers aided by the Spaniards held many dangers, and in England there was much deliberation whether the old soldiers in the Low Countries should join with the Germans, or whether a strong army should be sent to the Netherlands to stay the Duke of Parma, who was now proposing to come through France, but especially to keep the coast of France from the Spaniard, who was said to be practising to reduce Newhaven by corruption, and send a fleet into lesser Brittany.

In the midst of these consultations, the Duke of Parma entered France with a strong army, after the French King had won a notable victory at Ivry, overran Picardy, victualled Paris, then miserably famished, won Carboil and Laigny, that victuals might be carried into Paris, and led back his forces. On the other side, in the autumn, other companies of Spaniards arrived at Blavet in Brittany under the conduct of Don John D'Aquila, besieged Henebon, a little town on the sea, and took it with the aid of Philip Emanuel, Duke of Mercure, of the House of Lorraine. Against these Spaniards, Henry Bourbon, Prince de Dombes, who was Governor of Brittany with La Noue, craved aid from England, which the Queen and the Council thought not fit to send on the request of a subject, as the King himself did not then request it. Yet the danger was well understood that the Spaniard might bring under subjection a country so convenient for annoying or invading England, Holland or Zealand.

Some urged that the Queen should spare her money and put no trust in the French, alleging that they had been lately treacherous to their own kings, murdering the one who had been a most devout Catholic, and another, professing the reformed religion, they now pursued with popish curses and arms ; that within remembrance of their fathers they had unjustly withdrawn from the German Empire, Metz, Toul and Verdun ; and that they had so often deceived the English in money matters that those creditors whom they meant to deceive they called by a by-word '*les anglais.*' But the Queen, much affecting the safety and honour of the French, rejected these counsels, and when others put her in mind of that saying of Charles of Burgundy, 'that the neighbouring nations would be in happy case when France should be subject not to one sceptre but to twenty petty kings,' she rejected it with much stomach, saying, 'whensoever the last day of the Kingdom of France cometh, it will undoubtedly be the eve of the destruction of England.'

During this year died Ambrose Dudley, Earl of Warwick, and not long after Sir Francis Walsingham, the Queen's secretary.

In Ireland, Hugh Gairlock had accused the Earl of Tyrone of having had secret conference with some Spaniards, shipwrecked in 1588. To prevent this charge the Earl took him and caused him to be strangled, then being summoned to England, upon submission obtained the pardon of the Queen ; undertaking most religiously to keep the peace with his neighbours, not to put any man to death but by law, and to reduce Tyrone into more civility. Being sent back to Ireland, he confirmed these things before Sir William FitzWilliams, the Lord Deputy. Shortly before the Lord Deputy had taken Hugh Roe MacMahon, a great lord in the territory of Monaghan, and hanged him for that he had with banners displayed exacted contributions of his people. His lands were divided between the English and certain of the MacMahons, so that the family might be weakened, being strong and powerful through many tenants and adherents, and the tyranny of MacMahon blotted out together with the title.

Whereupon Brian O'Rourke, a great lord in the neighbouring County of Bren, fearing lest the same might happen to him, took arms against the Queen ; but being hunted and put to flight by Sir Richard Brougham, Governor of Connaught, fled into Scotland, and was by the Scottish King delivered into the Queen's hands when she required it, he protesting that he accounted all the Queen's enemies as his own.

1591

1st January. THE PRIVY COUNCIL.

At the beginning of this year the Lords and others of the Queen's most Honourable Privy Council are Dr. John Whitgift, Lord Archbishop of Canterbury; Sir Christopher Hatton, Lord Chancellor of England, Knight of the Garter; Sir William Cecil, Lord Burleigh, Lord High Treasurer of England, Knight of the Garter; Charles Howard, Baron of Effingham, Lord Admiral of England, Knight of the Garter; Henry Carey, Lord of Hunsdon, Lord Chamberlain, Knight of the Garter; Thomas, Lord Buckhurst, Lord High Butler of England, Knight of the Garter; Sir Francis Knollys, Treasurer of the Queen's Household; Sir Thomas Heneage, Vice Chamberlain to the Queen, Chancellor of the Duchy Lancaster; Mr. John Wolley, Esquire, Secretary for the Latin Tongue, Chancellor of the most Honourable Order of the Garter; Mr. John Fortescue, Esquire, Master of the Great Wardrobe, and Under Treasurer of the Exchequer.

DR. SUTCLIFFE'S 'TREATISE OF ECCLESIASTICAL DISCIPLINE.'

Dr. Matthew Sutcliffe dedicateth to the Earl of Bath his *Treatise of Ecclesiastical Discipline*, which is sent to the press, wherein is confuted article by article the doctrine and practice of those who attack the Church of England, either preferring the Presbyterial Government or disliking the disorders of the Church. Of these, some have consumed their own goods and devoured the late lands of Abbeys and are now so eager that they would digest not only tithes but also glebe and parish churches.

Others are moved by violent ambition, that although they talk much of equality, yet hope to be chosen presidents of the consistory, willing to hazard all and have a part in the government, for they disdain to be governed by others. Added thereunto are the stirring minds of men malcontent who however they fare always deem their present condition most burdensome, and so that they may see an innovation and change care not whether church or commonwealth be changed.

13*th January*. STEPNEY'S 'SPANISH SCHOOLMASTER.'

The Spanish Schoolmaster, by William Stepney, professor of the Spanish tongue in the city of London, is entered, containing seven dialogues, wherein is plainly shown the true and perfect pronounciation of the Spanish tongue, together with proverbs, sentences, the Lord's Prayer, the Articles of belief, the ten commandments and other necessary things. Mr. Stepney giveth many pithy and useful examples, meet for travellers on a great variety of occasions both at home and abroad. Noteth it as a new custom that divers dames in London do break their fast in their beds, and when they have broken it, they will lie down again, and sleep on it.

14*th January*. THE MURDER OF THE LORD BURKE.

Arnold Cosby, better known as Captain Cosby, a professional soldier, well known about the Court, hath stabbed to death the Lord Burke in a field near Wandsworth.

23*rd January*. WRIGHT'S 'PILGRIMAGE TO PARADISE.'

The Pilgrimage to Paradise, a book written by Leonard Wright, is entered, compiled for the direction, comfort and resolution of God's poor distressed children, in passing through this irksome wilderness of temptation and trial, and giving consolation to Christians in the warfare of their passage to Paradise.

25*th January*. THE TRIAL AND CONDEMNATION OF COSBY.

Arnold Cosby was this day brought from Newgate and taken over London Bridge to the Sessions on St. Margaret's Hill, where he was immediately put into the docket. He was wearing a yellow frieze doublet over which a loose nightgown had been thrown. A great pair of bolts was put on his feet and his arms were pinioned, though his hands were free.

Soon after there came to the Court, the Lord Chamberlain, the Earl of Wormwood, Sir George Carey, Knight Marshal of England, and Mr. Popham, the Queen's Attorney General.

For the Queen the chief witness was Mr. Powell of Wandsworth, who declared that the Lord Burke's footman coming to him had told him that his master and Cosby had gone out to fight. Thereon he had immediately taken horse and spurred as fast as he could until he came to a place where the Lord Burke lay wounded and on point of death. There he found a woman giving such help as she could; she had laid her frieze safeguard over him and was trying to stop the bleeding with cloths. The Lord Burke, being asked how he had come by his hurts, replied, 'Cosby hath villainously wounded me to death, I striking never a blow, nor giving thrust, but whilst I was striving to unbuckle one of my spurs, having unbuckled the other before through his persuasions, saying they would be some trouble, he most cowardly thrust me in at the top of the shoulder which ran far into the body; yet if I had striven but two blows with him, it would never have grieved me, had he manfully slain me in fight.' Then procuring a cart, Mr. Powell took the Lord Burke to his own house, where he died about two hours after, twenty-one wounds being found on his body.

In his defence, Cosby declared that the cause of the quarrel was that the Lord Burke had the night before pulled his nose. When they met in the field, having the Lord Burke at his mercy, he had offered him his life if he would break the point of his sword, return to the Court and acknowledge that he had wronged him, fought with him, and been spared by him.

While the jury were away, the Lord Chamberlain spoke to those present, showing how manifestly God had wrought in this case. When Cosby tried to escape on the Lord Burke's gelding, it had broken from him; even his own nag could scarcely be forced to take him to the wood at Wimbledon. Finally, when he passed behind the house where the body lay, the wounds began to bleed afresh.

The jury, after a short deliberation, gave in a verdict of guilty, and Cosby was condemned to be hanged.

27th January. Cosby Hanged.

Arnold Cosby was hanged at Wandsworth for the murder of the Lord Burke near to the place where his crime was committed.

30th January. Sir Edmund York sent to the French King.

Sir Edmund Yorke is to be sent to the French King to treat for the sending of English forces to Brittany. He is instructed when he shall have audience with the King to say her Majesty thinks it strange that in the four months since the Spaniards have invaded Brittany, she has not received any knowledge from him of what he means to do for the repelling of these forces, nor that he has sent any aid to the Prince de Dombes, who is unable with his present power to encounter the enemy though at this time reduced to 1800 men. But it appears from sundry sources that the King of Spain makes ready a greater number of ships, men and victuals to possess himself of all Brittany; whereof her Majesty is very mindful, first for the loss of so rich a dominion as Brittany, and by consequence of the evil neighbourhood of so mighty a Prince possessing so great enmity towards her.

Whilst she was in this doubtful state, there came a gentleman from the Prince de Dombes moving the French ambassador to be a means to her to help him with 2000 footmen to be sent into Brittany, whose charge should be answered by the King. To this she had answered the ambassador that it was a strange thing for her to be required of a subject to send forces into the King's country and more strange would it be for her to send them without the King's knowledge, or even request. Nevertheless having now heard that the succours which are coming in to the King are but few, and that the enemy prosper in possessing all the ports, saving Brest, where they have their galliasses and ships, and intend to fortify the mouths of the ports, the Queen hath told the French ambassador that she is content, if the King so wishes it, to prepare some 2000 or 3000 men or more to be sent into Brittany. For the ambassador's better information certain articles were delivered to him to be sent to the King, but no answer has been received. Sir Edmund Yorke is now to procure answer to every point in these articles and especially to procure for our shipping and people the use of the haven of Brest, the commodity of the roads for the ships, and the town and lodgings for the men; without this assurance neither ship nor men can be in any safety.

1st February. DRAYTON'S 'HARMONY OF THE CHURCH.'

The Harmony of the Church, containing The Spiritual Songs and Holy Hymns of Godly Men, patriarchs and prophecy; all sweetly sounding to the praise and glory of the highest, now newly reduced into sundry kinds of English metre; meet to be read or sung, for the solace and comfort of the godly, written by Michael Drayton, (a gentleman of the household of Sir Henry Goodere), is entered, being dedicated to the Lady Jane Devereux of Merivale. In this book are gathered nineteen songs and prayers from the Old Testament and Apocrypha rendered in English verse.

For an example, the Song of Deborah and Barach, from the fifth chapter of Judges, hath been thus reduced :

Praise ye the Lord, the which revenge on Israel's wrongs doth take,
Likewise for those which offered up themselves to Israel's sake,
Hear this, ye kings, ye princes all, give ear with an accord,
Smile, give thanks, yea sing the praise, of Israel's loving Lord.

And Sisera's death thus :

Jael the Kenit Heber's wife, most happy shall be blest,
Above all other women there, which in the tents do rest,
He asked water for to drink, she gave sweet milk to him,
Yea butter in a lordly dish, which was full trick and trim,
Her left hand to the nail she put, her right the hammer wrought,
Wherewith presumptuous Sisera unto his death she brought,
And from his corpse his head she cut, with mortal deadly wound,
When through the temples of his head, she nailed him to the ground.
He bowed then unto the earth, and at her feet gan fall,
And where he fell there still he lay, bereaved of senses all.

3rd February. FLESH PROHIBITED DURING LENT.

As in years past the killing and eating of flesh during the season of Lent is restrained. Six butchers only may be licensed to kill flesh for the City and liberties, to be bound by bonds of £200 to sell no flesh in Lent but to such sick persons as should show a special warrant from the Lord Mayor. Moreover they shall truly keep books of their daily sales and the names of those to whom they sell, with the quantities and the times.

The Lord Mayor will also cause to appear before him or his deputy before Lent all innkeepers, table keepers, victuallers, ale house keepers, and taverners and to take bonds of every one of them in good sums of money, not under £100 a piece to her

Majesty, not to dress any flesh in their houses this Lent time for any respect except for some person lying in their house that had licence through sickness or any other necessary cause.

As for the butchers and others that come out of the country, certain persons, of whom some shall be named by the Wardens of the Fishmongers' Company, are appointed to watch at the gates where flesh might be brought in to view, search, and intercept it. And if any flesh shall be found to be brought to a person not licensed to eat it, to be forfeited at the discretion of the Lord Mayor for the use of the poor in the Hospitals and prisons of the City, and the bringers imprisoned. If any of these watchmen be found negligent and corrupt in this charge, he is to be committed to prison, there to continue during the whole Lent.

A Proclamation against Piracy.

A proclamation is published to inhibit the offending on the seas of any persons in their ships or goods being subjects of any Prince, Potentate or State in amity with her Majesty. Certain complaints of late are made against some of the Queen's subjects, who have been this last summer under colour of recovering recompense on the Spaniard for the notable injuries by arrests and barbarous cruelties practised in Spain and Portugal, and have taken the ships and goods of the subjects of other princes and states. Lately one ship belonging to the Venetians and another claimed to belong to subjects of the Grand Duke of Tuscany were taken into some of the western ports but are certainly in safety.

Her Majesty doth now command that whosoever hereafter should break any bulk of the goods of any prize (though the prize be lawful) before the title thereto is allowed in the Court of the Admiralty shall be imprisoned, and his ship with the prize forfeited. Likewise any person whatsoever that shall knowingly take any ship belonging to any subjects of her friends and allies, and doth not forbear to keep them, or takes out of them any goods, shall be reputed and tried as a pirate, and receive the due punishment for piracy.

9th February. Job Hortop's 'Travels.'

A book written by Job Hortop is entered called *The Travels of an Englishman. Containing his sundry calamities endured by the space of twenty and odd years in his absence from his native country ; wherein is truly deciphered the sundry shapes of wild beasts, birds, fishes, fowls, roots, plants, etc.*

This Hortop being born at Bourne in Lincolnshire became servant to a gunpowder maker of Redriffe, in whose service he was pressed to serve in Sir John Hawkins' Guinea Voyage in 1567, and appointed to be gunner in the *Jesus of Lubec*. After many sufferings he returned to England in December last. Relateth many strange stories of things seen in his travels. In Guinea two of the company were slain by a sea horse who ate them ; this sea horse being a beast in form like a horse in all proportions, saving that his feet are very short, and his teeth very great, long, and crooked like to the tusks of a wild boar. In this place also be many elephants which the negroes take by policy, for in the day time they search out the haunt of the beast which is every night against a great tree. Then they sever the tree almost in sunder, whereby the elephant coming at night, leaneth against it and falleth on his belly, whereby he cannot rise, being of a huge bigness ; whereupon he roareth and the negroes come and kill him. The elephant hath a great trunk in his nose wherein he draws the negroes to him and kills them.

In the island of Corasa called the River de Latch, they took a monstrous aligarta ; a beast which hath a head like a hog, bodied like a serpent and full of scales on the back, every one as broad as a saucer, his tail long and full of knots, of which one was taken by seven men in the pinnace, using a dog as bait ; and as soon as the aligarta had swallowed the dog they rowed hard until it was choked. This beast was four and twenty feet long by the carpenter's rule ; and his skin after being flayed was stuffed with straw to have been brought to England, but the ship perished by the way.

The General and the other ships soon after came into the port of San Juan de Ullva through stress of weather, where hostages were exchanged with the Spaniards that no occasion for breach of the league might be given ; on our side six of the gentlemen, on the Spaniards' six arrayed in rich habits in the apparel of gentlemen but indeed the basest slaves in their company. But in a few days the Spaniards treacherously set upon the English ships and sunk four, Sir John Hawkins scarcely withdrawing with the Admiral, and Hortop himself escaping from the *Jesus of Lubec* to the General's ship. Hence in great distress through lack of victuals, they sought the river Pannico for water where the mariners mutinied, saying that they would rather be on shore to shift for themselves amongst their enemies than starve on ship board, so that ninety-six wishing to depart were set on shore, amongst whom was Hortop.

This company fell among the Indians and by them were robbed of all their goods, and many of them slain; but in the end Hortop and the remainder were carried to the city of Mexico, where they were examined by two friars and two priests, who willed them to cross themselves and say their prayers in Latin; this many of them did, so that the priest returned to the Viceroy and said they were all good Christians.

In Mexico they stayed two years until they were sent to Spain. On their voyage thither, they discovered a monster in the sea who showed himself three times from the middle upwards, in which part he was proportioned like a man, of the complexion of a mulatto or tawny Indian. When they came near the island called the Serres, Hortop and some others essayed to escape in the pinnace, but being discovered were like to have been hanged had not one of the Admirals of the Spanish ships declared that if he were a prisoner he would have done the like himself. When they came to Spain they were sent to the Contratation House at Seville. A year after Hortop and six others tried to escape but they were brought back, and condemned by the Inquisition. Two were burnt, but Hortop with one other was sent to the galleys, there to row at the oars for ten years, and then to be brought again to the Inquisition House, to have the coat with St. Andrew's cross put on their backs, and from thence to go to the everlasting prison remediless.

Thereafter Hortop served twelve years at the galleys, being thence returned to Seville where he wore the coat four years, but at great risk had it taken off for 50 ducats which Hornanda de Soria, treasurer of the King's mint, lent him; with whom he served as a drudge for seven years until in October 1590 he came away in a fly boat laden with Flemish goods, which was taken by an English ship, and Hortop set on shore the 2nd day of December 1590.

FRAUNCE'S 'COUNTESS OF PEMBROKE'S IVYCHURCH' AND 'EMANUEL.'

The Countess of Pembroke's Ivychurch, together with *The Countess of Pembroke's Emanuel*, by Abraham Fraunce, one of her gentlemen, is entered; *The Ivychurch* being a translation in English hexameters founded on Tasso's Italian and Mr. Thomas Watson's Latin. In his dedication to the Countess of Pembroke, Mr. Fraunce defendeth himself against those who mislike the reformed kind of verse, saying that as there is no penalty appointed for him that would not read, so if any begin to read, when he beginneth to take no delight, let him leave off and go no further. The first part of the *Ivychurch* is in form of a pastoral dialogue wherein Amyntas lamenting of the hardness of his Phillis is at last comforted by her love; the whole being written in such hexameters as these:

Once on a time when Nymphs and Pastors chanc'd to be sporting,
Standing all in a round, and each one whispered a secret,
Into another's ear, poor fool I began to be buzzing,
'Phillis, I burn with love. O take compassion on me;
Help, or I die, Phillis.' But Phillis straight with a lowring
Look and frowning face, and downcast eyes to the groundward,
Blush'd for spite and shame, and gave not a word for an answer,
But conveyed her away, and flew from the place in a fury.

Phillis having died after their betrothal, Amyntas laments her in twelve days of Eclogues.

In the *Countess of Pembroke's Emanuel* are related the Nativity, Passion, and Resurrection of Christ, together with certain psalms of David, all in rhymed hexameters.

13th February. A PETITION OF THE SKINNERS.

The handicraftsmen of the Mystery of Skinners presented a petition to the Queen, complaining of the decay of their trade, which is due in part to the lavish and unnecessary use of velvets and silks, partly to certain bad and ill-disposed persons that roam and range about the realm buying skins which they sell abroad. These men, not having the proper skill to choose or sort out skins, cause those at home, who would otherwise buy, to be put off with inferior skins so that foreign wares are come to be preferred to English.

20th February. THE SCOTTISH KING'S POOR ESTATE.

From Scotland it is reported that the King is in some peril of surprise by the Earls of Arroll, Moray and Athol which will not be prevented because the King is of such a disposition that he will not believe such matters until they are too evident; nor will he be restrained from the fields or in his pastime, for any respect. Such dangers might be avoided if the King had a guard, but this he is not by any means able to maintain, for his table and the Queen's are almost unserved through want. The Queen and her house are more costly to him than his own, all the servants of great place abuse him, serving one another's turn; and the King, being over frank and somewhat negligent, endureth this want and shame, for he hath nothing that he accounteth certain to come into his purse but what he receiveth from her Majesty.

26th February. HARINGTON'S 'ORLANDO FURIOSO.'

The English translation of *Orlando Furioso* upon which Mr. John Harington hath been long employed is this day entered for the press by Richard Field, the printer.

It is said that Mr. Harington first translated that story of Giacondo in the twenty-eighth book, in which are told the adventures of Jocundo and Faustus who discovered their wives to be false, and ranged over Europe to see if anywhere was to be found a faithful dame. But after their wanderings, having tried many ladies, and being at length beguiled even in their own bed by their maid Fiametta, they concluded that fidelity was no part of woman's nature.

'We had a thousand women prov'd before
And none of them denied our request;
Nor would and if we tried ten thousand more,
But this one trial passeth all the rest.
Let us not then condemn our wives so sore,
That are as chaste and honest as the best;
Sith they be as all other women be,
Let us turn home and with them well agree.'

The translation of this story being handed about among the ladies of the Court at length reached the hands of the Queen, who thereupon sent for her godson and severely censured him for endangering the manners of her ladies with so bawdy a tale, laying on him a punishment to translate the whole of the work before he should again be allowed to come into the presence.

11th March. PURITAN DISCONTENTS.

There is much discontent at this time amongst those that favour the Puritan principles; for the labouring and striving to bring in a uniformity causes, and seems likely to cause, nothing but desolation. The best and faithfullest preachers, say they, are cast into prison, sometimes being closely shut up from the speech and company of their dearest friends, degraded and deprived of their livings, some even having six or seven children, who are sent begging, for all the pillars of the church would do for them. Mr. Cartwright has lain in the Fleet since September; Mr. Fenne of Coventry with many more is in the Clink; Udall, a profitable preacher of Kingston-on-Thames, lies sentenced to be hanged for a book called *Demonstration of Discipline*; and having been condemned before as its author, they now try to make him acknowledge it as his doing. His life is spared hitherto by the intercession of Sir Walter Ralegh. All these things seem but a way to bring in popery, for atheism is here already, and soon will overflow the land. It is rumoured that a general demand is proposed not only of the ministry but of all who bear public office throughout the land to subscribe that the authority of the bishops is lawful by God's Word. When the Lord Treasurer was asked to subscribe to it, he answered, 'It is lawfully the positive law; but to say it is lawful by the Word of God, that is another matter.' There the matter stayed for the time.

12th March. RUMOURS.

The loans that are being levied are to meet the triple charge for the companies in Brittany, the ships at sea, and the army coming from Germany. Men are willing to pay because they see the necessity for helping the King of Navarre, and are angry that the Council did not help him more roundly.

The not naming of a Secretary to succeed Sir Francis Walsingham proceedeth from quietness at home, and the Queen's slowness in bestowing places of importance; the great ones about her would each have his friend. The Earl of Essex labours for Mr. Davidson's restitution; the Lord Treasurer for his son, Robert Cecil, and is like to prevail, and the Chancellor concurs, but either there is secret opposition or else the Queen is unwilling. The Lord Treasurer meanwhile executeth the office, as almost all other places of the realm, to the discontent of many.

There is a jar between the Lord Treasurer and the Archbishop of Canterbury because the Treasurer said the Spiritual Courts would fall into the *praemunire* for taking oaths of men against law. The Archbishop answered stoutly, as if the other affected patronage of the Puritans. The Treasurer was sick for a few days upon it.

The Earl of Essex and Sir Walter Ralegh are still rivals, but the Earl of Essex is like enough, if he have a few more years, to carry Leicester's credit and sway.

22nd March. TOWN GOSSIP.

It is said that the Attorney and Solicitor General are busied with proofs against Sir John Perrot, the same who was Lord Deputy in Ireland in '88, and now a prisoner in the Tower. There is much diversity of opinion about him, according as men incline to the Chancellor or the Lord Treasurer, who was said to be sick when Perrot was committed to the Tower and has not since left his chamber.

The Vice-Chamberlain and the Earl of Essex (whose sister is married to Sir Thomas Perrot) favour him; but the Chancellor has a great dependence, and, if his proofs be as evident as his accusations odious, they will weigh all down. He is said to have dealt with the King of Spain to be received into the Church of Rome, and to have practised with the Northern Lords of Scotland; but all the proofs rest on one priest, and he defamed. Advantages are now being taken from his insolent government in Ireland and his irreverent speeches against the Queen, which now come to light, as is usual when men are called in question, and being better proved, make the rest more probable.

The Earl of Cumberland is expected daily to depart with his fleet, but is detained by the lack of money, as the most part of his preparation is at his own charges. His design is upon the King of Spain's treasure. Some of the Low Country's forces are arrived; the rest to make up 2000 were expected daily with Sir John Norris.

The pique between the Archbishop and Lord Treasurer about Ecclesiastical proceedings is thought likely to cause a great quarrel between them. The Puritans are the weaker party but they hope well of the Earl of Essex, who makes Ralegh join him as an instrument from them to the Queen.

25th March. COCKAINE'S 'TREATISE OF HUNTING.'

Sir Thomas Cockaine hath written *A Short Treatise of Hunting: compiled for the delight of noblemen and gentlemen.* Sir Tristram, saith he, one of King Arthur's knights, was the first writer of the exact knowledge of hunting, whose terms in hunting, hawking and measures of blowing he holds to be best and fittest to be used. These first principles of Sir Tristram, joined with his long experience of hunting these forty-two years past, have moved him to write more at large concerning the breeding and training of hounds, terriers, and whelps for hunting the fox, the hare, the roe, the stag, the buck and the otter; together with a note of Sir Tristram's rules for blowing the horn in hunting.

30th March. THE CAPTAINS' PAY.

The schedule of the pay of the forces to be sent to France:

	Per diem.	Per mensem.
The General Captain of the English Forces - - - - - -	£5	£140
Lieutenant Colonel and for the regiment of one-third part of the forces - - - -	40s. and 10s.	£70
Two other Colonels of 2 regiments, besides the Captain of 2 bands at 10s. per diem, to each Colonel - - - -	20s.	£28
A Provost Marshall (6s. 8d.) to occupy the office of a Quartermaster - - - - -	10s.	£14
A Sergeant Major - - -	20s.	£28

	Per diem.	Per mensem.
A Commissary for Musters (6s. 8d.) and for munition (3s. 4d.) -	10s.	£14
Three Corporals at 6s. 8d. a piece -	20s.	£28
A Paymaster (6s. 8d.) with two clerks (3s. 4d.) - - -	10s.	£14

The two cannoneers sent with great ordnance to be paid 12d. per diem each, and two labourers 8d. each.

31st March. CAPTAIN GLEMHAM'S EXPLOITS.

News is come to London of the safety and exploits of Captain Edward Glemham who had been reported lost at sea in a fight with the Spaniards.

Edward Glemham, Esquire, of Benhall in Suffolk, set sail in August last in the *Edward and Constance* of the burden of 240 tons, and one pinnace, the *Falcon*, which alone at his own cost, he had equipped, furnished, and victualled in such sort and with such plenty as had seldom been known before. From Dover he shaped his course for the Islands of the Suryes and Canaries, leaving his pinnace at Dover for the repairing of some small fault which had appeared, but through the negligence of her master he never saw her again. Contrary winds drove them out of their course for two months, till, at the end of November, he returned to the Islands, having done little good, but being loath to return home without achieving some notable exploit for the honour of his country and the profit of his men, he resolved to land on St. George's Island.

Calling his company together and taking counsel with them he found them willing to follow him. So the long boat and the carvel were hauled up alongside, into which entered eighty-five men, sixty being musketeers, the rest armed with pikes or brown bills.

The watch of the island, seeing so large a company draw near, had given warning and the whole force of the island was ready to receive them when they should attempt a landing. But the gunner letting fly on them from the ship from a sacer charged with a chain, slew or dismembered ten or twelve of them, and continued to play upon them so that, after two hours' fight, the Spaniards sounded a retreat and fled with all speed into the high country, leaving our men to land with the loss of but two killed.

Thence they marched inland about a mile and made a camp, posting a strong watch for the night.

Day being come, the company divided into two parts, the General leading one, Mr. Edward Florecourt the other, at some distance so that their numbers might appear greater. So with colours displayed and drums and trumpets, they marched with easy pace, yelling terrible cries which might have terrified a great company.

When they had proceeded about half a league, the scouts brought word that a mounted man was approaching as if to speak with them; but the General sent forward a guard of musketeers to stay him from coming nearer to view his forces. He was a gentleman sent by the Governor to know what they were and what they required. The General answered that he was a gentleman of England, but would not say what he intended to any private man; but if the Governor himself should come, he promised, by the faith of an English gentleman, that he should pass and repass in safety.

After a time the Governor with twelve of his gentlemen approached the camp and halted about half a mile from the court of guard, where hostages were sent forward as pledges for his safety. The General having conferred for a while with the Governor declared that if the island should be surrendered to the Queen of England's use, the Spaniards might depart with their possessions; but if not, he would commit all to the hazard of the sword, for what advantage he had won and what spoil he could make he would keep or die for it. To this the Governor flat refused, but said that provided they neither spoiled the King of Spain's subjects nor their goods, he would give them what they wished from the island.

Hearing this the General went apart with his company and conferred with them, whether to accept the offer or to venture on force. They answered that they would ratify whatsoever he decided. But he, seeing the smallness of his own forces in the enemy's country, thought it best not to refuse what the Governor offered. So he returned to the Governor, and demanded victuals of all sorts for his ship and 1000 crowns as recompense for the loss of the two men slain at landing. To these conditions the Governor agreed and departed.

The next day the General feasted the Governor and his company in a brave manner to the honour of his country and his own worthy commendation, and, on the day following, wind and tide being favourable, they set sail and so ranged about the islands seeking their fortune.

The day after they had left St. George's Island two tall ships were discovered which they chased until the following noon when they came up with them, and commanded to strike for the Queen of England. Whereon as they showed the Leaguers' flag and refused to strike, the gunner shot one of them through, being the Admiral, so that she was forced to lie by the lee to stop her leak. Then the Vice-Admiral bare up to rescue her consort, whom the General commanded also to strike, but they answered despitefully they would not, but would sink in the seas ere they would yield or strike. So the company demanded who they were. They answered that they were the *Dolphins*, the *Great Dolphin* and the *Little Dolphin* of St. Malo, stout ships and well appointed, the least of them having two and twenty cast pieces.

'Well,' quoth the General, 'strike your flag, for never shall so base villains as you carry your flag where an English gentleman is.'

They said again that they would not.

Then the General bare with them and gave them his whole broadside and sheered close in to board, but by the negligence of the helmsman they fell off, to the General's great discontent. By this time the men in the Admiral had stopped her leak, and as they saw the General bearing upon them they made ready to fight, and first they gave a whole broadside which hit not the ship at all.

Then began a hot fight in which they suffered loss, for some of our men who entered the Admiral saw seven or eight men slain and hauled up in their forecastle. At the third encounter our men grappled with the Admiral so that she was not able to sheer away, and the General with twenty more boarded her ; but the Vice-Admiral coming up on the other side entered her men so that ours were forced to retire and break away, having given the enemy great damage but received little hurt themselves. For four hours longer the fight continued until night came on, when the General called his company together, first gave thanks to God for their preservation and then caroused with them, binding them all by their faith to fight it out with the enemy or die for it; but when day dawned, no Frenchmen were to be seen.

Their hurts being repaired, they made thence for the Northern Cape but were chased by six Spanish galligoes whom they shook off after a hot fight of three hours.

The General, having thus sustained great hurt and accomplished but small good for himself, being still unwilling to return to England, determined to make for the Straits of Gibraltar, whither they framed their course, but meeting with tempests by the way the main mast, which had been damaged by shot during the last fight, was lost. So they harboured in Algiers to repair the ship. Here they remained for nearly two months waiting for the company of the English Fleet; but then refusing to stay any longer, the General resolved to sail by himself with no other company than the *Flower de Luce*, a ship of Dieppe. But as they came near the mouth of the Straits, they met with four of the King of Spain's gallies which engaged the *Edward and Constance* alone, for the French ship was unwilling to put herself into any danger until the General had fought with all four and sunk one, when she came up and at her approach the rest of the Spaniards withdrew. The rigging was so much damaged by shot in this encounter that the General was forced to put back again to Algiers, leaving the *Flower de Luce* to go on to Dieppe alone.

3rd April. INSTRUCTIONS FOR SIR R. WILLIAMS.

On his leaving for Dieppe in command of 600 soldiers for service in Normandy, Sir Roger Williams is instructed to confer with the Governor of Dieppe in what sort his services shall be required, especially in defending the town, but unless some special and manifest cause for some good attempt against the enemy appears he may not hazard the Queen's people out of the town. If, however, other forces be joined to those of the Governor's, and opportunity of doing some good service should appear, he may join with him provided that he and his men be not further burdened with any action than the Governor himself should be.

A FRAY AT LIMEHOUSE.

A certain Edward Glasse made an attack on Mr. Thomas Andrews, who was appointed steward, overseer and paymaster of the workmen fitting out the ships for Mr. Thomas Cavendish. In the attack Andrews struck Glasse a blow in self-defence of which he died in a quarter of an hour.

14th April. A QUARREL IN THE PRESENCE CHAMBER.

The Earl of Essex and the Earl of Kildare, who had fallen out in the Presence chamber and used towards each other words very unfit to be uttered in that place and by persons of their quality, are summoned before the Council. Finding that the quarrel had arisen upon a very small matter the Council consider that the honour of the Queen may be greatly prejudiced by a fray begun so near her person and that great inconvenience would ensue if these noblemen pursue the cause in the heat of revenge. Therefore they enjoin them on their allegiance to keep the peace, binding each in securities of £10,000 not to assault, challenge or provoke the other.

16th April. SENTENCES AT THE SESSIONS.

At the Sessions Elizabeth Arnold, an unmarried woman, was found guilty of stealing an embossed ring worth 40s., a hollow ring with a whistle worth 40s., a turquoise ring worth 20s., a ring with a pearl worth 20s., a folding ring worth 13s. 4d., a black enamelled ring worth 6s. 8d., together with divers articles of wearing apparel from Thomas Collier of Turnhill Street. Also of stealing three silver whistles worth £5, seven silver spoons worth 40s., two gold rings worth £3, a gold ring with an emerald worth £5, with other articles of jewellery, and £7 in numbered money from John Smythe at Limehouse. At the same time Elizabeth Hawtrey, wife of John Hawtrey, was found guilty of feloniously receiving and comforting her after the first theft, and Elizabeth Johnson, spinster, after the second. Elizabeth Johnson pleaded guilty, and was sentenced to be hanged. The other two acknowledged the indictment but pleaded pregnancy ; a jury of matrons being empanelled both were found not pregnant and sentenced to be hanged.

The same day Edmund Chapman was found guilty of having seized and raped a girl of nine years old, and sentenced to be hanged.

24th April. A PROCLAMATION AGAINST TRADING WITH THE FRENCH REBELS.

A Proclamation by the Queen is published declaring that Henry the Fourth, King of France and Navarre, is justly entitled the King of France, being recommended to the realm by the last king before his death, in presence of all the Princes of the blood and of the rest of the nobility, to be his most lawful successor. It now manifestly appears that this unnatural rebellion is favoured by none of the ancient nobility of France but by a very few of a strange blood, lately brought in and planted by marriages in France, and only branches depending of the House of Lorraine. Her Majesty therefore is moved to yield to the King, her brother and confederate, her favour, both in approbation of his right and wishing to him prosperity against his rebels, as she thinks there is no Monarch nor Sovereign Potentate in Christendom but does the like, save only one, who not contented with all the kingdoms and dominions which his noble father left him, by reason of his abundant riches brought out of the Indies, attempts to augment his estate by encroaching to himself the Dominions of his neighbours.

This rebellion against the French King is fed and maintained in sundry port towns of France and especially in Normandy and Brittany, where the people live by exchange of merchandise and by receiving succours of victuals and munitions of war from foreign countries, without which the rebels in their ports could neither continue their rebellions nor yet relieve their fellow rebels in the land. Her Majesty therefore expressly commands all her natural subjects and all other persons resorting to her realm to forbear to trade with any of the King's rebels, either in France or fraudulently here in England, upon pain of being punished as traitors, and relievers and succourers of the Queen's enemies.

Her Majesty is informed that many of her subjects, outwardly making their entries with the officers of the Custom houses as if to repair to the ports of France which obey the French King, or to other ports of the realm, or to Jersey or Guernsey, craftily and by stealth carry powder, shot, copper and other habiliments of war to the ports held by the enemy. For the repressing of which abuse the officers of the Custom houses are to have good regard to the conditions of all that lade any wares to be transported out of the realm by sea.

26th April. A PROCLAMATION AGAINST UNAUTHORISED POSTS.

A Proclamation is published forbidding any to carry packets or letters to the countries beyond the seas except such as are ordinarily nominated to this service by the Master of Posts or otherwise show good warrant for their voyages and despatches under the hands of one of the principal Secretaries, an Ambassador, or others sufficiently authorised. All in authority, and especially the searchers, customers and controllers of the ports, shall make diligent search of all mails, budgets, and other carriages of such disavowed carriers, messengers and suspected persons coming or going out of the realm with packets of letters; all such discovered to be apprehended and kept in custody until by the view of their writings, sent up to the Privy Council, it is seen and advised what further should be done with them.

29th April. 'THE SHEPHERD'S STAR.'

The Shepherd's Star being a paraphrase dialoguewise upon the third of the Canticles of Theocritus, in prose, part with songs interspersed, is entered. It is written by Mr. Thomas Bradshaw, lately a gentleman of the company and retinue of the Lord Burgh at Brille.

30th April. FLORIO'S 'SECOND FRUITS.'

Signor John Florio, that wrote the *First Fruits*, being an induction to the Italian tongue, thirteen years since, now perfecteth his *Second Fruits* in twelve chapters, both in the Italian tongue and the English. In these witty and familiar discourses many subjects are treated of, such as the set at tennis, games of cards or chess, fencing, the thirty bodily parts of beauty in a woman; ending with a pleasant discourse of love and women. To this book is added *The Gardine of Recreation*, yielding six thousand Italian proverbs.

2nd May. LODGE'S 'ROBERT, DUKE OF NORMANDY.'

The famous, true and historical life of Robert, second Duke of Normandy, surnamed for his monstrous birth and behaviour, Robert the Devil, is sent to the press, being dedicated to Mr. Thomas Smith, and penned by Mr. Thomas Lodge, that last year wrote *Rosalynde, Euphues' Golden Legacy*.

This Robert, being the son of Aubert, Duke of Normandy, and Editha, his wife, was from his birth of a monstrous and devilish disposition; for while yet a boy he poisoned the son of his schoolmaster, afterwards cutting the throat of the father with his penknife. Being come to manhood he was to be knighted by his father, but being set to watch the night in the Abbey of St. Peter at Rouen, there to perform his vigil, when all had departed, issued from the church and walked in the fields until at last he arrived at a nunnery. Calling the Lady Abbess before him he commanded all the young nuns to be brought before him; then immodestly stripping them naked he made choice of the fairest, and dragged her by the hair of her head into a shady wood near adjoining, where in spite of her incessant intreaties he deflowered and afterwards slew her. After many other crimes and horrible murders he was outlawed by his father and betook himself to the woods, until his band was overcome by his father's cavaliers and he forced to wander away sore travailed by his wounds; and meditating upon his sins he thought that a voice sounded in his ear, 'The reward of sin is death.' In this desperate state a hermit who had long lived from the world found him and took him to his hermitage, where he was so schooled, that of a bad young man he became reconciled to a staid and holy course of life. At length being enjoined by the hermit for a penance to go barefoot to Rome, he came thither after many travels and served the Emperor as his fool, and afterward when the Sultan of Babylon would by force have married the Emperor's daughter, in disguise of a knight he saved the city from destruction. Absolved thereby of his penance, he was married to the Lady Eunice and returned to Normandy, his father being dead, to find his mother charged with the murder of her husband by the Lord Villiers. The lists being set for a champion to defend her, he defeated her adversary and reconciled himself to her, so that her sorrow was at last paid home with great solace, and Robert of being an irreligious person became the only royal paragon of the world.

3rd May. BRETON'S 'BOWER OF DELIGHTS.'

A book of Mr. Nicholas Breton's poems called *The Bower of Delights* is to be printed, containing his *Amoris lachrimae*, a discourse of the life, death and funeral of Sir Philip Sidney, with other poems to his memory, and pastorals and sonnets.

A POEM ON SIR P. S.

P Perfection peerless, Vertue without pride,
H Honour and Learning, linked with highest Love,
I Joy of the thought in true discretion tied,
L Love of the life that highest honours prove.
I In Angels' arms with heavenly hands embraced,
P Paradise pleased, and all the world disgraced.

S Seek all the world, oh seek and never find,
I In earthly mould, the mount of such a mind:
D Divinest gifts that God or man bestoweth,
N No glory such as of such glory groweth.
E End of the joys that hath all grief begun,
Y Yet let one weep when all the world is done.

8th May. THE FRENCH KING'S ORDINANCES.

Certain ordinances, which had been set forth by the French King two months since in the camp at Chartres, are published in English. These were afterwards proclaimed at Caen, being in the form of a proclamation, signed by the King and Monsieur Potier, and sealed in yellow wax with his Majesty's broad seal upon a single label. The King meaneth to take order against the complaints commonly made to him concerning the infinite oppression of his people through sundry imposts levied upon them by men of war that without his commission force them to contribute money, meat, and munition, whereby his poor subjects will be forced to abandon their habitations and the tilling of the earth, whereof there must ensue a general famine with the curse of God against the whole state. If any man of war shall levy troops or seize upon any place without the King's commission, the Governor or Lieutenant General shall with all speed besiege and force him; and all taken alive to be hanged up without other order of process.

CARTWRIGHT THE PURITAN BEFORE THE HIGH COMMISSION.

Mr. Thomas Cartwright, formerly master of the Hospital at Warwick, one of the chiefest of the English Presbyterians who has lain in prison since October, was brought before the High

Commissioners in Causes Ecclesiastical, the Bishop of London, the Attorney General, and four doctors. As it is now become a custom with the Puritans to refuse to take the oath before examination, the Bishop began in a long speech by demanding that he should take it.

Mr. Cartwright opening his mouth to speak, Mr. Attorney took the speech from him and also showed at length how dangerous a thing it was that men should upon the conceits of their own heads and yet under colour of conscience refuse the things that had been received for laws of a long time. This oath that was tendered was according to the laws of the land, which he commended above the laws of all other lands, yet because they were the laws of men, they carried always some stain of imperfection.

After much controversy, Mr. Cartwright still resolutely refusing to take the oath, the Bishop commanded an act thereof to be entered. Then Mr. Cartwright put the Bishop in mind that he had promised him leave to answer the charge which had been given against him; the Bishop replied that he had no leisure to hear his answer, and if he would answer it should be by private letter.

12th May. Ripley's 'Compound of Alchemy.'

The Compound of Alchemy is entered, showing the ancient hidden art of Alchemy, the perfectest means to make the philosopher's stone, *aurum potabile*, and other excellent experiments. George Ripley, sometime Canon of Bridlington in Yorkshire, first wrote this book, which he dedicated to King Edward the Fourth; but Mr. Ralph Rabbards, student and expert in alchemical arts, now sets it forth for the first time for the press. It is penned in twelve gates or books, each in verse, showing severally the properties of calcination, dissolution, separation, conjunction, putrefaction, congelation, separation, cibation, sublimation, fermentation, exhalation, multiplication, and projection. There is added also an Epistle to King Edward briefly summarising the whole and ending:

> First calcine, and after that purify,
> Dissolve, distill, sublime, discend, and fix,
> With *Aqua Vitae* oft times both wash and dry,

And make a marriage the body and spirit betwixt,
Which thus together naturally if you can mix,
In loosing of the body the water congealed shall be,
Then shall the body die utterly of the flux,
Bleeding and changing colours as you shall see.

The third day again to life he shall arise,
And devour birds and beasts of the wilderness,
Crows, popinjays, pies, peacocks, and mavois,
The Phoenix, with Eagle, and the Griffin of fearfulness,
The Green Lion, with the Red Dragon he shall distress,
With the White Dragon, and the Antelope, Unicorn and
    Panther,
With other beasts also, which almost each one doth fear.

In *bus* and in *nibus* he shall arise and descend,
Up to the Moon, and sith up to the Sun,
Through the Ocean Sea, which round is withouten end,
Only shippen within a little glass tun ;
When he is there come, then is the mastery won,
About which journey, great goods you shall not spend,
And yet you shall be glad that ever it was begun,
Patiently if you list to your work attend.

For then both body and spirit with oil and water,
Soul and tincture, one thing both white and red,
After colours variable it containeth, whatsoever man clatter,
Which also is called after he hath once been dead,
And is revived, our Markaside, our Magnet, and our lead,
Our Sulphur, our Arsenic, and our true Calx vive,
Our Sun, our Moon, our ferment and our bread,
Our toad, our basilisk, our unknown body, our man, our wife.

Our body thus naturally by craft when he is renovate,
Of the first order, is medicine, called in our Philosophy ;
Which often times again must be propertualicate,
The round wheel turning of our Astronomy,
And so to the Elixir of spirits you must come : for why,
Till the son of the fixed by the son of the fixer, be overgone,
Elixir of bodies, named it is only,
And this sound secret point deceiveth many one.

This natural process by help of craft thus consummate,
Dissolveth Elixir spiritual in our unctuous humidity,
Then in balneo Mare together let them be circulate,
Like new honey or oil, till perfectly they be thickened,
Then will that medicine heal all infirmity,
And turn all metals to Sun and Moon perfectly,
Thus you shall make the great Elixir, and *Aurum potabile*,
By the grace and will of God, to whom all honour and glory.

Wishing by all means possible to profit the Kingdom and State, Mr. Rabbards hath dedicated this work to her Majesty.

15th May. THE 'CENTURION'S' FIGHT WITH FIVE SPANISH SHIPS.

There has returned to London the *Centurion*, commanded by Mr. Robert Bradshawe, a very tall ship of burden yet weakly manned, that in November took a cargo to Marseilles. Here the master waited for about five weeks, and being about to sail, some ships of smaller burden entreated him to stay a day or two longer so that for their better safety they might sail in company, vowing together that they would not fly from each other if they should happen to meet with the Spanish galleys, but rather than be taken by the Spaniards to endure their accustomed cruelty, would fight it out to the end.

These small ships sailing along the Straits of Gibraltar upon Easterday, were suddenly becalmed, and immediately five galleys made towards them in very valiant sort, the chief leaders and soldiers bravely apparelled in silk coats, with great plumes of feathers in their hats and silver whistles round their necks. By ten o'clock they came up alongside the *Centurion* and grappled with her, two on either side and the Admiral at the stern which with her shot so sorely galled and battered the *Centurion* that the mainmast was greatly weakened, the sails filled with many holes, and the mizzen and stern almost unserviceable. In each of the gallies were about five or six hundred Spaniards, on the *Centurion* but forty-eight in all, men and boys.

For five and a half hours the fight continued, during which the trumpet of the *Centurion* sounded forth the deadly points of war and encouraged them to fight against their adversaries, but on the Spaniards' gallies there was no music, only the sound of the silver whistles. Many a Spaniard was turned into the sea, as they came crawling in multitudes and hung upon the sides of the ship intending to have entered into the ship. Five times was the *Centurion* fired with wild fire which the Spaniards threw in, yet by the diligent forcsight of the master no harm was done at all. Four of her men were slain, one being the master's mate, and ten others hurt by splinters which the Spaniards shot; until, when their shot was almost spent and they were now constrained to shoot at them with hammers and the chains from their staves, by spoiling and overwearying the Spaniards our men at last constrained them to ungrapple themselves and get going.

Whilst the two other small ships had fled away, the *Dolphin* lay aloof and durst not approach near, so that one of the gallies went from the *Centurion* and set upon the *Dolphin*, which immediately caught fire through her powder so that both ships and men perished. The next day six other gallies came and looked at the *Centurion* but durst not approach her.

16th May. AN INVASION EXPECTED.

The Lords-Lieutenant and others, charged with the defence of the places on the coasts, are warned to have all things prepared to resist any attempt that the enemy may make. Forces are to be put in readiness and reviewed, and immediate order taken to watch and guard the beacons as has been done before in time of danger.

19th May. A SEDITIOUS FELLOW.

At the sessions Nicholas Haselwood, yeoman, was found guilty of having spoken with malice and feloniously against the Queen, saying that he desired and wished her death; and further that he hoped to see his enemies burnt at Smithfield before Michaelmas. He pleaded not guilty of felony, but guilty of contempt and trespass and is sentenced to be put on the pillory, with a paper setting forth his offence over his head.

21st May. THE QUEEN AT THEOBALD'S.

On the 10th May the Queen came to Theobald's to stay with the Lord Treasurer, and there finding him very melancholy she caused to be delivered to him a charter addressed to 'the disconsolate and retired sprite, the eremite of Theobald's,' giving him leave to retire to his old cave, and abjuring desolations and mourning to the frozen seas and deserts of Arabia Petrosa. Amongst the shows there presented was a conference between a gentleman usher and a post, pretending to deliver letters from the Emperor of China. At her departure yesterday she knighted Mr Robert Cecil, the Treasurer's younger son, whom some expected to be advanced to the Secretaryship ; but in the Court it is said that the knighthood must serve for both.

RUMOURS.

It is rumoured that Sir John Norris has entered Brittany, taking an island near St. Malo, and has joined with the Prince de Dombes' forces ; and that 20 Spanish ships are off Cornwall. The Earl of Cumberland has sailed out from Plymouth to meet them with his ships. 1500 men are to go to Ireland, whither these ships are suspected of going, and 1500 more to be taken from Brittany ; Sir Walter Ralegh posts down to Cornwall. The Queen is much moved with this news, and was very melancholy at the Lord Treasurer's. In Scotland witches are discovered that, with the privity of Bothwell, have practised the King's death.

24th May. DR. GERVASE BABINGTON'S SERMON.

Dr. Gervase Babington, Bishop of Llandaff, preached before the Court at Greenwich on the Second of Kings, the fifth chapter ; he compared the Lords of Council to the servants of Naaman, advising him for the best though it were to their own hurt. And speaking of the present discontents in religion, 'Woe is me to speak it,' quoth he, 'some of us cry, and too many of us cry instead of this, "No church, no sacraments, no ministers, no discipline at all" ; and therefore we must leave all open assemblies in this land, and combine ourselves together to erect a form according to our wills, in woods, in fields, in holes and corners where we can. Yea, with more woe I speak it, some fear not to write, "Pharaoh of Egypt gave the Israelites leave to worship God truly, but our magistrates, IF they should give us leave, yet could we not be suffered for such and such." Making an IF after these infinite mercies poured upon us by God, in the gracious government we live under, and casting the governors in merit towards us, beneath Pharaoh of Egypt. O sinful IF! O damnable and undutiful IF!'

26th May. SIR R. WILLIAMS COMMENDED.

The Council have sent a special letter to Sir Roger Williams, Colonel of the English companies at Dieppe, commending him for the good service performed by him and those who served with him in the late encounter with the forces of the Governor of Rouen.

THE GALLANT ACTION OF SIR R. WILLIAMS.

In the beginning of May provisions being scarce in Rouen, two regiments of the enemy had been despatched to the village of Cingcens, to secure such supplies as they could. This village, which is nine leagues from Dieppe, they fortified with trenches and barricades, and lest they should be molested from Dieppe a troop of horse was sent out to a wood, two leagues off, covering the highway, so that if any force should come out from Dieppe they might either retire back to give intelligence or by making resistance should give those at Cingcens time to prepare themselves and to procure help from Rouen.

When news of this force was brought to the Governor, the Lord Chartres, formerly governor for the King in Malta, and Sir Roger Williams, who had lately arrived, they resolved to set out from Dieppe in the evening of 19th May with 400 Frenchmen and 300 English. After marching all night they came to the wood early the next morning, where they found the troop of horse waiting to stop their passage. On these they made so fierce an assault that all were slain and not one escaped. Accordingly, leaving the bodies in the wood and taking some of their horses, the Lord Chartres and Sir Roger Williams marched on, reaching Cingcens somewhile before noon; and there they descried the enemy with their ensigns displayed within the fort.

The Lord Chartres, seeing that the fortification was so strong, declared that it was impossible to enter it, and tried to persuade Sir Roger to go back again, considering that the enemy was two to their one. But Sir Roger answered that it were a great dishonour to him to so do, and declared that he would set on them with his own three hundred, though it should cost him and them their lives. The Lord Chartres, being much encouraged with this bold resolution of Sir Roger, protested that he too would take part with his four hundred, whatever should chance. Thereupon he displayed his ensign, and together with Sir Roger, he vowed, with God's assistance, to enter the barricades and charge the enemy. So he spoke to his soldiers, exhorting them to fight for their lawful king whose right they were bound to defend.

Sir Roger likewise encouraged his men, showing them that though they were few and had to fight a great multitude, skilful, stout, hardy and trained in martial discipline, yet their enemy was but a multitude of traitors, opposing themselves to God's ordinance, and therefore condemned of God to a shameful death both here and in the world to come. He assured them that in putting their confidence in God not one of their hairs should fall, and finishing his speech, he prayed to the Lord with great confidence. Having ended his prayer, he made them promise to die every man rather than that they would fly one foot.

Then they marched forward with great courage, displayed their ensigns, struck up their drums and with their trumpets sounded defiance. In this spirit of resolution they assaulted the enemy as freshly as if they had not marched all night. The fight continued for two hours until at length they entered the barricades; Sir Roger himself being one of the foremost fought hand to hand with the chief officers of the enemy; and from the other side, the Lord Chartres also behaved valiantly. At length the enemy began to give back, and being enclosed in their barricades like a flock of sheep in a sheepcote they were all put to the sword, not one man being suffered to escape alive.

Having obtained this victory, on their knees they gave thanks to God, who had subdued their enemies under foot, and praised Him with psalms.

The losses of the Lord Chartres and Sir Roger are eleven men killed and a few slightly wounded. The Generals then immediately took order to return speedily to Dieppe lest some fresh force from Rouen should come upon them, or by casting about should meet them on the way. They gave order also that the soldiers should leave all spoil behind them, except that which could easily be carried. Thus they returned safely to Dieppe. The enemy, as was afterwards learned, did indeed come with a large force to meet them, but they had passed that place four hours before.

31st May. RUMOURS.

Six ships are being victualled to be sent to Lord Thomas Howard who has sailed for the islands with charge to do somewhat upon the coast of Spain as he goes. The talk of the slaughter of the men of Rouen by Sir Roger Williams is in everyone's mouth.

1st June. SIDNEY'S 'ASTROPHEL AND STELLA.'

Sir Philip Sidney's *Astrophel and Stella* that hitherto is known but in private copies is now printed and set forth before the world with a preface by young Nashe. 'Put out your rush candles,' quoth he, 'you poets and rimers, and bequeath your crazed quatorzains to the chandlers; for lo, here he cometh that hath broken your legs. Apollo hath resigned his ivory harp unto Astrophel, and he, like Mercury, must lull you asleep with his music. Sleep Argus, sleep Ignorance, sleep Impudence, for Mercury hath Io, and only Io Paean belongeth to Astrophel. Dear Astrophel, that in the ashes of thy love livest again like the Phoenix; O might thy body, as thy name, live again likewise here amongst us: but the earth, the mother of mortality, hath snatched thee too soon into her chilled, cold arms and will not let thee by any means be drawn from her deadly embrace; and thy divine soul, carried on an angel's wings to heaven, is installed in Hermes' place, sole prolocutor to the Gods.'

THE FIRST SONNET OF ASTROPHEL

Loving in truth, and fain my love in verse to show,
That the dear *She*, might take some pleasure of my pain:
Pleasure might cause her read, reading might make her know,
Knowledge might pity win, and pity grace obtain.
  I sought fit words to paint the blackest face of woe,
Studying inventions fine, her wits to entertain,
Oft turning others' leaves, to see if thence would flow,
Some fresh and fruitful shower, upon my sunburnt brain.
  But words came halting out, wanting Invention's stay,
Invention, Nature's child, fled Stepdame Study's blows:
And others' feet still seemed but strangers in my way,

Thus great with child to speak, and helpless in my throes,
Biting my tongue and pen, beating myself for spite :
' Fool,' said my Muse to me, ' look in thy heart and write.'

Tempus adest plausus, aurea pompa venit, so ends the scene of idiots, and enter Astrophel in pomp.

5th June. THE TAKING OF GUINGCAMP.

From Brittany it is reported that Sir John Norris hath taken Guingcamp, a town very strongly fortified, with ditches and walls, and protected on one side with marshes.

The General having found that part of the town which was fittest for a breach, made a show on the contrary part, causing trenches to be dug at the south side, and passages to be made through the old houses, even up to the counterscarp itself. A long trench was likewise made on the east side of the town, with a platform of earth in the middle as if the cannon should have been placed there. In the meantime great labour was used in making a mine near to the intended breach, and in preparing passages and emplacements for the cannon. This was performed with such zeal that on the 20th May the artillery was brought down to the Jacopins' cloister, and there set up within less than a hundred paces of the wall. In this action the General exposed himself unceasingly.

On 21st May the battery began, and though it continued all day, yet by reason of the few pieces of artillery not able to make sufficient battery, the day's work brought no further effect than the crushing of two flankers and the beating down of the parapet so that but a very small breach was made, which was repaired continually by the soldiers and inhabitants within the town, who maintained the rampart with featherbeds, horse dung, and bags of earth almost to the lowest part of their parapet.

Very early the next day the battery began again, and continued until two or three in the afternoon, by which time the breach seemed very fair. Whereupon the French urged hotly to an assault and so importuned the Prince de Dombes that he consented. Sir John was not in favour of an immediate assault, as he learned from a sergeant, whom he had sent forward to examine the breach, that the approach was very steep, sliding, and difficult, but especially because his mine had not yet been pushed far enough forward. Nevertheless, seeing that if the Frenchmen offered to attempt the place themselves, it would be a disgrace to us, he instantly demanded the point and honour of the assault for the English. Such was the emulation of the English captains that to avoid contention the General caused the dice to be cast and it fell to Captain Jackson and Captain Heron to lead the first two hundred to the assault, which, after devout prayers recommending themselves to God, they performed very valiantly, scrambling up the slope, and standing for half an hour at the push of the pike in the face of a whole storm of small shot, but through the steepness of the place the soldiers were unable to get up, and in the end withdrew in as good order as they had assaulted. Captain Heron was killed by a shot in the throat, and about twelve others, Captain Jackson dangerously hurt, and some thirty were wounded.

The second attempt was made by the Baron de Molac, Colonel General of the French infantry in those parts, who attacked bravely with some few of the French gentlemen, the common soldiers advancing to the breach but coldly received greater hurt, and many were slain. Some others then presented themselves for a third assault, but it was considered best to stay until the next day when the battery should have made the breach larger. In these assaults, Captain Dennis, being sent to another part of the town with some forces to make a feint of scaling, advanced too near and received a musket shot in his stomach, whereof he died at midnight.

During the night those within the town demanded a parley, and when this was granted some deputies from the town came next morning to the Prince de Dombes. Terms of capitulation being agreed on, on Whitsunday the town was surrendered and on the 24th May the garrison marched out, being 120 horse, and about 260 foot. Great store of victuals was taken, 2000 weight of powder and some cannon.

The capture of this town of Guingcamp is of great import to the French king, for all lower Brittany depends on it, and the Courts of Parliament ordinarily held at Rennes have by the Leaguers been transferred thither.

6th June. UNLAWFUL GAMES TO BE PUT DOWN.

Unlawful games are again to be put down, since the Queen is informed that archery, though an exercise not only of good recreation but also of great use in the defence of the realm, is now greatly decayed; she knows that many at great charge furnish themselves with the muskets and harquebusses now come into use and that it will seem hard to lay on them the burden which the law imposes; yet, with very good reason, she requires those games and pastimes prohibited by law, that is, bowls, dicing, cards and such like, to be forthwith forbidden, and instead archery revived and practised; for by this ancient weapon hath our nation won great honour in times past. Moreover by this means those poor men whose living chiefly depends thereon, as bowyers, fletchers, stringers and arrowhead makers, will be maintained and set to work in their vocations.

23rd June. LEONARD DIGGES' 'TECTONICON.'

A new edition is entered of the book named *Tectonicon* by Leonard Digges, first published in 1556, briefly showing the exact measuring and speedy reckoning of all manner of land, squares, timber, stone, steeples, pillars and globes. The book further sets forth the use of the carpenter's rule, containing a quadrant geometrical, the use of the squire, and of the instrument called the staff.

25th June. TERMS OF AGREEMENT FOR THE DESPATCH OF FURTHER TROOPS TO NORMANDY.

At Greenwich this day articles of agreement were signed for the despatch of a further force of 3400 to be added to the 600 men under Sir Roger Williams at Dieppe in Normandy; by Monsieur de Beauvoir and Monsieur de Reau for the French King, and by the Lord Treasurer and the Lord Admiral for the Queen. The King to pay all the costs of the levying, furniture, transportation and wages of these soldiers, with a General Captain to govern them, and all accustomed officers; and to discharge this and the charges due for the men in Brittany with Sir John Norris, he grants the Queen all profit of the tolls, customs and taxes to be received from the towns of Rouen and Newhaven, which her Majesty shall begin to receive so soon as either town be restored in its obedience to the King.

There are in Brittany at this time 1675 men; with Sir John Norris 722, and with Sir Henry Norris 540, and Captain Anthony Shirley 413.

1st July. RUMOURS.

Sir John Norris was reported to have received a blow and his brother to be slain; but later letters show that there have been several skirmishes but no fight. The Earl of Essex is now to go to France, although the Queen was long unwilling, and his friends in England advised him to the contrary, wishing him rather to seek a domestical greatness like his father-in-law, but the Earl is impatient of the slow process he must needs have during the life and greatness of the Chancellor and the Lord Treasurer.

5th July. THE WAR IN BRITTANY.

After winning the town of Guingcamp, the purpose of the Prince de Dombes was to have assailed the town of Morlaix and to bring the rest of lower Brittany to the King's obedience; but, learning that the Duke Mercury, commanding the French rebels in those parts, had joined with 4000 Spanish, and was marching towards Morlaix by way of Corlay, he considered that it would be most dangerous to engage his army before the town until he had made himself master of the field, especially as the enemy were of greater strength, and he was in an unfriendly country where there were many peasants, armed and hostile. Accordingly he stayed at Guingcamp to repair the fortifications and the breach made by our artillery, and also to await the coming of two cannon and two culverin.

THE DUKE MERCURY BRAVES THE PRINCE DE DOMBES

On 7th June the Duke Mercury arrived at Corlay, within three leagues of Guingcamp, where the castle was treacherously yielded to him, and thence the Duke sent a trumpeter to the Prince de Dombes about some prisoners, who signified that he had in charge to entreat the Prince to appoint some day and place of battle. To this the Prince answered that it was the most acceptable news that could be brought, for it was a thing he had long sought and desired. He refused therefore to send an answer by word of mouth through the trumpeter lest it should afterwards be denied, but wrote a letter, signed with his own hand.

The next day the Duke removed from Corlay to St. Gilles, less than two leagues from Chateau Laudran, whither the Prince de Dombes moved with his army and encamped. There the trumpeter of the Duke met the trumpeter of the Prince and delivered the Duke's answer, signed with his own hand, which was that he would be ready with his army on the Thursday following at ten o'clock in the morning in the fittest place for action between Corlay and Guingcamp; and if the Prince should refuse this offer, he should show the world that his actions were not answerable to his brags.

Whereupon the Prince sent this reply, couched in such terms as to give the Duke all provocation possible to force him to give battle.

'The Prince de Dombes, Governor of Dauphine, Lieutenant General for the King in his Army in Brittany,

Having seen the answer of Duke Mercoeur of the eighth of this month signed with his own hand, upon the offer made of the day and place of battle to be given, saith: He was sent into this province to chastise and punish those that have traitorously rebelled against the King, of whom the said Duke, being chief, doth manifest how he shameth and feareth the presence of the said Prince and the pain and punishment of his rebellion: and in regard of the lewd imputations given by his answer to the King, and to the said Prince, he saith he lieth, and shall lie as often as he shall say so.

At the Camp at Chateau Laudran, the ninth of June, 1591.'

The cartel was sent by a trumpeter and delivered to the Duke in the presence of many of the principal men of his army.

The Skirmish near Quenelac

The Duke, being greatly moved, openly vowed a solemn oath to offer battle to the Prince within three days. On the 9th June (which was Wednesday) he moved his camp to Quenelac, a village about a league and a half from Chateau Laudran, situated at the foot of a high hill which by deep hedges, ditches, and inclosures, confronted a little heath of two miles' compass. As soon as he heard of the enemy's approach the Prince mounted on horseback to make choice of a place for battle between the enemy and the hill, and found about three-quarters of a league off the village, a large plain or heath, skirted on the side of the enemy with a coppice and a little hill, and the ground crossed by ditches, of great advantage for the enemy, who without any difficulty could enter the heath by three large passages.

The next day the enemy within a quarter of a league of the heath showed his whole army in order of battle on the top of a hill, and the Prince also set his troops within the heath, disposing of them, by the advice of Sir John Norris, into three battalions, of which the English infantry made two, the lance-knights the third. The day was spent in slight skirmishes.

On 11th June the enemy drawing his army to the foot of the hill, placed his artillery upon the side of the heath where it commanded the whole place, and bordered all the hedges with shot. By this time our army was marched into the heath, and immediately 200 infantry were sent out to view the contenance of the enemy. These advanced and charged the enemy, and, driving them back to their main body, cleared the hedges and barricades, and slew several; but on our men withdrawing, the Duke sent out 500 French and 200 Spanish to repossess these places, following them with main body of his army.

When the Prince, who remained in the plain with the advanced guard, perceived this, order was given for 300 infantry, commanded by Captain Anthony Wingfield, Sergeant Major, and Captain Morton, and the English horse under Captain Anthony Shirley, to be sent forward. Meanwhile, under cover of the hedges the enemy despatched a number of musketeers, thinking to lodge them on our left and to take some two or three houses and a small wood on the edge of the heath. Against this the Prince sent 100 men, musketeers and pikemen, and 150 French musketeers, led by the Baron de Molac, and supported by 40 light horse, under Monsieur de Tremblay.

The action was so gallantly performed, especially by our English, that the enemy's horse and foot in the plain were forced to fly, many being slain and the rest driven to save themselves within the artillery, where the whole strength of the Spaniards and the rest of the army was placed. In this charge, Monsieur de Guebrian, Colonel of the foot, was taken by Monsieur de

Tremblay; Don Roderigo, chief Marshal of the Spaniards, was killed, together with a Spanish Captain, 200 French and 60 Spanish. The attack so amazed the enemy that our men were allowed within ten paces of the cannon to disarm the dead, and lead away the prisoners, none ever offering to follow. The rest of the day was spent in slight skirmishes and cannonades.

Next day, the enemy made a great show but at last sent out some shot to skirmish, whom Captain Anthony Shirley, with 15 horse and a few foot, speedily put to their heels, pursuing them to their barricades, where his horse was shot. In the skirmish, Mr. Kempe, a gentleman of the cornet, was killed, and Mr. Charles Blunt had his horse killed under him with a cannon shot.

On 13th June, the enemy made some light skirmishes but would not abide a charge either of horse or foot. The day following, being St. John's day with the Spaniards, it was expected that the enemy would give battle, but nothing was done. In the night the Duke prepared to remove, and withdrawing his cannon, the next day he repassed the hill on which he had first appeared, and retired to Quenelac.

The Prince, having now waited with his army on the heath from Friday the 11th June to the 15th, in readiness to give battle, also withdrew his artillery and returned his troops to quarters.

16th July. A Conspiracy for Pretended Reformation.

There is much disquiet in the City by reason of three fanatical preachers, Hacket, Arthington and Coppinger. About ten o'clock this morning, these men, having met in a house in Broken Wharf, set out, and began to proclaim to passers-by that Christ was come again from heaven. Thence Coppinger led the way by Watling Street and Old Change towards Cheapside, all the time crying out, 'Repent, England, repent.'

Moved by the unwonted sight of these new prophets arisen in London, the people soon crowded about them until by the time that the Cross in Cheapside was reached, the throng was so dense that they could go no further. Whereupon they got up into a cart from which Coppinger and Arthington spoke to the people, declaring that Hacket was Christ's representative on earth by partaking of His glorified Body, by His Spirit, and by the office, which had been conferred upon him, of separating the good from the bad. They themselves were two prophets, the one of Mercy, the other of Judgment, sent and extraordinarily called of God to assist Hacket in his great work. Then one pronounced mercy, comfort, and joy unspeakable to those that should repent; the other denounced terrible judgments on those who refused to hear them.

They went on to declare that Hacket was King of Europe and that all other kings must obey him. The Queen of England had forfeited her crown and was worthy to be deprived. Finally they prayed God, in very unmannerly and saucy terms, to confound especially the Archbishop of Canterbury and the Lord Chancellor, cursing them even to the pit of hell.

They had at first hoped to repeat this declaration at different parts of the City, but as the people still increased, they were forced to go into the Mermaid Tavern in Cheapside. Here they rested for some time and then returned to the place whence they had set out, Arthington all the way repeating his cry of 'Repent, England, repent.'

When rumours of these happenings reached the Queen at Greenwich, two of the Council, Mr. Wolley and Mr. Fortescue, were sent post haste to the City to find out the truth and to take action. About one o'clock in the afternoon, Hacket and Arthington were arrested and taken to the Lord Mayor's house, where they were examined by the two councillors. Here they refuse to show any signs of respect to those present, even remaining covered until their hats are plucked off, though all the time Arthington treateth Hacket with the utmost reverence, even kneeling before him.

They say that this Hacket, in former time an evil-liver, who was converted to Presbyterianism, hath wrought himself into the belief that he is Christ's representative on earth. He has been the servant of a gentleman at Oundle, where his loose life and violent temper are notorious. Once his master, a certain Mr. Hussey, had quarrelled with a certain Freckington, an artificer of the town, whose son was the schoolmaster. Hacket taking up the quarrel and one day meeting with this schoolmaster at an inn, pretended to be exceedingly sorry that there should be bitterness between him and his master. The schoolmaster deluded thus into thinking that he meant friendship, was taken unawares and thrown on the ground, where Hacket having him now at his mercy, with great savagery, bit off his nose. Yet though both Freckington and a surgeon who chanced to be present, begged him to restore the nose so that it might be stitched on again while the wound was still green, he not only refused to part with it, but showed it exultingly to all who cared to look ; some even say that he ate it up.

19th July. RUMOURS.

The Queen herself is said to be going down to Portsmouth with the Earl of Essex, but his friends mislike the voyage, and wish that he had left it to some other in respect of the great charge it is to him to put himself forward according to his dignity ; but he and his think the cost well bestowed, conceiving that the coming of the Duke of Parma maketh worthy the adventure. The Queen allows him only 100 lances and 50 harquebusiers ; but there are 100 more of his own cost, and his friends have sent him bountifully, both horse and money. There are great expectations for him, and if he should return with honour from his voyage, he is like to be a great man in the state ; both soldiers and Puritans wholly rely on him.

The ships to be set forth for the supply of Lord Thomas Howard are yet not ready, wanting mariners who refuse to go upon the uncertainty who should pay them, whether the Queen or the merchants.

Hacket's conspiracy is in everyone's mouths, some liking him to John of Leyden who took on himself the kingdom of the Anabaptists, and thinking that Hacket plotted some such kingdom as these prophets might have assembled ; others take them to be mere fanatics ; but the enemies to the Puritans take great advantage against them, as these prophets have been great followers of their preachers and have solicited with their books and letters all those that they knew affected to their sect, especially the Lord Treasurer, the Earl of Essex, the Countess of Warwick and Mr. Davidson. Meanwhile the Queen is more troubled with them than it is worth.

24th July. SIR HENRY UNTON MADE AMBASSADOR TO THE FRENCH KING.

Sir Henry Unton is appointed ambassador to the French King, being furnished with certain instructions signed by the Queen's own hand.

He is commanded in all his behaviour to preserve the reputation and royal dignity of her Majesty, and especially by observing the rites of religion and following the form of Daily Prayer both himself and his household according to the Church of England as established by law. To acquaint himself with the ambassadors of Venice and of the Duke of Florence, and through them to learn of the affairs of Italy, as well as of the Pope and the King of Spain; and if any should come from the King of Scots or the King of Denmark or any other of the Protestant Princes of the Empire, to let them understand how friendly the Queen is to them. With regard to the money which is owing from the French King, not to press for it by any expostulation or to move any unkindness, but to put him in remembrance of the benefits he hath received.

He shall have especial regard to the actions of the Earl of Essex, giving him understanding from time to time what is thought of them, approving to him what are considered to be good, informing of such things as are to the contrary, and giving him good advice to reform them. He is charged on his allegiance not to fear to deal plainly with the Earl.

25th July. A RESTRAINT OF PLAYING.

Notwithstanding former orders to restrain the playing of interludes and plays on the Sabbath day, these orders are being neglected to the profanation of this day, and by reciting their plays on all other days of the week, the players cause great hurt to the game of bear baiting and like pastimes maintained for the Queen's pleasure. The Lord Mayor and the Justices of Middlesex and Surrey are required to take order that no plays be shown openly either on Sunday or on Thursday when the games are usually practised.

26th July. THE TRIAL AND CONDEMNATION OF WILLIAM HACKET.

This day Hacket was brought up from Bridewell to the Sessions house near Newgate for trial before the Commissioners, amongst them the Lord Mayor, Lord Wentworth, Sir Gilbert Garrard, Master of the Rolls, Sir Wolfstone Dixie, Sir Richard Martin, Mr. Sergeant Fleetwood (the Recorder), and Mr. Daniel.

He was arraigned on two indictments. Being asked to plead to the first, he answered, 'All must be as you will'; which was taken as a plea of guilty. To the second, he answered, 'You have wit enough to judge for me and yourselves too.' The question being put to him again, he replied, 'Few words are best; it is good to know much and say little.' It was shown that this answer would of itself condemn him of treason if he still refused to answer to the point, and being once more asked if he pleaded guilty or not guilty, he said, '*ambo*.' At last he was persuaded to plead not guilty to the second indictment.

He was next asked by whom he would be tried, but refused to give answer according to the form of the law, 'By God and my country.' Instead he replied, 'By the jury.' But realising that he now stood in very great danger, he began to blaspheme violently.

At last, seeing that Hacket obstinately refused to plead according to the form of the law, the Attorney General rose and demanded judgment.

As Hacket had pleaded guilty to one indictment and refused to plead to the second, there was no need to call witnesses or to enlarge on the case. Nevertheless for the better satisfaction of those present, both the Attorney General and the Solicitor General spoke at length. This done, the Recorder sentenced Hacket to death as a traitor, and he was taken away to Newgate.

28th July. THE EXECUTION OF HACKET.

In the morning William Hacket was brought from Newgate to execution for treason. All the way as he was dragged on the hurdle, he cried out continually, 'Jehovah Messias, Jehovah Messias,' and at another time, 'Look, look, how the heavens open wide and the Son of God cometh down to deliver me.'

The crowd was so vast that it was a long time before the officers could bring him to the gibbet which had been set up by the Cross in Cheapside. There, when silence had been called for, Hacket was exhorted to ask God and the Queen for pardon, and to fall to his prayers, but he began to rail and curse her Majesty. Being the more vehemently urged to remember his present state, he began to pray thus :

'O God of Heaven, mighty Jehovah, Alpha and Omega, Lord of Lords, King of Kings and God Everlasting, that knowest me to be the true Jehovah whom Thou has sent, send some miracle out of a cloud to convert these infidels and deliver me from mine enemies. If not, I will fire the heavens and tear Thee from Thy throne with my hands.' Then turning towards the executioner, he said, 'Ah, thou bastard's child, wilt thou hang William Hacket, thy king ?'

The magistrates and people were much angered by these speeches and called out to the officers to have him despatched ; so with much ado they got him up the ladder, where he struggled with his head, to and fro, to avoid the noose. Then he cried out very fearfully, 'O what do you, what do you ? Have I this for my kingdom bestowed on me ? I come to revenge thee, and plague thee——' and so was turned off.

But the people, unwilling in their fury that any mercy should be shown him, cried out that he should be cut down at once, being very angry with the officers for not showing more haste. As soon as he was taken down, almost in a trice, his heart was cut out and shown openly to the people.

29th July. COPPINGER DIES IN PRISON.

Coppinger, who had been Hacket's companion in the 'Conspiracy for pretended Reformation,' has died in Bridewell prison, having refused all food for more than a week.

Now that Hacket is dead there is much discontented murmuring. Some that seem moderate men, yet favour his opinions in Church government, think that he and his fellows intended good though they mislike the manner of the action. Others, extenuating the fault, believe that they were stark mad, and knew not what they said or did. Some even are heard to mutter that matters were made out to be worse and of greater peril and consequence than they were in fact, and that they were persecuted with greater sharpness than the offence deserved.

2nd August. Sir Robert Cecil a Privy Councillor.

Sir Robert Cecil, second son to the Lord Burleigh, Lord High Treasurer of England, was this day sworn of her Majesty's Privy Council.

3rd August. A Suspected Portuguese.

Mr. Mills, Signor Botello and Dr. Lopez, the Portuguese physician, are instructed to go to Rye to examine certain prisoners lately sent over from Dieppe. First, Emanuel Andrada, a gentleman of Don Antonio, who had previously offered to do the Queen some secret service but is suspected of designs against her. He is to be dealt with civilly at first, and then threatened with fear of his life to induce him to declare the truth; his papers are to be examined through Dr. Lopez. The second, John Semple, a Scot, to be examined about rebels and fugitives and his connexions in England and Scotland. The other two are Portuguese.

7th August. An Assault in St. Peter's, Westminster.

At the special Session of Oyer and Terminer, William Dethick, Garter King of English Arms, was indicted for assaulting Henry Brown in the Church of St. Peter's at Westminster, drawing his dagger and striking him on the head. He pleaded not guilty and was acquitted.

A Building allowed in Blackfriars.

Harman Buckhold, goldsmith, is by the Council's special licence, allowed to build on the little piece of waste ground in Blackfriars, though by the proclamation of ten years ago new buildings were prohibited within the City or three miles of it. This is allowed, being supported by most of the inhabitants of Blackfriars, for that this plot is very noisome not only to those who pass by it but also to the neighbours because of the great heaps of soil and filth continually laid there. By giving this licence the nuisance will be abated.

13th August. Andrada's Declarations.

Emanuel Andrada, the Portuguese prisoner, has declared to Mr. Mills that he is sent by King Philip to treat in his name with the Queen for a false peace, and to take her answer to the Duke of Parma who will write to the Council of Spain, the King replying by way of Italy. This is to while away time that by coming and going he may thoroughly understand what is happening in England. He was ordered by Don Christophoro Moro and Idiaques, the present rulers in Spain, to try by all means to kill Don Antonio, and there should be no lack of money or honour. To sound them he asked what should be done if any were willing to kill the Queen; they replied that King Philip had often been desired to do it, but he hoped before her death to see the ruin of her kingdom, and to have her in his hands, and would not therefore treat of her death.

Andrada further reporteth that in many ports of Spain and Portugal forty galleons are building, stronger than the King ever had. He has contracted with the Genoese at Madrid for forty Flemish ships, armed and victualled for six months, to be prepared at Antwerp and other free cities. From Germany and Biscay are coming this winter quantities of gunpowder, cordage, masts, munitions, and victuals to Brittany, where the King forms a magazine of ships, artillery and so forth; that province will furnish mariners, and then they will assault England. Don Juan, a captain of St. Malo, intends to assault Jersey in September.

20th August. A QUACK FIGURE CASTER.

Robert Henlack has petitioned the Council for redress against certain men who robbed him. He complains that while he was absent in the night a confederacy of certain evil disposed persons broke open his chamber door in the house of one Isabel Piggott in Thames Street and took away goods and money to the value of £400. Further, one Nathaniel Baxter hath since then robbed him of £12 more, pretending that by casting a figure he would help him to his goods and money again.

21st August. THE QUEEN ON PROGRESS.

On Saturday the 14th the Queen in her progress came from Farnham to Cowdray in Sussex, where she was royally entertained by the Lord Montague.

As the Queen and her train came into sight about eight o'clock in the evening, they were greeted with loud music which ceased suddenly as soon as she came to the bridge. Here a person in armour, standing between two porters carved out of wood, with a club in one hand and a golden key in the other, made a speech, after which he delivered the key to the Queen, who alighted from her horse and embraced the Lady Montague and her daughter, the Lady Dormir.

The next day being Sunday, the Queen rested and was most royally feasted, the portion for breakfast being three oxen and one hundred and forty geese.

On Monday, about eight o'clock in the morning, the Queen and her train rode out into the park to a delicate bower which had been prepared for her. Here while the musicians played, a nymph delivered her a cross-bow with which to shoot at the deer, some thirty in number, enclosed in a paddock. The Queen killed some three or four, and the Countess of Kildare one.

The rest of the week was spent in feasting and entertainment, and on Friday the 20th, the Queen moved from Cowdray to Chichester.

22nd August. The Bordeaux Wine Fleet to be Stayed.

An open placard is sent by the Council to all officers of the Port of London, the Cinque Ports and other ports on the south and west to stay all vessels about to trade with Bordeaux at the vintage time. It is credibly reported that certain merchants intend to set out in a very disorderly manner, and not in one or more fleets, forgetting that the state is interested in their private loss and that those ships which went unprotected last year have not yet returned.

28th August. Mr. Thomas Cavendish's Expedition.

Mr. Thomas Cavendish hath departed two days since from Plymouth with his fleet of three tall ships and two barks, *The Galleon*, wherein Mr. Cavendish himself sails, being the Admiral, *The Roebuck*, vice-admiral, whereof Mr. Corke is Captain, *The Desire*, with Mr. John Davis as Captain, *The Black Pinnace*, and a bark of Adrian Gilbert, commanded by Mr. Randolph Cotton.

31st August. Rumours.

The Queen is said to be at Portsmouth, having been at Chichester, whither she came from Lord Montague's at Cowdray, where she and the whole Court were magnificently entertained. Nothing is heard from Normandy from the Earl of Essex. From

Brittany it is reported that there hath been some quarrelling with the French, who laid in wait for the English and slew eight of Sir John Norris's horsemen ; whereupon he marched into the Prince de Dombes' camp, and slew a great number of his, and told the Prince that he would not serve under such rash heads. It is also said that 110 Spanish ships are at sea, to waft home the Indian fleet ; the Earl of Cumberland and the rest of the venturers are wished home again safe.

3rd September. ILLEGAL BUILDING IN LONDON.

The Justices of the Peace for Middlesex are sharply rebuked for allowing the Queen's express commandment to be broken, in that during this vacation when the Queen was on progress divers disobedient persons not only finish those buildings lately begun about the City of London but also begin new. The Council warn them how little the Queen will like this negligence, for not only did the magistrates refrain from removing the tenants of these cottages, according to the order given in the Star Chamber, but allow them still to be inhabited and others to be built.

4th September. THE EARL OF ESSEX IN FRANCE.

The news from France is that the Lord General (the Earl of Essex) leaving his army hath been to see the King and is at Pont de l'Arch, some three leagues from Rouen. On their way to the King not above ten people were seen ; the villages and houses were utterly abandoned, yet milk, cider, fresh water and bread were set ready to relieve our soldiers almost in every house, which the grooms and footboys brought their masters, for there was no straggling because the enemy followed from hill to hill, but only, as it seemed, to view and discover the size of the company.

At the gates of Noyon the Marshal Biron awaited him to conduct him to the King, who was in a garden attended by the Duc de Longueville, the Count St. Pol and many more. The King received my lord most kindly, and after a long discourse led him into the castle where he banqueted him. Afterwards, escorted by the Marquis Pisana and many other nobles, the Lord General was conducted out of the town and taken into a village a mile off ; but before the troops reached this place the King, accompanied by two or three, overtook them and said to all the train in English, 'You are welcome.' Having brought the Earl to his lodging, he remained half an hour and after was escorted back to his own quarters by the Earl and his company.

Next morning my Lord went to the King and attended a preaching in his house, being afterwards entertained to dinner. In the afternoon, the Earl accompanied only with a dozen gentlemen attended the King to Noyon (which he had recently besieged and taken), to consult with the Marshal Biron who lay there sick of the gout. Here the pitiful tokens of these lamentable wars were very manifest, the country being all spoiled, the bridges broken, all the suburbs of the town burned, orchards and gardens utterly destroyed, churches beaten down, the walls rent and the town within very filthy.

The Lord General came to the Pont de l'Arch on the 30th, where he held a council and determined to send for his army to Arques. He was advertised by letter that in his return from the King he was in great danger of being taken by Villiers, Governor of Rouen, who pursued him at the trot with at least 700 horses.

6th September. THE QUEEN DISCONTENTED AT THE ILL SUCCESS IN FRANCE.

The lack of all news from the ambassador in France breeds much disquietness, for though many rumours were noised abroad there hath been no certainty until the coming of Monsieur de Reauloc, which causeth the Queen to hold much offence both towards the King for not holding to his purpose to besiege Rouen, and the Earl of Essex for departing from his camp so long a journey without her licence. The Queen is therefore much discontented, saying that she wishes with all her heart, that she had never consented to it, though she had lost double the sum of money spent in the expedition.

10th September. NEWS FROM FRANCE.

It is reported that the Lord General sentenced a gentleman of his cornet to be disarmed for striking a woman. His army has now joined him at Pont de l'Arch.

12th September. MR. WALTER DEVEREUX SLAIN.

Mr. Walter Devereux, the only brother of the Earl of Essex, was slain with a small shot in the head four days since. The

Lord General being then at a village called Pavilly with his horse and foot marched, in a bravado, to see whether Villiers or any of his troops in Rouen durst come out and skirmish ; and in that skirmish Mr. Devereux was slain.

THE BORDEAUX WINE SHIPS TO SAIL IN CONSORT.

The Council order all who purpose to trade in wine or salt with Rochelle or Bordeaux to be ready with their ships, furnished with men and munitions, by the 25th of the month, either at the Downs or Dover, where there shall be a company of good ships with which they may pass safely. Those that cannot be ready by this time to forbear their voyage until they can go with a company of at least fourteen or fifteen good ships. Any disobeying this order of the Council shall be punished at their return for their contempt in putting in danger the Queen's people and the shipping of the realm, the owners of the ships, the masters and principal mariners ; and all the lading of the ships shall be arrested until full satisfaction has been made for the offence.

13th September. THE EARL OF ESSEX REBUKED.

The Council very sharply rebuke the Earl of Essex, for the Queen greatly dislikes that he left his army without any head except a Sergeant-Major and, not without danger, journeyed to the King, especially since she understands by letters from the French King that this journey was made voluntarily without any request from him. She therefore condemns him of rashness, reminding him that the purpose of his voyage was the recovery of Rouen and Newhaven. Moreover, she has contracted to pay the force but for two months from the time of their arrival, which was the 2nd August. She much misliketh that he came so near the town of Rouen to make a bravado upon the enemy in sight of the town, whereby to his own great loss and as a reward for his unadvisedness he hath lost his only brother.

Accordingly, considering how untowardly this action falls out under his government, the Queen is resolved that he shall return at the end of the two months. Moreover, she is determined to recall the force as well ; nevertheless if it appear probable that in one or two months more the King will retake either Rouen or Newhaven, and furnishes good assurance for the payment of the

English forces, then will she be content for some to stay, but not all.

16th September. A Proclamation against Supplying the King of Spain with Corn.

'For as much as it is manifestly seen to all the world how it hath pleased Almighty God of His most singular favour to have taken this Our Realm into his special protection these many years, even from the beginning of Our reign, in the midst of the troubled estate of all other kingdoms next adjoining, with a special preservation of Our own person, as next under his Almightiness, supreme Governor of the same, against any malicious and violent attempts :—'

It is commanded that no corn or grain nor any ordnance of brass or iron be carried to any foreign countries without special licence upon pain that the owner and master of the vessel so offending be committed to close prison for a year and further until they have answered fines to the quadruple value of the goods carried. And because this year there is such plenty of corn it is likely that some of the people near the sea coasts will desire to vent some part of the corn of their own growing for lack of sale in the country. Principal persons of wealth are advised and earnestly required to buy in the markets near the sea coasts such quantities of grain as the owners should be constrained to sell for their necessity, and to keep it in store to serve the markets in the latter end of the year.

This proclamation is very necessary because though the King of Spain hath abundance of treasure by his Indian mines yet his own country is greatly wanting in victual, especially of corn and of munitions of war, and of mariners, and other furniture for his navy. He hath attempted to corrupt some of the Queen's subjects and some strangers inhabiting the realm to satisfy his wants either directly by stealth to his own country, or indirectly and colourably first to some other countries next adjacent to his.

21st September. A Secret Marriage.

The Queen hath for some time been highly displeased with Mr. Thomas Shirley, son of Sir Thomas Shirley, her Majesty's Treasurer for the wars in the Low Countries, for that he secretly married Mistress Frances Vavasour, one of the Ladies in Waiting. When this became known Mr. Shirley was committed to the Marshalsea. She hath now somewhat abated her wrath, but Sir Robert Cecil is to write to Sir Thomas that her pleasure is that he shall make it publicly known that he cannot digest such an act of contempt to her Court, as well as wilful perjury and disobedience to himself, nor do for a son that has so highly offended her who always furthers any honourable marriage or preferment for any of hers, when broken to her without infamy and scandal. Should Sir Thomas come to Court, she will tell him her mind.

24th September. THE QUEEN, ON PROGRESS, VISITS ELVETHAM.

On Monday, 20th September, the Queen came to Elvetham to stay with the Earl of Hertford, where great preparations had been made for her worthy reception. As the house is small and unable to accommodate so large a company, there were built especially the following:

A room of estate for the nobles, with a withdrawing place for her Majesty; the outsides all covered with boughs, and clusters of ripe hazel nuts, and inside with arras, the roof with works of ivy leaves, the floor with sweet herbs and green rushes. Near to this were the special offices: the spicery, lardery, chandery, wine-cellar, ewery, and pantry, all of which were tiled. There were also a large hall for the entertainment of knights, ladies and gentlemen of account; a separate place for the Queen's footmen and their friends; a long bower for the Queen's Guard; another for the Officers of the Household; another to entertain all comers, suitors and others; another for the Earl's steward; another for his gentlemen that waited on him.

There were also made a great common buttery; a pitcher house; a large pastery, with five new ovens, some of them fourteen feet deep; a great kitchen, with four ranges and a boiling place; another great kitchen for all comers; a boiling house for the great boiler; a room for the scullery; and another for the cooks' lodgings.

Between the house and the hill, where these buildings were set up, was made in the valley a pond, cut to the perfect figure of a half moon. In this pond were three isles; the first the Ship

Isle, a hundred feet long and forty broad, with three trees for masts; the second the Fort, twenty feet square and overgrown with willows; the third the Snail Mount, rising to four circles of green privy hedges, twenty feet high, and forty feet broad at the bottom. In the water were boats prepared for musicians and a pinnace fully furnished.

Everything being in readiness, the Lord Hertford, calling his retinue apart, in a few words put them in mind of the quietness and diligence they were to use so that their services might bring her Majesty content and thereby his honour and their credit, with the increase of his love and favour to them. This done, the Earl with his train, amounting to the number of three hundred, most of them with chains of gold about their necks, and in their hats yellow and black feathers, rode out to meet the Queen, who entered the park between five and six in the evening. Proceeding towards the house, a poet met them and saluted them with a Latin oration. This poet was clad in green to signify the joy of his thoughts at her entrance, a laurel wreath on his head to express that Apollo was the patron of his studies, an olive branch in his hand to declare what continual peace and plenty he wished her Majesty, and booted to betoken that he was *vates cothurnatus*, and not a loose and creeping poet. His speech being ended, the poet presented the scroll to the Queen, who graciously received it with her own hands, and all moved on toward the house, being preceded by six maidens who strewed flowers, singing this song:

With fragrant flowers we strew the way,
And make this our chief holiday:
For though this clime were blest of yore,
Yet it was never proud before.
    O beauteous Queen of second Troy,
    Accept of our unfeigned joy.

Now th' air is sweeter than sweet balm,
And satyrs dance about the palm;
Now earth with verdure newly dight,
Gives perfect sign of her delight.
    O beauteous Queen of second Troy,
    Accept of our unfeigned joy.

Now birds record new harmony,
And trees do whistle melody;
Now everything that nature breeds,
Doth clad itself in pleasant weeds.
O beauteous Queen of second Troy,
Accept of our unfeigned joy.

After supper, a consort of six musicians was admitted to the presence and played before the Queen, who was so pleased with their music that she gave a new name to one of their pavans, made by Thomas Morley, formerly organist of St. Paul's.

The next day broke stormy and the rain continued until after dinner so that no devices could be shown in the morning. But the afternoon and evening were fine and the pageant was able to proceed. Immediately after dinner, a large canopy of estate was set up at the head of the pond for the Queen to sit under and view the sports. This canopy, which was held by four of Lord Hertford's chief gentlemen, was of green satin, lined with green taffeta sarcenet, every seam covered with broad silver lace; valanced about and fringed with green silk and silver, more than a hand's-breadth in depth; it was supported with four silver pillars, and decked above with four white plumes spangled with silver. All about the head of the pond was tapestry spread. The Queen came down to the pond about four o'clock and sat under the canopy, when a pageant of Nereus and the Tritons and Sylvanus was enacted in the water.

On Wednesday morning, as the Queen looked out of her casement window about nine in the morning, three musicians, disguised in the ancient country attire, greeted her with a country song of Coridon and Phillida:

In the merry month of May,
In a morn by break of day,
Forth I walked by the wood side,
When as May was in his pride.
There I spied, all alone,
Phillida and Coridon.
Much ado there was, God wot,
He would love, and she would not.
She said, never man was true!
He said, none was false to you.

He said, he had loved her long;
She said, love should have no wrong.
Coridon would kiss her then;
She said, maids must kiss no men,
Till they did for good and all.
Then she made the shepherd call
All the heavens to witness truth,
Never loved a truer youth.
Thus with many a pretty oath,
Yea and nay, and faith and troth,
Such as silly shepherds use,
When they will not love abuse;
Love, which had been long deluded;
Was with kisses sweet concluded:
And Phillida, with garlands gay,
Was made the Lady of the May.

This song was so acceptable to the Queen that she commanded it to be sung again.

The same day after dinner, about three o'clock, ten of the Lord Hertford's servants, all Somersetshire men, hung up lines in a green court in the form of a tennis court, making a cross line in the middle. In this square they played, five against five, with the hand ball at 'board and cord' to the great liking of her Majesty, who sat watching them for more than an hour and a half.

After supper, the two delights prepared were curious fireworks and a sumptuous banquet. During the time of these fireworks from the pond, two hundred of the Earl's gentlemen served the banquet, all in glass and silver, every one carrying so many dishes that the whole number amounted to a thousand; and there were to light them in their way a hundred torches. The dishes in the banquet were:—The Queen's arms and the arms of all the Nobility in sugar work; men, women, castles, forts, ordnance, drummers, trumpeters, soldiers of all sorts, lions, unicorns, bears, horses, camels, bulls, rams, dogs, tigers, elephants, antelopes, dromedaries, apes, and all other beasts; eagles, falcons, cranes, bustards, heronshaws, bitterns, pheasants, partridges, quails, larks, sparrows, pigeons, cocks, owls and all birds; snakes, adders, vipers, frogs, toads, and all kinds of worms; mermaids, whales, dolphins, congers, sturgeons, pikes, carps, breams, and all sorts of fishes. All these were in sugar work, some in standing dishes, some in flat work. There were also in flat sugar work and marchpanes, grapes, oysters, mussels, cockles, periwinkles, crabs, lobsters, as well as apples, pears and plums of all kinds, preserves, suckets, jellies, leaches, marmalades, pastes, and comfits.

On Thursday the day began with a song by the Fairy Queen, dancing round a garland with her maids, which so pleased the Queen that she caused it to be repeated twice over, graciously dismissing the singers with largess.

An hour later, the Queen and her nobles took their departure from Elvetham. On all sides as they went, the actors in the entertainment were grouped in melancholy postures, wringing their hands in dumb show at her going away. Last of all, as the Queen passed under the park gate, a consort of musicians, hidden in a bower, played while two sang:

O come again, fair Nature's treasure,
Whose looks yield joys, exceeding measure.

O come again, heaven's chief delight,
Thine absence makes eternal night.

O come again, world's starbright eye,
Whose presence doth adorn the sky.

O come again, sweet beauty's sun,
When thou art gone, our joys are done.

So highly was the Queen pleased with her reception at Elvetham, that she declared to the Lord Hertford that the beginning, process and end of his entertainment was so honourable that hereafter he should find reward in her especial favour.

29th September. The Beacon Watches.

To those asking that the watches at the beacons be discontinued, the Council answer that they would be very willing but that they have been advertised of the arrival of certain galleys of the King of Spain in the Narrow Seas, and some attempt may be made on the coast, especially on those parts that lay towards France. Nevertheless, that the charges may be diminished, the beacons need only be kept when there are land winds blowing and at spring tides, and at such times three or four only need be appointed to each beacon, provided they be vigilant.

30th September. DR. COSIN'S 'THE CONSPIRACY FOR PRETENDED REFORMATION.'

Dr. Richard Cosin hath written an account of the conspiracy and death of William Hacket that was executed on 28th July, called *Conspiracy for Pretended Reformation: viz. Presbyteriall Discipline. A Treatise discovering the late designments and courses held for advancement therefore, by William Hacket, yeoman, Edmund Coppinger, and Henry Arthington, Gent., out of others' depositions and their own letters, writings, and confessions upon examination. . . . Also, an answer to the calumniations of such as affirm they were mad men: and a remembrance of their action with the like, happened heretofore in Germany.* The book is now at the press to be printed by Christopher Barker, the Queen's printer.

2nd October. THE CAPTURE OF GOURNAY.

The town of Gournay having been besieged for some days by the troops of the Marshal and the Lord General is now taken. Those within had at first refused to yield, defending themselves in hope of relief until the cannon played and two fair breaches were made. When the English were ready to go to the assault, the town was yielded with very hard conditions; the composition being that the governor, captains, leaders, officers and gentlemen of quality should become prisoners, but not *de guerre*, for want of these words being at the King's mercy; the soldiers were to depart with white sticks only in their hands and the burgesses to be used as others of the King's subjects. It was agreed also that any of the Queen's subjects taken therein should be delivered, but only one was found, an Irishman who had run away from Sir Edward Norris.

4th October. THREE OF LYLY'S PLAYS TO BE PRINTED.

Three of Mr. John Lyly's plays are to be printed, being *Endimion*, *Galathea*, and *Midas*, that were formerly played before the Court at Greenwich by the Children of Paul's.

'So nice is the world,' saith he, 'that for apparel there is no fashion, for music no instrument, for diet no delicate, for plays no invention, but breedeth satiety before noon and contempt before night.

'Come to the tailor, he is gone to the painter's to learn how more cunning may lurk in the fashion than can be expressed in the making. Ask the musicians, they will say their heads ache with devising notes beyond Ela. Enquire at ordinaries, there must be sallets for the Italian; picktooths for the Spaniard; pots for the German; porridge for the Englishman. At our exercises soldiers call for tragedies, their object is blood; courtiers for comedies, their subject is love; countrymen for pastorals, shepherds are their saints. Traffic and travel hath woven the natures of all nations into ours, and made this land like arras, full of device, which was broadcloth, full of workmanship.

'Time hath confounded our minds, our minds the matter; but all cometh to this pass, that what heretofore hath been served in several dishes for a feast is now mingled in a charger for a gallimaufry. If we present a mingle-mangle, our fault is to be excused, because the whole world is become an hodge-podge.'

7th October. A Case of Sorcery.

Stephen Trefulack, gentleman, was indicted at the Sessions for having exercised certain wicked, detestable and diabolical arts called witchcrafts, enchantments, charms, and sorceries, with the intention of diabolically provoking George Southcott to the unlawful love of a certain Eleanor Thursbye. He pleaded guilty, but the judgment of the Court is deferred.

10th October. The Bordeaux Wine Fleet.

Sir John Hawkins, Sir George Barnes, Sir George Bond and William Burrows, Esquire, are to call in two of the Masters of the Trinity House and with them to view the fleet about to set sail for Bordeaux and to set down such orders for their strengthening as they thought necessary. Further to impress two suitable merchant ships of those lying in the Thames to be furnished in warlike manner at the charges of the merchants who trade for wines.

16th October. THE EARL OF ESSEX TAKES LEAVE OF HIS ARMY.

The gentlemen in the army in Normandy were much distressed on learning that they were to return to England.

It was hoped at this time to attempt some enterprise against Rouen, and on the 6th of the month every man was ordered to put himself in readiness to march by two o'clock in the morning. Very early next day, the Lord General with his voluntary gentlemen went to the Marshal Biron's quarters, where he found the Marshal ready and accompanied with many of the nobility.

The Lord General being very glistering with a great plume of feathers in his hat, the Marshal began to say to him merrily, 'What, you young gallant, are you come hither to brave me with your white feathers? I think I have white feathers too'; and with that called for a hat set with a mighty plume, and a horseman's coat of tawny velvet frill of silver lace; and thereupon put on the hat which caused him to look like an old cutting ruffian of Smithfield. This pleasant humour grew out of a confident hope he had of the good success of some intelligence received from Rouen, which was that one of the Colonels of the Governor of Rouen had promised, on account of some injury he had received from the Governor, to deliver a gate of the town to Monsieur Rollett, Governor of Pont de l'Arch.

An hour before day, Monsieur Rollett with the Lord General came to the rendezvous at Martinville. With him were about 2000 Gascons, harquebusiers on foot, two regiments of Swiss, Hallard Mountmorency with five troops of mounted cuirassiers; and the English under Sir Roger Williams, 2500 men with 140 horses. The troops that before were dull with sickness and discontent now grew into wonderful of hope of what the French promised, and after a short breakfast marched towards Rouen three leagues, but here, having reached a wood in sight of the town not half a league off, a messenger came from the Marshal to the Earl of Essex who was with the foremost troop that he should halt because there was treason in the intelligence; which much amated the soldiers.

After resting a while the Marshal came up and directed that they should march to a place called Direntoun, about as near as Mile End is to London from Rouen, which was reached so suddenly that many of the inhabitants were surprised in their homes. There much booty was taken, and in the morning great store of wine was found under the ground, of which the soldiers took as much as they could carry and let the rest run.

The next day (8th) the Earl of Essex took his horse very early and went to a hill near the town, not far from St. Katherine's Castle, bemoaning his fortune that he was recalled before he was master of the market place ; and there on a fair green in sight of the town (where there were 3000 soldiers besides the inhabitants), commanding all the gentlemen to dismount, he told them he was very sorry that no opportunity was offered him to have led them into a place where they might have gained honour ; but the fault was not his neither was it theirs, for he had received great good will in all, and thereof was determined to give notes of honour to some. And there he made twenty-four knights.

The Lord General then took his leave of the army and attended with all his gentlemen went to the Marshal's quarters, where he stayed an hour in consultation. Then the Marshal rode with him for a league on his way until they came to a windmill, where they halted for a while. They reached Dieppe about ten o'clock at night, and the Lord General scarcely stayed to eat, but went on board, leaving behind him a great many mourning but hoping for his return.

The next day Mr. Robert Carey came from England with good news, but the Earl was gone before him.

18*th October*. THE BORDEAUX WINE FLEET.

The Council having received Sir John Hawkins' report on the state and strength of the fleet about to sail for Bordeaux, order the ships to be stayed until further information is received of the disposition of Monsieur Lucon.

20*th October*. THE LOSS OF THE 'REVENGE.'

News is received in London of a great fight about the Azores, in which the Queen's ship, the *Revenge*, was lost. This report is confirmed by certain Spanish prisoners who fought in that action.

On 31st August, Lord Thomas Howard, with six of the Queen's ships (the *Defiance*, being the admiral, the *Revenge*, commanded by Sir Richard Grenville, vice-admiral, the *Bona-*

venture, commanded by Captain Cross, the *Lion* by George Fenner, the *Foresight* by Mr. Thomas Vavasour, and the *Crane* by Duffield, these two last being small ships), were riding at anchor near Flores, one of the westerly islands of the Azores, when news was brought of the approach of the Spanish fleet, and the report no sooner made than the enemy was in sight.

The English ships were all in confusion, many of the ships' companies being on shore, everything out of order, and in every ship half of the company sick and unserviceable. From the *Revenge* there were ninety men sick ashore ; in the *Bonaventure* not enough left to handle the mainsail, and, had not twenty men been taken out of a bark of Sir George Carey's, which was then burnt, she would never have reached England. In this plight the Spanish fleet, having shrouded its approach by the island, came upon them so swiftly that the English ships had scarcely time to weigh their anchors, some even being forced to slip their cables and set sail.

Sir Richard Grenville, having stayed to recover his sick men from the shore, was the last to weigh, and had by now delayed too long to recover the wind before the enemy was upon him. The master of the ship and others urged him to cut his mainsail and cast about, but Sir Richard refused to turn from the enemy and persuaded his company that he would pass through their two squadrons and force them to give way before him. This he did with the first ships, but the *San Philip*, a great ship of 1500 tons, coming towards him took the wind out of his sails so that the *Revenge* could neither keep way nor feel the helm. The *Revenge* being entangled with the *San Philip*, four other ships boarded her ; two on the starboard and two on her larboard.

The fight thus beginning at three o'clock of the afternoon continued very terrible all that evening. But the great *San Philip*, having received the lower tier of the *Revenge*, discharged with crossbar-shot, shifted herself with all diligence from her sides, utterly misliking her first entertainment. The Spanish ships were filled with companies of soldiers, in some two hundred, in some five, in others eight hundred, besides the mariners. In the *Revenge* there were none at all besides the mariners but the servants of the commander and some few voluntary gentlemen only. After many vollies had been interchanged from the great ordnance and small shot the Spaniards essayed to enter the *Revenge* by boarding, hoping to force her by the multitudes of their armed soldiers and musketeers, but were repulsed again and again, and at all times beaten back either into their own ships or into the sea.

In the beginning of the fight, the *George Noble* of London, having received some shot through her by the armados, fell under the lee of the *Revenge* and asked Sir Richard what he would command him; Sir Richard bad him save himself and leave him to his fortune.

After the fight had thus without intermission continued while day lasted and some hours of the night, many of our men were slain and hurt, and one of the great galleons of the armada, and the *Admiral of the Hulks* both sunk and in many other of the Spanish ships great slaughter was made.

The Spanish ships which attempted to board the *Revenge* as they were wounded and beaten off so always others came in their places, and having never less than two mighty galleons by her sides and aboard her. So that ere morning, from three of the clock the day before, there had been fifteen several armados assailed her; and all so ill approved their entertainment that they were by break of day far more willing to hearken to a composition than hastily to make any more assaults or entries. But as day increased, so our men decreased; and as light grew more and more, by so much the more grew our discomforts. For none appeared in sight but enemies, saving one small ship called the *Pilgrim* commanded by Jacob Whiddon, who hovered all night to see the success; but in the morning bearing with the *Revenge*, was hunted like a hare among many ravenous hounds.

All the powder of the *Revenge* to the last barrel was now spent, all her pikes broken, forty of her best men slain, and the most part of the rest hurt. In the beginning of the fight she had but one hundred free from sickness, and fourscore and ten sick, laid in hold upon the ballast; a small troop to man such a ship and a weak garrison to resist so mighty an army. By those hundred all was sustained; the volleys, boardings, and enterings of fifteen ships of war, besides those which beat her at large. On the contrary, the Spanish were always supplied with soldiers brought from every squadron; all manner of arms and powder at will. Unto ours there remained no comfort at all, no hope, no supply either of ships, men or weapons; the masts all beaten overboard, all her tackle cut asunder, her upper work altogether razed, and in effect evened she was with the water, but the very foundation or bottom of the ship nothing being left over either for flight or defence.

Sir Richard finding himself in this distress, and unable any longer to make resistance, having endured in this fifteen hours' fight the assault of fifteen several armados, all by turns aboard him, and by estimation 800 shot of great artillery, besides many assaults and entries; and seeing that he himself and his ship must needs be possessed by the enemy, who were now all cast in a ring about him, for the *Revenge* was not able to move one way or other but as she was moved with the waves and billows of the sea, commanded the master gunner, whom he knew to be a most resolute man, to split and sink the ship that thereby nothing might remain of glory or victory to the Spaniards, and persuaded the company, or as many of them as he could induce, to yield themselves unto God and to the mercy of none else; but as they had like valiant and resolute men repulsed so many enemies, they should not shorten the honour of their nation by prolonging their own lives for a few hours or a few days. The master gunner readily condescended and a divers few others; but the Captain and the Master were of another opinion and besought Sir Richard to have a care of them, alleging that the Spaniard would be as ready to entertain a composition as they were willing to offer the same; and that there being yet divers sufficient and valiant men still living, and whose wounds were not mortal, they might do their country and Prince acceptable service hereafter; and that where Sir Richard had alleged that the Spaniards should never glory to have taken one ship of Her Majesty's, seeing that they had so long and so notably defended themselves, they answered that the ship had six foot of water in hold, three shot under water which were so weakly stopped as with the first working of the sea she must needs sink, and was besides so crushed and bruised as she could never be removed out of place.

The matter being thus in dispute and Sir Richard refusing to hearken to any of those reasons, the master of the *Revenge* (while the Captain won unto him the greater party) was conveyed aboard to the General, Don Alfonso Bassan. Who finding none over hasty to enter the *Revenge* again, doubting lest Sir Richard would have blown them up and himself, and perceiving by the report of the master his dangerous disposition, yielded that all their lives should be saved, the company sent to England, and the better sort to pay such reasonable ransom as their estate would bear, and in the mean season to be free of the galley or imprisonment.

When this answer was returned and safety of life was promised, the common sort being now at the end of their peril, the most drew back from Sir Richard and the master gunner, it being no hard matter to dissuade men from death to life. The master gunner, finding himself and Sir Richard thus prevented and mastered by the great number, would have slain himself with a sword had he not been by force withheld and locked in his cabin. Then the General sent many boats aboard the *Revenge* and divers of our men fearing Sir Richard's disposition, stole away aboard the General and other ships. Sir Richard thus overmatched was sent unto by Don Alfonso Bassan to remove out of the *Revenge*, the ship being marvellous unsavoury, filled with blood and bodies of dead and wounded men, like a slaughter house. Sir Richard answered that he might do what he list, for he esteemed it not, and as he was carried out of the ship, he swooned, and reviving again desired the company to pray for him. The General used Sir Richard with all humanity and left nothing unattempted that tended to his recovery, highly commending his valour and worthiness.

The *Admiral of the Hulks* and the *Ascension of Seville* were both sunk by the side of the *Revenge*; one other recovered the road of St. Michael's and sunk there also; a fourth ran herself on the shore to save her men. Sir Richard died, as it was said, the second or third day aboard the General and was by them greatly bewailed; what became of his body, whether it were buried at sea or on land, is not known.

A few days after the fight was ended and the English prisoners dispersed into the Spanish and Indy ships, there arose so great a storm from the West and Northwest that all the fleet was dispersed, as well as the Indian fleet which were then come unto them as the rest of the Armada that attended their arrival, of which fourteen sail, together with the *Revenge*, were cast away upon the Isle of St. Michael. On the rest of the islands there were lost in this storm fifteen or sixteen more of the ships of war; and of a hundred and odd sail of the Indian fleet, expected this year in Spain, what in this tempest and what before in the Bay of Mexico and about the Bermudas there were seventy and odd consumed and lost with those taken by our ships of London, besides one very rich Indian ship which set herself on fire being boarded by the *Pilgrim*, and five other taken by Master Watts and his ships of London between the Havanna and Cape St. Antonio.

22nd October. AN AFFRAY AT WESTMINSTER.

This day one John Keckham, servant of Margaret Bray, a widow, was going on his mistress's business on the public way from Tuthall Street to the Gatehouse at Westminster when he met a certain Robert Crosyer, who crossed over to encounter him, and assaulting him with a cowlstaff, beat and struck him down, intending to slay him. Keckham seeing that he was in danger of his life, defended himself with his drawn rapier, and being unable to rise from the ground thrust at his adversary, giving him a mortal wound in the breast.

25th October. PRECAUTIONS AGAINST DISORDER AT THE PORTS.

News is received that the Lord Thomas Howard's ships have taken prizes from the Indian and Mexican fleet, laden with treasure and things of great value. Sir Thomas Gorges and Mr. Carmarden are to be sent down to take order in those ports where the ships shall arrive that no mariners be permitted to come on shore until the ships have been visited and the goods inventoried lest the sailors embezzle or take away short ends and such things as they may come by.

27th October. DISORDERS AT DARTMOUTH.

The mariners and other loose and dissolute persons have committed foul outrages and disorderly embezzlements of the goods brought in to Dartmouth by the two prizes newly arrived. Sir Francis Drake is required with all speed and circumspection to restrain these contempts and to recover from any party such parcels or portions as he can find by proof, suspicion or examination; and to this end to use the assistance there of any gentleman of quality.

28th October. THE TRIAL OF BRIAN O'ROURKE.

Brian O'Rourke was brought to trial and arraigned at Westminster. As he spoke no English, Mr. John Ly of Rathbride, a gentleman from Ireland, interpreted between him and the Judge. He was charged on several counts of having sought the deprivation of her Majesty from her royal seat, the destruction of her person and the overthrow of her realm of Ireland.

Amongst other accusations it is declared:

That at Dromaher he caused a picture of a woman to be made, setting to it Her Majesty's name, and causing it to be tied to a horse's tail and drawn through the mud in derision; and after he caused the galliglasses to hew it in pieces with their axes, uttering divers traitorous and rebellious words against Her Majesty;

That after the Spanish fleet sent by the King of Spain and Pope Sixtus V. had been dispersed by the English fleet till they came round Scotland and so into Ireland, O'Rourke entertained and succoured divers of the Spaniards who had been employed in the invasion; and that after proclamation was made by the Lord Deputy that upon pain of death no man should keep any of the Spaniards but send them to him by an appointed day, O'Rourke kept the prisoners and afterwards despatched them safe to Spain with a Spanish friar and an Irish friar;

That he violently entered and burned Ballingaffe and other villages in Roscommon, and the town of Knockmallen, murdering Her Majesty's subjects, and continuing these outrages until he was forced by the Queen's forces to fly to Scotland;

That at Glasgow he offered the King of Scots that if he would maintain him and suffer his subjects to join him he would bring the realm of Ireland to his subjection.

After many speeches had passed between O'Rourke and his judges, he declared that he would not consent to be tried by the jury unless he might have a week's respite to allow of papers from Ireland being sent to him, and a good man of law to be assigned to him who should swear to deal as truly for him as for the Queen's heir apparent if he were in his place; and besides he would have the Queen herself to be one of the jury. Upon this it was shown through Mr. Ly, that the law was that if he refused to be tried by twelve men he should be judged guilty forthwith and so be guilty of his own death. Yet for all this as he still refused trial he was condemned to death as a traitor. When the sentence was explained to him, he said nothing but if that were their will, let it be so.

31st October. RUMOURS.

Now that the loss of the *Revenge* is generally known, some condemn the Lord Thomas Howard for a coward, saying that he is for the King of Spain. The Lord Admiral and Sir Walter Ralegh have quarrelled and offered combat. Seven prizes have recently been brought in by the merchants who went to second Lord Thomas Howard.

The war in Normandy and Brittany is greatly liked, and 1000 pioneers are to be sent over to the siege of Rouen and 1000 new soldiers to the Earl of Essex, who has obtained leave to remain there till he has done something to revenge his brother's death ; but his making of twenty-four knights is greatly mocked. General musters were assembled on a rumour being received that the traitor Sir William Stanley would attempt an invasion. The Lord Chancellor is very sick with a strangury and not expected to recover. A proclamation against the Jesuits is being printed but is not yet published.

1st November. FATHER JENNINGS, A NOTABLE JESUIT, TAKEN.

Edmund Jennings, a Jesuit, hath been taken prisoner by Richard Topcliffe at the house of Mr. Swithin Wells in Holborn where he had been saying Mass. Topcliffe came on him while he was still in his vestments, and he, with some ten others who were present, was taken to prison. During the fray Topcliffe was thrown down the stairs by Mr. Brian Lacy's man.

3rd November. THE EARL OF ESSEX IN NORMANDY.

On 17th October the Earl of Essex, Lord General, returned to the army from England to the surprise and delight of most : that day he took counsel and resolved to send off to tell both the King and the Marshal of the success of his journey into England. The next morning Sir Roger Williams was sent to the King. News was now brought of the rendering up of Caudebec, by composition that all the men of war should depart to Rouen with a convoy for their security, the drums beating, ensigns flying, matches lighted and the horsemen with pistols in their hands.

On the 21st the Earl held a martial court where many grievances were heard and determined; some being condemned to die for going without passport to England and for other offences. On the 24th the Earl and his gentlemen were invited to dine with Monsieur D'O, where they were most sumptuously entertained, and so far from meaner things that they feasted on musk and amber in tarts; and the day following the Earl brought Monsieur D'O to see the army which was drawn up, over 2000 strong, besides 300 sick. On this day the English army began to draw their pay from the French King, but not to their content.

On the 28th the army marched towards Rouen and was well lodged in certain villages. That night Sir Roger Williams returned with letters from the King to the Earl showing his full determination to besiege Rouen with might and main and that he was marching thither with all expedition. Sir Roger was then despatched to England with the news, and the army moved to a village called Ophin, and the next evening marched towards Rouen which was about six miles off.

Next morning (29th) the point of the English army entered the village of Mount de Mallades about a quarter of a mile from the walls of Rouen, and looking down from thence they saw a great skirmish between the enemy from Rouen and the Marshal Biron's companies, the enemy holding on to a house and the hill until five in the evening when about 250 men issued out of the town to a place of advantage and assaulted the quarters of Hallard Mountmorency, which were next to the English, so sorely that he was forced to quit some part of them. The enemy so pursued him that they burned half his quarters, his troops offering no resistance, and would have burnt the rest if the Lord General had not sent certain harquebusiers to draw them into a skirmish, and offering to cut in between them and the town; which was so well performed that they were forced by our horse to wheel about, and by some pikes led by Sir John Wingfield to give ground. In this skirmish Captain Barton's lieutenant was slain, and two knights and one captain besides others wounded.

Several horses were hurt and the Earl's was shot dead under him. Towards night the fight was broken off and our men returned to their lodging.

THE EXECUTION OF O'ROURKE.

Brian O'Rourke was to-day drawn to Tyburn for execution. As they came to the gallows, while he was still standing in the cart, Mr. John Ly, with many good exhortations, bade him to remember the many odious treasons he had committed, and to ask Her Majesty and the world for forgiveness. But he obstinately refused, saying that if she would have given him time, and the writings which had been sent from Ireland against him so that he might answer them, and also if she would give him his life, then he would ask her forgiveness and henceforth serve her truly; adding further that he little thought the King of Scots would have sent him to the Queen without good assurance of his life and pardon for his offences.

Still Mr. Ly urged O'Rourke to repent and ask forgiveness, and likewise to forgive for that was the only way for him to come to the Heavenly Kingdom, and the standers by also urged him to repent. To all this he replied that they should make means for themselves to come to God, and he would look after himself; and with that fell to his prayers. The standers by then asked Meylerns, Lord Archbishop of Cashell, who was present, to counsel O'Rourke to call to God; but O'Rourke turning on him answered that he had more need to look to himself and that he was neither here nor there. So the cart went from him. His body was taken down, his members and bowels cut out and burned in the fire, and his heart taken out by the hangman, who showed it to the people as an archtraitor's heart; then his head was cut off and his body quartered.

4th November. AN AFFRAY NEAR WHITEHALL.

Thomas Coxon and Daniel Carter, yeomen, were going together between the two gates at Whitehall, when Coxon violently assaulted Carter, giving him several wounds with his dagger on the face. To this Carter said, 'What meanest thou to strike me? I have nothing to do with thee,' and did his utmost to withdraw from his adversary, who followed him with drawn sword until he reached the angle of a wall beyond which he could not go. After receiving divers wounds Carter drew his sword in self-defence, whereupon Coxon ran in on him and received a mortal wound in his body.

SPANISH DISASTERS.

News is received from the isle of the Tercera that there were three thousand men in the island saved from the Spanish ships which foundered in the great storm, and that by the Spaniards' own confession there were ten thousand cast away in that storm besides those that perished between the islands and the main.

'MEDIUS' PRINTED.

Medius, being the second book of sacred songs, some made for five, some for six voices, by William Byrd, the Queen's Organist, hath been printed with the music.

5th November. A PROCLAMATION AGAINST VAGRANT SOLDIERS.

A Proclamation is published against vagrant soldiers, declaring that there is a common wandering abroad of a great multitude, of whom the most part pretend that they have served in the wars on the other side of the seas, though it is known that very many of them neither served at all, or else ran away from their service and are justly to be punished and not relieved; some indeed have served, and, falling with sickness, are licensed to depart; these deserve relief.

Her Majesty therefore commands that discretion be used between unlawful vagrant persons and the soldiers now lawfully dismissed from their service. The vagrants, who have neither been brought to sickness or lameness in their service and are not able to show sufficient passport for their dismission, to be taken as vagabonds and so punished. And if any allege that they have been in the Queen's pay on the other side the seas and cannot show sufficient passport from the Lord General, he shall be indited and suffer as a felon, as a soldier that hath run away and left the service traitorously.

The Treasurer of Wars will make payment of sums of money to those who lawfully return to conduct them to the places where they were levied. Furthermore for the repressing of the great number of mighty and able vagrants now wandering abroad under pretence of begging as soldiers, by whom open robberies are committed, the Lieutenants of every county, who have sufficient warrant by their commissions to execute martial law upon such offenders, are charged to appoint Provost Marshals for the apprehension of such notable offenders, and to commit them to prison thereupon to be executed.

MEASURES OF RELIEF FOR RETURNED SOLDIERS.

Every soldier on landing, having the passport of the Lieutenant General or any special officer of commandment, to be paid five shillings for his conduct to the place where he was levied. Where there is no person of the Treasurer, the principal officer of the place to pay this sum immediately, which will be duly repaid by the Treasurer of Wars or the Council. On payment of the conduct money, the passports of the soldier shall be retained and a new passport given for his travel allowing sufficient time by convenient journeys from the place of landing to the place of his first levy. To be warned at the same time that if he lingers by the way in roguish manner or does not reach his former abode within the time limited, he shall be taken as a vagabond and punished according to the law.

8th November. SOUTHWELL'S 'MARY MAGDALEN'S FUNERAL TEARS.'

Mary Magdalen's Funeral Tears, written as it is said by Robert Southwell the Jesuit, though without his name inserted on the title-page, has been entered, wherein is expressed the sorrowful thoughts and lamentations of Mary Magdalen at the Sepulchre of Christ, in the manner of the writers of romantic tales. The author seeing how the finest wits are now given to write passionate discourses hopeth by his book to woo them to make choice of such passions as it were neither shame to utter nor sin to feel.

15th November. SPANISH LOSSES.

By examination of various Spaniards and Portuguese it appears that the King of Spain sustained very heavy losses this last summer. Of the Nova Spania fleet of 52 ships but 33 returned to Havannah, there being 2600 lost in 19 sail; of the Terra Firma fleet only 23 ships came to Havannah, having lost some 3000 men. As well as these 55, there met at Havannah 12 ships from S. Domingo and 9 from Funduras, 77 in all, and set sail on

17th July, keeping company till the 10th August, when they were scattered by tempests so that by the end of August all but 48 had been lost, 5000 men being thought to have perished in the ships cast away. The King of Spain's treasure is all landed at Havannah to be sent home in frigates in January.

20th November. THE DEATH OF SIR CHRISTOPHER HATTON.

This day Sir Christopher Hatton, the Lord Chancellor, died at Ely House in Holborn of a flux of his urine, aggravated with grief of mind because the Queen somewhat vigorously exacted of him a great sum of money collected of tenths and first fruits, whereof he had charge, and which he had hoped, in regard of the favour he was in with her, that she would have forgiven him. Neither could she once having cast him down with a harsh word raise him up again, though she visited and endeavoured to comfort him. He was reputed to be a man of pious nature, a great reliever of the poor, of singular bounty and munificence to students and learned men (for which reason those of Oxford chose him as their Chancellor of their University), and one who in the execution of the office of Lord Chancellor could satisfy his conscience in the constant integrity of his endeavours to do all with right and equity.

21st November. THE PROCLAMATION AGAINST JESUITS.

The Proclamation declaring the great troubles intended against the realm by seminary priests and Jesuits is now published though dated 18th October and printed some time since. The dangers and preparations made against the realm by the Pope and the King of Spain, and by English fugitives beyond the seas, are set forth and severer measures to be taken.

'And before all things, We do first require of the Ecclesiastical State, that the like diligence be used by the godly ministers of the Church, by their diligent teaching and example of life to retain Our People steadfastly in the profession of the Gospel and their duty to Almighty God and Us; as it is seen a few capital heads of treason are continually occupied within their Seminaries in withdrawing a multitude of ignorants to their inchantments.

'And secondly, for having sufficient forces in readiness by Sea, We hope by God's goodness and with the help of our subjects to have as great or greater strength on the seas as at any time we have had to withstand these puffed vaunts from Spain. And for Our forces by land, Our trust is that seeing We have distributed Our whole realm into several charges of Lieutenancies, that they by themselves when they may be personally present, and otherwise by their deputies and assistants of other Our ministers, will now after the general musters which have been by Our special order taken, consider of all things requisite to perform, and make perfect all defects that shall appear necessary, to make the bands both of horsemen and footmen fully furnished with armour, weapons and munition and with all other things requisite for their conduction to the place of service; and there also to continue as time shall require to defend their country. And so We do most earnestly require and charge all manner of Our subjects, with their hands, purses and advices; yea, all and every person of every estate, with their prayers to God, to move Him to assist this so natural, honourable and profitable a service, being only for the defence of their natural country, their wives, families, children, lands, goods, liberties and their posterities against ravening strangers, wilful destroyers of their native country, and monstrous traitors.

'And lastly, to withstand and provide speedy remedy against the other fraudulent attempts of the seminaries, jesuits, and traitors, without which as it appeareth his forces should not now be used, the same being only wrought by falsehood, by hypocrisy, and by undermining of Our good subjects under a false colour and face of holiness, to make breaches in men's and women's consciences, and to train them to their treasons: and that with such a secrecy, by the harbouring of the said treacherous messengers in obscure places, as without very diligent and continual search to be made, and severe orders executed, the same will remain and spread itself as a secret infection of treasons in the bowels of Our Realm; most dangerous, yea, most reproachful to be suffered in a well ordered Commonwealth.

'Therefore we have determined by advice of Our Council to have speedily certain commissioners, men of honesty, fidelity and good reputation, to be appointed in every shire, city, and port-town within Our realms to enquire by all good means what persons by their behaviours or otherwise worthy to be suspected to be any such persons, or have been sent, or that are employed in any such persuading of Our people, or of any residing within Our realm to treason, or to move any to relinquish their allegiance with Us, or to acknowledge any kind of obedience to the Pope or to the King of Spain ; and also of all other persons that have been thereto induced, and that have thereto yielded : And further to proceed in the execution of such their commission, as they shall be more particularly directed by instructions annexed to their commission.

'And furthermore, because it is known and proved by common experience upon the apprehension of sundry of the said traitorous persons sent into the realm, that they do come into the same by secret creeks, and landing places, disguised both in names and persons ; some in apparel as soldiers, mariners, or merchants, pretending that they have heretofore been taken prisoners, and put into galleys, and delivered. Some come in as gentlemen, with contrary names, in comely apparel, as though they had travelled into foreign countries for knowledge : and generally all, for the most part, are clothed like gentlemen in apparel, and many as gallants ; yea in all colours, and with feathers and such like, disguising themselves ; and many of them in their behaviours as ruffians, far off to be thought or suspected to be friars, priests, jesuits, or popish scholars. . . .

'And finally, We admonish and strictly charge and command all persons that have any intelligence with any such so sent, or come from beyond the seas to such purpose, to detect them to the commissioners, in that behalf to be assigned as aforesaid, within twenty days after the publication hereof, in the shire town, or city or port, within the precincts of the said commission : upon pain that the offenders herein shall be punished as abettors and maintainers of traitors : wherein We are resolutely determined to suffer no favour to be used for any respect of any persons, qualities or degrees : nor shall allow nor suffer to be allowed any excuse of negligence for not detection, or for not due examination of the qualities of such dangerous persons, according to the order hereafter prescribed, being no wise contrary, but agreeable to the most ancient laws and good usages of Our realm, devised for the good order of all manner of subjects in every precinct of every leet, to be forthcoming, to answer for their behaviours towards the Dignity of Our Crown, and the common peace of Our realm.

'Given at Our Manor of Richmond, the 18th of October, 1591, in the 33rd year of Our reign.'

Instructions set forth for the guidance of the commissioners show the form of questions to be put to those suspected of being recusants. The commissioners shall obtain from the *custos rotulorum*, the clerk of the peace, or the clerk of assizes, the names of those suspected, but their names not to be published unless some probable cause appear why they should be examined or apprehended. Nor shall suspected persons be pressed to answer any matter touching the conscience in religion, other than whether they usually come to Church or not; if they appear wilful recusants, then are they to be examined concerning their allegiance to the Queen, and of their devotion to the Pope or to the King of Spain, and whether they maintain any Jesuits, Seminaries, priests or other persons sent from beyond the seas to dissuade the Queen's subjects from their allegiance. In every town or large parish where the parsons or vicars are faithful and careful of their cures, they are to be urged to observe all such as refuse obstinately to come to Church. Those called before the commissioners, but not punished by the law, to be warned that their recusancy causeth them to be suspected of being disloyal in the duties towards the Queen and State or of favouring the common enemies.

25th November. The Siege of Rouen.

The Earl of Essex hath returned from Rouen, which is now besieged. There have been skirmishes but nothing of great moment.

On the 4th November in the night there sallied out of the Castle against the quarter of Monsieur Flavencourt 400 soldiers, burnt it over his head and slew as many as stood the defence, took his baggage, his horses and mules; but were at last forced to retire by certain Gascons and a regiment of French, leaving on the ground 26 dead and 8 prisoners, of whom two were English and one Spanish.

The next day one of the enemy's horse issued forth, a brave fellow all in crimson velvet, and called out one of ours to the sword on horseback, which he bravely answered and wounded his enemy in two places, and would have brought him in prisoner, had he not been rescued by his fellows. The Lord General the same day invited the three Colonels of the Switzers and there was general drinking of healths till some of them were sick and asleep. After dinner the General's party went out and came near a gate of the town where Villiers, the Governor of Dieppe, was quartered, and it happened that he was there with some twenty horse. Seeing the General's party he drew out certain shot and so began to come up the hill; but the General knowing who he was called to him and said he would speak with him at a blow with a sword or pistol, but he answered nothing except the shot of four or five harquebus. On the 7th our horsemen brought in some sixty kine, as well as sheep and swine. There came too a soldier from the Governor of Dieppe, sent from his master to the General, who reported that they had great desire to force the English quarter. There was a hot skirmish both of horse and foot near the castle of St. Katherine, where the people of the town stood on the bulwarks of the town, beholding as if it had been a triumph or a sport.

The Governor's Challenge

On the 9th a trumpet of one Jerpenville being sent into the town, Villiers the Governor desired him to signify to the Lord General that whereas he had sent unto Chevalier Pickard to break a pike with him, he would the next day bring him into the field, either armed or in his doublet, to answer his challenge; and if he listed he would bring sixteen of his gentlemen against sixteen of the General's.

To this the Earl of Essex answered in writing, that at his first coming into France he was occasioned to send his drums thither, understanding that the Chevalier Pickard was in the town, to tell him that he was sorry for old acquaintance that he should persist in so bad an action and against so brave a King. But since it were so, he would be glad to find him at the head of his troop with a pike. And he was to know that he was a General of an army from an absolute Prince in which there were many chevaliers, Pickard's equal at least. Besides, that if he or any others had desire to find him, all those of his could justify that the first day of his sitting down here he was twice at the head of his troop and offered to charge; and he refused and wheeled about. But for that he himself was in some respect of his government, he challenged him that he would make it good upon him either armed or in his doublet; that the King's cause was more just and honest than that he upheld of the League, that he himself was a better man than he, and his mistress fairer than his. And if he would have help and parley, he would bring twenty of like quality to Chevalier Pickard, or sixty, that the meanest of them should be a Captain in Chief.

The answer of Villiers was received on the 11th to the effect that, in saying the cause of the King was juster cause than that of the League's and that the General was a better man than he was, he did lie; and would fight thereon when the Duc de Mayne should come.

To this the Earl answered by trumpet that his lie was very frivolous and did no way concern him considering it was not given him upon a good ground; yet eftsoons he did call him to the maintenance of that he had denied, and if he did not answer now, he had no excuse; then shame and infamy must light upon him, which was generally spoken of him by all the French themselves.

The Governor also sent a challenge to any foot captain, man to man with shot and with rapier, which was accepted; and Captain Acton, desirous of that combat, had his name sent to the Governor. But in the end they made excuses and nothing came of it.

On the 13th after breakfast, the General went to the Marshal's quarters accompanied by sundry gentlemen in their best attire to meet the King, when all dismounted to kiss his hand, and he alighted to embrace the Marshal and the General; after which they brought him to his quarter and went to council.

The 16th it was rumoured, as it had been ever since he came, that the King was going to Dieppe to hasten provisions and necessaries; but some of his servants said that his journey was to meet a Saint (for he owed devotion to more than one Gabriel only) to whom he had long been devout, whose body was transported thither from Caen, that his devotion and his vows might be performed with more ease.

On the 19th about twelve o'clock at night some of the King's nobility and eight gentlemen approached the castle of St. Katherine, and there the pioneers began to build a fort, and, because it could not be finished in one night, the King's nobles and twenty-five of the Lord General's principal gentlemen, armed with pikes, came thither to guard against any sally that should be made out of the town or castle; and about an hour after day, the King himself came to cheer the pioneers to work and the rest to a resolute defence. The King seemed very desirous of some sport, and turning to Mr. Thomas Coningsby asked him whether the enemy would sally or no; who answered that if they were honest men they should, but if they were Englishmen they would; to which the King replied, 'By my faith, I believe it.' In the evening came news that the Lord General was to return to England in the morning.

On the 20th the Lord General rose very early and went towards the King's quarters, having first despatched and ordered many things for the army, and so accompanied with Sir Henry Unton and many others he alighted on a fair plain, and there he knighted Sir Henry Killigrew. After despatching his business in the King's quarters he took his journey towards Dieppe.

26th November. THE QUEEN'S LETTERS TO THE EMPEROR OF RUSSIA.

Sir George Barnes, who tradeth much with Russia, understanding that the Queen, at the request of the King of Scotland, is about to write to the Emperor of Russia for the enlargement of a Scottish Captain, a prisoner in Moscow, writes to the Lord Treasurer that since the Queen hath sent several letters for particular men and causes of little moment, it is said in the Emperor's Court that the Queen of England's letters are very cheap.

ABUSES IN THE CLOTH TRADE.

The Council being desirous of repressing certain abuses in the cloth trade have written to the Queen's Attorney General and others asking them for their advice. In the reign of King Edward the Sixth and of King Philip and Queen Mary certain laws were made concerning the true and perfect making of the cloth called Devonshire kerseys or dozens whereby a certain length, breadth and weight was presented, the penalty being laid on the clothier; but now slight and bad devices put in use by weavers prevent the good intended by that statute. These weavers escape because no provision was made in the statute for their punishment.

THE CHARGES OF THE BORDEAUX FLEET.

A charge of 3s. on the tun of all wines and other merchandise is to be levied on all wines and other merchandise arriving from the ports of Rochelle and Bordeaux at any port in England to cover the cost of waftage for the fleet. These charges fell formerly on the merchants of London, but as the ships of other ports take advantage of the convoy they shall be borne by all.

4th December. A PETITION OF THE PURITAN PRISONERS.

Thomas Cartwright and eight other Puritan prisoners have petitioned the Lord Treasurer praying that they may be allowed bail until the Council is pleased to call them for further trial of their innocency. His lordship, say they, will easily discern that over a year's imprisonment strikes deep into their healths. It is well known that divers papists, who not only deny the Queen's lawful authority but give it to a stranger, a sworn enemy of theirs and all other Christians, yet receive favour of freedom from their imprisonment. Never a one of them but has been sworn to the Queen's supremacy and is ready to take the oath again.

ORDERS FOR REFORMING THE ARMY IN NORMANDY.

Orders are sent by the Council for the better ordering and reforming of the army in Normandy under the Earl of Essex. He shall cause all captains of the foot bands to deliver on oath perfect rolls of all their officers and soldiers showing those now serviceable and any others remaining there sick and unable to serve; and in another roll the names of all that first came over with them but are not now present, making a distinction of those sent away by passport, those dead, and those that have run away; further they shall deliver in the roll a certain note of all the armour and weapons of those no longer in service, and where it is.

Having received these rolls the Lieutenant General shall consider how many bands of 150 (allowing 15 dead pays) or how many bands of 100 (allowing 10 dead pays) can be made of the whole number. And because this cannot be done without cassing some of the bands, he shall, for an example, cass his own band of 200, and also the bands of those receiving special allowance as officers of the army or colonels of regiments; also the bands which are weakest.

He shall take special care to preserve the ordnance and munition from water, and to recover, if he can, such as have fled away from the Queen's service. If they are apprehended in France they should be hanged as they deserve, and proclamation made that any who presume to come over to England will be hanged up whensoever he shall be apprehended.

5th December. AN UNSUCCESSFUL AMBUSCADE AT ROUEN.

From Rouen it is reported that the commanders taking at heart the ill success of a recent skirmish in which two brave soldiers had been killed and their bodies lost, planned to lay an ambuscade on the 30th November. Captain Barton with 24 shot hid in the cellar of a house pulled down near the ditch and town port; Captain Henry Power in another place with 16 pikes; and some shot of Monsieur Hallard Mountmorency on the other side of the port. This ambush being laid before day, about 8 o'clock the enemy opened the ports and came to the usual place of the court of guard, which was some six or eight score paces from the port.

After they had been there a while and set out their sentinels, Sir Roger Williams and the choicest of the gentlemen being in the trenches, caused some musketeers to shoot at their sentinels and sent other shot to beat them in. As the skirmish grew warm, our men according to directions retreated to bring the enemy more within danger of the ambuscade; then the sign was given, which was the throwing up of a hat with feathers of Sir Thomas Baskerville. But this was not observed by Captain Barton, who should first have discovered himself, so that our men were fain to call and cry, which caused the enemy to suspect and to retreat as fast as their legs could carry them to the port. Captain Barton, for want of better speed than they fell short of them, but some four or six were said to have fallen, and our men had the spoil of the court of guard, some cloaks and weapons.

As our men retreated some artillery were shot, one of which lighted upon Monsieur Hallard Mountmorency, slaying his horse and breaking his leg below the knee.

6th December. GREENE'S 'A MAIDEN'S DREAM.'

A Maiden's Dream ; upon the death of the Right Honourable Sir Christopher Hatton, written by Robert Greene, is entered, being dedicated to the Lady Elizabeth Hatton, to whom he noteth that, having long wished to gratify the father with something worthy of himself, he now takes opportunity to show his duty to him in his daughter. In this funeral elegy is shown the complaint of Justice, of Prudence, of Fortitude, Temperance, Beauty, Hospitality, and Religion ; and of primates, soldiers, and people for the loss of the Lord Chancellor, ending with the maiden's vision of the soul of Sir Christopher carried by Astraea among the hierarchies :

'With that methought within her golden lap,
(This sunbright goddess smiling with her eye,)
The soul of Hatton curiously did wrap,
And in a cloud was taken up on high.
Vain dreams are fond, but thus as then dreamt I,
And more, methought I heard the angels sing
An "Alleluia" for to welcome him.'

10th December. SEVEN CATHOLICS EXECUTED.

White, Plassden and Lacy, Jesuit priests, with two lay Catholics, taken by Topcliffe at the beginning of November, were executed at Tyburn. Edmund Jennings, the Jesuit, and Mr. Swithin Wells were dragged on hurdles to Holborn, over against Mr. Wells' house, where Jennings was discovered saying Mass. When Jennings arrived at the gallows he began to say, '*O Crux diu desiderata et iam concupiscenti animo praeparata.*' Being bade to confess his treason, for so the Queen would doubtless pardon him, he answered, 'I know not ever to have offended her. If to say Mass be treason, I confess I have done it and glory in it.' These words so enraged Topcliffe that he refused him leave to say any more, scarcely even to recite the *Pater noster*, but caused him to be turned off the ladder and the rope immediately cut. Jennings was thus thrown on his feet, but the hangman tripped up his heels, cut off his members and disembowelled him. In this agony Jennings began to call on St. Gregory to the great astonishment of the hangman, who cried out with a loud voice, 'God's wounds! his heart is in my hand and yet Gregory is in his mouth.'

13th December. GREENE'S 'NOTABLE DISCOVERY OF COSNAGE' AND 'THE SECOND PART OF CONNY-CATCHING.'

Robert Greene that was wont to write for the pleasure of our gentlemen and ladies hath penned a *Notable Discovery of Cosnage* and *The Second Part of Conny-Catching* now that riper days call him to repentance. These books are for the commodity of his countrymen, to warn them, and especially merchants, farmers, and honest-minded yeomen, against the practisers of the Art of Conny-Catching and the Art of Crossbiting.

For the Art of Conny-Catching, or cosening at card play, there be needed three parties, the setter to draw in the conny (that is to be cheated) familiarly to drink with him, the verser to join them in the tavern and to offer to play with them, and the barnacle appearing to be but a stranger that is invited to join them. The barnacle and the verser begin to cut the cards, and the verser, asking the conny secretly by signs if he will help him to cheat the barnacle, begins his game, and at the first winneth the stakes until the conny is also drawn in and venturing a high stake, by some sleight the cut falls against him and he is cheated of all.

The art of crossbiting is the practice of harlots and their mates that entice a young man into their houses and there either pick his pockets or else, on the woman sending for her husband or friend, the crossbiters fall upon him and threaten him with Bridewell and the law so that for fear he gives up his purse or makes them out a bill to pay a sum of money by a certain day.

In the *Second Part of Conny-Catching* are displayed the villainies of the nip and the foist, the priggar, the Vincent's law, the lifting law, the courber, and the black art.

The nip and the foist, though their subject, a well-lined purse, is the same, yet is their manner different; the nip using a knife to cut the purse, the foist his hand to draw the pocket. These foists holding themselves to be of the highest degree term themselves Gentlemen foists, and so much disdain to be called cutpurses that the foist refuseth even to wear a knife about him lest he be suspected to be a nip.

The priggar is the stealer of horses. The courber worketh with a hook or curb, made with joints (like an angle rod that he might hide it beneath his cloak), which he thrusteth through at a window to draw out what he shall find. The black art is the picking of locks, and Vincent's law the cheating at bowls.

It was objected by some that read the first book that Greene used no eloquent phrases as in his former works, and to this he answereth that it were an odious thing to apply a fine style to so base a subject.

15th December. The Defence of Plymouth.

The Council write to Sir John Gilbert, Sir Francis Drake and other gentlemen concerning the defence of the town of Plymouth against any sudden attempt that the enemy might make. As they are not resolved whether it is better to build a fort on the sea side within or near the town, or else to make a wall about the town, they instruct these gentlemen to seek the advice of some skilful engineer to view the circuit and to estimate the charge after a certain rate by the perch. Towards this charge besides the sums which the country might be induced to contribute the Queen will be pleased to grant an imposition to be laid upon each tun of pilchards taken out of Plymouth; and because the time is past for this season they deem it best that they should deal with the county to induce them to disburse by way of loan or otherwise such reasonable sums of money as may begin and maintain the work until the next season. But before they proceed with the work they should advertise the Council what they shall resolve and what hope they find of their endeavours with the county for beginning it.

A Negligent Commissary Dismissed.

Thomas Wyatt, commissary for the companies in the Low Countries dispersed under Sir Francis Vere, is dismissed from his post, having neglected to send over certificates or muster rolls of the companies whereby their strength might be discerned. By reason of his omission the strength of the companies lately sent into France was not known, so that instead of 1000 complete with the dead pays but 638 arrived, which numbers might have been redressed, if it had appeared before by his timely certificate.

16th December. SIR CHRISTOPHER HATTON'S FUNERAL.

Sir Christopher Hatton was this day honourably buried in St. Paul's; one hundred poor people having gowns and caps given them going before; of gentlemen, and yeomen, in gowns, cloaks and coats, more than three hundred, with the Lords of the Council and others, besides fourscore of the Guard which followed.

17th December. MASTERLESS MEN IN THE CITY TO BE TAKEN UP.

The Lord Mayor and Aldermen are required to take up within the City and liberties of London 100 loose and masterless men, there being at this time a great many, especially of those returned from service in France. These men are to be sent forthwith to Ostend in Flanders to complete the companies serving there under Sir Edward Norris. The men are to be bestowed in Leadenhall or some other fit place where they can be kept together and not allowed to slip away until the whole number is complete; and thence to be safely conveyed to their shipping near about St. Katherine's. The manner employed, either by privy search in the night or otherwise, is referred to their discretion. Orders have already been taken by Sir Edward for their victualling until they be embarked so that the City shall not be charged with them.

18th December. TWO SUSPECTED RECUSANTS.

The Attorney General and the Solicitor General are to examine two Englishmen, Anthony Skinner and Richard Acliffe, who were apprehended at Gravesend coming up the river in a small boat of Calais. These men are both recusants and had been absent from the realm for eight years, remaining for the most part at Rome, the one as servant to Cardinal Allen, the other with the Bishop of Cassano.

A NOTABLE INSTANCE OF THE CORRUPTION OF THESE WARS.

A gentleman that had a fair house in a village not far from Rouen was desirous to have protection from the Lord General, who promised to provide him with a certain quantity of oats and hay weekly. Two Englishmen were sent to guard his house, but certain of Monsieur Hallard Mountmorency's lackeys coming for forage to the village roughly intreated them and took away their horses. Whereupon, returning to their master, the following night at midnight, forty cuirassiers entered the house, with force took the two Englishmen prisoners, wounded the master to death, spoiled his house, took the Englishmen's horses and all his; and the next news heard was that the Englishmen were prisoners in Rouen, having been sold to the enemy.

19th December. FURTHER MEASURES AGAINST RECUSANTS.

The Commissioners specially chosen to inquire into the secret repair into the realm of Jesuits and seminary priests are warned that as the special commission will be renewed when necessary, they shall privately inform the Council whether any in the commission are suspected to be unsound in religion or have wives, children or any of their families known recusants or harbour persons suspected to be backward in religion. Moreover if they find the number not sufficient or not so placed for their habitations that they may divide the service, or that others meet to be employed in this service are omitted, they are likewise to certify their names and dwelling places, with their opinions of the men.

21st December. MASTERLESS MEN TO BE TAKEN UP IN KENT.

The Lord Mayor hath not been able to find above eighty masterless men in the City for service in the Low Countries. The Lord Cobham is now to give order to his Deputy Lieutenants in the County of Kent to take up loose and vagrant persons to make up the total number to one hundred.

24th December. A HIGHHANDED ARREST.

The Recorder of the City of London is summoned to appear before the Council on St. Stephen's Day to declare upon what foundation he subscribed a warrant whereby one Paine was taken out of his lodging in the night by a constable and a servant of his and a dozen persons, servants and friends of Sir Francis Willoughby, and conveyed to the Counter in Wood Street, there to be forthcoming to answer divers points touching high treason. They think it strange for him to be committed to prison upon treason that should hereafter be laid to his charge, as though a man should be made prisoner before his offence was known.

26th December. THE TRIPOLI MERCHANTS RECOMMENDED TO CHARITY.

There be six Turks lately arrived from France in an English vessel, of whom three are said to be of the guard of the Grand Signior. They allege that they have been retained more than twenty years as slaves in the galleys of the Spanish King before they found means to escape. These men have made humble suit to the merchants trading in Tripoli to be relieved by the loan of some hundred crowns, offering to be bound to repay the money when they come to the first place of Turkish dominion, before they set foot on shore. The Council recommend their request to the merchants, praying and requiring them to furnish this aid, which would be gratefully accepted by the Grand Signior and the other people in general of that country.

BEACON WATCHES.

Beacon watches are now to be discontinued until 15th March; but nevertheless the beacons to be kept in good order and furnished with sufficient fuel to be used if cause should require.

29th December. GOODS RIFLED FROM PRIZES IN CORNWALL AND DEVON TO BE RESTORED.

The captains of the London ships in the Lord Thomas Howard's fleet are reported to have carried their prizes into remote ports and havens and there enriched themselves by rifling the prizes and selling divers parcels to persons dwelling in the port towns, to the great slander and prejudice of sea discipline and wrong to the merchant adventurers of London. Her Majesty not willing to suffer so great a disorder now causeth proclamation to be made in Cornwall, Devonshire, Dorsetshire and Hampshire straightly charging all that in any ways have received any foreign coin, bullion of gold or silver, jewels, pearls, stones, musk, wrought or raw silk, cochenilia, indigo or other merchandise, within ten days to bring in a note of it in writing showing the prices they paid and the names of those off whom they bought, declaring also the day, time, and place. Those not obeying this order shall be held and taken as felons and abettors to pirates, and proceeded against as in the case of felony is customary to be done by the law of the realm.

THE SIEGE OF ROUEN.

From Rouen there is news of a sally made by the enemy on the 6th of the month, who came on with such speed that the sentinels had no leisure to give the court of guard any warning but by coming away without resistance. They quitted three of Hallard Mountmorency's courts of guard, not without the loss of their lives. The fourth court of guard, where the greatest strength lay, was a large house without a roof, the walls being a pike length high, with many loopholes to shoot out at. The enemy, with men for the purpose excellently well armed, by the advantage of the walls got to the top and leaped in amongst them most resolutely, putting to the sword all within, and those that escaped there fell upon the horsemen who had the like mercy. The horsemen advanced so far that our sentinels and the rest quitted the trenches, but Sir Thomas Gerrard at the instant drew out the guard of the day into the field to make stand, and gave alarm to all our army which came out full fast.

When the enemy perceived the fast stand of our pikes, they had no will to come nearer, but after some discharge of pistols towards our forward gallants, when Captain Barton was dangerously hurt in the face, seeing 150 of our pioneers coming out with their pikes, they retired and our men repossessed the trenches. After the fight nearly fifty dead were counted in the court of guard. Two captains in chief were slain, and two gentlemen of especial mark, both whose bodies the enemy took away. Soon after there grew a new alarm, and our men began to run in panic but were stopped by Sir Roger Williams, Sir Thomas Baskerville, Sir Thomas Gerrard and other gentlemen.

On the 7th Sir Richard Acton died of the disease of the camp, a pestilent ague, now very prevalent.

On the 12th, a sergeant of the pioneers was discovered to be conspiring to lead away fifty or sixty of the principalest into Rouen. Whereupon a Council of War was held, and all brought to the tree but the sergeant only executed for example in presence of them all.

On the 14th the Lord General returned to the army from England, and notwithstanding his long and great journey, he would needs before alighting go down to the trenches, and, hearing of the great threatenings which were expected, must call to a sentinel of the enemy and bid him tell Monsieur Villiers that he was come with some twenty gentlemen with him ; and that if he would enterprise anything against the English quarter he must do it that night or never, for the next day we should be too strong for him, there being 2000 English of the old bands of the Low Countries coming this night.

On the 17th and 18th muster was taken, and it was found that there were less than 200 horse. The 25 old companies were reduced to 8, and those short of their number. On the 19th the bands of the Low Countries were mustered, and five of them sent to another quarter where they watched every third night, and the Lord General himself with many other principal gentlemen also watching every third night within three pikes length of the enemy's guard, where they had continual shooting. The Lord General had great speech with Monsieur Pickard, who asked for his mistress that he had in England, and promised to come and dine with him one day.

On the 24th the Lord General went to the trenches with many, where they forced the enemy from the counterscarp and slew many, taking cloaks, weapons and the like. Marshal Biron took upon him to defend the ground that was won, which was of great importance, but the enemy sallying out in great numbers the next day about eleven o'clock forced the guard there. Our men fought bravely for about half an hour, never seconded of the French ; the soldiers spending all their powder and shot, and the enemy with great fury driving down the barrels of earth. Sir Thomas Baskerville saw no remedy, but to sally out, and beat them with the pike and halbert, but he was slenderly followed, and forced to retire, abandoned of too many of our common soldiers ; but seventeen gentlemen and officers rallied and made a stand.

SOMEWHAT TO READ FOR THEM THAT LIST

1591

CLAPHAM'S 'NARCISSUS.'

Narcissus, siue Amoris iuvenilis et praecipue Philautiae breuis atque moralis descriptio, written in Latin hexameter verses, and dedicated to Henry, Earl of Southampton, by John Clapham. Herein Narcissus,

quem luminis orba
Prosperitas genuit, peperit Superbia vana,
Et tepido erroris nutriuit Opinio lacte,

being smitten by the arrow of love came to the fountain Philautia, and there falling in love with his own image, cried out to it; but was answered back in mockery by Echo. Night coming on, the image vanished, and the infatuate youth unable anywhere to find his love, fell from the bank into the river and so perished.

COSIN'S 'APOLOGY FOR SUNDRY PROCEEDINGS.'

An Apology: of and for sundry proceedings by jurisdiction Ecclesiastical, of later times by some challenged, and also diversly impugned by them, written by Dr. Richard Cosin, though without the name either of author or printer on its title. He noteth that of late certain disturbers of Her Majesty's happy reformation had rested themselves most in advancing a new-found discipline and in discrediting the present government Ecclesiastical by their speeches and writings, as well by impugning the callings and form of Ecclesiastical government as by defaming the persons of the governors with unchristian gibes, contumelies and other indignities. But when these had not succeeded according to their wish, they pursue a more politic course; for by themselves, and others more simple excited cunningly by them, they challenge divers received proceedings in Courts Ecclesiastical as not justifiable by law; and by their frequent clamours, some very grave, wise and learned (no way affected to their other fancies), either not being well informed of proceedings Ecclesiastical, or not weighing for want of leisure certain points doubtfully reported in the book of common law as their learning doth afford. In a kind of commiseration toward some of those who seem distressed and to be otherwise well meaning men divers proceedings Ecclesiastical have lately been called in question, both for matter and for circumstance and manner, that they are contrary to the laws of this realm.

Therefore he taketh in hand to show the reasons for the contrary based on the law and the Scriptures.

DIGGES' 'PANTOMETRIA.'

A new edition of *A Geometrical practical treatise named Pantometria*, revised by the author, Mr. Thomas Digges and his son, Mr. Leonard Digges. This book besides giving the theories of Geometry, addeth many engravings showing the practical use of measuring distances and heights with such instruments as the quadrant geometrical, the geometrical square, the theodolitus, the measuring of plane surfaces, the contents of solids, and so forth.

GARRARD'S 'ART OF WAR.'

The Art of War, written by William Garrard, gentleman, who had served the King of Spain in his wars of fourteen years and died in 1587, corrected and finished by Captain Hitchcock, dedicated to the Earl of Essex. Herein are five books, of which the first treateth of the behaviour of a good soldier, disnier or corporal, together with the martial laws of the field; the second, adorned with many figures, the office of a sergeant, ensign bearer, lieutenant, and gentlemen of a band; the third of the governing f bands, squadrons and battles, of captains, colonels, and sergeant-majors-general; the fourth of the general of horsemen, the scout-master, and the office of the marshal of the field; the fifth of the great master of the artillery, of the master gunner, and of general notes of fortification; of the besieging, expugning and defending of a fortress.

GIBBON'S 'WORK WORTH THE READING.'

A Work worth the Reading, by Charles Gibbon, of Bury St. Edmunds, dedicated to Sir Nicholas Bacon, wherein is contained five profitable and pithy questions, *videlicet*: 1st, whether the election of the parents is to be preferred before the affection of their children in marriages; 2nd, whether the father may lawfully disinherit his first born; 3rd, whether a reasonable allowance may be taken for lending of money; 4th, whether the rich or the poor are to be accounted most blessed; 5th, whether there be degrees of glory in Heaven or differences of pains in Hell. These questions are argued by Philogus and Tychicus, two lovers of learning, the latter supporting his arguments more from the Scriptures, the former rather from common experience.

Of the rights of parents in marriage Tychicus saith that if a man may bestow his goods to whom he will, he may as well bestow his children where he thinketh best, for children are the goods of the parents. To which Philogus answereth that if parents impose upon their children a match more to content their desire for more than their children's godly choice for love then they should not be obeyed, for what greater occasion of incontinency could be given than to match a young and lusty maid against her own mind with an infirm and decrepit person to satisfy another's pleasure? To this Tychicus replieth that to match a young maid and an old man is indeed most miserable.

Giles Fletcher's 'Of the Russe Commonwealth.'

The Book of the Russe Commonwealth, by Mr. Giles Fletcher (that was employed in the Queen's service to the Emperor of Russia in 1588), being dedicated to the Queen. Herein is described the cosmography of the country; the ordering of the state, with the condition of the commonality or vulgar sort; the judicial procedure; their warlike provisions and martial discipline; the ecclesiastical state; ending with a chapter upon the œconomy or private behaviour of the people of that nation.

The Emperor of the country is a person of mean stature, somewhat low and gross, of a sallow complexion, and inclining to the dropsy, hawk nosed, unsteady in his pace by reason of some weakness of his limbs, heavy and inactive, yet commonly smiling, almost to a laughter. For quality otherwise simple or slow witted, but very gentle and of an easy nature, quiet, merciful, of no martial disposition, nor greatly apt for matter of policy, very superstitious, and infinite that way.

The Russe because he is used to extremities both of heat and cold beareth both very patiently. They can be seen coming out of their bath stoves, all on a froth, and fuming as hot almost as a pig at a spit, and straightway to leap into the river stark naked, and that in the coldest of winter time. The women to mend the bad hue of their skins, use to paint their faces with white and red colours so visibly that any man can perceive it. But this is no matter, because it is common and liked well by their husbands, who make them an ordinary allowance to buy colours to paint their faces, delighting themselves much to see their foul women become fair images. This practice parcheth the skin, and helpeth to deform them when their painting is off.

Of the vulgar sort he noteth that they are much oppressed by the nobility so that though otherwise hardened to bear any toil, they give themselves to idleness and drinking, as passing no more than from hand to mouth.

QUERCETANUS' 'SPAGERIC PREPARATION OF MINERALS, ANIMALS, AND VEGETABLES.'

The true and perfect spageric preparation of minerals, animals and vegetables, originally written by Dr. Josephus Quercetanus of Armenia, now set forth with divers rare secrets not heretofore known of many, by John Hester, a practitioner in the spagerical art; and dedicated to Sir Robert Carey.

Amongst those remedies especially recommended for the plague is a preparation of mummy (in former times prepared of bodies embalmed with pitch, frankincense, myrrh or aloes, but now made only of dried flesh), either in liquid, balm or tincture; also *balsamum urinae*, which Mr. Hester regardeth almost as *catholicum* in its uses.

This tincture to be made thus: 'Take the urine of young children about the age of twelve years, that hath drunk wine for certain months if it be possible; the same putrefy *in balneo* or dung a philosopher's year; then distil it with a gentle fire in sand, being also luted, the which ye shall note diligently. The flame ye shall put upon the feces four times; then the last water keep close shut, the which is white and stinking, and therefore ye may give it both taste and smell with cinnamon and sugar. The feces that remained in the bottom being black ye shall sublime by degrees of fire, and you shall have a most precious salt, the which some affirm will dissolve gold, silver and other metals; some philosophers call it their *menstrua*.'

'THE TROUBLESOME REIGN OF KING JOHN.'

The two parts of *The Troublesome Reign of King John*, a play that hath been sundry times acted by the Queen's players in the City of London. In the first part is shown the discovery of King Richard Cordelion's base son (commonly named the Bastard Faulconbridge), the wars in France and the supposed death of Arthur, being a play very fitting to the times, as the prologue proclaimeth:

> You that with friendly grace of smoothed brow
> Have entertained the Scythian Tamburlane
> And given applause unto an Infidel,
> Vouchsafe to welcome, with like courtesy,
> A warlike Christian and your countryman.
> For Christ's true faith indured he many a storm,
> And set himself against the Man of Rome,
> Until base treason (by a damned wight)
> Did all his former triumphs put to flight,
> Accept of it, sweet gentles, in good sort,
> And think it was prepared for your disport.

In the second part is portrayed the death of Arthur Plantagenet, the landing of Lewis, and the poisoning of King John at Swinstead Abbey.

WILMOT'S 'TANCRED AND GISMUND.'

The Tragedy of Tancred and Gismund, compiled and acted by Robert Wilmot and other gentlemen of the Inner Temple before the Queen more than twenty years before, being newly revised and polished according to the decorum of these days, on the importunity of some of Mr. Wilmot's friends. This tragedy, whereof the story is taken from Boccaccio, is written after the pattern of the ancients, the action being related and not shown upon the stage.

1592

1st January. SPENSER'S 'DAPHNAIDA.'

Mr. Edmund Spenser hath sent his *Daphnaida, an Elegy upon the death of the noble and virtuous Douglas Howard, daughter and heir of Henry Howard, Viscount Bindon, and wife of Arthur Gorges, Esquire,* to the Lady Helena, Marquess of Northampton, wherein in the form of a pastoral Alcyon complains of the death of his Daphne.

3rd January. ANOTHER PROCLAMATION AGAINST THE DISORDERS AT PORTS.

Information hath now been given that some of the Captains, Masters and Mariners besides those in the west broke bulk and made spoil of goods on the seas before their ships had come to port. Another proclamation in terms similar to that of the 29th December is now published, commanding all such offenders to declare themselves in writing within twenty days.

7th January. THE LEVANT COMPANY.

The Levant Company are granted a patent allowing them with other privileges the sole right of trading to the Levant Seas, Turkey and Venice, and of importing the small fruits called 'currants,' being the raisins of Corinth.

THE COMMISSION AGAINST JESUITS RENEWED.

The Commission for enquiry of Jesuits and Seminaries is renewed for the counties of Kent, Buckingham, Middlesex, Surrey and Durham.

MR. HENRY CAESAR RELEASED.

Mr. Henry Caesar that was committed to the charge and custody of Sir Richard Martin for his recusancy is now to be released, since the Council learn that through conference of learned preachers he now conforms himself in religion, professing that he is indeed resolved in his conscience according to the truth. They therefore let him understand that they see no cause but that he may be set at liberty to be at the disposition of his brother, Dr. Julius Caesar, who means to place him at the University for his better instruction and furtherance in learning.

9th January. A Protest on behalf of the Puritans.

Sir Francis Knollys hath written to the Lord Treasurer on behalf of the Puritans still in prison that he marvels how the Queen can be persuaded that she is in as much danger of the Puritans as of the Papists; for she cannot be ignorant that the Puritans are not able to change the government of the clergy but by petition; and even then the Queen could not do it but she must call a parliament for it, and no act could pass unless she give her royal assent thereto. As for their seditious conduct, if the bishops or the Lord Chancellor or any of them could have proved *de facto* that Cartwright and his fellow prisoners had gone about any such matter seditiously, then they had been hanged before this. But the Queen must keep a form of justice as well against Puritans as any other subjects, and they tried in convenient time, whether suspected for sedition or treason or Puritanism or by whatever name it is called.

An Attorney's Unseemly Apparel.

One King, an attorney in the Court of Common Pleas, that was committed to prison for his misdemeanour in raising and laying the street for the assisting of an arrest with lewd words which were likely to have bred some tumult, was brought before the Council. And because he appears before their Lordships in apparel unfit for his calling, with a gilt rapier, extreme great ruffs, and like unseemly apparel, they certify the Lord Chief Justice of the Common Pleas of his behaviour that he shall be dismissed of his office and place in that Court.

16th January. A Case of Contraband Goods.

This day the Privy Council heard a cause between the Earl of Cumberland and one Harman Langerman, factor for certain merchants of the Stoad Towns, of whom some ships and goods appertaining were taken on the seas by the Earl. He claimed them as good prize going into Spain by the North Seas, being laden with prohibited goods of divers sorts for the use of the enemy. Amongst these was canvas of six sundry sorts which was claimed as prize being fit for use as sails for ships of war, for cartilages for powder and like use for the wars; but which Langerman said served only for merchandise.

The controversy had been referred to Sir John Hawkins and William Burrows, officers of the Admiralty, and to four men skilful in these matters, two chosen by each party. Whose report being heard and also what Langerman could say on his own behalf, the Council consider that the fourth and fifth sort of these canvases, called euphards or soutages, might be used for sails and other necessary purposes for the seas and for wars; yet, because Langerman shows that the merchants of the Steeds did not understand the sorts of canvases to be prohibited, they offer that either Langerman shall receive of the Earl the sum of £300 for all the two sorts of canvases, or shall give the Earl £300 and himself take the canvases, or else that they shall be sold to the uttermost value and one half to be given to Langerman. The sixth sort of canvas called guttings, which they judge to be of the nature of merchandise and not for any use in war, shall be delivered back to Langerman.

They also require Langerman to certify his countrymen that the kind of canvas called euphards as well as the other three kinds of canvas are reputed as wares prohibited, and may not be carried into Spain so long as the King of Spain should continue his hostility against the Queen's majesty and her dominions.

Certain Goods prohibited to be carried to Spain.

Notwithstanding former warnings to the citizens of the Hanze Towns and Stade that they should forbear to send into Spain or Portugal any kind of provision fit for the wars upon pain of confiscation, the enemy is daily being furnished with corn, munition, and other things. The Council now add to the list of prohibited wares iron, steel, all sorts of weapons, planks, deal boards, wainscot, pipe staves, flax, tow, hemp and resin.

19th January. The Earl of Essex returns to Court.

The Earl of Essex on his return from France hath come to the Court, and being received very graciously by the Queen is able to allay her anger with Sir Henry Unton, the ambassador, for that he had allowed the Earl to see a certain letter of hers. This letter was sent to Sir Henry by Sir Robert Cecil, written in Her Majesty's own hand, and to be shown to the Earl only if he refused to return to England. When the packet of letters reached the ambassador, being brought by one of my Lord's servants and delivered in his presence, he required the packet to be opened forthwith, saying that he hoped there were letters for him. Upon Sir Henry opening the packet, my Lord seeing a letter addressed to himself, snatched it out of his hands before he had time to read that letter of Sir Robert Cecil's which accompanied it. The Queen hath hitherto been much displeased that her letter should have reached the Earl's hands thus, and by the hands of the Lord Treasurer had severely censured the ambassador. Moreover the Earl speaketh very highly of the ambassador's good services to the Queen, who is thus appeased. It is believed that his return to Court will make the Queen more favourable to helping the French King.

22nd January. A PROCLAMATION TO REFORM ABUSES IN THE CLOTH TRADE.

A proclamation is published for the reformation of sundry abuses about making of cloths, called Devonshire kersies or dozens, ordering that from the Feast of the Annunciation of Our Lady these cloths as they come raw from the weaver's beam shall weigh fifteen pounds at the least and contain between fifteen and sixteen yards in length.

8th January. A SPECIAL COMMISSION TO DEAL WITH IMPRISONED RECUSANTS.

Owing to matters of greater weight and importance, to which the members of the Council are bound to attend, some prisoners suspected of being Jesuits or Seminaries from over seas remain for a long time without being thoroughly heard or examined. A special commission of twelve gentlemen, amongst them Sir Richard Martin, Mr. Sergeant Fleetwood, the Recorder of London, Richard Topcliffe and Richard Young, is now appointed. On any special cause three or more of them shall summon such persons before them, and for their better proceeding the keepers of the prisons shall deliver weekly the names of such prisoners as they have received. They meet once a week in some convenient place, either at the prison or some place near, to examine them on such information as they receive. Moreover as some are prisoners at large, and some may be bestowed in prisons not fit for them to remain by reason of favour shown to them, the commissioners will take order, as they think fit, for their more straight keeping or removing to other prisons.

30th January. FLESH PROHIBITED DURING LENT.

The Lords-Lieutenant of the counties near London are charged that the orders restraining the use of flesh during the time of Lent shall be put in execution and not as in former years so neglected that at this time of the year wherein young cattle should most be spared for increase a greater quantity is killed than in any other season. The money received from the butchers for their licences is reserved for the use of poor soldiers, lame, impotent or maimed in the wars.

4th February. DANIEL'S 'DELIA.'

Delia, containing certain sonnets, by Samuel Daniel, is entered. In the Epistle Dedicatory to the Lady Mary, Countess of Pembroke, Mr. Daniel writeth that although he rather desired to keep in the private passions of his youth from the multitude, as things uttered to himself and consecrated to silence, yet seeing that he was betrayed by the indiscretion of a greedy printer and had some of his secrets betrayed to the world uncorrected, doubting the like of the rest, he is thus forced to publish that which he never meant.

6th February. NEWS FROM FRANCE.

The news from France is that the Duke of Parma is likely to give battle, and if he doth not besiege some town by the way will reach Rouen within a week. Sir Henry Unton, the ambassador, is not only out of favour with the Queen over the matter of her letter to Essex, but with the King, who is advertised that he hath done ill offices for him with the Queen.

SIR FRANCIS WILLOUGHBY BEFORE THE COUNCIL.

Sir Francis Willoughby was called before the Council at the suit of Robert Paine, a prisoner in the King's Bench, for certain hard and unconscionable dealings offered by his servants, which appeared to their Lordships to be rather of malice than of any good ground or proof. They move him to have a charitable consideration of the poor man's estate, to which he willingly consenteth, promising to write letters to his servants to cease their negotiations and to redeliver his writings, goods, and other things taken away, if they should be found wrongfully detained. Sir Francis is accordingly dismissed of his farther attendance, but Paine remitted to the prison of the King's Bench to follow his trial for the criminal matters alleged against him.

7th February. GREENE'S 'THIRD PART OF CONNY-CATCHING.'

Greene hath written a *Third and last part of Conny-Catching, with the newly devised knavish art of fool-taking.* Herein are set forth notes of the devices of the conny-catchers delivered to him by a certain justice of the peace, and showing how divers had been beguiled.

12th February. THE QUEEN REFUSES FURTHER AID TO THE FRENCH KING.

Notwithstanding the letters of the King, and the solicitations of the French ambassador to yield more succour, the Queen will in no wise be induced to consent, though no more than 1500 men are required, 3000 having been asked for at first. Some fourteen days since the Lord Treasurer made ready letters and warrants for the Queen to have sent over one or two thousand pikemen; but when they came to the signing, she changed her mind, and ever since denies it, putting forward these reasons:

Firstly, her former offence against the King for that the last summer he neglected the taking of Rouen which he might have done, and yet wasted his own people and her treasure to no purpose.

Secondly, she thinketh so hardly of the King's fortune and success that she is loath to adventure any more of her people with him.

Thirdly, she thinketh it impossible to levy and send any power out of the country to be able to join with the King's forces before the Duke of Parma should force the King to battle.

Lastly, she is loath to send 2000 of her men out of the Low Country, and to hazard and waste her disciplined soldiers; for if need be to have their service in England she will be greatly disappointed by the loss of them.

But in truth the Queen and her realm are become very weary with the great expense both in loans of money, and in waging of men both by land and sea.

14th February. NEWS FROM FRANCE.

From France it is reported by the ambassador that the Duke of Parma hath captured Neuchâtel upon honourable composition, a place of great advantage to the enemy.

On the 7th the King was engaged with the enemy, and in the fight the Count Challigny (the Duke Mercury's brother) who commanded them was taken prisoner by Chicott, the King's fool, and very sore hurt. Many were slain and some captured; the rest escaping gave the alarum to the Duke of Guise's quarter, who barricaded their lodgings, and armed themselves. Most of their horse and foot sallied out, but by this time many shot had come up to the Baron de Biron and the enemy were forced back into Bures, where the King's men entering pell-mell with them slew two hundred in the village and took divers prisoners. The rest were forced to retire to the other side of the river. All the Duke of Guise's baggage was taken, his plate and money, and all he had there.

In this engagement Sir William Sackville is either taken or slain, having been separated from the rest. For himself the ambassador declareth that he is in great straits; all his horses are dead or harried out, for they never rest, being on horseback almost day and night; his servants die daily, and many of them are very weak and sick and cannot live long.

The King meanwhile anxiously expects succour from England.

15th February. FLESH PROHIBITED IN LONDON DURING LENT.

As in former years, killing and eating flesh in London during Lent is restrained.

19th February. PLAYING RESUMED.

The Lord Strange's Players now begin to play at the Rose Theatre on the Bankside, and act this day *Friar Bacon.*

THE QUEEN RESOLVES TO SEND SOLDIERS TO FRANCE.

The Queen having now resolved that 1600 soldiers shall be sent with diligence to Dieppe to the aid of the French King, the Council have ordered 300 to be levied in Sussex, which in heads are to be only 270, deducting the dead pays after the usual rate of 10 in the hundred, to be coated and armed forthwith and embarked at Rye; similarly another 300 from Kent to be embarked at Dover on the 28th of the month.

20th February. NEWS OF ROUEN.

Two lackeys of Monsieur Villiers, Governor of Rouen, taken returning from the Duke of Parma, who has now advanced to Cinqsens, declare that he would succour Rouen or force the levying of the siege.

21st February. THOMAS PORMORT, A JESUIT, EXECUTED.

Thomas Pormort, a seminary priest, was executed for high treason. This Pormort, being lodged in the house of Topcliffe after his arrest in October 1591, had been pressed very straightly to give information. He declared that in the course of these examinations Topcliffe, hoping to persuade him to recant, used very lewd and familiar speeches to him to show his favour with the Queen. Topcliffe said that all the Stanleys in England were to be suspected as traitors; he himself was so familiar with Her Majesty that he hath very secret dealing with her, having not only seen her legs and knees but felt her belly, saying to her that it was the softest belly of any womankind. She had said unto him, 'Be not these the arms, legs and body of King Henry?' to which he answered 'Yea.' She gave him for a favour a white linen hose wrought with white silk. He said that he was so familiar with her that when he pleased to speak with her he might take her away from any company; and that she was as pleasant with anyone that she loved. The Archbishop of Canterbury, he declared, was a fitter councillor in the kitchen among wenches than in a Prince's Court; as for Justice Young, he would hang the Archbishop and three hundred more if they were in his hands.

At the execution Pormort was forced to stand in his shirt almost two hours on a very cold day while Topcliffe pressed him to deny these words; but he would not.

23rd February. A LITIGIOUS FELLOW.

The magistrates of Essex are directed to look into the case of one, John Feltwell, of Great Wendon. This man, a very contentious person, cited certain inhabitants of the parish into the

Ecclesiastical Courts of London for tithes which had been answered, and, purposely to undo them, put in long and tedious libels, the copies of which were for the most part eighty sheets of paper, so that the poor men were not able to take them out by reason of the charges, much less to follow the causes at law. As this Feltwell, to avoid arrests and processes to be served on himself at the suit of sundry persons whom he has wronged, often removes as a fugitive to unknown places, the magistrates are to examine the matter and to make such good end therein that the poor men shall have no further cause to trouble the Council.

Sir R. Williams in Command in Normandy.

On the return of the Lord General from Normandy Sir Robert Williams succeedeth to the command.

24th February. Victuals sent to Normandy.

It is said that some hard measure was offered to the Vice-Treasurer by the captains of bands in Normandy for refusing to satisfy them in their undue demands of pay for soldiers under them. Sir Roger Williams is instructed to cause this matter to be reformed and to require the captains to forbear to demand their pay till a muster can be made; and also to let them know that the matter is very offensively taken.

As there hath been so great waste and spoil made in Normandy that victual will be scant and dear, a supply to the value of £1000 is being sent over with the 1600 men under Sir Edmund Yorke, to remain in magazine at Dieppe for the relief of the forces when needful but not otherwise. The price of this victual is to be defalked accordingly from the captains' weekly payments.

The rates to be charged for victual:

Beer, 3 pints	2d.	Cheese, 1 lb.	3d.
Biscuit, 1 lb.	1½d.	Beef, 1 lb.	3d.
Butter, 1 lb.	5d.	Bacon and Pork, 1 lb.	5d.

25th February. A Petition against Plays.

The Lord Mayor of London hath complained to the Archbishop of Canterbury of the daily and disorderly exercise of players and playing houses erected in the City whereby, saith he, the youth is greatly corrupted and their manners infected by the wanton and profane devices represented on the stages prentices and servants withdrawn from their work; and all sorts in general from their daily resort to sermons and other godly exercise, to the great hindrance of the trades and traders of the City and the profanation of religion. To the playing houses resort great numbers of light and lewd persons, harlots, cutpurses, coseners, pilferers, and such like. The Lord Mayor understandeth that the Queen must be served by this sort of people, and for this purpose did licence Mr. Tilney, the Master of the Revels, to reform, exercise and suppress all manner of players, by which he first licensed the playing houses within the City, for the Queen's service. But the Aldermen conclude that the Queen's players might as conveniently exercise in some private place, the City be freed from these continual disorders, and the great offence to the Church removed which would be to the contentment of all good Christians, especially the preachers and ministers who have long time made complaint for the redress of these abuses.

26th February. PLAYS OF THE WEEK.

The plays acted at the Rose Theatre this past week were *Muly Mullocco*, *Orlando Furioso*, *The Spanish Comedy*, *Sir John Maundeville*, *Harry of Cornwall*, *The Jew of Malta*.

THE DUKE OF PARMA RETREATS.

The ambassador now reporteth that on the 18th the King dislodged his whole army from Claire, fully resolved to give the Duke of Parma battle rather than to suffer his siege to be raised, for he had heard that the night before the Duke had marched from his camp near Cinqsens, with the greatest part of his vanguard to Cinqsens and Bellencombre with intent to raise the siege or thrust succours into Rouen. But the enemy, having received news of this intent, and being advertised of the effect of the last sally, retired with all possible diligence to Aumale, intending to go along the river to Abbeville. The next day the enemy lodged at Sinarpoint; and the next day still continued his way to Abbeville. This sudden retreat and the diligence used therein cannot be understood, neither is the siege raised nor the town succoured, except that a few men are sent in by stealth, 15 or 20 in a company at several times.

28th February. MAIMED SOLDIERS TO BE EXAMINED.

A proclamation signed by the Lords of the Privy Council is published ordering all soldiers who allege that they have served in the wars and still remain in London to be brought before those appointed at the Sessions Hall in the Old Bailey on Saturday next at one o'clock. They are to be examined and viewed so that some good order may be taken for the maimed in service, and for the punishment of the others, common beggars, rogues and able persons, counterfeiting the name of soldiers.

29th February. THE SCOTTISH WITCHES.

A pamphlet is printed called *News from Scotland* declaring the damnable life and death of Doctor Fian, a noted sorcerer who was executed at Edinburgh in January last, together with the examination of the witches, as they were uttered in the presence of the Scottish King.

The conspiracy of these witches was first brought to light by one David Seaton, deputy bailiff of the town of Trewent. This Seaton had a maid servant called Geillis Duncan that used secretly to be absent from her master's house every other night when she took in hand almost miraculously to help all that were troubled with any kind of sickness or infirmity, which caused such wonder that her master began to suspect these things to be done by some unnatural or extraordinary means. Whereupon he began to be very inquisitive, and when she gave him no answer, that he might the better learn the truth, with the help of others he tormented her with the torture of the pilliwinks upon her fingers and by binding a rope round her head. Still she would not confess anything, which made them suspect that she had been marked by the devil, and making diligent search about her they found the enemy's mark in her throat, whereon she confessed that all her doings were done by witchcraft through the wicked allurement of the devil.

After her confession she was committed to prison, where through her accusations she caused certain other notorious witches to be apprehended, notably Agnes Sampson of Haddington, and Dr. Fian, *alias* John Cunningham, master of the school at Saltpans in Lowthian. This Agnes Sampson was brought to Holyrood House before the King and others of the nobility of

Scotland, but stiffly denied all that was alleged against her, whereon they caused her to be taken back to prison, there to receive the tortures which had lately been provided for witches. Moreover it has been found by careful examination of witches and witchcraft, and by the confession of the witches themselves, that the devil marketh them with some secret mark; for when he receives them as his servants he licketh them with his tongue in some privy part of the body, which is commonly covered with hair, so this mark may not easily be seen, and so long as the devil's mark is not seen by the searchers the witch will not confess to anything.

For over an hour this Agnes Sampson was grievously tortured with a rope thrawen round her head, according to the Scottish custom, but would confess nothing until the devil's mark was found upon her privities, when immediately she confessed all that was demanded of her. And now being again brought before the King she confessed that on All Hallowe'en last she with a great company of other witches, to the number of two hundred, had gone to sea, each one in a riddle or sieve, drinking and making merry as they sailed until they came to the kirk of North Berwick in Lowthian, where they landed and danced a reel; Geillis Duncan going before them playing on a small trumpet, called a 'Jews' trump,' until they entered the kirk. This declaration so astonished the King that he sent for Geillis Duncan, who played this dance upon the trumpet before him, much delighted to be present at such strange examinations.

Agnes Sampson said further that the devil in likeness of a man had waited for their coming at North Berwick kirk, and being vexed that they tarried over long in the journey had enjoined on them a penance, which was to kiss his buttocks in sign of duty to him. Then he made an ungodly exhortation, greatly inveighing against the King of Scotland; and took their oaths for their good and true service. So they returned to sea and home again. At this time the witches asked the devil why he so hated the King of Scotland, and he replied that the King was his greatest enemy in all the world.

Sundry other things Agnes Sampson confessed before the King so strange and miraculous that he said they were all extreme liars. Whereupon she answered that she would discover a matter whereby he should not doubt. So taking him a little aside, she declared the very words which had passed between him and his Queen at Upslo in Norway the first night of their marriage, with their answers one to the other; whereat the King wondered greatly and swore by the living God that he believed all the devils in hell could not have discovered the same, acknowledging that her words were most true. Thereafter he gave more credit to what she confessed.

The examination of Dr. Fian also showed the great subtlety of the devil; for being apprehended at the accusation of Geillis Duncan, when he was tortured with the accustomed torments his tongue would not serve him to speak until the rest of the witches bad them search under his tongue, where two pins were found thrust up to the head. At this the witches cried, 'Now is the charm stinted.' Then he was immediately released and brought before the King; his confession was taken, and he willingly set his hand to it. Amongst other things confessed, he declared that he had sought the love of a gentlewoman by witchcraft and sorcery. This gentlewoman being unmarried had a brother who went to his school. Calling the boy to him he asked if he slept with his sister; he answered that he did. Therefore Dr. Fian secretly promised the boy that if he would bring three hairs of his sister's body he would teach him without stripes, giving him a piece of conjured paper to wrap them in.

The gentlewoman being asleep with the boy suddenly cried out to her mother that her brother would not let her sleep; whereon her mother, having a quick understanding, for she was a witch herself, rose immediately and asked the boy very closely what he meant, and the better to extort the truth she beat him. The mother recognising the doctor's purpose thought it best to answer him in his own art, so she took the paper from the boy in which he should have wrapped his sister's hair and went to a young heifer which had never gone to the bull and clipping off three hairs from the udder she told the boy to deliver them to his master, which he immediately did.

As soon as the schoolmaster had received them, he wrought his art upon them, thinking that they were the maiden's hairs; but no sooner had he conjured than the heifer whose hairs they indeed were came to the door of the church where he was, and made towards him, leaping and dancing upon him, and following him out of the church and wherever he went, to the great astonishment of all the townsmen of Saltpans.

Having signed this confession Dr. Fian was taken back to prison, where for a time he appeared very penitent, but in the night he found means to steal the key of the prison door, which he opened and fled away to Saltpans. Hot pursuit was made after him, and he was taken and brought back to prison. There being called before the King he was again examined concerning his flight and what had happened before. But notwithstanding his former confession, he utterly denied all. The King therefore thinking that he had made a fresh league with the devil, commanded a new and most strange torment to be applied to him. The nails on his fingers were split and pulled off with a pair of pincers and under every nail were thrust two needles up to the heads. But for all this, and for the torments of the boots which followed, he would not confess, but said that what he had said and done before was for fear of the pains which he had endured. After great consideration by the King and his Council, Dr. Fian was arraigned and condemned to be burned according to the law of the land. Whereupon he was put in a cart, and being first strangled was cast into a fire made ready and so burned on the Castlehill in Edinburgh on a Saturday at the end of January last past.

1st March. MEN TO BE IMPRESTED FOR SERVICE IN FRANCE.

As well as the 330 already impressed, the Lord Mayor is to cause 200 able and sufficient men to be taken up and delivered to Sir Matthew Morgan; and because there are but 400 men musketeers in the whole 1600 soldiers and it is thought that more shots in proportion to the number of the pikes are needful, so these 200 serve as shot.

SIR EDMUND YORKE'S INSTRUCTIONS.

Sir Edmund Yorke is required immediately on his arrival at Dieppe to muster all his companies and to deal very earnestly with the Governor of Dieppe in the Queen's name to take strict order that no bark or vessel whatever receive any English soldier that cannot show his licence to depart.

ANOTHER PETITION OF THE PURITAN PRISONERS.

Thomas Cartwright and the other Puritan prisoners have again written to the Lord Treasurer asking for release from imprisonment on bail. If, say they, they have transgressed some of the laws of the land, whereof their consciences set in the presence of God do not accuse them, yet seeing it plainly appears by their own answers on oath and by the depositions of witnesses that they have special care in their meetings to keep within obedience of the laws, their transgression, being of ignorance, may find the easier pardon.

Since their coming to prison, divers papists, known enemies of the state, of the Church and commonwealth, have been delivered without renovation of any error ; and it is universally granted to any, either papist or schismatic, that upon promise of coming into the Church, they enjoy the same freedom as other subjects. Their hope therefore is that they who not only come to church but labour to the utmost to entertain men in the fellowship of the Church and to reduce others estranged from it, should not be more hardly dealt with in being forced to any confessions or submissions against the testimony of their consciences. Moreover by réason of their long imprisonment and lack of convenient air some five or six of them are sore and dangerously sick.

2nd March. SIR WALTER RALEGH'S EXPEDITION.

A proclamation is published ordering all mariners, who are pressed to serve with Sir Walter Ralegh, Captain of her Majesty's Guard, to repair to their ships immediately, upon pain of death, so that the service be in no way delayed.

3rd March. MUSTER ROLLS IN THE COUNTIES.

The Lords-Lieutenant of the Counties of Somerset, Wiltshire, Monmouth, Pembroke, Anglesey, Cornwall, Chester, Devon, Huntingdon, Sussex, Rutland, Leicester and York, are rebuked for their slackness in rendering a certificate of the forces of their several counties and again required to certify how many able men there are, how many trained and received into bands, how many untrained, under what captains and officers, and how furnished with horse and weapon. The numbers of those taken out of the trained bands for foreign services, to be supplied by good and able men sorted with such arms and weapons as the others so that the trained and enrolled bands be whole and complete for the defence of the country.

At the same time the Council commend the zeal of the Lords-Lieutenant of Berkshire, Cambridge, the Isle of Ely, Suffolk, Norfolk, Surrey, Kent, Buckingham, Bedford, Dorset and Gloucester.

THE FISHMONGERS REBUKED FOR NEGLECTING TO SUPERVISE THE BUTCHERS.

The Wardens of the Fishmongers' Company are rebuked for their negligence in carrying out the restraint of the killing and uttering of flesh in Lent, for where they were authorised to appoint some trusty and discreet persons to search the houses and shops of victuallers, they did appoint but some mean men for that purpose who negligently execute it. Though but one butcher is licensed for the County of Middlesex and six for the City, there are twenty about the City and suburbs that licentiously and contemptuously kill and utter flesh. The Wardens are therefore to appoint at least six discreet persons of their company to repair at least twice a week to the houses of those butchers not licensed to sell flesh, and if any be found offending they shall not only lose the flesh found in their shops but be carried before the Mayor or some of the Justices and by them committed to prison, bonds being taken of them to answer the same at the next Sessions.

4th March. PLAYS OF THE WEEK.

The plays at the Rose Theatre this past week were *Cloris and Ergasto*, *Muly Mullocco*, *Pope Joan*, *Machiavel*, *Harry the Sixth* (for the first time), *Bindo and Richardo.*

5th March. RUMOURS OF PEACE.

The ambassador in France reporteth that the French King is resolved to conclude a peace with his subjects upon any reasonable conditions, to which they are now as much inclined as himself, being weary of the Spanish yoke, and that it is likely to take effect.

7th March. REPORT OF SIR JOHN NORRIS ON THE STATE OF FRANCE.

Sir John Norris, who has been called home from Brittany to report on the state of affairs in France, saith that the retreat of the Duke of Parma is not because he intendeth to desert those of his party besieged in Rouen but to join certain troops that come to him under conduct of the Duke of Brunswick and the Count Mansfield, nor is it because of some fear of confusion in the Low Countries, nor of dislike or disagreement with the French. Had this been so he would have hastened to his own Government, and not have taken care to fortify the Bridge of St. Remy where he passed. Seeing his obstinacy in continuing enterprises and his jealousy for reputation, it is likely that he will venture the extremity of his fortune rather than that Rouen be taken.

He doubteth whether the King's army can hope for any good event of the siege. His French disband very fast, all those of Normandy being already retired, his rutters are diminished and will shortly want pay, his lance-knights so decayed with want and sickness that not above 3000 are left, his Switzers ready every day to mutiny. The greatest ground of the siege lies upon the English and Dutch, and whether they are strong enough to take the town when the Duke of Parma shall seek to succour it must be advised on; or whether the King, leaving the siege if the Duke of Parma should approach, should be able to compel him to fight.

Brittany is in worse case, for the King of Spain has continual care to see his party strengthened; they are possessed of the best towns, and have but weak enemies; only the Queen's assistance kept them well the last year, and as that decayed, so they prevailed; and if it be not now increased, the whole province will be lost, for it is a vain hope to attend any succour from the King. Its maintenance must proceed from her Majesty, and the longer it is deferred, the more difficult will it be; and if much time passes before it is looked into it will be irrecoverable.

Orders against those who aided Deserters.

The Lord Mayor is required to cause verbal proclamation to be made throughout the City and suburbs that all victuallers, innkeepers, alehouse keepers and others having in their houses any soldier that has been levied shall upon severe penalties bring him forth to receive punishment according to the laws. Likewise if any soldier hath run away from his captain and sold or pawned his armour and furniture, it shall be seized and the party with whom it is found committed to prison.

8th March. UNDUTIFUL GENTLEMEN.

Some of the inhabitants of Middlesex, divers of them gentlemen of good calling, and some being her Majesty's servants, very wilfully refuse to bear their contribution in the levy of sums of money for the setting forth of soldiers and other public services, so that oftentimes for the expedition of the service the Justices are themselves constrained to disburse money for armour, weapons, and other provisions, whereof some are not yet satisfied for money disbursed three years since. The Council have instructed the Justices to will and require these persons, of what quality and sort soever, to contribute the sums demanded of them (excepting only the ordinary yeomen and grooms of her Majesty's Chambers). If by this gentle disposition they be not drawn to do that which in all duty and good respects they ought to do, their names to be sent to the Council that their perverse disposition may be made known to her Majesty.

9th March. A SPANISH PRISONER'S ACCOUNT OF THE STATE OF ENGLAND.

A certain Spanish prisoner that was released about a month since hath declared that many of all conditions, men and women, assured him of their good wishes for the success of the Spanish in England, and their zeal for the Catholic faith. If they do not openly avow their sympathy it is that they may not lose homes and possessions ; others confess themselves Catholics, and, though they have suffered many punishments, yet openly say that they will remain firm and die in the faith. Many complaints, saith he, are made of the large number of declared Catholics, and the Queen is petitioned to have them punished, but she hath ordered that such complaints should not be made against them, and that they shall be allowed to live freely as they wished. There is great fear of the galleys and their commander. Sir Francis Drake is very unpopular, the people of quality saying that he is but of mean origin to have risen so high, the common people regarding him as the cause of the wars ; but the Queen esteemeth him highly. They cannot bear the name of

Don Antonio, who is called 'The King of Portugal,' as he is considered the cause of all the wars in Portugal. They threaten to stone him, and it is said that the Queen keeps him in a castle which he does not leave. He is miserably poor, lacking both money and servants.

11th March. PLAYS OF THE WEEK.

The plays at the Rose Theatre this past week were *Four Plays in One, Harry the Sixth, A Looking Glass for London, Zenobia, The Jew of Malta, Harry the Sixth.*

12th March. THE EARL OF BOTHWELL AND THE SCOTTISH BORDER.

The Wardens of Border are bidden to keep watch for the Earl of Bothwell and his complices in the late treasonable attempt on the Scottish King at Holyrood House, since they are reported to have been received into the northern parts of the kingdom. Thus is the Queen's government maliciously slandered as though her realm by her permission or offer were a refuge to the rebels of the Scottish King, with whom she is in good amity. Special search is to be made at the races and running of horses in the wardenry of the Lord Scroop, and knowledge of this order to be given to the opposite Wardens or their deputies, requiring them to advertise if they know or suspect any of the rebels to be in this realm.

18th March. PLAYS OF THE WEEK.

The plays at the Rose Theatre this past week were *The Spanish Comedy, The Spanish Tragedy, Harry the Sixth, Muly Mullocco, The Jew of Malta.*

21st March. HOPEFUL NEWS FROM FRANCE.

The Ambassador in France reporteth that the King and his Council resolve to batter Rouen, though everything is done by the Catholics in his army to hinder that resolution. The King now awaiteth the coming of the English, and then will immediately begin his approaches. The Governor of Rouen hath lately much angered the burgesses by a stratagem to enrich himself by a trick. Some days since a part of the wall of the town fell down, leaving a breach of forty paces. Thereupon Monsieur Villiers assembled the people, using feigned persuasions to them to make a composition with the King and alleging that the late succours were not sufficient for their defence, the Duke of Parma had retired and that the King was resolved to batter the town. On this speech sixty of the burgesses, best inclined to the King's service, answered that they would very willingly agree to his motion; then these men, well noted by the Governor, were sent for from their houses, and made prisoners, being forced to pay great ransoms at his pleasure for their release.

The late offer of a peace is likely to come to nothing, for the first part of the Leaguers' demand will be for the King to become a Catholic. They have proffered it but to confuse the King, distaste his Catholics, and to better their condition with Spain.

24th March. VOLUNTEERS TO BE LEVIED IN LONDON.

The Lord Mayor and the Justices of Peace for the County of Middlesex now begin to imprest and take up 200 voluntary men to fill up the companies of the bands remaining in Brittany under Sir John Norris.

25th March. DISTRESS IN ROUEN.

The garrison of Rouen are reported to be daily thrusting out forty or fifty women and many prentices; they want wine and have forbidden the making of beer because they would spend no corn in drink. They cannot hold out longer than two months if the King do not force them otherwise to yield. Two thousand French that had disbanded have rejoined the army and more return daily in hope of spoil at Rouen. Sir Edmund Yorke with twelve companies arrived at Dieppe on the 18th.

PLAYS OF THE WEEK.

The plays at the Rose Theatre this past week were *The Spanish Tragedy*, *Constantine*, *Jerusalem*, *Harry of Cornwall*, *Friar Bacon*.

COMPLAINTS AGAINST THE GOVERNOR OF OSTEND.

Complaints against Sir Edward Norris, Governor of Ostend, have been renewed by the Council of the States of the United Provinces. The Council now give orders that he shall repair to them when they should send for him to satisfy their demands and yield account of how the contributions of the country have been expended, and to clear himself of the imputations preferred against him; but they in requiring his presence should make choice of a fit time so that the enemy may have no advantage by his absence. When they have viewed his accounts and heard what he can say in his own defence and excuse, they shall not give any sentence or decree against him until the Queen hath been duly informed. She hath given order in respect of the dislike which they conceive of him, that, if they be not satisfied with his answers, he shall be recalled home as soon as he is dismissed by them to be charged with those matters wherein they find fault with him.

Recusancy in the North.

The Earl of Derby is much commended for his zeal in the reformation of his tenants from their sinfulness in not resorting to their parish churches. He hath also joined with the Commissioners to reduce the recusants throughout Lancashire, now almost overflown with a multitude of obstinate persons, offending publicly in the sight of the world, as it seemeth without any fear of punishment. Her Majesty greatly allows of their honourable, wise and politic proceedings; and the Council pray him not to stay the good cause begun in restraining the principal obstinate recusants either by imprisonment or by committing them to the custody of such as be sound in religion.

This course is a most necessary to be taken in the present dangerous state of the country; nor should the reformation be delayed by following a long course in answering strictly all the statutes, howsoever any of the Justices may have delivered their opinions upon the strict point of law, not respecting what is most necessary at this time and in that county. If any should repine against his former proceedings upon conceit that any Justice or learned man showeth opinions to the contrary, he is to be forthcoming and caused to declare the name of the Justice who shall be charged therewith, as a matter not any wise allowable.

27th March. The Case of Robert Paine.

Dr. Aubrey and Mr. Justice Peryam are to examine the controversies between the widow of Robert Paine, lately deceased, and Sir Francis Willoughby, and either to conclude a final end between them or to report their full proceedings and opinions to the Council.

CAPTAIN GLEMHAM'S SHIPS TO BE STAYED.

It appeareth that certain goods and merchandise have lately been taken out of a Venetian argosy at sea by Captain Glemham and his consorts. The Council order that any of his ships that be found shall be stayed and the goods in them sequestered, and six of his chiefest ships stayed.

31st March. THE PURITAN PRISONERS RELEASED.

The Puritan prisoners are now released from prison, the Council being pleased that the charges against them should no further be proceeded with.

1st April. PLAYS OF THE WEEK AT THE ROSE.

This past week were played *The Looking Glass for London*, *Harry the Sixth*, *Muly Mullocco*, *The Spanish Comedy*, *The Spanish Tragedy*, *Sir John Maundeville*.

2nd April. MERCY TO BE SHOWN TO DEBTORS.

Some time since Commissioners were appointed to inquire into the causes of poor prisoners detained a long time in prison for debt. They report that the adverse parties will not be reduced to conformity or commiseration. Now are the Council moved by the pitiful complaints of the prisoners, and by reports that of late very many of them are dead in prison, whereby their creditors lose all their debts, whereof in time they might have received a good part if not the whole sum.

But if no persuasion or intreaty shall move the creditors to compassion, then shall they be plainly let to understand, that, if at any time information be brought against them upon a penal statute, or other advantage taken against them in any matter by the strictness of the law, let them look for no favour but all extremity that may be used.

If they refuse still, the Commissioners shall advertise the Judges of the Queen's Bench and Common Pleas to send for the parties to see what they shall be able to prevail with these wilful and hard hearted persons ; and if they will still by no means be brought to reasonable order, the Judges to let them understand that they must look for like measure and to have no favour at their hands.

7th April. TWO PRISONERS' RANSOM.

Some time since John Dipford and Walter Horsey, merchants of Exeter, sent their servants John Gupwell and Thomas Dipford to the town of Lanyon in Brittany with lawful merchandise. Not only did the Leaguers take their goods but committed the men to prison to the Castle of Callett near Morlaix, whence Thomas Dipford was released on ransom, but Gupwell is held to ransom by the first of May or else is threatened with execution. For the relief of their losses and the discharge of their servants' ransoms, the Council instruct the customers of Dartmouth and Opsam to permit these merchants to transport 20 packs of kerseys, 4 packs of broad cloths, 3 packs of bays, and 3 packs of coarse cloth stockings, after paying the customs due, in a bark of twenty or thirty tons.

DISTRESS IN ROUEN.

It appeareth that Rouen is in some distress for victual by the disbanding of many soldiers of the garrison who daily leave the town and submit themselves to the King's mercy, whereby the King and his Council have great hope of the timely rendering of the town if it be not relieved by the return of the Duke of Parma.

8th April. PLAYS OF THE WEEK.

The plays at the Rose Theatre this week were *Machiavel*, *The Jew of Malta*, *Harry the Sixth*, *Brandimer*, *The Spanish Tragedy*, *Muly Mullocco*.

12th April. BRETON'S 'THE PILGRIMAGE TO PARADISE' AND 'THE COUNTESS OF PEMBROKE'S LOVE.'

The Pilgrimage to Paradise, joined with *The Countess of Pembroke's Love*, compiled in verse by Nicholas Breton, gentleman, is sent to the press. The first telleth of the journeyings of the Soul, with his five servants the senses, past the snaring temptations of the flesh until he reaches an angel by whom he is forewarned against the beast with seven heads which are ambition, avarice, gluttony, sloth, lechery, malice, and murder, and protected with seven books by which, after long debate, the monster is slain. At length the pilgrim comes to a fisherman with whom he sails and who tells him his story. And continuing their way they meet a world of people making piteous moan:

The courtier, he complained of love's disgrace,
The soldier, he cried out of lack of pay,
The lawyer, lack of hearing of his case,
The client, how his coin went to decay,
  The merchant of the loss of his adventure,
  The prentice of the bands of his indenture.

The landlord, of his tenants' beggary,
The passenger, of lack of amity,
The tenant, of the landlord's misery,
The beggar all of lack of charity,
  The churchmen of their small possessions,
  The laymen of the Church transgressions.

And past these to an army set out in the field, and to a city sacked till the pilgrims reached the true Church

Where sacred Mercy first did solemnise
The Spirit to the Flesh in marriage,
  And here the heart did find his spirit blest
  To bring the senses to eternal rest.

In *The Countess of Pembroke's Love* he likeneth her to a phœnix in rarity, aspiring to the Heavenly Love and despising all earthly gifts which men of all kinds and degrees brought in to her.

15th April. PLAYS OF THE WEEK.

At the Rose Theatre this week past *The Spanish Comedy*, *Titus and Vespasian* (for the first time), *Bindo and Richardo*, *Harry the Sixth*, *The Jew of Malta*, *Sir John Maundeville*.

16th April. A FRAY AT FULHAM.

William Arnold, yeoman, was journeying to his father's house at Fulham between six and seven in the evening when a certain Peter Jones came up to him, calling out, 'Sirrah, sirrah, you with the long sword, stay for I must talk with you.' To whom Arnold answered, 'I have nothing to say to thee'; whereon Jones assaulted Arnold, and in the ensuing affray received a blow in the breast of which he died then and there.

English Mariners Forbidden to Sail with a Stranger.

Information has been given that there is at Dartmouth a flyboat of Enghuizen called *The Dolphin* prepared to go to Flushing and the Newfound Land, that, for her better conduct, intends to be furnished with English mariners. The Council order that no English pilot, master or mariner, in any wise be permitted to go either in that ship or in any other strange bottom to the Newfound Land. If (notwithstanding the Queen's straight commandment) any person be hired for lucre by a stranger, he shall be committed to prison for his contempt.

17th April. The Siege of Rouen Raised.

It is reported from France that the siege of Rouen is raised, the King having been suddenly advertised that the Duke of Parma was marching towards his camp with 12,000 foot and 4000 horse. He was within four leagues of Rouen before the army rose, using all possible diligence in his march to surprise the King and defeat his army of rutters in their lodgings and the English troops in their quarters. This was only prevented by the discovery and advertisement of the Duke of Boullion, who made his retreat with the rutters in view of the Duke of Parma's army with great hazard and no loss. Thus the King's army was forced to march away with all haste, and at its rising had very hot skirmishes but without loss. Sir Roger Williams' horse was shot, and his hat in two places ; he served very honourably with great courage and discretion in the view of the King, greatly to his commendation, as did many of the English who were the last to retreat.

That night the army encamped within a league of Pont de L'Arch, expecting the coming of the Duke of Parma to give battle whereunto the Duke of Mayne and Villiers earnestly pressed him. Whereupon the King was immediately advertised and made choice of the place of battle, fortifying and trenching the place.

The Duke of Parma lodged at Croissett, and his army along the river. He sent to all castles and gentlemen's houses where was great store of corn to cause them to bring it to Rouen.

21st April. 'The Defence of Conny-Catching.'

The conny-catchers have one 'Cuthbert Connycatcher' that answers Greene in a book called *The Defence of Conny-Catching, or a Confession of those two injurious pamphlets published by R. G. against the practitioners of many nimble witted and mystical sciences.* Herein Greene is attacked for having touched small scapes but let gross faults pass without any reprehension, and himself accused of conny-catching; 'ask the Queen's players if you sold them not *Orlando Furioso* for 20 nobles, and when they were in the country sold the same play to the Lord Admiral's men for as much more?' And to show the nature of more gross abuses examples are given of the villainy of an usurer; a miller; a serving man, counterfeiting to be gentlemen to make a good match; a man that was married to sixteen wives but well cured by the last; and a tailor.

22nd April. Plays of the Week.

The plays at the Rose this past week were *Muly Mullocco*, *The Jew of Malta*, *The Looking Glass for London*, *Titus and Vespasian*, *Harry the Sixth*, *The Comedy of Jeronimo.*

The Enghuizen Ship Released.

Notwithstanding direction formerly given, the Council order that a ship called *The Lion of London*, with the master and mariners, may be allowed to pass to the fishing at the Newfound Land, and likewise the ship of Enghuizen now at Dartmouth to go on her intended voyage, provided that she hath in her no English masters or mariners soever.

27th April. The French King attacks Parma.

The Ambassador reporteth that on the 17th Caudebec surrendered by composition to the Duke of Parma, who had encamped his army within a league of Ivetot in open field where he was strongly entrenched; the Dukes of Mayne and Guise with 2000 horse and 1200 foot, lodging at Ivetot. Hereupon the King marched towards them with all his army in order of battle, and ten pieces of artillery, until he was within a mile and a half. There he made a stand, and himself with 500 horse advanced further to discover the enemy. The Duke of Mayne showed himself with 1000 horse, whom the King charged with two troops of horse and pursued to their quarter, in which charge Monsieur Coutenan, a special commander of horse, was taken prisoner, who assured the King that the Duke of Parma had but then taken the alarm of his coming and would not believe that the King durst look upon him; if he did, he was resolved to give battle.

This news much contented the King, who retired in time to lodge his army in the villages, preparing the next day to give the Duke of Parma battle, if he would accept it, near Ivetot in a fair champaign field.

Early in the morning (18th) the King drew all his forces together waiting for the enemy; but finding no likelihood of their preparation to fight, he resolved to force their lodging of Ivetot, and to lodge there himself in despite of them or else to force them to accept the battle. He therefore marched with his whole army, advancing certain cuirassiers and harquebusiers on horseback to observe the enemy's countenance who were now marching towards him with horse and foot. On perceiving the King with his forces to come on so resolutely, they retired most dishonourably, quitting their quarter and setting it on fire, and fled in disorder until they came to the Duke of Parma's camp. The King with his horse had them in chase, himself conducting them, killing many and taking some gentlemen prisoners, amongst them the Baron of Chastre, son of Monsieur Chastre. The Duke of Mayne hardly escaped, for he fled so fast that his horse was like to have failed him for want of breath.

That night the King lodged at Ivetot, and the rest of the army in the villages a league beyond it, within three-quarters of a mile of the Duke of Parma's intrenchment, who was much amated with this dishonour, imagining that he was betrayed by his French.

The 19th the King's army stayed at Ivetot, offering many skirmishes to the enemy, which they coldly entertained.

The 20th the King dislodged with his army and marched to Varqueville, a mile and a half from Ivetot towards Newhaven, which way the Duke of Parma's army most lodged, in order to cut off his victuals from Newhaven and for want thereof to force him to a battle.

After the King's army was quartered and lodged, the enemy's

horse made towards them; whereupon the King sent for Sir Roger Williams to come to him with 200 muskets and 150 pikes of his best, who were no sooner come to the King but five cornets of Spanish and Italian horse charged them before any horse could succour them. The English encountered them with so great resolution and courage that they took two or three cornets; whereof one the King sent to the Queen, another was torn by the soldiers. Divers of the chief leaders of the horse were slain, and many other of the enemy. 600 Spanish foot, with muskets and pikes, came to second their horse and entered a very hot skirmish with the English; in the meantime other English companies came to their succour. In the end they forced the enemy's horse and foot to retire into their quarters with very great dishonour and loss. Of the English, 40 were hurt and 8 slain; Captain Rush was hurt in the thigh, no other men of quality hurt or slain.

Sir Roger Williams unarmed served most honourably and unhorsed their best leader, and, encountering besides with George Basta, did, as it was thought, hurt him in the neck, giving him a very great blow with his sword. The King commended him highly and did more than wonder at the valour of our nation. Sir Matthew Morgan and his brother also served very valiantly, and Captain Henry Poore. This action greatly encouraged our men, who had very good spoils of the enemy and discouraged the enemy. The King gave great honour to Sir Roger Williams and his men, whom he had held as lost, and caused public thanks to be given to God.

A letter of the Duke of Parma to the King of Spain was intercepted wherein he represented his misery for want of sufficient forces to encounter the King, and his want of victuals and means to return. He complained greatly of the Duke of Mayne and the French, concluding that he must hazard the loss of his army, for without fighting he could not return.

The Duke of Parma had been wounded some days before, being shot in the arm between the bones; the hurt is not dangerous of itself, yet his sickly body and the accidents that usually follow such hurts give some cause of doubt to physicians. Many troops are now daily coming to the French King, and more daily expected.

THE TRIAL OF SIR JOHN PERROT.

Sir John Perrot, who hath lain a prisoner in the Tower for more than a year past, was brought to his trial before the King's Bench Bar, before the commissioners being the Lord Chamberlain, the Lord Buckhurst, Sir Robert Cecil, the Lord Chief Justice and other judges. He was charged on two indictments; the first that in 1587 he went about to depose and raise rebellion against the Queen, that he had promised help to the King of Spain, and that he had procured and moved Sir Brian O'Rourke to rebellion. The second indictment charged him with having conferred with Sir William Stanley in 1586 about his treasonable practices.

To these indictments he pleaded not guilty very vehemently. The jury was then sworn, and the indictments having been read, Sergeant Puckering for the Queen rehearsed the principal points of the indictment. But before he came to the particular offences, he told them that the origin of these treasons proceeded from the imagination of the heart; which imagination was of itself high treason, albeit the same proceeded not to any overt fact; and the heart being possessed with the abundance of his traitorous imagination and not being able so to contain itself, burst forth in vile and traitorous speeches and from thence to horrible and heinous actions.

At this Sir John prayed Sergeant Puckering to lay aside words and proceed to the matter of the indictment; to which he answered that he would proceed by degrees, but would first begin with his contemptuous words which in themselves contained the high treason.

Amongst other speeches, it was reported that when Sir Nicholas Bagnol, Marshal of Ireland, was with Sir John in his house, hot words had broken out and Sir John cried, 'If it were not for yonder pilled and paltry sword that lieth in the window I would not brook these comparisons,' meaning her Majesty's Sword of Justice which was carried before him.

Sir John answered that he had called the sword 'pilled and paltry' because the scabbard was old and worn; and within a week after he had caused a new scabbard to be made. Then falling into other idle discourse, the Lord Buckhurst begged him not to speak from the purpose for it would but hurt his cause.

Then it was shown that Sir John, having called a parliament in Dublin, moved, amongst other matters, to suppress the Cathedral Church of St. Patrick; and her Majesty then sending letters to the contrary he said, with a stern countenance, 'Nay, God's wounds, I think it strange she should use me thus.' With these words the Bishop of Meath was moved to find fault with his undutiful demeanour, for he spoke as though the kingdom were his own and not the Queen's.

Sir John answered that the Archbishop of Dublin was his mortal enemy, and the reason why he was moved to suppress the Cathedral was to have a University created thereon, but he was withstood by the Archbishop because he and his children received 800 marks a year from the Cathedral, and further the Archbishop bore him great malice because when the Queen had sent him letters to discharge idle and unnecessary pensioners he had discharged among the rest one of the Archbishop's sons.

Then it was shown that when the office of the Clerk of the Exchequer was empty and letters were sent from the Queen that Mr. Errington should be admitted to this office, Sir John said, 'This fiddling woman troubles me out of measure: God's wounds, he shall not have the office, I will give it to Sir Thomas Williams.' This was proved by the oath of Philip Williams.

Sir John declared that this Williams was his mortal enemy, a naughty, lewd man of no credit who had abused the Lord Treasurer in a letter, for which he had beaten him in his chambers.

It was also shown that when the Queen had written him a letter about the time that the Spaniards should come, to look well to his charge, he said, 'Ah, silly woman, now she shall not curb me, she shall not rule me; now, God's lady dear, I shall be her white boy now again: doth she think to rule me now?' Shortly after John Garland brought Sir John a letter, which so greatly displeased him that he broke forth into these terms: 'God's wounds, this it is to serve a base bastard pissing kitchen woman; if I had served any prince in Christendom, I had not been so dealt withal.'

All these speeches Sir John denied very vigorously with oaths.

Next Mr. Attorney proceeded to open the treasons which were alleged against Sir John. He declared that when Dr.

Craugh, a known traitor and papist, should have been arrested, Sir John sent out warrants that he should be sought in all places except the White Knight's country, where he knew Craugh to be. To this Sir John answered that there was a God above all, and he marvelled that he who had known religion these forty-six years should be charged with favouring of papists and mass-mongers.

But Mr. Attorney willed him not to stand upon religion; 'for then,' said he, 'we shall prove you irreligious. Will any men of religion seek to have men murdered? Will any men of religion stab a man in the cheek, and after bring him to the fire to be roasted, to make him confess that he knoweth not, and afterwards hang him by martial law?'

Mr. Attorney further to prove him of no religion showed that Sir John being once in his chamber in the Castle at Dublin had looked out at the window and espied Sir Dennis O'Roughan who knew all his secret treasons, and willed his chamberlain to call to him Stephen Seager. When he came, Sir John commanded away his chamberlain and locking the chamber door willed Seager to look out at the window, saying, 'Seest thou not one beneath in a black mantle?' Seager answered that he saw none. Sir John said, 'There is one there; you see how I am crossed by some of the Council here, and he is going to the North with letters from some of the Council to move them against me: I would have thee take those letters from him, kill him, cast him aside, and bring those letters to me.' Seager answered that he would take those letters from him, but he would not kill him; but if Sir John should give commandment to hang him by martial law he would see it done. Whereupon Sir John said, 'Go thy ways, thou art a paltry fellow; I did it but to prove thee.' This was proved by the oath of Seager.

Sir John then called for Seager to speak to him face to face, when he justified all he had said. Then the Lord Chamberlain said, 'Now you see you bad him kill one.' Sir John answered, 'Because he hath sworn I will not reprove him; it may be I spake such words, but I remember it not.'

Other witnesses showed that he had favoured traitors, amongst them Sir Brian O'Rourke, lately executed at Tyburn, whom he might have arrested had he wished.

Then Sir Dennis O'Roughan was called to testify against

Sir John, and the book being offered him to swear, Sir John said it was no matter whether he swore or not, for his word and his oath were all one ; for there was neither truth nor honesty in him. Sir Dennis testified amongst other things that Sir John had used extreme malice towards the Cavener, and the better to execute his purpose, he had found means that the Cavener should offend the law by making an escape out of prison, and, being afterwards taken, he was hanged for having escaped.

Sir John now began to discredit the evidence of Sir Dennis, declaring he had changed his religion five times in six years ; was a common drunkard, a common liar, and had been forsworn a thousand times. Sir Dennis, being again called, swore that Sir John Perrot and Sir Brian O'Rourke had been confederates together in the last Parliament and that each had sworn to the other to help the King of Spain. Here Sir John grew very angry with O'Roughan and declared that he was a lousy villain, a rogue, and had the pox on him.

Other witnesses declared that Sir John had exchanged letters with Sir William Stanley, and that when he came to England he went about to get a pardon, wherein he showed his guilty conscience.

After the Queen's Counsel and Sir John had addressed the jury, they departed from the bar and within three-quarters of an hour they returned with a verdict of guilty. Then Sergeant Puckering in the Queen's name began to pray judgment ; but Sir John desired most humbly that he might speak with some of their honours before sentence should be pronounced.

To this after some conference they agreed, and judgment was deferred until the Queen's pleasure should be known. Then the Court was adjourned until the 2nd May.

29th April. PLAYS OF THE WEEK.

The plays at the Rose Theatre this past week were *The Spanish Tragedy*, *Jerusalem*, *Friar Bacon*, *Muly Mullocco*, *The Second Part of Tamar Cam* (for the first time), *Harry of Cornwall*.

30th April. THE COUNCIL DECEIVED.

Some days since John Dipford and Walter Horsey, merchants of Exeter, were allowed to transport certain merchandise in a bark to Morlaix to recover their losses when their goods and servants were seized by the Leaguers. Now the Council are credibly informed that the suggestion is false, for that the parties came safely from Morlaix without ransom. The bark is to be stayed and no goods hereafter to be taken to Morlaix or St. Malo.

A CONTEMPTUOUS SEA CAPTAIN.

On the 25th March, Mr. Leman, on behalf of certain merchants of Amsterdam, appeared before the Council in the matter of a Dutch ship called the *Jonas*, laden with sugars and other goods coming from Barbary, that was taken at sea by the *Prudence* of Barnstable, whose captain was Captain William Batten. Both parties had willed their case to be referred to Drs. Aubrey, Herbert and Caesar, who decided in favour of Mr. Leman. The Council ordered the *Jonas* to be delivered to him. It now appeareth that Captain Batten, to avoid the ship being given up, hath practised with certain lewd persons who violently seized her and took her to some places unknown, to the great offence of the Queen; and it is greatly to be suspected that they mean to carry the ship and the goods to some remote part of the realm or into Ireland and there to make sale of the goods. The ship is to be stayed and delivered to Mr. Leman if she shall arrive at any port; and Captain Batten to be apprehended and required to appear before the Council or the Judge of the Admiralty within fourteen days.

4th May. AN ACCIDENT AT GREENWICH.

A tiltboat of Gravesend carrying some forty persons was run down by a hoy near Greenwich, where the Court now remains. Most of the passengers were drowned in sight of the Queen, who hath been much frightened.

6th May. PLAYS OF THE WEEK.

The plays at the Rose Theatre during this past week were *Muly Mullocco*, *The Spanish Tragedy*, *Titus and Vespasian*, *Harry the Sixth*, *The Jew of Malta*, *Friar Bacon*.

7th May. THE DUKE OF PARMA'S CAMP PILLAGED.

From France the ambassador reporteth that the Duke of Parma, who intended by stealth to regain Rouen and to pass from thence to Neuchâtel, was pursued with such diligence by the King that he was forced to retire towards Caudebec, where for want of a bridge he resolved to cross over in boats, having gathered together all the boats of Rouen. But the weather is so tempestuous that they cannot as yet pass many over.

On 30th April, the King assembled early in the morning 1000 English, as many Scots and Netherlands, 800 lance-knights, 1500 Switzers, 2000 French shot, 1500 French cuirassiers and as many rutters, causing three small pieces of artillery to march with them. The rest were left at their quarter. The King gave the leading of 200 cuirassiers and as many rutters and 300 shot to the Baron of Biron, and 1500 French shot to Grilion. Sir Roger Williams was appointed to second him with 200 English and 400 Scottish and Netherlands; the Marshal D'Aumont with 300 cuirassiers; the rest of the force remained with the King for their retreat. The Baron Biron and the others were commanded to give in to the quarter where the Duke of Parma's horse were lodged, to defeat them, to take spoil of their baggage and burn their quarter; which they accordingly performed. But the Baron's overhastiness, entering the quarter with the troops before the rest could come to second him, and the greediness of the soldiers to spoil, hindered the performance of the enterprise and was the occasion that the enemy escaped and that few were killed; and had not Sir Roger Williams with his 200 English withstood the enemy better, the Baron with his companies and the Marshal D'Aumont had been overthrown. But God gave them very good success, for the enemy wanted courage, and our men, forcing the quarter, killed 150, taking the spoils of 500 waggons, and all the baggage, and brought away 1000 horse of all sorts, and as much spoil as is worth 50,000 crowns at least. The rest of the quarter and spoils our men set on fire and then retired without loss. The attempt was most desperate and resolved by the King to force the enemy to fight, which nothing could work.

The English soldiers in these days are much harried and many disband daily for want of money and victuals.

8th May. FURTHER REINFORCEMENTS FOR FRANCE.

The Queen upon the present great and urgent occasion determines to have 2000 footmen complete, and 100 horsemen from the troops in her pay in the Lowlands to be speedily transported by sea into France.

13th May. An Unlucky Gaoler.

Richard Mudford, Keeper of the Counter in Southampton, had in his custody one Edmund Mellish, imprisoned for debt. This Mellish escaped some two years since, and, notwithstanding the Council's warrant for help and assistance in the speedy recovery and apprehension of the prisoner, and Mudford's diligent travail in search of him, yet is he still at large; and the keeper, unless some charitable course be taken, liable to pay his debt of two hundred crowns and £14 in costs, besides the loss of his great expenses and travail, amounting to no less sum. The Council therefore write to Mellish's mother, the Lady Allot, moving her charitably to consider the poor keeper's distress by discharging him of the whole payment of her son's debt.

Deserters from France at Dover.

It is credibly reported that, notwithstanding the Council's orders for the restraint of such soldiers as without passport draw themselves from the service of the French King in Normandy, above two hundred men of strong and able bodies are landed at Dover and the places near without passport, in the company of some few sick men, and without stay. These men are allowed to beg in the county with the passport of the Mayor, using most slanderous speeches of the Queen's service and entertainment, tending to the great discouragement of such as be willing to serve. Mr. Verney, Mr. Edward Boyes, and Mr. William Pertridge, Esquires, are to repair to Dover, and discover the truth of the matter; and in case they shall find the Council's orders have been neglected, good bonds are to be taken of the Mayor and such others who are found culpable for their personal appearance; and to cause all soldiers that of late are landed without passport to be stayed and punished.

Plays of the Week.

The plays at the Rose Theatre during this past week were *Brandimer*, *Harry the Sixth*, *Titus and Vespasian*, *The Spanish Tragedy*, *The Second Part of Tamar Cam*, *The Jew of Malta*.

17th May. A CLAIM AGAINST CAPTAIN GLEMHAM.

In the Admiralty Court was heard the cause between John de Riviera, a merchant stranger residing in London, acting on behalf of certain Venetians, and Captain Edward Glemham of the *Edward and Constance*, touching sugars and other goods taken in the Levant Seas, which Riviera claims, though without proof, as belonging to Venetians. The judges order that the goods shall be appraised by six experienced men chosen by de Riviera and Glemham, and the inventory lodged in the Admiralty Court; Glemham to have possession and to dispose of them at his pleasure in a bond in double their value to pay their first value within two months after proof has been made or for so much as can be proved to belong to Venetians or others not the subjects of the King of Spain.

20th May. PLAYS OF THE WEEK.

The plays at the Rose Theatre this week past were *The Spanish Tragedy*, *Harry the Sixth*, *Titus and Vespasian*, *Sir John Maundeville*, *Muly Mullocco*, *Harry of Cornwall*.

21st May. THE WEAKNESS OF THE NORMANDY COMPANIES.

It appears from the certificates sent by Sir Edmund Yorke before his death that on the first of the month the companies in Normandy are so decayed that there are not above 1500 men, and since then these are much more weakened by sickness, famine, escaping and other indirect means. By good estimation the numbers remaining there, though in the name of nineteen captains, will not make above eight companies, whereby her Majesty is much abused both in her opinion of the strength of the forces there and in the greatness of her charge, as much by weekly pays and lendings as if the companies were full and complete. Sir Roger Williams is now ordered to take a general muster and to reduce all unto eight companies or according to the numbers of able men, appointing 100 men to serve under such captains of the old bands from the Low Countries as by their valour and by careful preserving their companies together best deserve. The captains of every band to be caused to be paid and discharged without unnecessary delay.

25th May. A Rumour.

This morning it is said that the Queen is out of quiet with her foreign foes and home broils. It is expected that the new Lord Chancellor will be nominated to-day, and the choice believed to be between the Solicitor-General and Sergeant Puckering; but the Queen is not yet determined.

Puckering made Lord Keeper.

John Puckering, Esquire, one of her Majesty's Sergeants at Law, about three o'clock in the afternoon was by the Queen made a Knight in the Privy Chamber, and straightway going into the Council Chamber he took the oath of supremacy and of a privy councillor at the Council Board. Thereupon being placed in the lowest place of the Council according to his calling, and having signed a letter as Councillor, he returned to the Queen, in company with the rest of the Council, into the Privy Chamber, where, after some grave speeches and admonitions how to use such a great office to the pleasing of God and the content of all people having any causes afore him, her Highness delivered into his hands the Great Seal, to have and keep the same as Lord Keeper of the Great Seal of England. And so he came down again into the Council Chamber, took his place as Lord Keeper and signed letters accordingly.

27th May. Plays of the Week.

The plays at the Rose Theatre during this past week were *Harry the Sixth*, *The Jew of Malta*, *The Spanish Comedy*, *The Spanish Tragedy*, *The Tanner of Denmark*, *Titus and Vespasian.*

28th May. Seditious Books from Abroad.

There have recently been divers traitorous and seditious books brought into the country by most lewd persons, who the better to colour their vile doings wrap them up in merchandise and after disperse them to evil disposed persons, infecting them and others with their poisoned libels. All ships arriving in the realm are to be searched, as well as any houses or places where it is suspected that such slanderous books may be hidden.

31st May. A Disaster in Brittany Rumoured.

Sundry rumours are abroad of a great success of the enemy under the Duke Mercury against the Princes of Conde and

Dombes, who were besieging the town of Craon in Brittany. The Princes have been compelled by the Duke's Bretons and Spaniards to leave their siege and forced to fly with the loss of the most part of their footmen, amongst them many English, about whom there is no certain news how many be lost, taken or escaped. Sir Henry Norris, that is lieutenant to his brother, the General in that part, is to repair thither with all speed to understand the true estate of the Queen's people. To take with him a quantity of arms and powder, and order from Sir Thomas Shirley, the Treasurer for Wars, for a proportion of money so that the English who want weapons may be furnished, and those saved may have money to relieve them for their victualling and other necessaries. He carries a special letter from her Majesty to Monsieur Hallard Mountmorency, Governor of Caen, requesting his advice and assistance. Also he shall resort to both the Princes (if he finds it convenient), declaring to them how much her Majesty is discomfited with this great loss, and requiring them to show all favour to her people that be saved.

MR. JOHN HARINGTON AND THE PRINTER.

Mr. John Harington, High Sheriff of the County of Somerset, some time since did withdraw one Thomas Wells, a prentice, from his master Augustine Rither, printer and graver of London, to serve him in his profession. The man with much ado was restored to his master, but by indirect means Mr. Harington hath lately gotten him away from his master, to his utter impoverishing, whose living consisteth solely in his occupation, wherein with much travail and many charges he brought up his apprentice. The Council rebuke Mr. Harington for so uncharitable an action, not fitting a gentleman of his quality. He is strictly charged to redeliver Wells to his master or to make personal appearance without delay to answer his default.

1st June. SIR WALTER RALEGH DISGRACED.

It is rumoured that Sir Walter Ralegh hath been recalled from the fleet which is now at sea and hath been cast into the Tower. He hath offended with Mistress Elizabeth Throckmorton, one of her Majesty's Ladies-in-Waiting.

2nd June. Foreign Artisans in England.

Monsieur Caron, Agent for the States of the United Provinces of the Low Countries, hath lately made suit to the Queen and the Council on behalf of divers poor men of those countries living in London, some of them candlemakers or exercising like manual trades. He petitioned that certain proceedings under penal statutes made against them might be stayed, and these poor men permitted to continue their accustomed trades whereby they maintain themselves and their families. Hereupon those that laid the informations, being called before the Council, brought in their defence some requests from the Lord Mayor showing that of late years the numbers of handicraftsmen of strangers are so much increased within the City and suburbs that the freemen of the City are supplanted and their living taken from them. These strangers who came hither in these times of trouble abroad the better to enjoy the free exercise of their consciences are so extraordinarily favoured that some are grown to great wealth. Some of them convey beyond the seas the commodities of this realm, whereby the prices of divers things are increased and the Queen deceived in her custom.

The Council now instruct Sir Henry Killigrew and other gentlemen to make inquisition how many strangers of every nation use handicrafts that are not allowable in the City and suburbs, where they inhabit, what occupations they use, how many both men and women they keep in their houses, how long they have been in the realm, to what churches they resort, and whether they keep any English born in their houses.

This inquisition is to be made with as much secrecy as may be whereby neither the English artisans and apprentices take any comfort or boldness to contemn the strangers, or the poor strangers be made afraid to be hardly used.

3rd June. Plays of the Week.

The plays at the Rose Theatre during this past week were *Harry the Sixth*, *Tamar Cam*, *The Spanish Tragedy*, *Machiavel*, *The Jew of Malta*, *Muly Mullocco*.

5th June. The Disaster in Brittany.

Sir Henry Unton, the ambassador in France, hath now reported at length upon the disaster in Brittany. It appeareth that on the 13th May, the Princes of Conde and Dombes raised their siege from Craon, understanding of the approach of the Duke Mercury towards them with all his forces; and intending to retire (for they were too weak to encounter their enemies) they were suddenly surprised through want of advertisements, of counsel and good resistance, being charged by the enemy both before and behind, they having taken an unfit, straight passage to retire with their cannon and their forces. The English and lance-knights only came to blows who served with great courage and paid for it accordingly, being most of them slain. The rest of the French ran away at the first and saved themselves until the Duke Mercury coasted them, and then overtaking some of them in rout killed many but took the most part prisoners. Of the artillery they saved not one piece, having seven cannon and four demi-culverin, without ever making shot with them.

The Princes' forces were about 3500 foot and 400 horse, and the enemy between 5 and 6000 foot and 800 horse. The Duke Mercury hath since pursued his victory and taken Chateau Goutyer and Le Val, which surrendered voluntarily, both being passages of the Mayne and therefore of very great importance. He is now before Mayne, the chief town.

This unhappy accident hath struck a great fear and terror into all the hearts of the King's subjects in Brittany, and therefore will hazard the loss of the towns and places there if they be not relieved immediately and better assured. The King's designs of blocking Rouen and Newhaven and clearing Normandy are frustrated, he is diverted from following the Duke of Parma, as before he intended, and hath now been forced to return to Vernon to take counsel for his best course to succour Brittany. The Leaguers are animated and the Parisians receive 1200 Spaniards, Italians and Walloons into garrison, and in a manner become less willing for peace.

Immediately after the receipt of these news the King sent for Sir Henry Unton and imparted them to him at length with great passion and discontent, discoursing at large of his miserable estate, of the factions of his servants, and of their ill dispositions. Then he required the ambassador's opinions touching his course for Brittany, and also what further aid he might expect from the Queen, alleging that unless he were immediately strengthened from England, it was impossible for him to resist the greatness of Spain who assailed the country by Brittany, Languedoc, by the Low Countries, by the Duke of Savoy and the Duke of Lorraine.

The ambassador replied mildly, humbly craving pardon from the delivery of any opinion as a public minister, but not refusing as a private person to deliver his conceit by way of discourse, not of advice. On this being granted by the King he began to set out the importance of Brittany; the King's want of providence therein; his breach of promise in not sending forces thither; the King of Spain's great desire to have that country and how much his honour, profit, and safety might be specially impeached and endangered. He then delivered such reasons as might urge the necessity of his defence of that country; and lastly peremptorily pressed his going in person with an army into Brittany to resist the enemies' pursuit of victory, concluding by giving him neither any manner of comfort nor discomfort of the Queen's resolution.

To this the King gave a willing ear, and replied with many thanks, yielding many excuses of his want of means, not of disposition to provide a remedy. In the mean season, he said he would take counsel and then acquaint the ambassador with his resolution.

Soon after this, the Queen's letters for the ambassador's revocation (for which he hath long petitioned) came to hand; whereupon he took occasion to repair to the King and to crave his leave to depart, which the King very willingly granted, requesting him, partly for his better safety, but chiefly for the better understanding of his further resolution concerning his affairs, to attend him to Vernon, where within six days he should meet his Council.

6th June. Lewdness in a Conduit.

A man and a woman, both aged persons, were set in the pillory in Cheapside towards Paul's upon a scaffold with papers on their heads, the man being keeper of the conduit there. These two lewd persons in the night entered the conduit, washed themselves, and evacuated their bowels therein.

10*th June.* PLAYS OF THE WEEK.

The plays at the Rose Theatre this past week were *Bindo and Richardo*, *Titus and Vespasian*, *The Looking Glass for London*, *Tamar Cam*, *The Spanish Tragedy*, *A Knack to Know a Knave* (for the first time).

12*th June.* RIOTS IN SOUTHWARK.

There was great disorder in Southwark last evening, until about 8 o'clock at night, when the Lord Mayor, taking with him one of the Sheriffs, came down upon the rioters, finding great multitudes of the people assembled, especially some apprentices of the feltmakers, out of Barmsey Street and the Blackfriars, together with a number of loose and masterless men. Whereupon proclamation was made and, the multitude having been dismissed, the Lord Mayor apprehended the doers of the disorder and committed them to prison. This morning, examinations being taken, it is found that the disorder began upon the serving of a warrant from the Lord Chamberlain by one of the Knight Marshal's men upon a feltmonger's servant who was committed to the Marshalsea without any cause of offence. Whereupon the apprentices, under pretence of meeting at a play, assembled themselves to make a rescue. The inhabitants of Southwark of best reputation complain that the Knight Marshal's men in serving their warrants use not themselves with good discretion and moderate usage, but by their most rough and violent manner provoke them whom they have to arrest by their rough and violent manner. In this case they entered a house where a warrant was to be served with a dagger drawn, affrighting the good wife of the house who sat by the fire with a young child in her arms; and afterwards taking the party and several others committed him to prison where they lay five days without making their answer. When therefore the apprentices' men assembled themselves before the Marshalsea, the Knight Marshal's men issued forth with their daggers drawn and bastinadoes in their hands, beating the people, of whom some came, as their manner was, merely to gaze; and afterwards drew their swords, whereby the tumult was incensed and they themselves endangered but that help came to prevent further mischief.

15th June. SOME ENGLISH SAILORS ILL-TREATED.

Sir Henry Unton, the ambassador in France, is to make complaint to the King of the hard treatment offered to certain English sailors. It seemeth that in August last a ship called the *Mary of Waterford*, laden with salt, pepper, suckats, marmalade, and other commodities, about 60 leagues from Cape Finisterre was taken by one Govant, Captain of the *Salamander* of Dieppe, and other subjects of the French King. This man spoiled them of all their goods, worth £800, beside the hindrance and damage to the extent of £200, and so left the company of the ship, being sixteen persons, only with a basket of broken bread and a small roundlet of cider mixed with water. In this state they continued at sea twenty-five days before they could recover any land, so that two died with hunger and the rest were brought in so weak that they were greatly endangered.

DISTRESS AT CANTERBURY.

After deliberate consideration of some good means to be used for the present relief of the decayed estate of the City of Canterbury and the great number of poor people there inhabiting, the Council think it best to put into execution an Act of Parliament, made for this purpose in 6th of Henry VIII. (1515) for the making of the river running from the City of Canterbury navigable for craiers, boats and lighters to pass to the town of Fordwich, as at present from Fordwich to Sandwich, whereby the inhabitants of the City might have more trade to employ them. But as this work far exceedeth the abilities of the inhabitants of the City, the magistrates of Kent are required at some speedy convenient time to assemble themselves and consider an estimate of the whole work; and first to set down a liberal contribution themselves, and afterwards to exhort also the gentlemen and wealthiest inhabitants to bestow rateably such convenient proportion of money as should be laid upon them.

17th June. SIR HENRY UNTON RETURNS.

Sir Henry Unton, ambassador to the King of France, hath come to London, having received his despatch on the 10th.

PLAYS OF THE WEEK AT THE ROSE.

This past week were played *Harry the Sixth*, *Muly Mullocco*, *The Jew of Malta*, *A Knack to Know a Knave*, *Sir John Maundeville*.

19th June. RECUSANCY IN WALES.

The Council write to the Earl of Pembroke praying him certify the names of those gentlemen in the Principality of Wales, that be sound in religion and well affected, to be appointed commissioners for the inquiry of Jesuits, Seminaries and other suspected persons. Since no commission is appointed for Wales numbers of recusants flee thither so that there is daily infection and falling away from religion in those parts.

In Carmarthen many, both men and women, in the night season and by day repair to certain places where in times past were pilgrimages, images or offerings; they assemble sometimes in great numbers, a thing intolerable to be permitted after so long a time of the preaching of the Gospel. These superstitious and idolatrous monuments are to be pulled down, broken, and quite defaced so that no remnant, token or memory may remain. Should any hereafter repair to those places they shall be apprehended and severely punished for their lewd behaviour that others may be warned by their examples to take heed of such intolerable abuses.

21st June. A COZENER PILLORIED.

One Kirby, a gentleman in countenance, but a cozener by quality, was set in the pillory without Aldersgate and there lost one of his ears.

22nd June. FATHER SOUTHWELL THE JESUIT.

Topcliffe hath written to the Queen concerning Father Southwell the Jesuit that he took prisoner a few days since, saying that he keeps him very straitly in his strong chamber at Westminster; and if her Majesty wishes to know anything in his heart, then shall he be made to stand against the wall, his feet standing upon the ground and his hands put as high as he can reach against the wall—like a trick at trenchmore—shall enforce him to tell all.

23rd June. PLAYING CEASES AT THE ROSE THEATRE.

The Lord Strange's men have ceased from playing at the Rose Theatre, their plays during the five days past being *The Spanish Tragedy*, *Harry the Sixth*, *The Comedy of Jeronimo*, *Tamar Cam*, *The Knack to Know a Knave*.

Rumours of Peace in France.

It is reported that peace in France is expected and the King has sent M. de Saucy to acquaint her Majesty therewith or else to see how he may be helped at her hands to stand the war. The Duke de Mayne is at St. Denis with the King on safe conduct, the terms offered by the League being liberty of religion on both sides where it is, and, where it is not, no inquisition; the Protestants to have churches in the fauxbourgs, and the Leaguers to have in every province certain towns of caution for certain years.

Abuses in the North.

It is reported that in the north those evilly disposed towards religion hold May games, Morris dances, plays, bear baitings, ales and other pastimes on Sundays and holy days at the time of Divine Service and other godly exercises to draw away the people when men assemble together for the hearing of God's Word and to join in common prayers. The Council have prayed the Earl of Derby to give special direction to all Justices to forbid these and the like pastimes to be in any place whatsoever on Sunday or holy days at the time of Divine Service, sermons, or other godly exercises; and to cause the favourers, maintainers or chief offenders to be sent up to answer their contentious and lewd behaviour.

Small reformation has been made in those parts by the Ecclesiastical Commissioners as appeareth by the emptiness of churches on Sundays and holy days, and the multitude of bastards and drunkards; great sums have been levied under pretence of the commission, but the counties are in worse case than before and the number of those that do not resort to Divine Service greater. The people lack instruction, for the preachers are few, most of the parsons unlearned, many of those learned not resident, and divers unlearned daily admitted into very good benefices by the Bishop. The youth are for the most part being trained up by such as possess papistry; and no examination made of schools and schoolmasters. The proclamation for the apprehension of seminaries, Jesuits, and mass priests, and for calling home children from parts beyond the sea is not being executed. Some of the coroners and justices and their families do not frequent church, and many of them have not communicated at the Lord's Supper since the beginning of the Queen's reign. In many places the seminaries have lately offered disputations against the settled religion, but nothing is said to them.

They that resort to church are so few that preachers who were determined to preach on Sundays and holy days refrain from lack of auditors; the people so swarm in the streets and alehouses during service time, that open markets are kept and in many churches only the curate and the clerk are present.

Marriages and christenings are celebrated by seminary and other priests in corners, and in some parts children baptized according to law have afterwards been rebaptized by priests. Divers mass priests, being apprehended, refuse to be examined npon oath as to where they frequent. Alehouses are innumerable, and the law for suppressing and keeping them in order not executed, whereby toleration of drunkenness, unlawful games and other abuses follow. Small or no reformation has followed the letters of the Council. The recusants have spies about the Council to give intelligence when anything is intended against them so that they may shift out of the way and avoid being apprehended.

RIOTING EXPECTED IN LONDON.

The magistrates of the City of London and the suburbs are warned that certain apprentices and other idle people their adherents, the same that were the authors and partakers of the late disorder in Southwark, have a further purpose on Midsummer evening or night to renew their lewd assembly by colour of the time and to commit a breach of the peace or other foul outrage. To prevent this mischief, a strong and substantial watch, sufficient to suppress any tumult, is to be kept both on Midsummer evening, Midsummer night and Sunday night of householders and masters of families, to continue from the beginning of evening to the morning. All masters of servants to be straightly charged, as they shall answer to their perils, to keep their servants in their houses for these two nights, and not to let them have any weapons if they be disposed to execute any evil purpose. If, notwithstanding this strait charge, any servants, apprentices or suspected persons be found in the streets they shall immediately be committed to prison. Moreover for avoiding of these unlawful assemblies, no plays may be used at the Theatre, Curtain or other usual places, nor any other sort of unlawful or forbidden pastime that draws together the baser sort of people from henceforth until the Feast of St. Michael.

26th June. SIR JOHN PERROT CONDEMNED.

Sir John Perrot, that was found guilty of high treason on 27th April, appeared to-day before the Commissioners for judgment. He was brought in a coach from the Tower to the Old Swan, thence conveyed by water to Westminster Bridge where he landed and so into Westminster Hall between 8 and 9 in the morning. He was accompanied by Mr. Blunt and Mr. Cooke, son and son-in-law to the Lieutenant of the Tower, and strongly guarded by divers of the yeomen of the guard with halberds and the Lieutenant's men all round him. In this fashion he was brought to the Queen's Bench bar where he stood for a quarter of an hour waiting for the Commissioners. He was clothed in a doublet and hose of plain black satin and a gown of wrought velvet furred, with a plain white ruff and wearing a square, or flat crowned, black felt hat with a small band ; and he carried a carnation in his hand.

The Commissioners having taken their places, Sergeant Snagg for the Queen prayed that judgment might be given. Then the Clerk of the Court asked Sir John whether he had anything to say why judgment to die should not be given.

Sir John made protestation of his innocence in a speech of about a quarter of an hour in which he complained very bitterly of the hard and false dealings of the witnesses against him. He said that he knew of her Majesty's mercy which proceeded from the providence of God, who knew his innocence and so stayed him so long from judgment. Whereupon the Lord Chamberlain, conceiving his meaning to be that the Queen had deferred judgment being persuaded of his innocency, interrupted his speech and declared that he had received more favour than any traitor he ever saw. But Sir John prayed the Lord Chamberlain not to misconstrue his meaning.

Mr. Attorney Egerton now stood up, and directing his speech to the Commissioners urged that Sir John Perrot by protesting his innocency thought to deceive the audience into believing that he was not guilty of treason.

To this Sir John angrily replied, 'Mr. Attorney, you did me wrong now as you did me before.'

'I never did you wrong,' said Mr. Attorney.

'You did me wrong,' said Sir John.

'Instance where I did you wrong,' answered Mr. Attorney.

'You did me wrong,' again said Sir John.

'I never did you wrong,' replied Mr. Attorney.

Both the Lord Buckhurst and the Lord Chamberlain spoke to Sir John declaring that he had been most manifestly proved guilty of treason by a number of witnesses. Sir John answered that the matter had been set forward by his enemies in Ireland, and that he was condemned by Irish witnesses all; and further, that the Irish witnesses had no respect of an oath, and for a small value, a man might procure a number to swear anything.

After further talk with the Commissioners, Anderson, the Lord Chief Justice of the Common Pleas, asked him whether he had anything to say in arrest of judgment. Sir John answered that seeing it had pleased God and the Queen to bring him to that pass he had nothing to say, but humbly submitted himself to the law and their lordships.

Then the Lord Chief Justice began with a long discourse, showing how God from time to time had revealed the treasons that had been practised at home and abroad. He said that he agreed with the others that Sir John was justly condemned of treason, and so proceeded to judgment: that he should be carried by the Lieutenant of the Tower to the Tower which was the place from which he came, and thence to be drawn upon a hurdle through the City of London to the place of execution, and there to be hanged, and to be cut down alive, and his bowels and privy members to be cut off and cast into the fire in his sight, his head to be cut off and his body to be cut in four quarters, to be disposed at the Queen's pleasure, and God have mercy upon him.

Sir John then again declared his innocency very fervently and concluded by asking that certain petitions might be granted. He asked that, if it would please the Queen to grant him his life, he might have a better room, for his lodging was a small chamber, room only for his chair and table. To this the Lord Chamberlain answered that the room was fit for such a man as he was. He begged that if he should suffer death he might die a gentleman's death and be spared from drawing through the streets and the rest of the judgment. He also asked, amongst other petitions, that their Lordships would enlist the Queen to be good to his son and his wife, and, as he heard, to a little son which they had who might hereafter do her Majesty service.

Then Sir John was taken away from the bar in the same manner as he had been brought thither, and so back to the Tower. The Commissioners having sat a little longer after his departure caused proclamation to be made that the present commission of Oyer and Terminer was ended, and on the stroke of ten o'clock at night, the court broke up.

28th June. THE MURDER OF JOHN BREWEN.

This day Anne Brewen and John Parker were executed in Smithfield for the murder of John Brewen.

Two and a half years before Anne Welles (as she then was) by divers young men was beloved, but especially by John Brewen and John Parker, both goldsmiths, being bachelors and good friends. Brewen had the favour of her friends and kinsfolk, but notwithstanding his long suit and the gifts of gold and jewels that he gave her he was disdained in favour of Parker, who enjoyed her love in secret. At length seeing his suit despised and having no hope of her favour, Brewen determined to demand again his gold and jewels, and coming to her he requested that his gifts might be given back; to this she answered contemptuously that he should stay for it. Without more ado the young man had her arrested for the jewels.

The damsel was so astonished and dismayed that she promised if he would let his action fall nor ever think the worse of her, she would marry him and make him her husband by a certain day; and this before witnesses she vowed to perform. Brewen therefore was not a little joyful and made preparation for his marriage; but when Parker heard of it he was grievously vexed and taunted her so bitterly that she repented of the promise made to Brewen, and began to hate him; and after this Parker would never let her rest but continually urged her to make away with him.

She had not been married above three days to Brewen when she put in practice to poison him. Although her husband loved her dearly she would not stay with him after the first night of their wedding, saying she had vowed not to lie with him until he had got her a better house, and the more to cover her treachery and to show her discontent with him she provided a lodging near to the place where Parker lived, so that he had free access to her.

Two days after her marriage Parker brought her a deadly poison that would work speedily on the heart without any swelling on the body or outward sign of infection. This poison she carried secretly to her husband's house, and, coming in the next morning with a pleasant countenance, she asked him if he would have a mess of sugar sops that cold morning. 'Ay, marry, with all my heart,' said he, 'and I take it very kindly that you will do so much for me.' Then she prepared a mess for him with the poison, but in rising from setting the pot back on the fire her coat spilled the mess, and she began to lament that so good a mess of sugar sops should be wasted. But her husband said, 'What, woman, vex not at the matter, your ill luck go with them.' 'Marry, amen,' answered she. Then she asked him to fetch her a pennyworth of red herrings.

When he came back, he found that she had made ready a fresh mess of sugar sops for him, one for herself and another for a little boy that she brought with her.

In a little while Brewen began to wax very ill about the stomach, with a grievous inward griping ; and immediately after to vomit exceedingly so that he requested her to help him to bed. When it grew somewhat late, she told her husband that she must return to her lodging, and though he begged her to stay with him, she said she could not and would not ; and so left the poisoned man all alone for the whole night without comfort or company. All that night he was extremely sick, worse and worse, never ceasing to vomit until (as was afterwards supposed) his entrails were all shrunk and broken within him. The next morning she came to him again but made little show of sorrow. When he rebuked her for her unkindness, she asked him if he would have her forsworn. 'Well, Anne,' said he, 'stay with me now, for I am not long to continue in this world.' 'Now God forbid,' she replied, affecting a great show of sorrow. Then she made a caudle with sugar and spices which she gave him, and immediately after he had eaten it, he died. The next day he was buried, none of the neighbours suspecting that any evil had been done to him.

Parker now became very bold with the widow so that ere long she durst deny him nothing or he would threaten to stab her with his dagger. In this state he kept her unmarried for two years after her husband's death until at length she was with child. And now, to save her credit, she begged him to marry her, but he reviled her most shamefully, taunting her with Brewen's murder. While they were thus quarrelling very vehemently, some of the neighbours overheard their words and revealed them to the magistrate. Whereupon the woman was carried before Alderman Howard to be examined, and the man before Justice Young; but both denied the deed very stoutly until the woman was made to believe that Parker had confessed, when she revealed all. She was therefore taken into the country to be delivered of her child and then brought back to prison. Both were arraigned and condemned at Newgate; the woman to be burnt in Smithfield, the man to be hanged before her eyes.

10th July. SIR W. RALEGH'S COMPLAINTS AGAINST THE DEPUTY OF IRELAND.

Sir Walter Ralegh hath written from the Tower to Sir Robert Cecil complaining that when his disgrace was known in Ireland, the Deputy, Sir William Fitzwilliams, an enemy of his, dealt very despitefully with him. Pretending a debt to the Queen of £400, he sent a sheriff to take away all the cattle of Sir Walter's tenants in Munster and unless the money were paid the same day to sell them on the next. The debt was but for 50 marks, and paid; but the sheriff did as he was commanded, and took away five hundred milch kine from the poor people; of whom some had but two, and some three, to relieve their poor wives and children, and in a new country set down to milch and plant. He had forcibly thrust Sir Walter out of possession of a castle because it was in law between him and his cousin, and would not hear his attorney speak. He had admitted a ward (and given it to his man) of a castle which was the Queen's, which Sir Walter had built and planted with English these five years; and to profit his man with a wardship, lost the Queen's inheritance; and would plant the cousin of a rebel in the place of an English-man, the castle standing in the most dangerous place in all Munster.

18th July. A PROGNOSTICATION.

In the *Calendar* for the next twelve months that James Carre, Master of Arts, hath penned, it is prognosticated that in the winter months sickness, engendered of cold humours and of phlegmatic matter, will this quarter afflict divers persons; and the trembling ague will cause many to tremble, not only those that have it, because they have it, but such also as have it not, lest they should have it. For the spring, the weather will be very seasonable and temperate, but notwithstanding there shall be some painful and perilous sicknesses, together with wars and rumours of wars. In the summer the drought less than in the two former summers: and yet greater store of drought in divers places to dry up the strong ale, than of strong ale to quench the drought: the winds at this season likely to be very variable. The harvest time will be inclined unto sundry wet and unexpected perries of rain, growing still from hot and dry exhalations to cold and moist vapours.

21st July. MILITARY EQUIPMENT IN THE COUNTIES.

The Lords Lieutenant of certain Counties are directed to enquire how much of the armour and furniture given to soldiers sent into foreign services has been returned; for it is reported to the Council that there is not such honest regard as there should be for the return of this armour, for which cause the country might be unfurnished. The armour that has not been returned shall be replaced as soon as possible by some general and reasonable contribution which the Queen earnestly desireth shall not be levied on the meaner sort but on those best able to bear it, such as farmers, landed men, and persons grown in wealth by any other trade.

It is also reported that some recusants have good quantity of armour in their houses. In 1585 special commissioners were chosen to receive the armour and weapons belonging to recusants until such time as they should conform to the laws; but since that time others have declared themselves recusants who are thought to have armour. The armour and weapons of all certified as recusants is to be collected into safe custody to be returned again to the owners when they shall conform. This is especially necessary at this time because the enemy make great brags of the assistance which they shall receive from those backward in religion.

21st July. GREENE'S 'QUIP FOR AN UPSTART COURTIER.'

Greene's *Quip for an Upstart Courtier*, or *A Quaint Dispute between Velvet Breeches and Cloth Breeches* is entered, being dedicated to Mr. Thomas Barnaby, Esquire, wherein in the form of a dream are set down the disorders in all estates and trades.

Velvet Breeches and Cloth Breeches coming upon each other began to dispute which was of the more ancient lineage. They agreed therefore to impanel a jury to try the title of Velvet Breeches, and as men of all occupations passed by so were they examined and accepted or challenged by both parties. The jury having at last been impanelled the case was put to them and in a short space they found that Cloth Breeches had the better title, being one that had been formerly a companion to Kings, an equal with the nobility, a friend to gentlemen and noblemen, a patron of the poor, a true subject, a good housekeeper and as honest as he was ancient, whereas Velvet Breeches was an upstart come out of Italy, begot of Pride, nursed by Self Love, and brought into this country by Newfangledness; that of late he was a raiser of rents and an enemy to the commonwealth, and not in any way to be preferred in equity before Cloth Breeches.

In some copies of this book is printed a very bitter satire on ropemakers, aimed at the father of Dr. Gabriel Harvey, who hath caused offence to Greene and his friends; but in others this leaf is cancelled either because Greene thinketh better of it or because he feareth lest that he bring himself within the law.

23rd July. A MONOPOLY IN STARCH.

The Council have granted to Mr. Richard Young an open letter preventing all persons from buying or bringing starch into the country contrary to the special grant giving him sole licence and authority for the making, bringing in and selling of starch in the realm.

28th July. ROBERT SOUTHWELL SENT TO THE TOWER.

Southwell, the Jesuit, is now committed to the Tower by order of the Council to be kept a close prisoner, and to see none but the keeper that Mr. Topcliffe shall appoint.

31st July. SIR WALTER RALEGH'S LAMENTABLE COMPLAINT.

Sir Walter Ralegh, writing to Sir Robert Cecil from the Tower, complaineth in very extravagant terms of the departure of the Court and of the Queen from London. 'My heart was never broken,' saith he, 'till this day that I hear the Queen goes so far off; whom I have followed so many years with so great love and desire, in so many journeys, and am now left behind her, in a dark prison all alone. While she was yet near at hand that I might hear of her once in two or three days my sorrows were the less; but even now my heart is cast into the depth of all misery. I that was wont to behold her riding like Alexander, hunting like Diana, walking like Venus, the gentle wind blowing her fair hair about her pure cheeks, like a nymph; sometimes sitting in the shade like a goddess; sometimes singing like an angel; sometimes playing like Orpheus.' He concludeth, 'Do with me now, therefore, what you list. I am more weary of life than they are desirous I should perish, which if it had been for her, as it is by her, I have been too happily born.'

6th August. DESERTERS IN HERTFORDSHIRE.

Many soldiers of a company levied in Hertfordshire have deserted their captain without leave, both before embarking and after landing. These men now lurk in very riotous and disordered sort in the remote places in the county, not only to the harm and prejudice of peaceful subjects but also showing a dangerous example. The magistrates from whose divisions the men come are ordered to apprehend the ringleaders and commit them to the common jail.

7th August. ABLE-BODIED IRISHMEN TO BE DEPORTED.

Certain able-bodied Irishmen, masterless men, that now for a long time frequent the City and the suburbs begging, are to be despatched to Ireland and set to work by Mr. William English, that complains that by reason of his long imprisonment in England his tenants and followers have left his lands and possessions waste and unpeopled.

8th August. NASHE'S 'PIERCE PENNILESS.'

Nashe hath written a book called *Pierce Penniless; his Supplication to the Devil,* being a satirical pamphlet on the abuses of the times.

Seeing that now gentle Sir Philip Sidney is dead and no one left to care for poor scholars, Pierce Penniless in despair pens his supplication to the devil, wherein he writeth invectively of usurers, the deadly sins of greediness, nigardize, and pride (attacking by the way the antiquaries for their rusty wits in so doting upon worm-eaten eld), envy, murder, wrath, and railery, and especially those that rail upon playing. For the policy of playing, saith he, is very necessary for a state, since those that are their own masters (as gentlemen of the Court, the Inns of Court, captains and soldiers) needs must spend their afternoons upon pleasure, either gaming, following of harlots, drinking, or seeing a play, of which the last is the least evil. Nor are plays evil, though some petitioners of the Council dislike them; for no play encourages any man to tumults or rebellion but lays before him the halter and the gallows; or praises or approves pride, lust, whoredom or prodigality but beats it down utterly; and besides they bring upon the stage our forefathers' valiant acts. Thence Pierce passeth to gluttony, drunkenness, sloth and lechery, and so to a discourse on the nature of Hell and the Devil. Amongst many others attacked in this book are Dr. Gabriel Harvey and his brother Richard.

11th August. THE COUNT MOMPELGARD IN LONDON.

This day Frederick, Count Mompelgard, is come to London, having set out from Mompelgard with his train of servants to travel and see the world. They reached Dover two days since, being much frightened at sea through their unfamiliarity with the waves, and distressed through their frequent horrible vomitings. Having landed, noting on the way the wrecks of the Spanish Armada still lying on the beach, they took post horses for Gravesend. The journey hath been very wearisome to them by reason of our English saddles, which being covered only with bare hide are painful to strangers and hard to ride upon, especially for the Count who is corpulent and heavy.

They are much amazed with the throngs of people in London,

and their magnificent apparel, but they complain that the inhabitants are extremely proud and overbearing; and because the greater part, especially the tradespeople, seldom journey into other countries but always remain in their houses in the City attending to their business, they care little for strangers, but scoff and laugh at them.

Moreover, say they, no one dare oppose our citizens else the street boys and apprentices collect together in great crowds, and strike right and left unmercifully without regard to person.

13*th August.* THE COUNT MOMPELGARD FEASTS WITH THE FRENCH AMBASSADOR.

Being Sunday the Count Mompelgard attended the French service and afterwards at midday partook of a magnificent banquet provided by the French Ambassador. The French wine did not agree with the Count, though he relished the beer exceedingly.

15*th August.* A SCURRILOUS JESUIT PAMPHLET.

Some copies have been found in England of a book written in Latin by Father Parsons, the Jesuit, under the name of 'Andreas Philopater,' answering the proclamation made against the Jesuits and seminary priests dated 18th October, 1591. There is also a digest in English, pretended to be put forth by an English Intelligencer in a letter to the Lord Treasurer's secretary. The Latin book hath been translated into French and circulated amongst the Queen's enemies. In this book the proclamation is answered point by point in a preface and six sections, and some of the Council and principal men of the state very slanderously described.

Of Sir Christopher Hatton, Philopater saith that he departed very unwillingly from this life on the very day before this edict was published, which he was said to have resisted so long as he lived and would never have assented to, partly because, being a more moderate man, he would not have approved such cruelty, partly because he differed so heartily from Cecil and the Puritans, to whom Cecil showed patronage, nor would he that they should be increased to oppressing of the Catholics. Hence arose that suspicion of poison for his removal which was written in divers letters from England. Being born of a family honest rather than famous, he had come to London to study the municipal laws of the kingdom ; but when the labours of study seemed to him too heavy to be borne of an equal mind he did, what now a great part of the youth of England are wont to do who come to London to study, but frequent the presence chamber rather than the school. It happened not long after the accession of Queen Elizabeth to the throne, when there was much rejoicing, with merriment, shows, mummings and other childish exercises, that on the very birthday of Our Lord a comedy with the utmost show was presented in the Queen's hall in the name of the University by the students themselves. On this occasion when many acquitted themselves very fairly, Christopher Hatton was thought to have excelled them all in beauty of person and grace of action, by which he so pleased the Queen that henceforward she always had him in the presence chamber, and promoted him through all the grades of honour to the very top, which is the Chancellorship ; for first he was Captain of the Queen's Body-guard, then of the Bed-chamber, finally Chancellor.

Of Cecil it is written that though he is Treasurer, guardian of the wards of nobles, and controls almost all things in England by his own judgment, yet he came of humble and obscure origin. For his father, whose name was David Cecil, served almost in the meanest rank in King's Wardrobe ; his grandfather was one of the Guard of the King's Person, and kept a public tavern in the town of Stamford. After spending some time in the study of letters at the University of Cambridge, where for a time he sought part of his living by tolling the bell in St. John's College, at the beginning of the reign of King Edward the Sixth Cecil insinuated himself into the household of the Duke of Somerset, the Protector.

After thus running through the Lord Treasurer's life from his youth, this Philopater declareth though he would not deny that the Queen assented to the Proclamation (for which she would render her account to God), yet it was not of her own accord, but extorted from her by the importunity of others and especially by the fraud and importunity of Cecil, who is believed to be not only the instigator and procurer of the proclamation but even the writer, because as well as other offices which he has ambitiously grasped, he alone has usurped the office of Secretary after the death of Walsingham. From him proceeded the framing of the whole affair; from him the odious names and phrases newly applied to the Catholics, and not taken over from previous proclamations; from him the insults and lies against Catholic Princes which in the eyes and judgments of all are manifestly false and impudent.

Of Sir Walter Ralegh it is written that he keeps a school of Atheism much frequented, with a certain necromantic astronomer as schoolmaster, where no small number of young men of noble birth learn to deride the Old Law of Moses as well as the New Law of Christ with ingenious quips and jests; and among other things to spell the name of God backwards.

He compareth the seminaries, which the proclamation denounced, with the colleges in the two Universities of England, declaring that the students come out of England neither for lack of living nor for crimes committed, for they are commonly gentlemen, or wealthy peoples' children, and might easily have had preferment if they would apply themselves to the protestants' proceedings. Moreover he showeth that a great multitude of gentlemen's sons leaving their inheritances and other hopes of worldly possibilities at home come over daily to study and to be made priests with infinite desire to return again quickly to England. He declareth that there are more gentlemen at this time in the English seminaries of France, Rome and Spain than in all the clergy of England twice told, to which no gentleman will afford his son to be a minister and much less his daughter to be a minister's wife.

With the order and studies observed in the seminaries are compared the loose proceedings of the English Universities and Colleges where Cecil, Leicester and such like, cancellers of virtue rather than Chancellors of Universities, have overthrown all. The porters are taken away from College gates which used to keep students in awe, whence come confusion and immodesty in apparel, every man wearing either as his pride or his fancy serve, or his purse and ability permit. To this is attributed the filling up and pestering all colleges with harlots to be baits for the young men, headships given to light and wanton companions, fencing and dancing schools crowded, taverns filled with scholars, statutes of founders condemned and broken, leases embezzled, the goods made away, and the places of fellows and scholars publicly sold.

17th August. THE COUNT MOMPELGARD SUMMONED TO COURT.

The Count Mompelgard being summoned to the Court which is now at Reading, arrived there about noon and lodged with the Mayor. Hardly had he changed his apparel when the Earl of Essex visited him in his lodging, welcoming him in the Queen's name and inviting him to take dinner in his apartments, whither the Count was conveyed in a coach. After being most sumptuously feasted, he was entertained with sweet and enchanting music. The repast being ended, he was again accompanied by the Earl of Essex to his lodging, but shortly afterwards he was summoned by the Queen and conducted to her own apartments.

18th August. THE COUNT MOMPELGARD AGAIN VISITS THE QUEEN.

In the afternoon the Count had another audience with the Queen, when she herself made and delivered an appropriate speech in the French language in the presence of Monsieur de Beauvoir, whom she holds in especial favour. After he had been conversing with her in a very lively and good-humoured manner he so far prevailed on her that she played very sweetly and skilfully on her instrument, the strings of which are of gold and silver.

20th August. THE COUNT MOMPELGARD AT WINDSOR.

The Count was conducted to Windsor, and the day being Sunday, he visited the Chapel where he listened for more than an hour to the music, the usual ceremonies and the English sermon. He noted especially the beauty of the playing of the organ and the singing of a little boy, finding the ceremonies very similar to the papists'. Dinner being ended the Count with the English and French deputies went to inspect the Castle of Windsor, and on the lead of the highest tower of all he hath cut his name. After this, he was shown the beautiful royal bed-hangings and tapestries of gold and fine silk, also a unicorn's horn and other costly things.

21st August. GREENE'S 'BLACK BOOK'S MESSENGER.'

Greene's *Black Book's Messenger* is entered, wherein is laid open the life and death of Ned Browne, one of the most notable cutpurses and crossbiters that ever lived in England. This is the messenger to that Black Book, giving a beadroll of all the notable conny-catchers about London which Greene promised in his *Disputation*. Telleth the merry tales of Ned Browne's villanies until he went over to France, where being condemned for robbing a church near Aix he was hanged at a window, in default of a gallows; and his body being buried without the town was in the night torn out of his grave by a company of wolves and devoured.

24th August. CONDEMNED CRIMINALS AS SOLDIERS.

Some of the prisoners remaining in the common jails in Oxford and Berkshire on criminal charges and in danger of capital sentences have promised that if they be sent abroad as soldiers they will not return without special leave. Since some of these men are able and strong, and may prove good subjects to the State, the Council have ordered that means be taken in the discretion of the Lord Chief Baron to deliver them to Sir John Norris after examination of their charges.

27th August. A PRIEST'S INFORMATIONS.

James Young, *alias* Dingley, an arrested priest, hath declared to the Lord Treasurer that he heard from Father Parsons that the King of Spain had promised Sir William Stanley to invade England, but not till 1593, because of the hindrances in France. By which time he hoped to have brought in Brittany and have thence 16 great ships and 10,000 men, and more commodity to come to the Irish kerns; thence Sir William Stanley could go to his own country, where the Earl of Derby would be ready to assist him. He hoped that the young Lord Strange would also help; but now he discloses every one that moved in the matter. The King of Spain said that he remembered the Earl very well, as he was one of the last noblemen married in his time, and that if Lord Strange had been unmarried, none would have been more fit to have been proclaimed King at their first arrival.

A certain Captain Cripps, that came to the Jesuits' College at Seville, spoke to Father Parsons on an embassy wherein Lord Derby was sent, and of a minister that came there from whom a soldier stole a portmanteau; whereupon Parsons replied, he would rather he had stolen my Lord's golden breeches with which he had been known these thirty years at least.

The assault of Stanley is to be attempted next April, and as soon as his arrival is reported, the whole Spanish fleet is to be ready; Parsons is to be present, and Cardinal Allen to come from Rome, but not to England until the event of the navy is seen.

ANXIETY FOR OSTEND.

Great anxiety is felt that the enemy will attempt to surprise the town of Ostend. The Council have ordered that the companies in Ostend which were to have proceeded to Brittany to reinforce Sir John Norris be retained. Further, that Sir Francis Vere and Sir Thomas Morgan who are in command of the companies in Holland shall have everything in readiness at Flushing by the 6th September to embark for Brittany.

29th August. SIR ROGER WILLIAMS' COMPLAINTS.

Sir Roger Williams writeth to the Lord Treasurer from France that the estate of the poor King is now very desperate and our own far from any hope of peace, for in time the greater purses will eat and consume the lesser. The Spaniard will not greatly feel the matter unless the war is made in his own country, or his Indian navy (the armadas and not the merchant ships) defeated, or the Duke of Parma defeated in battle. It seems strange to him to see how we entered into war for the Netherlanders' defence, who traffick freely with the Spanish, whilst we ourselves are barred; by which means Holland and Zealand grow rich, and England greatly impoverished, and will be far greater if it continue any time. Holland and Zealand are rich and invincible, France ruined and poor, ready to be conquered; wherefore the Queen's forces in the Low Countries, saving strong garrisons in Flushing and Brille, should be transported for service in France.

1st September. AN INVASION EXPECTED ON THE SOUTH COAST.

It is credibly reported that a large fleet of ships with a great store of men and munitions have been sent out by the King of Spain and the Leaguers and are now in the Sleeve, which forces are believed to be intended against the Isle of Wight or one of the seaports of Sussex. All armour, furniture, munitions and weapons in those parts are forthwith to be put in readiness, and upon the first notice or discovery of their arrival the forces shall immediately assemble to repulse the enemy; beacon watches also to be renewed and diligently kept.

3rd September. The Death of Robert Greene.

Robert Greene, author of plays, poems and pamphlets, is dead, having lain sick for a month of a surfeit which he had taken with drinking, and though he continually scoured, yet his body continued to swell upward until it swelled him at the heart and in his face. All this time he hath continued most patient and penitent, with tears forsaking the world, renouncing oaths and desiring forgiveness of God and men for all his offences, so that throughout his sickness he was never heard to swear, rave or blaspheme the name of God as he was accustomed to do before, but he was continuously calling on God even until he gave up the ghost, to the great comfort of his well willers to see how mightily the grace of God worked in him. It is noted that his sickness did not so greatly weaken him, for he walked to his chair and back again the night before he died.

About nine o'clock last night as he lay in bed a friend of his told him that his wife sent her commendations, whereat he greatly rejoiced, and, confessing that he had mightily wronged her, wished that he could see her before he died. But, feeling that his time was short, he took pen and ink and wrote her this letter:

'Sweet Wife,

As ever there was any good will or friendship between me and thee, see this bearer (my host) satisfied of his debt. I owe him ten pound, and but for him I had perished in the streets. Forget and forgive my wrongs done unto thee, and Almighty God have mercy on my soul. Farewell, till we meet in heaven, for on earth thou shalt never see me more. This 2nd of September, 1592.

Written by thy dying husband,

Robert Greene.'

4th September. THE COUNT MOMPELGARD DEPARTS.

The Count Mompelgard after visiting the Universities of Oxford and Cambridge hath received his passports and is embarked at Gravesend for Flushing.

5th September. DR. HARVEY AND ROBERT GREENE.

Dr. Gabriel Harvey is at this time in London, intending to prosecute Greene at law for what he wrote of his father and brothers in *The Quip for an Upstart Courtier.* But learning that Greene was lying dangerously sick in a shoemaker's house in Dowgate he was speaking of the matter with some friends when he heard that Greene was dead.

Accordingly he went down yesterday to Dowgate to speak with Mrs. Isam, the shoemaker's wife, who told him of Greene's poverty and miserable end: how in his extremity he would beg a penny pot of malmsey, and how none of his old acquaintances came to comfort him except a certain Mistress Appleby and the mother of his bastard son, Fortunatus. Even Nashe, his fellow writer, that was his companion at the fatal banquet of rhenish and pickled herring never after came near him. Mrs. Isam also told Dr. Harvey, with tears in her eyes, how he was fain, poor soul, to borrow her husband's shirt whilst his own was a-washing; and how his doublet and hose and sword were sold for three shillings; and besides the charges of his winding sheet, which was four shillings; and the charge of his burial in the new churchyard near Bedlam, which was six shillings and fourpence; how deeply he was indebted to her poor husband as appeared by his bond for ten pounds, and how, for a tender farewell, she herself crowned his head with a garland of bays.

All these things Dr. Harvey spreads about to his friends.

Greene's lamentable end is much talked of, for he was notorious in London for his dissolute and licentious living, his unseemly apparel and his loose companions, his monstrous swearing and impious profanation of sacred texts, his outrageous surfeiting. He had in employment one 'cutting' Ball, till he was hanged at Tyburn, to levy a crew of his trusted companions to guard him from arresting, and kept this Ball's sister as his mistress, of whom was born his bastard son, Fortunatus Greene, having forsaken his own wife a few months after marriage.

6th September. GREAT WINDS.

To-day the wind blowing west and by south as it hath for two days past, very boisterous, the Thames is so void of water by forcing out the fresh and keeping back the salt, that in divers places men have gone over two hundred paces and then flung a stone to land. A certain collier on a mare rode from the north side to the south and back again on either side of London Bridge; but not without great danger of drowning. This unusual event causeth much wonder especially among the Dutch, who fear lest the sea by some violent inundation has broken the banks in some of the Low Countries.

THE RETURN OF SIR MARTIN FROBISHER'S FLEET EXPECTED.

Sir Martin Frobisher's fleet is expected to return soon, and it is likely that on news of his coming merchants from the city of London will resort to Plymouth and Portsmouth to buy up the goods, and thereby carry the plague from London to those parts still free from infection. No one may be allowed to go to these towns unless licensed by the Council or the Lord Admiral; and as some of them may come in disguise, sufficient guards are, by the Council's order, to be set at the gates to examine all who repair thither.

7th September. THE PLAGUE IN LONDON.

The soldiers levied in Nottinghamshire, Leicester and the neighbouring counties are not to enter the City because of the infection, but to march by land to Southampton.

10th September. THE TAKING OF THE GREAT CARRACK.

The *Madre de Dios*, the great carrack, that was taken at the Islands of the Azores, was brought into Dartmouth the 7th, and the manner of her taking reported.

The season being so far advanced before the expedition set sail, Sir Walter Ralegh abandoned his enterprise upon Panama, and before leaving the fleet, gave directions to Sir John Burgh and Sir Martin Frobisher to divide the ships into two parts; Sir Martin, with the *Garland*, Captain George Gifford, Captain Henry Thin, Captain Grenville and others to lie off the South Cape and thereby to amaze the Spaniards and keep them on their own coasts; while Sir John Burgh, Captain Robert Cross,

Captain Thompson and others should attend at the Islands for the carracks or other Spanish ships coming from Mexico or other parts of the West Indies. This direction took good effect; for the King of Spain's Admiral receiving intelligence that the English Fleet was come on the coast, attended to defend the south parts of Spain, and to keep himself as near Sir Martin Frobisher as he could to impeach him in all things that he might undertake, and thereby neglected the safe conduct of the carracks.

Before the fleet severed themselves, they met with a great Biscayan on the Spanish coast, called the *Santa Clara*, a ship of 600 tons, which after a reasonable hot fight was entered and mastered, being found to be freighted with all sorts of small iron work as horse shoes, nails, plough shares, iron bars, spikes and the like, valued by our men at £6000 or £7000 but worth to them treble the value. This ship, which was sailing towards St. Lucar, there to take in further provision for the West Indies, was first rummaged and after sent for England.

The fleet now coasted along towards the south cape of St. Vincent, and on the way about the Rock near Lisbon, Sir John Burgh in the *Roebuck* spying a sail afar off gave her chase, which being a flyboat and of good sail drew him far southwards before he could fetch her. Not long after, sailing back toward the rest of his company he discovered the Spanish fleet to seaward of him, and they also having espied him between them and the shore spread themselves before him; but trusting to God's help only he thrust out from among them; and knowing that it was but folly to expect a meeting there with Sir Martin Frobisher (who when he understood of this armada as well as himself would be sure not to come that way) he began to shape his course towards the Azores.

Arriving before Flores upon Thursday, the 21st of June, towards evening, accompanied only with Captain Caulfield and the master of his ship, for the rest were not yet arrived, he made towards the shore with his boat, finding all the people of Santa Cruz in arms to bar their landing and ready to defend their town from spoil. Sir John contrariwise made signs to them by advancing a white flag which was answered with the like. Whereupon ensued intercourses of friendship, and pledges were taken on both sides, the Captain of the town for them, Captain Caulfield for ours; so that whatsoever our men wanted which the place would supply either in fresh water, victuals or the like, was very willingly granted by the inhabitants; and good leave given to refresh themselves on shore as much and as oft as they would without restraint.

At this Santa Cruz Sir John was informed that there was indeed no expectation of any fleet to come from the west but from the east, three days before his arrival a carrack had passed by for Lisbon, and that there were four carracks behind of one consort. Sir John being very glad of this news, stayed no longer on shore but at once embarked himself and quickly discovered one of the carracks. Meanwhile, part of the rest of the English fleet drew also towards the Azores, so that the same evening Sir John descried two or three of the Earl of Cumberland's ships (whereof one Mr. Norton was captain), which having in like sort perceived the carrack pursued her by that course which they saw her run towards the Islands. But on no side was there any way made by reason of a great calm, so that to discover what she was Sir John took his boat and rowed the space of three miles to make her out more exactly: and being returned he consulted with the better sort of the company upon boarding her in the morning.

But a very mighty storm arose in the night, the extremity whereof forced them all to weigh anchors; yet their care not to lose the carrack in wrestling with the weather was such that in the morning the tempest being now qualified, and our men bearing in again with the shore, they perceived the carrack very near the land and the Portugals confusedly carrying on shore such things as they could in any manner convey out of her. Seeing the haste our men made to come upon them, they forsook her, but first set fire to that which they could not carry away, intending wholly to consume her that neither glory of victory nor benefit of ship might remain to our men, and, lest the English should extinguish the flames, they entrenched themselves on the land, being four hundred men, to protect the carrack and keep our men aloof so that the carrack might be utterly destroyed. When Sir John Burgh noted this, he landed one hundred of his men, whereof many did swim and wade more than breast high to shore easily scattering those that guarded the coast, and he no sooner drew towards their new trenches but they fled immediately, leaving as much as the fire had spared to be the reward of our men's pains.

Here was taken among others one Vincent Fouseen, a Portugal, purser of the carrack, with two others, one an Almain, the other a Low-Dutchman, both cannoneers, who refused to make any voluntary report of those things which were demanded of them till the torture was threatened ; the fear whereof at last wrested from them the intelligence that within fifteen days three other greater carracks would arrive at the same island. Five carracks had set out from Goa, being specially commanded by the King of Spain not to touch at the island of St. Helena, where the Portugal carracks were always wont to refresh themselves, because of the English men-of-war who (as he was informed) lay there in wait to intercept them. The last rendezvous for them all was the Island of Flores, where the King assured them not to miss his armada sent thither to waft them to Lisbon.

Upon this information Sir John drew to counsel, meeting there Captain Norton, Captain Bownton, Captain Abraham Cock, Captains of three ships of the Earl of Cumberland, Mr. Thompson of Harwich, the Captain of the *Dainty* of Sir John Hawkins, one of Sir Walter Ralegh's fleet, and Mr. Christopher Newport, Captain of the *Golden Dragon*, newly returned from the West Indies, and others. These being assembled, he communicated with them what he had learned and what great presumption of truth the relation did carry, wishing that forasmuch as God and good fortune had brought them together in so good a season, they would show the uttermost of their endeavours to bring these Easterlings under the lee of the English obedience. Hereupon a present accord on all sides followed not to part company or leave of those seas till time should present cause to put their consultations in execution. The next day, the Queen's good ship, the *Foresight*, commanded by Sir Robert Cross, came in to the rest, and he, being likewise informed of the matter, was soon drawn into the service.

Thus Sir John with all these ships departing thence six or seven leagues to the west of Flores, they spread themselves abroad from north to south, each ship two leagues at least distant from another, by which order of extension they were able to discover the space of two whole degrees at sea.

In this sort they lay from 29th June to 3rd August, what time Captain Thompson in the *Dainty* had first sight of the huge carrack called the *Madre de Dios*. The *Dainty* being of excellent sail got the start of the rest of the fleet, and began the conflict, somewhat to her cost, with slaughter and hurt of divers of her men. Within a while after Sir John Burgh in the *Roebuck* of Sir Walter Ralegh's was at hand to second her, who saluted her with shot of great ordnance and continued the fight within musket shot, assisted by Captain Thompson and Captain Newport, till Sir Robert Cross, Vice-Admiral of the fleet, came up, being to leeward. At his arrival Sir John demanded of him what was best to be done, who answered that if the carrack were not boarded she would recover the shore and fire herself as the other had done.

Whereupon Sir John concluded to entangle her and Sir Robert promised also to fasten himself at the same instant; which was accomplished. But after a while Sir John Burgh receiving a shot with a cannon perrier under water and being ready to sink desired Sir Robert to fall off that he might also clear himself and save his ship from sinking, which with much difficulty he did; for both the *Roebuck* and the *Foresight* were so entangled that they had much ado to clear themselves.

The same evening Sir Robert Cross finding the carrack then sure and drawing near the island persuaded his company to board her again, or else there was no hope to recover her. And they after many excuses and fears were by him encouraged and so fell athwart her foreships all alone and so hindered her sailing that the rest had time to come up to his succour. Toward the evening after he had fought with her for three hours alone, the Earl of Cumberland's two ships came up and with very little loss entered with Sir Robert Cross, who had in that time broken their courages and made the assault easy for the rest.

The General having disarmed the Portugals and stowed them for better security on all sides, now saw the true proportion of the great carrack which did then and may still justly provoke the admiration of all men; yet the sight of so many bodies slain and dismembered drew each man's eye to lament and hands to help.

No man could step but upon a dead carcase or a bloody floor, especially about the helm; for the greatness of the steerage required the labour of twelve or fourteen men at once, and some of our ships beating her in at the stern with their ordnance, oftentimes with one shot slew four or five labouring on either side the helm. Whereupon our General moved with singular commiseration of their misery sent them his own surgeons, denying them no possible help that he or any of his company could afford.

Sir John intending not to add too much affliction to the afflicted, at length resolved freely to dismiss the captain and most part of his followers to their own country, and bestowed them in certain vessels furnished with all kinds of necessary provisions. This business thus despatched, he had good leisure to take a more convenient view of the goods, having first, to prevent the pillage to which he saw many inclined, seized upon the whole to the Queen's use.

The carrack is in burden estimated at 1600 tons, of which 900 tons are stowed with merchandise. Her length from the beak head to the stern (whereon is erected a lantern) is 165 feet; her breadth at the widest in the second close deck (whereof she hath three) is 46 feet 10 inches. She drew in water 31 feet at her departure from Cochin in India but not above 26 at her arrival in Dartmouth. She carries in height seven several stories, one main orlop, three close decks, one forecastle, and a spar deck of two floors apiece. The length of the keel is about 100 feet, of the main mast 121 feet, and the circuit about at the partners 10 feet 7 inches; the main yard is 106 feet long. There were between 600 and 700 persons on board.

THE PLAGUE IN LONDON.

The plague is greatly increased, and it is feared that the infection may grow with the prisons pestered with the great numbers committed for debt or on small charges. The Lord Mayor is required in common charity to cause speedy inquiry to be made, and, having summoned debtors and creditors, to persuade them to come to some composition; for if the imprisoned die, the creditors will lose their whole debt.

Two Rich Spanish Prizes brought in.

Mr. Thomas White in the *Amity* is returned to London with two Spanish prizes which he reporteth to have taken on the 26th July off the coast of Barbary.

At four in the morning, having sighted two ships about three or four leagues distant, that proved to be a Biscayan and a flyboat, they came within gunshot by seven, supposing by their boldness in having the King of Spain's arms displayed that they were ships of war.

The enemy having placed themselves in warlike order, one a cable's length from the other, the *Amity* began the fight, in which our men continued as fast as they were able to charge and discharge for the space of five hours, being never a cable's length distant from either.

In this time they received divers shot both in the hull of the ship, masts and sails to the number of 32 great, besides 500 musket shot, and harquebuses a crock at least. And because they perceived the enemy to be stout, our men thought good to board the Biscayan which was head on to the other, where lying aboard about an hour and playing their ordnance, in the end they stowed all the enemy's men. Then the other in the flyboat, thinking our men had entered into their fellow, bare room with the *Amity* meaning to have laid her aboard and so entrapped her between them both. But the *Amity*, quitting herself of her enemy, hoisted top sails and weathered them both. Then coming hard aboard the flyboat with her ordnance prepared, gave her whole broadside and slew several so that our men saw the blood running out at the scupper holes. After that they cast about, new charged all the ordnance, and, coming upon them again, willed them to yield or else they would sink them : whereupon the one would have yielded, which was shot between and water, but the other called him traitor. To whom our men made answer that if he would not also yield immediately, they would sink him first. Thereupon, understanding their determination, he put out a white flag and yielded, yet they refused to strike their own sails because they were sworn never to strike to any Englishman. The captains and masters were then commanded to come aboard, which they did ; and after examination and stowing some, certain of our men were sent aboard who struck their sails and manned their ships, finding in them 126 persons living and 8 dead, besides those whom they themselves had cast overboard. Our men were but 42 and a boy. These two ships are rich prizes, laden with 1400 chests of quicksilver with the arms of Castile and Leon fastened upon them, and a great quantity of bulls or indulgences, and gilded missals or service books, besides a hundred tuns of excellent wines, so that what with his silver which should have delivered from the quicksilver and his taxes on the bulls at 2 reals the piece, the King of Spain's loss amounts to £707,700.

14th September. SPANISH HOPES.

The priest, George Dingley, is again examined before the Lord Keeper, Lord Buckhurst and Mr. John Fortescue about the things he had heard in Spain. He declareth that many of our nobility were believed to be discontented at not being advanced and would easily be moved to follow the Spaniard, who would promise to put them in places of authority if he should possess England. The Earls of Oxford and Cumberland, and the Lords Strange and Percy are much talked of as alienated by discontent. Their chief hope is the Queen's death; wherefore the Spaniard lingers in his attempt at again assaulting England because time will call her away, when they have certain hope of a debate between the two houses of Hertford and Derby, who will seek the throne, each for himself; during which contention the Spaniard thinketh entry into England would be without danger.

They greatly rejoiced in the mutterings of the Martinists, translating the book into Spanish and presenting it to the King, judging from its hot words that some uproar would shortly be moved by that faction which would find favour amongst the noblemen in hopes of enjoying the bishops' and other spiritual revenues.

They think Lancashire and the north will soonest favour them, and Sir William Stanley would have the Spanish navy come to Milford Haven rather than to the narrow seas.

Though there are many beyond sea who wish this new assault attempted, yet Father Parsons is the only man England need fear; he by his travail and credit with the Spaniard, solicits the

King and his councillors by all means possible, and maintains Cardinal Allen and Stanley with accounts. There is not a man executed in England for religion who is not known there, and sermons openly preached in his praise, with bitter inveighing against the cruelty of our present governors.

16th September. THE GREAT CARRACK.

The sailors are making great pillagings of the spoil of the Great Carrack. Sir Robert Cecil and Mr. Thomas Middleton are sent down in haste to take charge of the matter, being instructed to inquire into the proceedings of Sir Ferdinand Gorges and the other Commissioners; to cause all lading to be viewed and entered in registers and especially to search out all precious things; and also to hire sufficient ships to bring the goods into the Thames. Sir Walter Ralegh, in the charge of Mr. Blunt, is also despatched from the Tower to join them on the Commission.

17th September. THAME FAIR PUT OFF.

Thame fair that is usually held on Michaelmas day is postponed for 15 days lest the Londoners resorting thither should spread the plague, to the danger of the Queen who proposes at that time to visit Lord Norris at Ricott on her progress.

19th September. THE SPREAD OF THE PLAGUE.

The plague is now reported at East Greenwich. Sir John Hawkins is to take special measures to prevent it from spreading to Deptford and Lewisham, lest the Queen's service should be hindered; also to cause the making of starch at a house in Deptford Strand to cease because of the number of dogs used therein which, being a noisome kind of cattle, especially at this contagious time, are very apt to draw on the infection.

20th September. GREENE'S 'GROAT'S-WORTH OF WIT.'

Chettle hath sent to the press *Greene's Groat's-worth of Wit, bought with a million of repentance*, collected out of certain papers that Greene left at his death. In the forepart of the book are displayed the adventures of one Roberto, a scholar, that despising the wealth heaped by his dying father, a miser and an usurer, was left but a groat. The money thus passing to his younger brother Lucanio, Roberto practised to fleece him with the help of Mistress Lamilia, a courtesan, and found small difficulty in bringing the two together. But no sooner hath Lamilia enticed Lucanio into her power than she betrayed Roberto to his brother, who cast him out of doors. Then Roberto, being in extremities, began to lament his woes in verse when a player, chancing to come, offered him employment, which, seeing no other remedy, he accepted; and thereafter falling into bad company, mingled with thieves and harlots, until by immeasurable drinking and the scourge of lust he now lay comfortlessly languishing. Here, noting that Roberto's story agreed in most parts with his own, Greene broke off his tale, adding certain rules for young gentlemen that are delighted with the like fantasies, warning them of God's judgment on those who follow their own lusts.

To his fellow scholars in the City that also made plays he wrote a very invective letter, especially warning two of them, the one termed a 'famous gracer of tragedians' to beware of atheism, the other, a 'young Juvenal that biting satirist,' that with him lately wrote a comedy, to avoid getting enemies by bitter words. To these is joined a third, that also dependeth on the making of plays, to shun the ingratitude of the players, for, saith he, 'there is an upstart crow, beautified with our feathers, that with his *Tiger's heart wrapped in a player's hide*, supposes he is as well able to bombast out a blank verse as the best of you; and being an absolute *Johannes factotum*, is in his own conceit the only Shake-scene in a country.'

These words are very offensively taken by those intended.

22nd September. THE GREAT CARRACK.

Sir Robert Cecil having now reached Exeter writeth that he has brought back everyone he met within seven miles of Exeter that had anything in a cloak, bag or mail, which did but smell of the prizes (for he could smell them almost, such had been the spoils of amber and musk). He stays anyone, who might carry news to Dartmouth or Plymouth, at the gates of the town; he compels them also to tell him where any trunks or mails are, and finding the people stubborn, has committed two innkeepers to prison; had this been done a week ago, it would have saved the Queen £20,000. In a Londoner's shop, he found a bag of seed pearls, pieces of damask, cypresses and calicos, a very great port of musk, and certain tassels of pearl.

He hath left an impression by his rough dealing with the Mayor and orders a search of every bag coming from the west. There never was such spoil; letters have been intercepted to friends in London to come down, all which he keeps to charge the parties at Dartmouth, and over two thousand buyers are assembling; them he will suppress.

In his search he hath found an armlet of gold, and a fork and spoon of crystal with rubies, which he reserves for the Queen. Sir Walter Ralegh came after him; but having outridden him will be at Dartmouth first.

THE QUEEN AT OXFORD.

The Queen, on her progress, leaving Woodstock is gone to Oxford.

She entered the bounds of the University at Godstow Bridge about three o'clock in the afternoon, where she was waited for by the Vice-Chancellor of the University, the Heads of Colleges in their scarlet gowns, and the proctors and beadles. As soon as the Queen learned that the Vice-Chancellor and the rest were ready to present their duties to her, she caused her coach to be stayed, notwithstanding the foulness of the weather, and signified her pleasure to hear a speech, provided it were not too long. Whereupon Mr. Saville, the Senior Proctor, being then on his knees with the rest of the company, entered into a short speech signifying the great joy of the University. This done, the Queen with the nobility and the rest of her royal train went towards the City, being met by the Mayor, with the Aldermen and Bailiffs, the Recorder and the townsmen, who received her in a short speech, offering in the name of the city a cup of silver gilt containing sixty angels. As she entered the City, she was received with great applause from the crowds of scholars that thronged the streets from the North Gate to Christchurch, signifying their joy by speeches and singing. Then as she passed by St. John's College she was presented with a private speech on behalf of the College and so to the Carfax, where the Reader in Greek offered a short speech in Greek, being thanked by her Majesty in the same tongue. Thence they moved to the great quadrangle of Christchurch where the Public Orator declared the abundant joy of the University. After a short time the Queen entered the Cathedral Church under a canopy borne by four doctors, where the *Te Deum* was sung and thanksgiving offered for her safe arrival.

CONSTABLE'S 'DIANA.'

Mr. Henry Constable hath sent to the press his *Diana*, eight decads of sonnets, dedicated in a sonnet by Mr. Richard Smyth to 'Her Sacred Majesty's honourable Maids.'

23rd September. THE QUEEN AT OXFORD.

Between two and three o'clock in the afternoon the Queen went to the Church of St. Mary, riding in a rich carriage and attended by the nobility on horseback with foot cloths. The Queen being placed under her cloth of estate upon a very fair stage, purposely erected for her in the east end of the church, a philosophy act was provided for her, which was begun on the word '*incipiatis*' being uttered by her. Whereupon the proctors called on the first replier, who after three conges to the Queen propounded the questions unto the answerer. Hereupon the answerer, Mr. Thomas Smith, Orator of the University, repeated the questions, which were :

i. '*An anima cuiusuis fit in se praestantior anima alterius?*' (Whether the soul of one man be more excellent than the soul of another.)

ii. '*An, ob mundi senectam, homines minus sunt heroici nunc quam olim?*' (Whether, on account of the age of the world, men be less heroic now than formerly.)

And so entered into his position, which continued for almost half an hour, which the Queen thought somewhat long, for when the Proctors said to the replier, in the accustomed words, '*procede magister*,' she supposing that they spoke to Mr. Smith said that he had been too long already.

Upon these words Mr. Gwynne first addressing himself to her Majesty to excuse his disability to speak in that honourable presence, spoke discreetly and wittily for about a quarter of an hour, and was then cut off by the Proctors. After the others had spoken the argument was ended by Mr. Saville, who determined the questions in a very good speech though somewhat long, ending with thanks to her Majesty for her great patience in hearing. This done the Queen returned to her lodging attended as she had come.

A PROCLAMATION ABOUT THE GREAT CARRACK.

A proclamation is published charging all who have taken or received goods of any value out of the Spanish carrack lately brought to Dartmouth, either while she was on the seas or since her coming into the haven, that within ten days they discover to the principal officer of the place where they reside what they have received or sold.

Likewise all innkeepers, householders, or owners of any vessels, where any person shall come with any carriage wherein they may suspect any portion of the commodities from the carrack to be bestowed, shall cause the same to be stayed.

Further, that if anyone who claims any portion of the goods by reason of his consort or adventure in the late service be proved to have taken or bought anything from the carrack without revealing it to the Commissioners, he shall lose all the benefit he might claim from the adventure.

24th September. THE QUEEN AT OXFORD.

Being Sunday the sermon was preached before the Queen by the Dean of Christchurch, Dr. James; and at night a comedy, called *Bellum Grammaticale*, was acted in the hall of the College which was most graciously and patiently heard by the Queen, though but meanly performed.

SIR ROBERT CECIL AT DARTMOUTH.

Sir Robert Cecil now writeth from Dartmouth of his dealings with the Great Carrack. As soon as he came on board the carrack with the rest of the Commissioners, Sir Walter Ralegh arrived with his keeper, Mr. Blunt. His poor servants to the number of 140, and all the mariners came to him with such shouts of joy that he was much troubled to quiet them. But his heart is broken, and he is extremely pensive unless he is busied, in which he can toil terribly. The meeting between him and Sir John Gilbert, his half-brother, was with tears on Sir John's part; but Ralegh finding that it is known that he hath a keeper, whenever he is saluted with congratulation for his liberty answers, 'No, I am still the Queen of England's poor captive.' Sir Robert wished him to conceal it, because it diminished his credit, which was greater among the mariners than he had thought; therefore he graces him as much as possible, finding Ralegh very greedy to anything to recover the conceit of his brutish offence.

They have found a thing worth looking on, rats, white and black, and a drink like smoke in taste.

25th September. THE COURT AT OXFORD.

At nine in the morning a divinity lecture was read by Mr. Holland, her Majesty's Reader in Divinity, at which many scholars were present but few of the nobility. The Lords of the Council dined with Mr. Saville at Martin College in the common hall, where, after dinner, they heard a disputation in philosophy which was determined by Mr. Saville, who because one of the questions had been '*An dissensiones ciuium sint respublicae utiles?*' (Whether the disagreements of citizens are useful for the state) took occasion to commend by name the Lord Treasurer, who was present, the Lord Chamberlain, the Lord Admiral and the Earl of Essex. This done the Lords went to sit in Council.

27th September. THE QUEEN AT OXFORD.

In the afternoon the Queen came again to St. Mary's and listened to questions in Law and Divinity, the last act being determined by the Bishop of Hereford, who argued against the question, '*An licet in Christiana respublica dissimulare in causa religionis?*' (Whether it be lawful in a Christian commonwealth to feign in the cause of religion). Upon which he made so copious and eloquent an oration that the Queen twice sent to him to cut short his words because she meant herself to make a speech that night. But he either would not, or else could not, put himself out of a set methodical speech for fear lest he should have marred it all and perhaps confounded his memory. The Queen was so tired that she forbore her speech that day.

28th September. THE QUEEN LEAVES OXFORD.

About ten in the forenoon the Queen sending for the Vice-Chancellor and the Heads of Houses made them a speech in Latin in which she thanked them for their entertainment; but in the middle of her oration casting her eye aside and seeing the Lord Treasurer standing for want of a stool, she called in all haste for a stool for him, and would not proceed in her speech till she saw he was provided with one. Then she fell to it again as if there had been no interruption, whereupon one, who might be so bold with her, afterwards told her that she did it of purpose to show that she could interrupt her speech and not be put out although the Bishop of Hereford durst not do so for a less matter the day before. Shortly afterward, about eleven in the forenoon, the Queen and her train left the University, and heard, lastly, a long tedious oration made by the Junior Proctor of the University, at the very edge of their boundaries near Shotover.

1st October. THE INCREASE OF THE PLAGUE.

The plague still grows in the City. The Lord Mayor and Aldermen are straightly warned that if the infection do not abate the Queen will remove the Term to some other place, to the great hindrance of the City. Moreover, by the Queen's special direction, the Council demand what means are being taken to keep the sick from the sound, and to relieve those whose houses were shut up; and why the Lord Mayor and Aldermen refuse to allow fires to be lit in the streets which has been found by good experience very effective in purging the air in places infected.

REINFORCEMENTS FOR BRITTANY.

A further reinforcement of 1000 men is to be enrolled for Sir John Norris in Brittany; of whom one-third to be armed with pikes and halberds, the remainder furnished with harquebusses and calivers, of which one-fourth were to be muskets. In choosing men especial care is to be taken that they be of able body and fit for service and not, as is too common, so light or so fearful that, after they have marched to the seaside or to their destination, they either run away from their captains, or offer them money to be discharged and suffered to return.

6th October. 'THE REPENTANCE OF ROBERT GREENE.'

The Repentance of Robert Greene is entered, being written by himself as he lay dying, in which he relates the story of his life and the misery of his end brought on himself by loose company, drunkenness, swearing, contempt of the Word, and other gross and grievous sins.

KYD'S 'SPANISH TRAGEDY.'

The Spanish Tragedy, written by Thomas Kyd some years before, that was lately played at the Rose Theatre, is to be printed.

11th October. CITY FEASTS TO BE FORBORNE.

Because of the infection the Lord Mayor sought directions for the keeping or omitting of the feasts and ceremonies usual at the taking of the oath. The Council now approve the omitting of the feasts at the Guildhall and in other Halls of Companies, and desire that the money so saved be given to relieve those whose houses are infected. For this end the preacher at Paul's Cross on the Sunday following shall notify to the people why the feasts are for this time to be forborne, and let them understand that it is not to spare charge but because of the inconvenience that might come from drawing together assemblies; and also that the money is being put to a use more acceptable to God and for the good of the City. Moreover those poor men who are thereby relieved will be more willing to keep within their houses.

12th October. PRECAUTIONS AGAINST THE PLAGUE.

That the Court may be the better preserved from the infection, it is proclaimed that no one, except those who have cause to come thither for their ordinary attendance on the Queen's person, repair to the Court or within two miles of it.

Nor shall anyone attending on the Queen repair to London or the suburbs or places within two miles of the city without special licence in writing, upon pain to be imprisoned by attachment of the Knight Marshal. He is to cause search to be made for all vagabonds, commonly called rogues, that haunt about the Court or within the verge.

18th October. PLAGUE DEATHS.

This last week 198 persons died of the plague in London.

19th October. Sir John Norris Delayed.

The weather at Southampton remains contrary so that the soldiers with Sir John Norris are unable to sail. Upwards of one hundred men have run away, and though Sir John has written to the justices thereabout to apprehend them, yet such is the slender care found in them and in the constables and other officers charged to follow the hue and cry that not a man has been returned. They are received into houses in the country, and helped to convey themselves and their furniture away. Sir John hath asked the Council that one hundred men may be pressed in Hampshire to fill up their places and to give the county better minds than to hinder the soldiers and assist them to escape.

Not finding sufficient shipping at Southampton, Sir John wrote to the Mayor of Poole, who showed himself very willing, charging the masters and owners of some suitable shipping in the road to put themselves in readiness; but they disobediently and contemptuously took down their masts and rigging, using very bad language and threatening revenge. For this the Mayor has committed them.

21st October. A Proclamation concerning the Plague.

A proclamation is published that, as the infection in London and Westminster is but little abated, the remainder of the term is adjourned to Hertford, and all with causes or suits in the Courts of Chancery, Starchamber, Exchequer, Wards and Liveries, the Duchy of Lancaster or Court of Requests to proceed thither.

Further if there should be any access at the Castle or Town of Hertford of those that have the plague in their houses or have been infected with it, there may ensue great evil and damage to the rest of the realm. It is commanded that no persons who have had the plague in their houses or have been infected themselves since the 1st of July shall repair to the town of Hertford unless summoned by special process for their personal appearance. Any one so summoned shall openly notify by some message his state to those appointed by the Lord Keeper of the Great Seal to keep the gates. If the party then be ordered to come into the town or castle, to bear in his hand, upright to be seen, one red rod of the length of a yard or more.

20th October. THE DEATH OF COUNT MONTAIGNE.

News is received in London of the death of Count Michael de Montaigne, which occurred on the 13th September from a quinsy.

THE GREAT CARRACK.

Certain persons from Antwerp and other towns of the Low Countries, subjects of the King of Spain, are lately arrived in London to buy part of the goods taken in the Carrack. As they have come without licence or safe conduct, the Lord Mayor is to make immediate search within the City that it may be known who they were; and, when any are found, their hosts to be made chargeable that they be forthcoming to obey such directions as shall be given them. Also they are to be searched for jewels, and if any be found in their possession these are to be taken away and kept in safe custody.

22nd October. EDWARD ALLEYN MARRIES.

Edward Alleyn, the tragedian, hath married Joan Woodward, step-daughter to Philip Henslowe that built the Rose Theatre.

23rd October. BEACON WATCHES TO BE DISCONTINUED.

Now that the nights grow very long and cold with the approach of winter, the watching of beacons is become very tedious and troublesome, and no longer necessary. The Council have ordered it to be discontinued until the spring.

27th October. THE NORMANDY FORCES TO BE SENT TO BRITTANY.

The companies in Normandy are ordered to be sent to Brittany in the conduct of Sir Roger Williams to serve under Sir John Norris in Brittany. On arrival Sir Roger shall be appointed a Marshal of the Field in place of Sir Henry Norris, and Colonel of one of the regiments of 400.

30th October. ABUSES AT HERTFORD.

Now that the Michaelmas Term is adjourned to Hertford excessive prices are being demanded by the inhabitants for chambers and lodgings. Her Majesty hath caused her Clerk of the Musket to repair thither and to set reasonable prices on all manner of victuals, as dear at least as in London, and likewise on the houses, lodging, stables, shops and other rooms; and for the convenience of those that repair thither, a harbinger of the Queen's to inform them of these prices. Moreover divers Londoners have already hired houses and lodgings, intending to offer victuals for sale, retail wares, and let out chambers for their own private gains. The magistrates shall suffer no one from the City of London, Westminster, the suburbs, or Southwark to hire any houses or chambers or other rooms that is not a professed Counsellor, Attorney or Solicitor of the law.

THE LORD MAYOR REBUFFED.

In answer to the suit of the Lord Mayor and Aldermen that the term might be held in London, the Council have written that they wish with all their hearts that the Lord Mayor had observed the orders prescribed for preventing the spread of infection, and then the Queen would have had no cause to remove the Term. Had their suit been made earlier it might have been considered, but her Majesty is now fully resolved on it and the preparations are too far forward for them to be recalled without great inconvenience.

4th November THE DEATH OF SIR JOHN PERROT.

Sir John Perrot died last night in the Tower, where he has remained under sentence of death since June.

THE CHARACTER OF SIR JOHN PERROT.

Sir John Perrot was exceedingly tall and big in stature, yet his body was very compact and well proportioned, and as he exceeded most men in stature so did he in strength of body. His countenance was full of majesty, his eye marvellously piercing and carrying a commanding aspect, insomuch that when he was angry he had a very terrible visage, but when he was pleased or willing to show kindness, he had then as amiable a countenance as any man. His mind was answerable to his body, for he was of an undaunted spirit, never regarding his adversaries were they never so many or so great. In time of danger he showed himself always resolute and valiant; he had a very sharp wit and was naturally wise. But he had also some defects; for he was by nature choleric and could not brook any crosses or dissemble the least injuries although offered by the greatest personages, and thereby he procured to himself many and mighty adversaries who in the end wrought his overthrow. In anger he would sometimes deal roughly, and so long as any man did oppose him he would contend with him by sword or by law: but if submission were offered by an inferior or reconciliation by his equal he would receive it readily. When moved by wrath he would swear excessively, partly from custom, partly from choler. He was also addicted to incontinence, leaving children by several ventures, as well as his lawful son, who succeeds him.

Many declare that his fall was brought about through the malice of Sir Christopher Hatton, the Lord Chancellor, whom Sir John had taunted because, as he said, he danced himself into favour. But the Chancellor hath a greater injury against Sir John, in that he seduced his daughter. On his return from his trial he cried with oaths and fury to Sir Owen Hopton, the Lieutenant of the Tower, 'What, will the Queen suffer her brother to be offered up as a sacrifice to the envy of my flattering adversaries?' These words being carried to the Queen, she refused to sign the order for his execution, and swore that he should not die, for he was an honest and faithful man. His mother was a lady of great honour in the Court of King Henry the Eighth who was married to Sir Thomas Perrot, a gentleman of the Privy Chamber, but Sir John in his person, qualities, gesture and voice so much resembled the late King that it is very generally believed that he was indeed a surreptitious child of the blood royal.

4th November. HARWARD'S 'SOLACE FOR THE SOLDIER AND THE SAILOR.'

The Solace for the Soldier and the Sailor, written by Simon Harward, that was a Chaplain in the Earl of Cumberland's fleet, is to be printed, being dedicated to the Archbishop of Canterbury. In the preface to the Christian Reader, Mr. Harward saith that he hath written this pamphlet for three causes; the first because he is thereunto requested by certain godly and valiant captains and shipmasters amongst whom he laboured on the Spanish seas; the second, to answer the obloquies and reproachful speeches of many that affirm that his voyages are a blot and discredit to the doctrine which he delivereth on land; and thirdly because of the many seditious malcontents who by their unthankful grudgings will not afford a good word to those that are willing to undergo so many dangers abroad to procure peace and quietness at home. In his book he justifieth from Scripture the lawfulness of the profession of arms, and especially of the war against the Spaniard.

13th November. MR. HERRICK'S GOODS.

Mr. Nicholas Herrick, a goldsmith, hath of late fallen from an upper window in his house in the City and is dead, whereupon some credibly think that he cast himself out wilfully, whereby his goods and chattels are forfeited to the Queen's Almoner, though by others the matter is endeavoured to be found casual. The coroners of the City of London are straightly charged that they receive no verdict until the evidence which the Almoner shall bring is thoroughly known and examined.

14th November. SIR JOHN NORRIS'S COMPLAINTS.

Sir John Norris writeth that fresh Spaniards to the number of 2500 have appeared in Brittany, but his own men run away infinitely, so that when all shall come together there will not be 3000, wherewith he will not spare himself, but he can make them no more worth than they are, for he never saw men more fearful. The King has sent for these troops to assist him to the recovery of the Castle of Pont de l'Arch, and Sir John awaiteth the Queen's instructions thereon.

17th November. CORONATION DAY.

Upon the Coronation Day, at night, there came into the Privy Chamber two armed knights (being the Earl of Essex and the Earl of Cumberland) and there made a challenge that upon the 26th February next they will run all comers to maintain that their mistress is the worthiest and fairest Amadis of Gaul.

20th November. A FAVOURITE LADY-IN-WAITING.

Her Majesty is so pleased with the behaviour of the Lady Bridget Manners, one of her Ladies-in-Waiting, and daughter of the Countess of Rutland, that she hath caused Sir Thomas Heneage, her Vice-Chamberlain, to write to the lady's mother to this effect:

'The exceeding good, modest and honourable behaviour of my Lady Bridget your daughter with her careful and diligent attendance of her Majesty is so contenting to her Highness and so commendable in this place where she lives (where vices will hardly receive vizards and virtues will most shine) as her Majesty acknowledgeth she hath cause to thank you for her, and you may take comfort of so virtuous a daughter, of whose being, love and attendance, her Majesty hath bidden me to tell your Ladyship that you shall have no cause to repent.'

'SOLIMAN AND PERSEDA.'

The Tragedy of Soliman and Perseda is entered for printing.

7th December. UNWILLING CAPTAINS TO BE PUNISHED.

Certain captains and soldiers of the forces ordered to pass from the Low Countries to Brittany excuse themselves for frivolous reasons. It is ordered that the Deputy-Treasurer in the place shall withhold the pay and imprest money of any who refused to embark, and also inform the Governor, requiring him to commit the offender to prison, not to be released until he hath certified the Council and received direction.

8th December. CHETTLE'S 'KINDHEART'S DREAM.'

Chettle hath entered his *Kindheart's Dream*, wherein he taketh occasion to clear himself of the charges made against him for having allowed the letter in Greene's *Groat's-worth of Wit* to be printed. 'With neither of them,' saith he, 'that take offence was I acquainted, and with one of them I care not if I never be. The other, whom at that time I did not so much spare as since I wish I had, for that as I have moderated the heat of living writers, and might have used my own discretion, especially in such a case (the author being dead); that I did not, I am as sorry as if the original fault had been my fault, because myself have seen his demeanour no less civil than he excellent in the quality he professes; besides, divers of worship have reported his uprightness of dealing, which argues his honesty and his facetious grace in writing that approves his art. For the first, whose learning I reverence, and at the perusing of Greene's book stroke out what then in conscience I thought he in some displeasure writ; him I would wish to use me no worse than I deserve. I had only in the copy this share: it was ill written, as sometimes Greene's hand was none of the best; licensed it must be, ere it could be printed, which could be never if it might not be read.

To be brief, I writ it over, and, as near as I could, followed the copy, only in that letter I put something out, but in the whole book not a word in; for I protest it was all Greene's; not mine nor Master Nashe's as some unjustly have affirmed.'

16th December. THE FUNERAL OF THE DUKE OF PARMA.

The Duke of Parma died of his wound on the 3rd of this month and on the 10th his body was brought with great pomp and solemnity from Arras to Brussels. The soldiers and fraternities, all the clergy, the Counts Von Mansfield, Arenburg, Barlaimont, and de Fuentes, with all the rest of the nobility, and the members of the Council came out to meet the corpse with lighted lanterns in their hands, and escorted it to the Castle Chapel.

18th December. 'ELIOT'S FRUITS FOR THE FRENCH.'

Mr. John Eliot hath written *Orthœpia Gallica or Eliot's Fruits for the French*, being penned for the practice, pleasure, and profit of all English gentlemen, who will endeavour by their own pain, study and diligence, to attain the natural accent, the true pronunciation, the swift and glib grace of this noble, famous and courtly language.

In the first part of the book are three dialogues, showing the words and sentences used by the scholar and traveller, followed by the two books of *The Parliament of Prattles*, giving the words and sentences needed by gentlemen on two and thirty kinds of occasion. In the former of these books the French words are shown in the first column; in the second the way of pronouncing them; and in the third the English.

30th December. PLAYING RESUMED.

Yesterday the Lord Strange's players began again to play at the Rose Theatre after their inhibition in the summer, and played *Muly Mullocco*; and to-day *The Spanish Tragedy*.

31st December. THE BILLS OF MORTALITY FOR THE YEAR.

This year first beginneth a custom of keeping weekly bills of mortality for the City of London and the parishes immediately adjoining. When anyone dies either the tolling and ringing of the bell or the bespeaking of a grave intimateth it to the searchers (who keep a strict correspondence with the sextons);

and thereupon the ancient matrons sworn to that office repair to the place where the corpse lies, and upon their own view and others' examination, make a judgment of what disease or casualty the corpse died, which judgment they report to the parish clerk. He on every Tuesday night bringeth to the clerk of the Hall an account of every christening and burial that week; whence on Wednesday the general account is made up, and printed. During this year 1592, there have died in London from March to December 25,886 persons, whereof of the plague 11,503.

SOMEWHAT TO READ FOR THEM THAT LIST

1592.

COLONNA'S 'HYPNEROTOMACHIA.'

Hypnerotomachia : the Strife of Love in a Dream. Written in Italian by Francisco Colonna, and translated into English by Richard Dallington, being dedicated to the thrice honourable and ever living virtues of Sir Philip Sidney, Knight, and to the right honourable and others whatsoever, who living loved him, and being dead gave him his due, and the epistle written to the Earl of Essex. The story telleth of the amorous visions of the monk Potiphilus, and the first Italian copy is much noted for the beauty of its cuts.

GREENE'S 'DISPUTATION.'

A Disputation between a He Conny-catcher and a She Conny-catcher, written by Robert Greene, in which Lawrence, a foist, and Nan, a traffic, dispute for a supper whether a thief or a whore is more prejudicial to a commonwealth, both alleging instances out of their experience until Lawrence confesseth that he is beaten.

Appended to the *Disputation* is the *Conversion of an English Courtesan*, relating how a certain young woman, the daughter of wealthy parents, became a strumpet. Being from childhood cockered by her parents, she flouted the warnings of her kinsmen, and refused the wealthy farmer whom her parents chose for her husband but fell in with the humour of the odd companion of a gentleman that dwelt hard by, a fellow of small reputation and no living, that had no excellent qualities save thrumming on the gittern, and the singing of quaint and ribald jigs. Having yielded herself to him, he carried her away to an Inn, when as his money ran short, he left her to see how her parents took their departure. The report of her beauty being spread abroad, many youthful gentlemen came to the Inn to seek her favour, with one of whom she went off to the Bath, where she lived as his wife ;

until growing tired of her new lover, she inveigled one of his friends to take her to London, and here after a time he left her, and she betook herself to a place of good hospitality as a common strumpet.

Hither came a sober young clothier with whom she fell violently in love, but he refused at first to have aught to do with her. Coming a second time he asked for a chamber, and she gladly took him apart into the fairest room where they fell to dalliance. But he complained that the room was too light; whereupon she took him to another room and drawing the curtain asked if that was too light. Still he asked for a darker room, so that she took him into a back loft, so dark that at noon it was impossible for a man to see his own hands.

'How now, sir,' quoth she, 'is not this dark enough?'

He, sitting on the bed, fetched a deep sigh and said, 'Indifferently, so, so; but there is a glimpse of light in at the tiles; somebody may see us.'

'In faith, no,' quoth she, 'none but God.'

'God,' said he, 'why, can God see us here?' and so entering into talk with her so wrought upon her that she was struck with remorse and fearful terror of her sins, and besought him that he would help her out of her misery. Hereupon, after further talk, they went down together and he provided her with another lodging, where she used herself so honestly that after a time he took her to his wife.

In writing these two discourses Greene declared that he was acting for the good of his countrymen at the peril of his own life, for the conny-catchers had protested his death, and one evening had beleaguered him being at supper in the Saint John's Head within Ludgate, and thought to have slain him, but that the citizens and apprentices took his part, so that two or three of them were carried to the Counter, although a gentleman in his company was sore hurt.

Greene also promiseth that he will print a bead-roll of all the foists and conny-catchers about the City.

'THE GROUNDWORK OF CONNY-CATCHING.'

The Groundwork of Conny-catching, purporting to be a new book, but in fact Thomas Harman's *Caveat for Common Cursetors* (first printed in 1567).

JOHNSON'S 'NINE WORTHIES OF LONDON.'

The Nine Worthies of London: explaining the honourable exercise of arms, the virtues of the valiant, and the memorable attempts of magnanimous minds; pleasant for gentlemen, not unseemly for magistrates, and most profitable for prentices: compiled by Richard Johnson, being dedicated to Sir William Webb, Knight, Lord Mayor of the City of London. Herein Fame and Clio, meeting together, cause the ancient worthies of the city to rise from the ground and declare their own fortunes in verse. First Sir William Wallworth, fishmonger, who slew Wat Tyler; Sir Henry Pritchard, vintner; Sir William Sevenoake, grocer; Sir William White, merchant tailor; Sir John Bonham, mercer; Sir Christopher Croker, vintner; Sir John Hawkwood, merchant tailor; Sir Hugh Caverley, silk weaver; and Sir Henry Maleveret, grocer, surnamed Henry of Cornhill, which last having fought in the Holy Land, to rescue the oppressed Jews, was by envious tongues defamed, and maketh complaint:

The good that I had done was clean forgot,
  Ingratitude prevailed against my life,
And nothing then but exile was my lot,
  Or else abide the stroke of fatal knife;
    For so the ruler of the Jews concluded,
    His Grace by false reports was much deluded.

There was no striving in a foreign soil,
  I took it patient, though 'twere causeless done,
And to avoid the stain of such a foil,
  That slanderous tongues had wickedly begun,
    Where, to the holy well of Jacob's name,
    I found a cave to shroud me from their blame.

And though my body were within their power,
  Yet was my mind untouched by their hate,
The valiant faint not, though that Fortune lower,
  Nor are they fearful at controlling fate,
    For in that water none can quench their thirst,
    Except he meant to combat with me first.

By that occasion for my pleasure sake,
  I gave both knights and princes heavy strokes:

The proudest did presume a draught to take,
  Was sure to have his passport sealed with knocks :
    Thus lived I till my innocence was known,
    And then return'd ; the King was pensive grown,

And for the wrong which he had offered me,
  He vowed me greater friendship than before,
My false accusers lost their liberty,
  And next their lives ; I could not challenge more :
    And thus with love, with honour and with fame,
    I did return to London whence I came.

1593

3rd January. RUMOURS.

There is great disagreement about the goods of the Great Carrack. The Earl of Cumberland would claim them, having taken her when she was like to have carried away the Queen's ship, and had beaten Sir John Burgh's; but for the Queen's part it is alleged that by her prerogative she may challenge the services of all her subjects' ships, that are bound to help her at sea, and recompense them according to her princely bounty, which she would do liberally enough to the Earl, but for some that would make a profit by buying it at her hands. All the others, that served the Queen, and Sir Walter Ralegh, receive only their pay, and are discontented at receiving so little out of so rich a prize, worth £150,000, though indeed much of the richest is purloined and embezzled.

The Lord Treasurer is much offended with the libels printed against him and lately brought over; it is thought that they will do no good to the Catholics, against whom a book is being written.

6th January. PLAYS OF THE WEEK.

The plays at the Rose Theatre this past week were *A Knack to Know a Knave* (twice), *The Jew of Malta, Sir John Maundeville, The Jealous Comedy* (for the first time), *Titus and Vespasian.*

8th January. THE WAR IN FRANCE.

Fresh levies are demanded of the Lord Mayor of London and the Lords Lieutenant of ten counties for Normandy to the number of 1200, of which 450 are from the City, to be ready to embark on the 12th February. It is commanded that special care be taken in the choice of the men and their appointments.

From Brittany it is reported that the English Captains are still prisoners, being held at extreme ransoms, especially the Sergeant-Major, for whom they demand 10,000 crowns. If they be not relieved, others will be discouraged from undergoing the like dangers.

12th January. NASHE'S 'STRANGE NEWS.'

Nashe hath replied to Dr. Gabriel Harvey in a book called *Strange News of the intercepting of certain letters and a convoy of verses as they were going privily to victual the Low Counties*, where, in the form of a commentary paragraph by paragraph upon the *Four Letters*, Dr. Gabriel Harvey is very abusively handled.

In Greene's defence Nashe noteth that he inherited more virtues than vices; a jolly long red peak like the spire of a steeple, he cherished continually without cutting, whereat a man might hang a jewel, it was so sharp and pendant. Why should art answer for infirmities of manners? 'He had his faults, and thou follies. Debt and deadly sin who is not subject to? With any notorious crime I never knew him tainted (and yet tainting is no infamous surgery for him that hath been in so many hot skirmishes). In a night and day would he have yarked up a pamphlet as well as in seven year, and glad was that printer that might be so blessed to pay him dear for the very dregs of his wit.'

To Dr. Harvey's praise of the English hexameter Nashe answereth that the hexameter verse is a gentleman of an ancient house (so is many an English beggar), yet this clime of ours he cannot thrive in: our speech is too craggy for him to set his plough in, he goes twitching and hopping in our language like a man running up quagmires, up the hill in one syllable and down the dale in another, retaining no part of that stately smooth gait which he vaunts himself with amongst the Greeks and Latins.

13th January. PLAYS OF THE WEEK.

The plays at the Rose Theatre this past week: *The Spanish Tragedy*, *Muly Mullocco*, *Friar Bacon*, *The Comedy of Cosmo*, *Sir John Maundeville*, *The Knack to Know a Knave*.

18th January. RUMOURS.

The Parliament that hath been summoned for 19th February is said to be only for money to maintain the troops in Brittany and elsewhere, the last payment of the last Parliament's subsidy being now due, and almost all spent already if the soldiers' debts were paid.

The mariners of the Earl of Cumberland are angry that the Great Carrack should have been awarded to the Queen, for were the prize the Earl's they would have their shares by the composition made with him before going out; whereas those who went with Sir John Burgh, on the Queen's adventure, Sir Walter Ralegh's, or the City of London's are to be paid wages. These mariners, being much discontented, have combined to seize upon the goods in London, and it is thought they will take occasion to be slack in some action hereafter, divers of them even threatening to go to the enemy. The whole prize is offered to the City of London, but they expect so great a pennyworth and the State affords them so little that nothing is likely to come of it.

Now that the Duke of Parma is dead, it is thought that the King of France will have the upper hand, and 3000 men under Sir Roger Williams are being sent to him.

The Lord Treasurer is now well recovered of his dangerous sickness, at which there is much satisfaction, for on him the whole state of the realm dependeth; and if he were to go there is no one about the Queen able to wield the State.

20th January. PLAYS OF THE WEEK.

The plays at the Rose Theatre this week past were *The Comedy of Cosmo*, *Titus and Vespasian*, *Harry the Sixth*, *Friar Bacon*, *The Jew of Malta*, *Tamer Cam*, *Muly Mullocco*.

21st January. THE PLAGUE AGAIN INCREASES.

The weekly returns of the plague which for some weeks past were diminishing now show an increase, so that the Lord Mayor and Aldermen of the City are sharply rebuked for their neglect, because either they do not observe good order for preventing the plague or else the orders themselves are insufficient. They are commanded by the Council at their utmost peril to cause immediate note to be taken of all houses infected or suspected to be infected and themselves to see them shut up either by locks hanging outwardly in the doors or by a special watch on every house. Thus the infected shall be prevented from resorting abroad to mix with the sound. Those so shut up shall be provided with sufficient food and other provision, to be paid for by those of ability; but the poorer sort, artificers or those who live by handiwork or by alms, to be relieved with the charity of the parish and of the City, especially to be collected for that purpose. The Lord Mayor and the Aldermen are further warned that if they continue to be careless, her Majesty, in addition to the punishment she meaneth to inflict on them, will remove the Parliament away from the City.

27th January. PLAYS OF THE WEEK.

The plays at the Rose Theatre this past week were *The Spanish Tragedy*, *Cosmo*, *The Knack to Know a Knave*, *Titus and Vespasian*, *The Massacre at Paris* (for the first time), *Sir John Maundeville.*

28th January. EVASION OF SERVICE IN PRIVILEGED PLACES.

Many of late resort to St. Martin's, Blackfriars, Whitefriars, and other places privileged and exempt from the authority of the Lord Mayor to avoid the imprest for service. The officers and principal inhabitants of these places are now required to assist the Lord Mayor and his deputies to imprest suitable men and to contribute towards their charges.

SIR HENRY KNIVETT'S SUBMISSION.

Sir Henry Knivett was this day called before the Council and after he had confessed his fault in showing contempt for the authority of the Lord Keeper was admonished to beware of such presumption hereafter and given leave to depart.

He had been committed to the Fleet by the Lord Keeper for having allowed his servants to commit an outrage upon a person coming to serve a process on a gentlewoman then residing in his house. Being released he wrote a letter to some of her Majesty's Privy Council in which he slandered the proceedings of the Lord Keeper, alleging them to have been unjust; which letter being read at the Council Board in his presence, the Lord Keeper, although not liable to render account for his sentences given in the Queen's Court to any but her Majesty, was nevertheless willing that their Lordships should hear the proofs of the accusation.

Accordingly Sir Henry was called to the Council Board and required to show proofs of his allegations; which being carefully heard, it appeared that he had unjustly, undutifully and indiscreetly slandered the Lord Keeper, and for this offence he was committed to the Fleet; whence after some days he wrote a letter of submission, acknowledging his offence, beseeching the pardon of their Lordships and their favourable mediation with the Lord Keeper.

PLAYS AND GAMES PROHIBITED BY REASON OF THE PLAGUE.

As the plague increaseth continually all manner of concourse and public meetings of the people (preaching and Divine service at churches excepted) at plays, bearbaiting, bowling and other assemblies for sport are inhibited.

2nd February. PLAYING CEASES.

At the Rose Theatre *The Jew of Malta* was played, and on the days before *Friar Bacon* and *Harry the Sixth.* Owing to the increase of plague the theatre is now shut up.

3rd February. 'GREENE'S NEWS FROM HEAVEN AND HELL.'

Greene's News both from Heaven and Hell, commended to the press by B. R., is to be printed, being dedicated to Gregory Coolle, chief burgomaster of the Castle of Clonars. In this collection of merry tales B. R. saith that he met the ghost of Robert Greene which popped into his hands his papers to be committed to the press. Herein, Greene, speaking in his own person, declareth that his ghost wandering breathless up a steep hill there found Velvet Breeches and Cloth Breeches fast together by the ears. Having parted them, all three made their way to Heaven Gate, where St. Peter demanded of Greene his name, but learning that he was Robert Greene, he rebuked him for describing the pilfering cosenages of petty varlets whilst looking with indifference on the corruption of great ones, refusing entrance to Heaven to a man that could look with one eye and wink with the other. Nor would he allow Velvet Breeches to enter, but seeing the simplicity of Cloth Breeches he was for letting him in. Whereupon, Cloth Breeches hastily demanded whether his wife had come to Heaven, and learning that she had, he replied that all Heaven would be too small for the two of them: so he turned away with the other two toward Purgatory. Nor would Lucifer allow Greene to remain in Hell, for as he entered there an infinite number of conny-catchers gathered together and exclaimed against him, so that Lucifer was fain thrust him out, charging him to remain a restless spirit, wandering through the world and never after to make any return again to that place.

7th February. LAWLESSNESS ON THE SCOTTISH BORDER.

The Bishop of Carlisle and others have sent to petition the Council by the gentlemen of the county chosen to sit in the Parliament complaining of the spoils and robberies made not only by the Scottish borderers but the English also, especially since Michaelmas. Divers gentlemen have been invaded in their dwelling-houses, their goods and chattels taken by violence and carried into Scotland, and themselves put to ransom. Most of the gentry dwelling within twenty miles of Carlisle go in fear of their lives and goods, so that not only they but justices of the peace even are forced to keep their cattle within their houses nightly, and dare not suffer them to pasture on their grounds. The justices and sheriffs are unable to give any relief, nor can the Warden help them.

8th February. AN INVASION EXPECTED.

Reliable information is received that the Spaniard will attempt an invasion of the realm by means of some dangerous conspiracy with some of the nobility of Scotland. As they will pass the seas between Ireland and England, it is thought likely that they will try to surprise the Isle of Man, and fortify it as a place very convenient for their victualling and watering. The Earl of Derby is therefore to send trustworthy persons straightway to put the island in a state of defence, but especially to take care of any trusted with the charge of any place because some be suspected. Good heed especially to be taken of one Mr. Dudley that hath of late been in Scotland to some evil purpose.

11th February. CONTRIBUTIONS EVADED.

Many persons of quality, having houses in the City, and especially most of the Doctors of the law, now refuse to contribute to the charges of the Lord Mayor in the present public services. The Council order that anyone refusing to contribute to the defence of the realm be informed of their wish ; and if he still refuse, bonds shall be taken of him to appear before them. Further, if he refuse to enter into a bond, it is necessary that her Majesty be acquainted with his unwillingness and to this end the Lord Mayor shall commit him to prison.

12th February. Rumours : the Great Carrack.

The goods taken in the Great Carrack are said to have amounted to £150,000, whereof the Earl of Cumberland receiveth £37,000 by way of reward, Sir Walter Ralegh for his adventure £24,000, the City of London £12,000, some others £7000 or £8000, and the rest to be the Queen's. £10,000 worth of goods are already sold at Dartmouth to pay the mariners' wages, besides other booty plundered at sea. The Queen's share is £80,000 with all the pepper.

14th February. Insufficient Men Impressed as Soldiers.

Sir George Carew, Lieutenant of the Ordnance, Sir Thomas Baskerville and Sir Thomas Morgan, that were appointed to view the levies from the counties and to report the sufficiency of the men and their furniture, find that of 50 men sent by the County of Bedford 14 were unable and insufficient, and most of them very evilly apparelled, their coats of very bad cloth and unlined. Of the 50 men levied in the County of Cambridge but 49 had arrived in London, one having run away, and of the rest ten were insufficient; most of them are ill and nakedly apparelled, wanting doublets, hose, stockings, shirts and shoes, their cassocks also of very bad cloth and unlined. Yet from Buckinghamshire, Essex and Middlesex come men able and sufficient, well furnished with armour and weapons.

18th February. Regulations for Butchers during Lent.

The Lord Mayor is advised to take strict charge that the orders concerning the eating of flesh in Lent be duly enforced and the disorders of last year avoided, wherein over 12,000 lbs. of the meat of calves, sheep and lambs were sold in the space of five weeks to the great prejudice of the State by the spoil of the breed of young cattle. Every butcher having licence to sell meat at this time shall pay £10 for the relief of poor maimed and impotent soldiers. The Lord Mayor is also to join the Wardens and chief of the Butchers with those of the Fishmongers that are willing to travail and take pains in the reformation of these abuses more exactly than last year.

19th February. Parliament Assembles.

Parliament having been summoned for this day, in the morning the knights and burgesses came to Westminster, where each one, after declaring his name to the Clerk of the Crown who entered it in his book, went into the House.

The House being set, the Earl of Derby, Lord High Steward for this Parliament, came in to take their oaths, being instructed by Sir Thomas Heneage as to what order he should use. First, all removed into the Court of Requests where the Lord High Steward, sitting at the door, called the knights and burgesses of every county according to the letters of their names in the alphabet. Each one, having answered as he was called, went next to the Parliament House door and there took the Oath of Supremacy given to him by one of the Privy Councillors; this done he entered again and took his place as a member of the House.

There was no further proceeding until two o'clock in the afternoon, about which time the Queen, having come privately by water, entered the House of Lords, accompanied by Sir John Puckering, Lord Keeper of the Great Seal, and many of her lords spiritual and temporal. The members of the Lower House, having received intelligence that the Lords had taken their places, went to attend in the Upper House before the Bar, and, when as many had been admitted as conveniently could be, the door was shut, and the Lord Keeper, by command of the Queen, began to speak to the effect that the assembling of Parliament hath anciently been, and still was, for the enacting of laws and reforming of grievances and abuses of the subjects of the Realm; yet at this time the Queen was chiefly desirous to have the advice of her loving people concerning the defence and preservation of herself, her realms and subjects from the power and oppression of a foreign enemy.

At this point the Lord Keeper's speech was interrupted by the murmuring outside. It appeared that the place of the Lower House in the chamber had been filled by those who came in privately before the Commons had been summoned, so that when the rest came up they found the door shut, contrary to custom, and were so discontented that the noise reached the Queen's ears. When she understood the cause of the discontent, she immediately commanded the doors to be set open, and the Lord Keeper continued his speech.

This enemy, he said, was the King of Spain, and his malice

was increased by his loss and shame received in '88. That his resolution still was to invade this kingdom did plainly appear by his building and getting together many ships of less bulk, which would be fitter for service in our seas, than those greater galliasses and galleons had been in '88. He desired some nearer place from whence to invade England, and therefore at that time he was labouring to plant himself in Brittany, a part of France. He had also raised factions in Scotland and conspiracies against the King there, finding him an enemy to his ambitious designs.

'And therefore,' quoth the Lord Keeper, 'we, her Majesty's subjects, must with all dutiful consideration think what is fit for us to do; and with all willingness yield part of our own for the defence of others, and assistance of her Majesty in such an unsupportable charge. Were the cause between friend and friend, how much would we do for the relief of one another? But the cause is now between our Sovereign and ourselves; seeing there is so much difference in the parties, how much more forward ought we to be?

'The aid formerly granted to her Majesty in these like cases is so ill-answered, and with such slackness performed, as that the third of that which was granted cometh not to her Majesty. A great show, a rich grant, and a long sum seems to be made; but little it is, hard to be gotten, and the sum not great which is paid. Her Majesty thinks this to be for that the wealthier sort of men turn this charge upon the weaker and upon those of worst ability; so that one dischargeth himself, and the other is not able to satisfy that he is charged withal. These things should be reformed by such as are commissioners in this service.

'Wherefore it is her Majesty's pleasure that the time be not spent in devising and enacting new laws, the number of which is so great already as it rather burdeneth than easeth the subject; but the principal cause of this Parliament is that her Majesty might consult with her subjects for the better withstanding those intended invasions, which are now greater than ever before were heard of. And where heretofore it hath been used that many have delighted themselves in long orations, full of verbosity and vain ostentations, more than in speaking things of substance; the time that is precious would not thus be spent. This session cannot be long; the spring time is fit that gentlemen should repair to their counties; the Justices of Assize also to go their circuits; so the good hours should not be lost in idle speeches, but the little time we have should be bestowed wholly on such business as is needful to be considered of; and Thursday next is appointed as the day to present the Speaker.'

As soon as the Lord Keeper's speech was ended, the Clerk of Parliament read the names of receivers of petitions, and, after the other business was ended, the Parliament was adjourned by the Lord Keeper in these words: '*Dominus Custos Magni Sigilli ex mandato Dominae Reginae continuat praesens Parliamentum usque in diem Jovis proximam futuram.*'

20th February. PRECAUTIONS AGAINST DESERTION.

The officers of ports on the south and east are ordered to search any ship from beyond seas in which deserters might be carried, and all suspected to have come from Normandy or Brittany without sufficient passport from Sir John Norris or Sir Roger Williams to be committed to prison.

21st February. THE FRENCH AMBASSADOR ALLOWED MEAT.

The French ambassador with his family is specially allowed by the Council to be served with meat by his own butcher during Lent, but bonds are put in that the butcher do not sell meat to others under colour of this order.

22nd February. THE SPEAKER PRESENTED.

The Queen herself came to Westminster about three o'clock this afternoon accompanied by the Lords spiritual and temporal; there being present the Archbishop of Canterbury, Sir John Puckering, Lord Keeper of the Great Seal, William, Lord Burleigh, Lord Treasurer of England, the Marquis of Winchester, twelve Earls, two Viscounts, fifteen bishops and twenty-three barons.

The Queen and the Lords having taken their places, the members of the House of Commons were summoned, and immediately came up with their Speaker, Edward Coke, Esquire, the Queen's Solicitor, into the Upper House. The Speaker being led up to the Bar at the lower end of the House between two of the most eminent personages of the Lower House, as soon as silence was made and the rest of the House of Commons had placed themselves below the bar, spake as follows:

'Your Majesty's most loving subjects, the knights and burgesses of the Lower House, have nominated me, your Grace's poor servant and subject, to be their Speaker. This their nomination hath hitherto proceeded that they present me to speak before your Majesty; yet this their nomination is only a nomination yet and no election until your Majesty giveth allowance and approbation; for, as in the Heavens a star is but *opacum corpus* until it hath received light from the sun, so stand I *corpus opacum*, a mute body, until your bright shining wisdom hath looked upon me and allowed me.

'How great a charge this is, to be the mouth of such a body, as your House of Commons represent, to utter that is spoken, *grandia regni*, my small experience, being a poor professor of the law, can tell. But how unable I am to undergo this office, my present speech doth tell that of a number of this House, I am most unfit: for amongst them are many grave, many learned, many deep wise men, and those of ripe judgments; but I am untimely fruit, not ripe, nay, but a bud not scarce fully blossomed, so as I fear your Majesty will say, *neglecta fruge, liguntur folia*; amongst so many fair fruits, you have plucked a shaking leaf.

'If I may be so bold to remember a speech used the last Parliament in your Majesty's own mouth, "many come hither *ad consulendum qui nesciunt quid sit consulendum*"; a just reprehension to many, as to myself also, an untimely fruit, my years and judgment ill befitting the gravity of this place. But howsoever I know myself the meanest and inferior unto all that ever were before me in this place, yet in faithfulness of service and dutifulness of love, I think not myself inferior to any that ever were before me: and amidst my many imperfections, yet this is my comfort; I never knew any in this place but if your Majesty gave him favour, God, Who also called them to this place, gave them also a blessing to discharge it.'

The Lord Keeper having received instructions from the Queen made answer:

'Mr. Solicitor, her Grace's most excellent Majesty hath willed me to signify unto you that she hath ever well conceived of you since she first heard of you, which will appear when her Highness selected you from others to serve herself: but of this your modest, wise and well composed speech, you give her Majesty further occasion to conceive of you above that she ever thought was in you: by endeavouring to deject and abase yourself and your desert, you have made known and discovered your worthiness and sufficiency to discharge the place you are called to. And whereas you account yourself *corpus opacum*, her Majesty by the influence of her virtue and wisdom doth enlighten you, and not only alloweth and approveth you, but much thanketh the Lower House and commendeth their discretions in making such a choice, and electing so fit a man.

'Wherefore, Mr. Speaker, proceed in your office and go forward to your commendation as you have begun.'

Then began the Speaker a new speech wherein, after expressing his loyalty to the Queen for the great and wonderful blessings which had been enjoyed under her rule, he related the great attempts of the Queen's enemies against us, especially the Pope and the King of Spain, from whom we were wonderfully delivered in '88. Then having touched on the supremacy which the Kings of England since Henry the Third's time had maintained, he went on to speak of the laws that are so many and great that they are fitly to be termed *elephantinae leges*; wherefore it might seem superfluous to make more laws, yet the malice of the devil, though it is always great, was never so great as now; and, *dolus* and *malum* being crept in so far amongst men, it was necessary that sharp ordinances should be provided to prevent them, and all care used for her Majesty's preservation.

'Now,' quoth he, 'am I to make unto your Majesty three petitions, in the names of your Commons. First, that liberty of speech and freedom from arrests, according to the ancient custom of Parliament, be granted to your subjects: that we may have access to your Royal Person to present those things which shall be considered of amongst us: and lastly, that your Majesty will give us your Royal Assent to the things that we agreed upon. And, for myself, I humbly beseech your Majesty, if any speech shall fall from me, or behaviour be found in me not decent and unfit, that it may not be imputed blame upon the House but laid upon me, and pardoned in me.'

To this speech the Lord Keeper, having received new instruction from the Queen, replied that he commended the Speaker greatly for his speech ; and he added some examples for the King's Supremacy in Henry the Second's time, and Kings before the Conquest. As for the deliverance we received from our enemies, and the peace we enjoyed, he said the Queen would have the praise of all those to be attributed to God only. To the commendations given to herself, she said well might they have a wiser Prince, but never should they have one that more regarded them, and in justice would carry an evener stroke without acceptation of persons ; and such a Princess she wished they might always have.

'To your three demands,' he concluded, 'the Queen answereth, liberty of speech is granted you, but how far, this is to be thought on. There be two things of most necessity, and those two do most harm ; which are, wit and speech : the one exercised in invention, the other in uttering things invented. Privilege of speech is granted, but you must know what privilege you have, not to speak everyone what he listeth, or what cometh in his brain to utter ; but your privilege is to say, "Yea or no."

'Wherefore, Mr. Speaker, her Majesty's pleasure is that if you perceive any idle heads which will not stick to hazard their own estates, which will meddle with reforming of the Church and transforming of the Commonwealth, and do exhibit any Bills to such purpose, that you receive them not until they be viewed and considered of by those whom it is fitter should consider of such things and can better judge of them.

'To your persons all privilege is granted with this *caveat*, that under colour of this privilege no man's ill doings or not performing of duties be covered and protected.

'The last, free access is also granted to her Majesty's person, so that it be upon urgent and weighty causes, and at times convenient, and when her Majesty may be at leisure from other important causes of the Realm.'

The Parliament was then adjourned to the Saturday following.

24th February. Mr. Wentworth's Petition.

Mr. Peter Wentworth and Sir Henry Bromley delivered a petition to the Lord Keeper, desiring the Lords of the Upper House to join with the Lower House as suppliants to the Queen that she would entail the succession to the Crown ; and for this purpose they have a bill already drawn. When the Queen heard of it, she was so highly displeased, for this is a matter directly opposite to her commands, that she charged the Council to call the parties before them. Sir Thomas Heneage therefore hath sent for them, and they are commanded to forbear coming to Parliament and not to go out of their lodgings.

24th February. THE SPEAKER SICK.

This day the House being set and Mr. Speaker not coming to the House, some said that they had heard that he was sick, whereon it was moved that the Clerk should in the meantime proceed to the saying of the Litany and prayers. Which done, the Sergeant of the House brought word that the Speaker had been this last night and also the present forenoon extremely pained with a wind in his stomach and looseness of the body so that he could not as yet without great peril adventure into the air. Whereupon all the members of the House being very sorry for Mr. Speaker arose and departed away.

SIR ROGER WILLIAMS' COUNSEL.

Sir Roger Williams writeth his opinion that the greatest danger to England may proceed by the Scots or the Irish, especially by Ireland, where it stands her Majesty upon to make sure of those people by cutting off the principal instruments and persuading the rest of the faction by fair means; if not, immediately with good squadrons of horsemen and footmen, for there is such meanings in them that if 8000 strangers, with the treasure they would carry with them, join them, there will be great mischief. The state of France is not too desperate so long as the King keeps the field, and the Spanish do not possess the rest of the parts of Brittany and Normandy; if this were to happen, then will there be wars in England.

25th February. MR. WENTWORTH BEFORE THE COUNCIL.

Mr. Wentworth, Sir Henry Bromley and two others have been called before some of the Council, being the Lord Treasurer, the Lord Buckhurst and Sir Thomas Heneage, who treated them favourably and with good speeches. But so highly was the Queen offended that they said they had no choice but to commit them. Whereupon Mr. Wentworth is sent to the Tower, Sir Henry Bromley and the others to the Fleet.

THE EARL OF ESSEX ADMITTED TO THE COUNCIL.

This day the Earl of Essex, Master of the Horse, having taken the Oath of Supremacy, and of a Privy Councillor, took his place at the Council Board.

DESERTERS IN GLOUCESTERSHIRE.

It is reported from Gloucestershire that of 150 soldiers that were impressed in that county and await a favourable wind at Southampton, 40 have escaped or been released by the indirect means of the officers that have the conducting of them.

26th February. A COMMITTEE OF THE HOUSE APPOINTED.

In the House it was proposed that a grave Committee should be elected to consult about the provision of treasure in this present time of danger.

Sir Robert Cecil spoke first, showing that when the King of Spain sent his navy against us, it was almost upon our banks ere we were aware of it; yea, and we were so slack in provision that it was too late to make resistance, had not God preserved us. Now he hath gone about to win France, wherein he hath greatly prevailed, and specially in Brittany, having most part of the port towns in his possession, whither he sendeth supply daily, and reinforces them every four or five months. This province he specially desireth, for it lieth most fit to annoy us, whither he may send his forces continually and there have his Navy in readiness; and besides may keep us from traffic to Rochelle and Bordeaux; as he hath done in the Straits from Tripoli and St. Jean de Luce. And so he hindereth us from carrying forth and bringing into this land any commodities from those parts, where the realm might be inriched and her Majesty's impost ever eased, being one of the great revenues of the Crown. In Scotland also the King of Spain's malice daily increaseth against us, and at home the number of papists, or at leastwise becomes more manifest.

After him Sir John Wolley exhorted the House to a speedy agreeing of a subsidy, and then Sir John Fortescue spake showing the great charges that her Majesty had been at, insomuch that the burden of four Kingdoms rested upon her, which she maintained with her purse, England, France, Ireland and Scotland. She had assisted the French King with men and money which hath cost her about £100,000; and as for the Low Countries, they stood her in yearly, since she undertook the defence of them, £150,000.

'All which,' quoth he, 'her Majesty bestowed for the good of the Realm, to free us from war at home. Besides when her Majesty came to the Crown, she found it £4,000,000 indebted; her Navy, when she came to view it, greatly decayed: yet all this hath discharged, and (thanks be to God) is nothing indebted, and now she is able to match any Prince in Europe, which the Spaniards found when they came to invade us. Yea, she hath with her ships encompassed the whole world whereby this land is famous throughout all places. She did find in her Navy all iron pieces, but she hath furnished it with artillery of brass, so that one of her ships is not a subject's but a petty King's. As for her own private expenses, they have been little in building; she hath consumed little or nothing in her pleasures. As for her apparel it is royal and princely, beseeming her calling, but not sumptuous or excessive. The charges of her house small, yea, never less in any King's time.'

After Sir Edward Stafford and Mr. Francis Bacon had spoken, the whole House agreed to the committee.

27th February. UNREASONABLE DEMANDS FROM PRISONERS.

The Queen hath been credibly given to understand that some that receive grants for the keeping of gaols and others to whom the charge of gaols is assigned have leased them out at exceeding great rents or other profits. Thus their assigns are constrained to exact excessive prices for victual, bedding, fire, fees of irons and other things from poor prisoners, who for want of means to satisfy these unreasonable demands, so perish through famine: for they remain in prison a long time after they are discharged of the principal cause of their commitment only for lack of ability to defray the great sums exacted of them for such intolerable impositions.

The Justices of the Assizes at every place of gaol delivery in the next circuit shall inform themselves thereof; and because they will not have leisure themselves they shall appoint certain of the discreetest Justices of the Peace, and such as be not interested with the granters of the goods, to examine strictly the prisoners in every place and bolt out what hath been laid on them for their meat, drink, bedding and so forth. These being recorded in writing, a reasonable rate and prices shall be set down to be paid by the prisoners from time to time.

A Bill against the Bishops.

Mr. Morris, Attorney of the Court of Wards, delivered a Bill to the Speaker which touched on the abuses of the Bishops in the matter of lawless inquisition, injurious subscription and binding absolution, asking that, if the House thought well of it, they might petition the Queen to have it allowed. Thereupon Mr. Dalton and Sir John Wolley spoke against the Bill, but Sir Francis Knollys was for reading it. Sir Robert Cecil, putting the House in mind that her Majesty had strictly forbidden them to meddle in such cases, the Speaker, perusing the Bill, answered that it was so weighty and long that he needed time to consider it, and to this end asked the leave of the House to keep it for a while. It was therefore put to the House whether the Bill should be committed to the Speaker only, or to the Privy Council and to him ; but as it was held to be against the Order of the House that a Bill should be committed before it was read, it was agreed that the Speaker should keep it.

About two o'clock in the afternoon the Speaker was summoned to the Court, where the Queen herself gave him commandment what to deliver to the House.

27th February. The Subsidies.

The committee of the House yesterday appointed have agreed that, should the House assent thereto, the treasure to be provided for her Majesty be two entire subsidies and four fifteenths and tenths. After consultation the House agreed that the Bill to this effect should be drawn, with a preamble signifying that so great and extraordinary supply is at this time given for resisting the power and preventing the malice of the King of Spain.

Roger Rippon's Corpse.

Roger Rippon, a Barrowist, having died in Newgate, his body was taken by his friends and enclosed in a coffin which they laid at the door of Justice Young, bearing this inscription :

'This is the corpse of Roger Rippon, a servant of Christ and her Majesty's faithful subject, who is the last of sixteen or seventeen which that great enemy of God, the Archbishop of Canterbury, with his High Commissioners, have murthered in Newgate within these five years, manifestly for the testimony of Jesus Christ. His soul is now with the Lord; and his blood crieth for speedy vengeance against that great enemy of the saints and against Mr. Richard Young, who in this, and many the like points, hath abused his power, for the upholding of the Romish Antichrist, Prelacy and priesthood.'

Many copies of this libel are spread about the City.

28th February. THE BILL AGAINST THE BISHOPS.

Mr. Morris hath been sent for to Court and committed into Sir John Fortescue's keeping.

In the Lower House the Speaker showed that he had kept the Bills delivered him the day before by himself and no one else had seen them. A little after he had perused them, he was sent for by special messenger from her Majesty, who commanded him to deliver a message to the House.

'I protest,' he declared, 'a greater comfort never befell me than that this my integrity and faithful promise to this House is not violated; for her Majesty, in her gracious wisdom, before my coming determined not to press me in this, neither indeed did she require the Bill of me; for this only she required of me: what were the things spoken of by the House? Which points I only delivered as they that heard me can tell.

'The message delivered me from her Majesty consisteth of three things: First, the end for which Parliament was called. Secondly, the speech which her Majesty used by my Lord Keeper. Thirdly, what her pleasure and commandment now is.

'For the first it is in me and my power (I speak now in her Majesty's person) to call Parliaments, and it is in my power to end and determine the same; it is in my power to assent or dissent to anything done in Parliament.

'The calling of this Parliament was only that the Majesty of God might be more religiously served, and those that neglect this service might be compelled by some sharper means to a due obedience and more true service of God than there hath been hitherto used.

'And, further, that the safety of her Majesty's person, and of this realm, might be by all means provided for against our great enemies, the Pope and the King of Spain.

'Her Majesty's most excellent pleasure being then delivered unto us by the Lord Keeper, it was not meant that we should meddle with matters of State, or in causes ecclesiastical, for so her Majesty termed them. She wondered that any should be of so high commandment to attempt (I use her own words) a thing contrary to that which she had so expressly forbidden; wherefore with this she was highly displeased. And because the words then spoken by my Lord Keeper are not now perhaps well remembered, or some be now here that were not there, her Majesty's present charge and express commandment is *That no Bills touching matters of State, or Reformation in Causes Ecclesiastical, be exhibited.* And upon my allegiance, I am commanded if any such Bill be exhibited not to read it.'

FLESH IN LENT.

The Lord Mayor is rebuked for his forwardness in giving leave to certain butchers to kill and utter flesh during this season of Lent.

The Council have asked that a butcher may be admitted to provide flesh for the use of Don Antonio, who hath never used to eat fish.

A PLOT TO KILL THE QUEEN.

Gilbert Laton, a recusant, that was taken, hath voluntarily confessed that he was sent over to England by Father Parsons, Sir Francis Englefield, and Don Juan de Idiaques to kill the Queen. It was to be performed while she was still on progress, with a wire made with jemos or with a poniard.

1st March. ROGER RIPPON'S CORPSE.

Christopher Bowman, goldsmith, being examined before Justice Richard Young concerning the corpse of Roger Rippon, declareth that his whole congregation consented to the making of the coffin, for which they paid 4s. 8d. He will not disclose who the congregation are, nor their secrets, nor the place of meeting. He will not be persuaded to go to his parish church, nor to Paul's Cross to hear a sermon, seeing that any man, however wicked he might be, is admitted to receive the communion; and he would not join with the minister who gave holy things to dogs. Moreover, he refuseth to sign his examination.

EXTREME TENETS OF THE PURITANS.

Amongst the more extreme opinions of the Puritans, shown either in their writings or examinations, it appeareth that in Church matters they would take away all gifts of bishoprics and deaneries from the Queen by dissolving them, and all patronages; for they hold that all ecclesiastical functions should be elective by the people or their elders. When supremacy was restored to the crown, one chief supereminency was that the final appeal in all ecclesiastical causes should be made to the King in chancery; this they would take away, making the appeal from an Eldership Consistory to a Conference, thence to a Provincial Synod, lastly to a National Synod which should be final.

They would have the Queen, being a child of the Church, subject to the censures of examination by their elderships as well as any other person, and that all, great or small, must willingly be ruled and governed, and must obey those whom God had set over them. If the Prince without God's warrant intermeddle with the Church, he must think it none injury to be disobeyed; for we are not bound to obey the Prince's law for conscience' sake, because only God's laws bind men's consciences. The Prince must take heed that he pass no weighty matter of the Commonwealth without the assembly of all the estates of the realm, whereby he is debarred from treating or capitulating, either for war, peace or league with any other prince without the Parliament being privy to it. In all matters of the Church the highest ecclesiastical authority belongeth to the eldership.

They would administer baptism to no known papist's children, to none excommunicate person's children and to none but to their children that be within the Church, that is, to those who submit themselves to their order of discipline, all others being accounted out of God's covenant and so no true Christians.

They would have the judicial law of Moses for punishing divers sins with death to be in force, so that no prince nor law could save the lives of those who offend wilfully as blasphemers of God's Name, conjurers, soothsayers, persons possessed with an evil spirit, heretics, perjurers, breakers of the Sabbath day, neglecters of the sacraments without just reason, any that disobeys or curses his parents, incestuous persons, daughters who commit fornication in their fathers' houses, adulterers, and all incontinent persons, save single fornicators, and any who conspire against any man's life. The *lex talionis*, that is an eye for an eye, ought to be observed in every commonwealth.

They would cut off the state ecclesiastical, being one of the three in Parliament, and have all laws made by the lords temporal and the commons only. It is unlawful, say they, for any State to tolerate the present Government Ecclesiastical, for it is false, unlawful, bastardly and unchristian, and can be defended by no good or sound subject; those that do so are traitors to God and His Word, enemies to the Queen and the land, and shall answer for the blood which the Spaniard or other enemies might spill, for they bring in hazard the Queen's life and the prosperity of the kingdom, being its greatest enemies.

The sect called the Barrowists holdeth all these positions and besides, that it is not lawful to use the Lord's Prayer publickly in church for a set form; for all set prayers are a mere babbling in the sight of the Lord. The Church of England in its public prayers and worship is false and superstitious, and, as now established, antichristian and popish.

If the Prince or Magistrate should refuse or defer to reform the faults in the Church, the people may take the reforming of them into their own hands before or without his authority. The Presbytery and Eldership may for some causes, after admonition, excommunicate the Queen if there ensue no reformation. They will not communicate with those in the Church of England, neither in prayer nor in sacraments, nor come to church because they hold that the Church of England as by law established possesses neither a true Christ nor a true religion nor has it indeed ministers nor sacraments.

3rd March. DR. UDALL'S PETITION.

Dr. John Udall, the Puritan preacher, hath petitioned the Lord Treasurer for release from prison, where he hath lain these three years. He hath consented with the Turkey merchants to go to Syria and remain there two years with their factors if his liberty may be obtained.

The Archbishop hath consented and the Lord Keeper promised his furtherance; the Earl of Essex hath the draft of a pardon ready when the Queen would sign it; but unless he have liberty out of hand the ships will be gone.

3rd March. THE SUBSIDY.

This morning in the House of Commons was received a message from the Lords to the effect that they did look to have heard something from the Commons before this concerning the provision of treasure; and desiring that according to former usage a committee of some grave and settled members of the House be appointed to have conference with a committee of the Lords. It was agreed accordingly that a committee should be appointed to meet with the Lords at two in the afternoon.

A STRANGER IN THE HOUSE.

In the House of Commons it was found that a certain man, being no member, had sat there during the greater part of the forenoon. He was brought to the Bar and examined by Mr. Speaker of his name and place of abode. He answered that his name was John Legg, a servant to the Earl of Northumberland; and pleading simplicity and ignorance for his excuse, alleged that he had some business from his master to Mr. Dr. Herbert, the Master of Requests; and therefore he entered the House, not thinking any harm nor knowing the danger thereof. After humbly praying pardon he is committed to the custody of the Sergeant of the House till the House shall upon further examination take other order.

4th March. PENRY TO BE ARRESTED.

A warrant directed to all public officers is issued by the Council for the arrest of John Penry, that is said to have written *Martin Marprelate.*

THE SUBSIDY.

In the House of Commons Sir Robert Cecil showed that at the conference had yesterday between the committees of the two Houses their Lordships signified that they would by no means assent to pass any Act for less than for three entire subsidies to be paid in the next three years. Sir Robert urged therefore that further conference should be held with their Lordships. Whereupon arose a question on the matter of privilege, Mr. Francis Bacon showing that the custom and privilege of the House was to make offer of a subsidy or else to assent to a Bill presented to the House, but not to pair with them in this motion.

After much debate it was agreed that the committee should have further conference with their Lordships.

5th March. 'THE GARLAND OF GOODWILL.'

A collection of ballads and songs is to be printed, entitled *The Garland of Goodwill*, amongst them *A Mournful Ditty on the Death of Rosamond; The Lamentation of Shore's wife; How Coventry was made free by Godiva, Countess of Chester; Locrine; A Song of Queen Isabel, wife to King Edward the Second; A Song of the Banishment of the two Dukes, Hereford and Norfolk; Patient Grissel.* Also *A Dialogue between plain Truth and blind Ignorance*, wherein Ignorance lamenteth the passing of the old religion:

TRUTH

God speed you, aged Father,
  And give you a good day:
What is the cause, I pray you,
  So sadly here to stay?
And that you keep such gazing
  On this decayed place,
The which for superstition
  Good Princes down did rase?

IGNORANCE

Chile tell thee by my vazon
  That sometime che have known
A vair and goodly Abbey
  Stand here of brick and stone:
And many holy Friars,
  As ich may say to thee,
Within these goodly cloisters
  Che did full often zee.

TRUTH

Then I must tell thee, Father,
  In truth and verity:
A sort of greater hypocrites
  Thou couldst not likely see;
Deceiving of the simple
  With false and feigned lies:
But such an order truly
  Christ never did devise.

IGNORANCE

Ah, ah, che smell thee now, man,
  Che know well what thou art;
A fellow of new learning,
  Che wis not worth a vart:
Vor when we had the old Law
  A merry world was then:
And every thing was plenty,
  Among all zorts of men.

TRUTH

Thou givest me an answer,
  As did the Jews sometime
Unto the prophet Jeremy,
  When he accused their crime.
' 'Twas merry,' said the people,
  'And joyful in our realm,
Which did offer spice cakes
  Unto the Queen of Heaven.'

IGNORANCE

Chile tell thee what, good vellow;
  Bevore the vriers went hence,
A bushel of the best wheat
  Was sold for vorteen pence:
And vorty eggs a penny,
  That were both good and new:
And this che zay my self have seen
  And yet ich am no Jew.

But in the end Truth prevaileth over old Ignorance.

6th March. Legg Released.

John Legg, that has remained prisoner at the bar of the House these three days, after good exhortation given him by the Speaker, and the Oath of Supremacy pronounced by him, is upon his humble submission and craving of pardon, set at liberty by the order of the House, on paying his fees.

6th March. The Subsidy.

After further debate yesterday, it was today agreed that the committee of the House of Commons should confer with the committee of the Lords, but not in anywise to conclude or resolve of anything in particular without the privity and consent of the House.

7th March. Musters to be held in the North.

The Earl of Huntingdon, Lieutenant in the North Part and President of the Council of the North, is to muster and view the strength of the counties towards Scotland as well for men and horses as for castles and houses of strength, and to cause all wants to be supplied.

7th March. The Subsidy.

In the House of Commons to-day there was further debate concerning the subsidy and of the poverty of the country.

Sir Henry Knivett affirmed that the principal reason of our poverty was because we bring in more foreign wares than we vent commodities, and so by this means our money is carried out of the country. He made two motions; first, that the Queen should be helped by a survey taken of all men's lands and goods in England, and so much to be levied yearly as to serve the Queen to maintain wars, the proportion being set £100,000 yearly; secondly, if this were misliked, every man upon his word and power to deliver what were the profits of his lands and worth of his goods, and so a proportion to be had accordingly.

Sir Walter Ralegh, answering those who argued the poverty of the realm by the multitude of beggars, said that those who came back maimed from the wars in Normandy and the Low Countries never went back to the towns whence they came. For a multitude of clothiers now have their own looms and spin wool for themselves, and unless these men could spin for them cheaper than they could for themselves, they will never give them work to do. This engrossing of so many trades into their hands beggareth many that usually live by trade. He thought it inconvenient to have men's lands surveyed because many are now esteemed richer than they are, and if their land and goods were surveyed they would be found beggars; and so their credit, which is now their wealth, would be bound nothing. But he agreed to three subsidies, for the longer we defer aid, the less shall we be able to yield aid, and in the end the greater aid will be required of us.

Sir Francis Drake described the King of Spain's strength and cruelty where he came, and wished a frank aid to be yielded to withstand him; and he agreed to three subsidies.

In the afternoon the House considered of the subsidies in committee and after long debate it was agreed for three subsidies payable in four years.

9th March. BARROWISTS ARRESTED.

Many of the sect called Barrowists have been taken at one of their meetings at Islington. One, Daniel Buck, a scrivener, was to-day examined before Justice Young. Concerning the bishops he thinketh that they have no spiritual authority over the rest of the Church. Being demanded who was their pastor, he said one Mr. Francis Johnson; and about six months since this Johnson delivered the sacrament of baptism to seven persons; but they had neither godfathers nor godmothers. He took water and washed the faces of them that were baptised, saying only in the administration of the sacrament, 'I do baptise thee in the name of the Father, of the Son, and of the Holy Ghost,' without using any other ceremony therein, as is usually observed according to the Book of Common Prayer.

Being further demanded the manner of the Lord's Supper administered among them, he saith that five white loaves or more were set upon the table. The pastor did then break the bread, and delivered it to some of them, and the deacons delivered to the rest; some of the congregation sitting and some standing about the table. And the pastor delivered the cup unto one, and he to another, till all had drunken, using the words at the delivery thereof as it is set down in the eleventh of the Corinthians, the 24th verse.

10th March. The Subsidy Agreed.

After further deliberations of the committee of the House of Commons, the articles which they have drawn up were read before the House. It was resolved that a triple subsidy and six fifteenths and tenths to be paid in four years should be yielded to her Majesty towards the provision against the great and imminent perils of this Realm.

11th March. The Butchers Defiant.

Many butchers, apart from those six specially licensed, do kill and make open sale of flesh. The Warden of the Fishmongers is ordered to call them before him and to examine them by what authority they do the same, certifying their names and dwelling-places, and from whence they received their licence. He shall also examine the six licensed upon their oath what money they have paid to the Lord Mayor for their licences.

12th March. A Bill against Recusants.

A Bill against recusants was read in the Lower House for the first time. When this Bill had been presented to the committee of the House, divers hard penalties in goods and lands were set down ; but many of these were altered before the Bill came before the House. Among the penalties proposed are these :

> A recusant shall be disenabled to be Justice of Peace, Mayor, Sheriff, etc.
>
> He shall forfeit for keeping a recusant in his house, either servant or stranger, £10 every month.
>
> His children being ten years old shall be taken from him till they be sixteen to be disposed of at the appointment of four Councillors, the Justices of Assize, the Bishop of the diocese or the Justices of the Peace.
>
> He shall be disenabled to make any bargain or sale of his goods or chattels.

Mr. Darcy's Unseemly Conduct.

There have of late been complaints made of Mr. Edward Darcy's patent for sealing of leather. Yesterday he went to the house of the Lord Mayor to confer with him and with Sir George Barnes and Dr. Fletcher, who usually attend the Lord Mayor in such cases. They having said that in some things Mr. Darcy's fees were hard and excessive, he in a very unseemly and unreverent manner '*thou'd*' Sir George Barnes (who had used him with very moderate and friendly terms), preferring himself above the knight in birth and degree, which in good discretion and modesty he might have forborn. Not content withal he suddenly strake Sir George with his fist on the face in most violent manner, wherewith the blood gushing out and embruing his face, his eye also was in great danger by the force of the stroke.

Moreover Mr. Darcy would hardly have escaped without great hurt and peril of his life, especially if his abuse and outrage had been known to the apprentices and those dwelling thereabout; but the Lord Mayor thought good to dismiss him with all present speed and to be conducted part of his way before the fact was rumoured abroad.

To-day the Lord Mayor maketh complaint to the Council of this injury towards an ancient Alderman of the City of London, begging them to take notice of it, and showing what great mischiefs and tumults might have arisen, especially seeing the original cause of Mr. Darcy's negotiation was a thing not very grateful to the common sort of the City, nor, as he supposeth, to any other of her Majesty's subjects.

13th March. A SPANISH NOBLEMAN SENT HOME.

Don Pedro Valdes, a Spanish nobleman, that was taken prisoner at sea by Mr. Richard Drake during the fighting in 1588, is given leave to depart. A few days ago he was taken to Court by orders of the Queen and treated very handsomely, being visited by the Council, the nobles and the captains of ships. All request, saith he, that when he shall reach the Spanish King's Court he will use his best offices in favour of peace. He was then taken to the City and entertained to a banquet by the Lord Mayor and the Aldermen. Next day he visited the Lord Treasurer, who also pressed him to use his influence for peace. The Lord Treasurer is now very ill, and the doctors give up hope of saving him.

16th March. MEASURES AGAINST THE BUTCHERS.

When the Wardens of the Fishmongers' Company called on the butchers to appear before them, they withdrew themselves and would not be found when they were sent for, to the contempt of the Council's orders. The butchers' shops are to be shut up.

19th March. BUNNY'S 'TRUTH AND FALSEHOOD.'

There is entered a book by Mr. Francis Bunny, Fellow of Magdalen College in Oxford, called *Truth and Falsehood, or A Comparison between the truth now taught in England, and the Doctrine of the Romish Church,* to which is added *A Short Answer* to reasons which commonly the popish recusants in the north parts allege why they will not come to our churches. At the head of each chapter is set the doctrine of the protestants and beside it the answer of the papists, upon which is argued the position, thus running through the chief points of variance between the reformed and the Catholic doctrine. The magistrates are exhorted not to show lenity to recusants, seeing that God commands idolaters to be stoned, nor to atheists, though nothing so dangerous as papists.

21st March. KELLWAY'S 'DEFENSATIVE AGAINST THE PLAGUE.'

Mr. Simon Kellway hath written *A Defensative against the Plague,* containing two parts, the first how to preserve from the plague, the second how to cure those that are infected, with a short treatise of the smallpox, is entered, being dedicated to the Earl of Essex.

The causes of the plague are great and unnatural heat and dry or great rain and inundations of waters; great store of rotten and stinking bodies lying unburied which corrupt the air so that corn, fruit, herbs and waters are infected; dunghills, filthy and standing pools of water; by thrusting a great number of people into a close room, as in ships, common gaols, and in narrow lanes and streets where many dwell together. But for the most part it cometh from clothes and such like that have been used about some infected body. It may also come by dogs, cats, pigs and weasels.

Certain signs foreshow the plague, as when the spring time is cold, cloudy and dry, the harvest stormy and tempestuous with mornings and evenings very cold, and at noon extreme heat; fiery impressions in the firmament, especially in the end of summer, such as comets; great store of little frogs in the beginning of harvest, or of toads creeping on the earth having long tails, or when there is abundance of gnats, caterpillars, spiders and moths, showing the air to be corrupt. Also when young children flock together in companies, and feigning one of their members to be dead, solemnise the burying in mournful sort.

Our magistrates are advised to observe certain rules :

To command that no stinking dunghills be allowed near the City.

Every evening and morning in hot weather to cause cold water to be cast in the streets, especially where there is infection, and every day to cause the streets to be kept clean and sweet, and cleansed from all filthy things.

Where the infection is entered to cause fires to be made in the streets every morning and evening, wherein should be burnt frankincense, pitch or some other sweet thing.

Not to suffer any dogs, cats or pigs to run about the streets.

To command that all excrements and filthy things voided from the infected places be not cast into streets or into sewers that are daily used to make drink or dress meat.

No surgeons or barbers that use to let blood should cast it into the streets or rivers. Nor should vaults or privies be emptied therein, for it is a most dangerous thing.

All innholders should make clean their stables every day and cause the filth and dung therein to be carried out of the City, for by suffering it in their houses as some use to do a whole week or a fortnight, it putrefies so that when it is removed there is such a stink as is able to infect the whole street.

To command that no hemp or flax be kept in water near the City or town, for that will cause a very dangerous and infectious savour.

To have special care that good and wholesome victuals and corn be sold in the markets, and to provide that no want thereof shall be in the City, for there is nothing that more increases the plague than want and scarcity of necessary food.

In the remainder of the book are given receipts for perfumes, pomanders, preservatives, purges, cataplasms, powders, unguents and so forth for the various occasions of the plague, with directions for its prevention and cure.

22nd March. BARROW, GREENWOOD AND OTHER PURITANS CONDEMNED.

Yesterday at the Session Hall without Newgate, Henry Barrow, John Greenwood and three others were indicted of felony before the Lord Mayor, the two Lord Chief Justices of both benches and others of the commission. To-day they are arraigned and condemned, Barrow and Greenwood for writing sundry seditious books, the others for publishing and setting them forth.

23rd March. A DISHONEST CAPTAIN.

Sir John Norris is to call before him one Captain Joshua Hilliard, and to command him to appear before the Council. This Hilliard, when the 150 men levied in Gloucestershire were sent to Southampton under their proper officers, taking upon himself to be their captain received £10 for the discharge of certain of the company.

24th March. GYER'S 'ENGLISH PHLEBOTOMY.'

The English Phlebotomy or method and way of healing by letting of blood, written by Nicholas Gyer, minister of the Word, is published, being dedicated to Mr. Reginald Scott that wrote the *Discovery of Witchcraft.* This book is directed against those that for want of skill in blood-letting either straightway kill or leastwise accelerate the immature deaths of divers faithful Christians. Giveth the reasons for phlebotomy; the method of practice; the proper astrological observation, showing what members and parts of the body are to be opened according to the several seasons of the year; the observation of the blood with the signs of the excess or deficiency shown therein.

25th March. ABUSES OVER IMPRESSMENTS IN GLOUCESTERSHIRE.

The Queen is greatly offended that certain soldiers, levied in Gloucestershire for service in France, were licensed to depart after their arrival at Southampton and on their way thither for certain sums of money. The Sheriffs shall cause the constables to bring before them those that dwell not far off, and examine them on their oaths by whom and where they were discharged, and what they gave to their conductors or to any other to purchase licence; and the Justices should do the same. The examinations to be sent up to the Council.

27th March. A RECUSANT EXECUTED AT WINCHESTER.

Two days since James Bird, a young layman, was executed at Winchester for recusancy, having been condemned some time before, after enduring ten years in prison. When he was arraigned at the General Assizes, the Lord Chief Justice Anderson addressing the jury said, 'Here you have James Bird, a recusant. You know what a recusant means. A recusant is one that refuseth to go to church; this no one refuseth unless he hath been reconciled to the Church of Rome. The man that hath been reconciled to the Church of Rome is a rebel and a traitor. Now you know your evident duty.' After a short retirement, they pronounced Bird to be a traitor.

The execution having been long delayed, at length the men arrived to lead Bird to the gallows, and he went down to meet them with joy and gaiety, when a messenger came to say that the execution was again put off; at which he showed evident signs of grief.

When at length the day arrived, as he was on the ladder, he said to the Sheriff, 'I beg you, Mr. Sheriff, seeing that I am a native of this city, that you would grant me one favour before I die.'

'What favour?' said he.

'Tell me what I die for,' answered Bird.

'I know not,' quoth the Sheriff; 'you received the sentence of death in the presence of the Judge; who can know better than you the reason for which you were condemned?'

'Nay,' said he, 'I do not understand it at all.'

Then said the Sheriff, 'Come now, confess your crime, promise to go to church, and the Queen's pardon will be begged for you.'

'Right heartily do I thank thee,' then answered Bird; 'if by going to church I can save my life, surely all the world will see this, that I am executed solely for faith and religion, and nothing else. It was just this that I wished to elicit from you. Now I gladly die.' And with these words he was thrown from the ladder.

31st March. BARROW AND GREENWOOD RESPITED.

Barrow and Greenwood, that were condemned on the 22nd March, were brought in a cart to Tyburn, but respited as they were about to be trussed up.

1st April. A Counterfeit Captain.

From Rutland it is reported that one calling himself Captain Bayton hath been in that county, and by colour of a counterfeit commission to levy men and horse for the Queen's service taken sums of money from sundry of the inhabitants.

2nd April. Maimed Soldiers to be Examined.

A Commission is appointed to meet in two days' time to view and examine a number of captains and soldiers that claim to have been maimed or sore hurt within the last four years' war in France, the Low Countries or on the seas. The names of the men are to be enrolled, showing their names and surnames, the counties where they were born, and where they were levied, with the times and places, and under what captain or leader they were hurt.

4th April. A Bill against the Brownists.

The question of the Brownists again arose in Parliament on the Bill for the explanation of a branch of a Statute made in the 23rd year of the Queen's reign, entitled '*An Act to retain Her Majesty's subjects in their due obedience*.' After divers members had spoken, Sir Walter Ralegh said that in his conceit the Brownists are worthy to be rooted out of a Commonwealth; but what danger may grow to ourselves, if this law passed, it were fit to be considered. 'For it is to be feared,' said he, 'that men not guilty will be included in it; and that law is hard that taketh life, or sendeth into banishment, where men's intentions shall be judged by a jury, and they shall be judges what another man meant. But that law that is against a fact is just, and punish the fact as severely as you will.

'If two or three thousand Brownists meet at the seaside at whose charge shall they be transported? or whither will you send them? I am sorry for it; I am afraid there is nearly twenty thousand of them in England; and when they are gone, who shall maintain their wives and children?'

5th April. Charitable Contributions for Maimed Soldiers.

It is agreed in the House of Lords that there shall be a charitable contribution made towards the relief and help of soldiers maimed and hurt in the wars of France, the Low Countries and on the seas. To this end every Archbishop,

Marquis, Earl and Viscount shall pay 40s., every Bishop 30s., and every Baron 20s. The Queen's Almoner, the Bishop of Worcester, is appointed to collect the money of the Bishops, and the Lord Norris of the Lords Temporal. These sums are willingly being paid by all who attend the Parliament. Further, it is agreed that those who have saved their charges by not attending the Parliament shall pay double, that is, the Archbishop of York and every Earl £4, Bishops £3, and Barons 40s.; and those who have been present but seldom shall pay a third part more than those who have attended regularly. And if any Lord Spiritual or Temporal should refuse or forbear to pay (which it is hoped in honour none will) the ordinary means to be used to levy the money.

PRECAUTIONS AGAINST PLAGUE.

The Lord Mayor is bidden take extraordinary care to prevent the increase of the infection in the City, and to keep the streets clean and sweet, especially because the Queen proposes to stay longer at St. James's, being near the City. All infected houses are to be shut up and watched, the other orders which have been devised to be obeyed.

The Justices of Middlesex shall do the like, giving strict charge that such as have grounds where there are laystalls have them removed at once; and that they allow no dung or filth to be laid in any of the highways, being a great annoyance both to breed infection and to her Majesty riding sometimes in the fields to take the air.

6th April. BARROW AND GREENWOOD HANGED.

Barrow and Greenwood, that were respited last week, were hanged early this morning. It is said that the execution proceeded through the malice of the Bishops towards the Lower House because the dislike shown yesterday to the Bishops' Bill against the Puritans. The reprieve was through a supplication to the Lord Treasurer that in a land where no papist was ever put to death for religion theirs should not be the first blood shed who concurred about faith with what was professed in the country and desired conference to be convinced of their errors. The Lord Treasurer spoke sharply to the Archbishop of Canterbury, who was very peremptory, also to the Bishop of Worcester, and wished to speak to the Queen, but none seconded him.

7th April. SPECIAL WATCH TO BE KEPT FOR TRAITORS.

Now that the King of Spain dischargeth many English, Irish and Scotch fugitives and rebels of the pensions given by him, many of them are likely to come into the realm in secret and covert manner. The officers of the Cinque Ports are ordered to make diligent search and enquiry upon the arrival of any shipping, causing all suspicious persons to be stayed and examined.

8th April. THE DISORDERLY BUTCHERS.

The Justices of the Peace of Middlesex are to call before them the butchers who have killed and uttered flesh contrary to the proclamation and to the wrong of those poor men that paid good sums of money for licences for the use of maimed soldiers. They shall be indicted by a jury and for their contempt fined in good round sums of money to be converted to the use of maimed soldiers.

The Lord Mayor is forthwith to send the sum of £90, being the balance of £120 collected for maimed soldiers from the butchers' licences to the Council, that it may be distributed; otherwise the Council will send a number of the maimed soldiers with tickets to receive money from him, and to be relieved until they be satisfied of the sum. Further, seeing that the Lords of the Upper House, and the Bishops and Clergy of the Convocation House have made a charitable contribution for this purpose, the Lord Mayor and the rest of the Aldermen are required to show the same forwardness amongst themselves and the City Companies. Hereby the poor men may have some reasonable relief, and the City be eased of the clamour and trouble of these lame, maimed and poor creatures, going up and down the streets begging.

9th April. 'CHURCHYARD'S CHALLENGE.'

Churchyard's Challenge, being a collection of twenty pieces of prose and verse written at divers times by Thomas Churchyard, and by him presented to different gentlemen and ladies at Court, is to be printed, the whole being dedicated to Sir John

Wolley, secretary of the Latin Tongue and one of her Majesty's privy councillors. Among these discourses are 'The Tragedy of Shore's Wife,' much augmented; 'A commendation to them that can make gold'; 'A warning to the wanderers abroad, that seek to sow dissension at home'; 'The man is but his mind,' a prose discourse of the different kinds of mind; 'A discourse of true manhood'; 'The honour of a soldier.'

THE WITCHES OF WARBOYS.

On the 7th April Alice Samuel and her husband, John, and her daughter, Agnes, were executed at Huntingdon for having bewitched to death the Lady Cromwell, wife of Sir Henry Cromwell, and for bewitching the daughters of Robert Throckmorton, Esquire.

It appears that for many months past, beginning at the end of the year 1589, the daughters of Mr. Throckmorton have been thrown repeatedly into strange fits, wherein they accused Mother Samuel of bewitching them, and of having a spirit in the form of a chicken which snatched at her chin. Soon after the beginning of this time, the Lady Cromwell, who then lay at Ramsey, a town two miles distant from Warboys, came with her daughter-in-law, Mrs. Cromwell, to visit the children and to comfort the parents. She had not been long in the house before the children all fell into their fits, to the great distress of the lady, who could not abstain from tears. She therefore caused the old woman Samuel to be sent for, who, because her husband was a tenant of Sir Henry Cromwell, durst not refuse; but so soon as she was come the children grew much worse. Then the Lady Cromwell took her aside and charged her deeply with the witchcraft, using hard speeches to her, which she stiffly denied, declaring that Mr. Throckmorton and his wife did her great wrong to blame her without cause.

The lady answered that neither Mr. Throckmorton nor his wife accused her, but the children in their fits did it, or rather the spirit of them. One of the children, by name Joan, being then in her fit, when she heard the old woman clearing herself (though by reason of her fit she heard neither the Lady nor any other), said that it was she who caused all this, 'and something there is,' said she, 'doth now tell me so,' asking if nobody heard it but she, affirming that it squealed very loud in her ears.

Mother Samuel still continuing in her denial, the Lady Cromwell would have taken her into a chamber where Dr. Hall, a doctor of Divinity, was present, to examine her more closely, but she refused to go with them. At length, when the Lady perceived that she could not prevail with her, she suddenly pulled off Mother Samuel's kercher and taking a pair of shears clipped off a lock of her hair and gave it privily to Mrs. Throckmorton together with her hairlace, willing her to burn them. Mother Samuel seeing herself thus dealt with spake to the Lady, 'Madam, why do you use me this? I never did you any harm as yet.'

Towards night the Lady departed, leaving the children much as she had found them. That night the Lady Cromwell suffered many things in her dreams concerning Mother Samuel and was very strangely tormented by a cat (as she imagined) which Mother Samuel had sent to her which offered to pluck off all the skin and flesh from her arms and body. Such was the struggling and striving of the Lady in her bed and the mournful noise which she made, speaking to the cat and to Mother Samuel, that she awakened her bedfellow, who was Mrs. Cromwell, wife of Mr. Oliver Cromwell. Not long after, the Lady fell strangely sick and so continued until her death which occurred in about a year and a quarter. The manner of her sickness, except that she always had her perfect senses, was much like the children's, the pains taking her sometime in one part of the body, sometime in another, but always the grieved part shook as if in a palsy. But the saying of Mother Samuel would never go out of her mind: 'Madam, I never hurt you *as yet*.'

Some time after Mother Samuel, who was then staying at Mr. Throckmorton's house, became very sick, and being very penitent in her sickness she confessed her witchcraft. Mr. Throckmorton sent to Dr. Dorrington, the minister of the town, relating the whole circumstance and desiring him to console her. The next day being Sunday, and Christmas Eve, Dr. Dorrington to comfort her chose his text of repentance out of the Psalms, and there declared in the whole assembly all the matter of Mother Samuel's confession, applying himself especially to the consolation of a penitent heart. All through this sermon Mother Samuel did nothing but weep and lament, and was so loud in her passion, that she caused all in church to look at her. That night she returned to her husband and daughter, who thereon set upon her for having confessed, so that the next day she denied all.

Then Dr. Dorrington and Mr. Throckmorton went to her house to learn the truth, and there found the husband and daughter talking of the matter. Being asked whether she had not confessed, she now answered, 'I confessed so indeed, but it is nothing so.' This so angered Mr. Throckmorton that the next morning early he went to Dr. Dorrington and told him he would not let the matter rest there lest the worser sort of people should imagine that it was some device of theirs against the old woman. Therefore they sent for the constables, and giving both mother and daughter in their charge ordered them to provide for the journey, for they should go before the Bishop of Lincoln at Buckden. They were therefore taken before him the same day (26th December) and there examined.

She was then asked whether a dun chicken did ever suck on her chin and whether it was a natural chicken. She answered that it had sucked twice, and no more, since Christmas Eve. She declared that it was a natural chicken, for when it came to her chin she scarce felt it, and when she wiped it off with her hand, her chin bled, and further she declared that all the trouble that had come to Mr. Throckmorton's children had come by means of this dun chicken.

Mother Samuel was again examined three days afterwards before the Bishop of Lincoln, and Francis Cromwell and Richard Fryce, Justices of the Peace. At this examination she declared that she knew the dun chicken had now gone from the children because it had returned to her with the rest and was now at the bottom of her belly with the others, which made her so full that she could scarce lace up her coat, and that the way as she came they weighed so heavy that the horse fell down. She said also that she had five spirits given her by an upright man in the shape of dun chickens, three she called to her by the names of Pluck, Catch and White; the others by smacking her lips. She was then committed, with her daughter, to the jail at Huntingdon till the Assizes; but Mr. Throckmorton, hoping to get something out of the daughter, persuaded the Justices to let her out on bail to come home with him.

The fits continued very grievous with the children all the while she was in prison. On Wednesday, 4th April, Mistress Joan Throckmorton went to Huntingdon, and was very well on her way, but half an hour after they had entered the Crown Inn, she fell again in her fit, and neither saw nor heeded any. In the evening after the Court had broken up, Mr. Justice Fenner, the Judge, who was lodging at the same inn, went into the garden to see the girl, still greviously tormented by her fit. Mr. Throckmorton told the Judge that if he would command Agnes Samuel, who was standing by, to say certain words his daughter would immediately be well. The words were these: 'As I am a witch and a worse witch than my mother, and did consent to the death of the Lady Cromwell, so I charge the devil to let Mistress Joan come out of her fit at present.' But first, the Judge himself and others to make trial of these words repeated them themselves without avail.

Then the Judge bade Agnes Samuel pray for the girl, and whenever she named God or Jesus Christ in her prayer, Mistress Joan was more troubled than before. Then she was commanded to say, 'As I am no witch, neither did consent to the death of the Lady Cromwell, so I charge the devil to let Mistress Joan come out of her fit at this present'; but all was to no purpose until Agnes Samuel repeated the first words, when Mistress Throckmorton immediately wiped her eyes and came out of her fit, and made a low reverence to the Judge. But a short while after she fell into another fit, first shaking one leg, then another, with many other extraordinary passions. When the Judge and others had prayed without avail, Agnes Samuel was ordered to speak these words: 'As I am a witch and would have bewitched to death Mistress Joan Throckmorton in her last week of her great sickness, so I charge the devil to let Mistress Joan to come out of her fit at this present.' This said, Mistress Joan was immediately well again.

The next day Mother Samuel, her husband, and her daughter were indicted with having bewitched to death the Lady Cromwell, and having bewitched Mistress Joan Throckmorton and others, contrary to God's Laws and the Statute made in the 15th year of the Queen's reign. These things and many others were sworn in testimony against them, and the jury brought in a verdict of guilty.

Then the Judge, passing sentence, asked old Father Samuel what he had to say for himself; he answered that he had nothing to say but the Lord have mercy on him. Then he asked Mother Samuel what she had to say to stay judgment; she answered that she was with child, which set all the company laughing, for she was nearly eighty years old, and she herself more than any, because she thought that for this reason no judgment should be given. The Judge moved her to leave that answer; but she would not be driven from it till at length a jury of women was empanelled, who gave up their verdict that she was not with child, unless, as some believed, by the devil.

All three were therefore condemned to be hanged and shortly executed in Huntingdon.

10th April. THE PARLIAMENT DISSOLVED.

Between five and six this afternoon, the Queen accompanied by her Officers came to the Upper House, and as soon as she was seated with the Lords Spiritual and Temporal, the knights, citizens and burgesses of the Lower House were summoned, and came up with their Speaker, bringing the Bill of Subsidy. The Speaker being placed at the Bar of the Upper House with as many of the Commons as could be admitted, after humble reverence to the Queen, spoke thus:

'The High Court of Parliament, most High and Mighty Prince, is the greatest and most ancient court within this your Realm; for before the Conquest in the high places of the West Saxons we read of a Parliament holden, and since the Conquest they have been holden by all your royal predecessors, Kings of England and Queens of England. In the times of the West Saxons, a Parliament was held by the noble Queen Ina by these words: "I, Ina, Queen of the West Saxons, have caused all my fatherhood, aldermen and wise commons, with the godly men of my kingdom to consult of weighty matters, etc.," which words do plainly show the parts of this Court still observed to this day. For in Queen Ina is your Majesty's most royal person represented ; the fatherhood in ancient time were those whom we call Bishops, and still we call them reverend fathers, an ancient and free part of our State. By aldermen were meant your noblemen ; for so honourable was the word alderman in ancient time that the nobility only were called aldermen. By wisest commons is signified your knights and burgesses, and so is your Majesty's writ *De discretioribus et magis sufficientibus.* By godliest men is meant your Convocation House, it consisteth of such as are devoted to religion and as godliest men consult of weightiest matters ; so is your Highness writ at this day *Pro quibusdam arduis et urgentissinis negotiis nos, statum et defensionem regni nostri et ecclesiae tangentibus.* Your Highness's wisdom and exceeding judgment with all careful providence needeth not our counsels, yet so urgent causes there were of this Parliament, so importunate considerations as that we may say (for we cannot judge) if ever Parliament was so needful as now or ever so honourable as this.

'If I may be bold to say it, I must presume to say that which hath been often said, but what is well said cannot be too often spoken ; this secret counsel of ours I would compare to that sweet Commonwealth of the little bees ; *Sic enim paruis componere magna solebam.* The little bees have but one governor whom they all serve ; he is their king. *Quia latrea habet latiora;* he is placed in the midst of their habitations *ut in tutissima turri ;* they forage abroad sucking honey from every flower to bring to their king : *ignavum fucos pecus a principibus arcent*, the drones they drive out of their hives *non habentes aculeos ;* and whoso assails their king in him *immittunt aculeos et tamen rex ipse est sine aculeo.*

'Your Majesty is that Princely Governor and noble Queen whom we all serve ; being protected under the shadow of your wings we live ; and wish you may ever sit upon your throne over us ; and whosoever shall not say Amen, for them we pray *ut convertantur ne pereant et ut confundantur ne noceant.* Under your happy government we live upon honey, we suck upon every sweet flower ; but where the bee sucketh honey, there also the spider draweth poison. Some such there be ; but such drones and door bees we will expel the hive and serve your Majesty, and withstand any enemy that shall assault your own lands or goods.

Our lives are prostrate at your feet to be commanded ; yea, and thanked be God and honour to your Majesty for it, such is the power and force of your subjects that of their own strengths they are able to encounter your greatest enemies ; and though we be such yet have we a Prince that is *sine aculeo*, so full of that clemency is your Majesty. I must now to your laws.

'The laws we have conferred upon this session of so honourable a Parliament are of two natures ; they are such as have life but are ready to die, except your Majesty breathe life into them again. The other are laws that never had life, but being void of life do come to your Majesty to seek life.

'The first sort are those laws that had continuance until this Parliament and are now to receive new life. The other that I term capable of life are those which are newly made but have no essence until your Majesty giveth them life.

'Two laws there are, but I must give the honour where it is due, for they come from the able, wise lords of the Upper House, the most honourable and beneficial laws that could be desired ; the one a confirmation of all Letters Patents from your Majesty's most noble father of all Ecclesiastical livings, which that King of most renowned memory took from those superstitious monasteries and priories, and translated them to the erecting of many foundations of Churches and Colleges, thereby greatly furthering the maintenance of learning and true religion. The other law to suppress the obstinate recusant and the dangerous sectary; both very pernicious to your Royal Government.

'Lastly, your most loving and obedient subjects, the Commons of the Lower House, most humbly and with dutiful thanks stand bound unto your gracious goodness for your general and large pardon granted unto them, wherein many great offences are pardoned, but it extendeth only to offences done before Parliament.

'I have many ways since the beginning of this Parliament by ignorance and insufficiency to perform that which I should have done offended your Majesty, I most humbly crave to be partaker of your most gracious pardon.'

The Lord Keeper then received instructions from the Queen and afterwards replied to the Speaker that her Majesty did most graciously accept of these services and devotions of this Parliament, commending them that they had employed their time so well, and spent it on necessary affairs; save only that in some things they had spent more time than was needed; but she perceived some men did it more for their own satisfaction than the necessity of the thing deserved.

She misliked also that such irreverence was shown towards Privy Councillors (who were not to be accounted as common knights and burgesses of the House that were but councillors during the Parliament); whereas the others were standing councillors, and for their wisdom and great service were called the Council of State.

Then he said that the Queen's Majesty had heard that some men in the case of great necessity and grant of aid had seemed not to regard their country and made their necessity more than it was, forgetting the urgent necessity of the time and dangers that were now eminent.

Her Majesty would not have the people feared with reports of great dangers but rather to be encouraged with boldness against the enemies of the State. And therefore she charged and commanded that the mustered companies in every county should be supplied if they were decayed and that their provisions of armour and ammunition should be better than heretofore it had been used.

For this offer of three subsidies her Majesty most graciously in all kindness thanketh her subjects; but except it were freely and willingly given she did not accept it; for her Majesty never accepteth anything that is not freely given.

If the coffers of her Majesty's treasure were not empty or if the revenues of the Crown and other Princely ornaments could suffice to supply her wants and the charges of the Realm, in the word of a Prince she did pronounce it, she would not now have charged her subjects nor accepted of this they gave her.

The Lord Keeper's Speech being ended, after some intermission, the Queen herself, sitting in her chair of State, spoke to the two Houses:

'This Kingdom hath had many wise, noble and victorious Princes: I will not compare with any of them in wisdom, fortitude or any other virtues, but saving the duty of a child that is not to compare with his father, in love, care, sincerity and justice, I will compare with any Prince that ever you had or should have.

'It may be thought simplicity in me, but all this time of my reign I have not sought to advance my territories and enlarge my dominions; for opportunity hath served me to do it. I acknowledge my womanhood and weakness in that respect, but though it had not been hard to obtain yet I doubted how to keep the things so obtained; that hath only held me from such attempts, and I must say my mind was never to invade my neighbours or to usurp over any.

'I am contented to reign over mine own and to rule as a just Prince.

'Yet the King of Spain doth challenge me to be the quarreller and the beginner of all these wars, in which he doth me the greatest wrong that can be; for my conscience doth not accuse my thoughts wherein I have done him the least injury; but I am persuaded in my conscience, if he knew what I know, he himself would be sorry for the wrong that he hath done me.

'I fear not all his threatenings; his great preparations and mighty forces do not stir me, for though he come against me with a greater power than ever was his *Invincible Navy*, I doubt not (God assisting me, upon Whom I always trust) but that I shall be able to defeat and overthrow him. I have great advantage against him; for my cause is just.

'I heard say, when he attempted his last invasion, some upon the sea coast forsook their towns and flew up higher into the country and left all naked and exposed to his entrance. But I swear unto you by God if I knew those persons, or of any that shall do so hereafter, I will make them know and feel what it is to be fearful in so urgent a cause.

'The subsidies you give me I accept thankfully, if you give me your goodwills with them; but if the necessity of the time and your preservations did not require it I would refuse them. But let me tell you that the sum is not so much but that it is needful for a Prince to have so much always lying in her coffers for your defence in time of need, and not be driven to get it when we should use it.

'You that be Lieutenants and gentlemen of command in your counties, I require you to take care that the people be well armed and in readiness in all occasions. You that be judges and justices of the peace, I command and straightly charge that you should see the laws to be duly executed and that you make them living laws when we have put life with them.'

And so with most gracious thanks to both Houses, her Majesty ended her speech.

Then the titles of all the Acts were read in order, beginning with the Bill of Subsidies, to which the Clerk of the Parliament, standing up, did read the Queen's answer: *La Royne remercie ses loyaule Subjects, accept leur benevolence, et ainsi le veult.*

Next the Clerk pronounced the thanks of the Lords and Commons in these words: *Les Prelates, Seigneurs et Communes en ce present Parliament assembles, au nomes de touts vous autres subjects, remercient tres humblement vostre Majesty, et prient Dieu que vout il done en sante bonne vie et longue.*

At each Public Act, to everyone allowed by the Queen the Clerk said, *Le Royne le veult*; to every Private Act, he said, *Soit fait come il est desiré*; and to such Acts as the Queen forebore to allow, *Le Royne se advisera.*

After which the Parliament was dissolved by the Lord Keeper of the Great Seal in Latin with these words: *Dominus Custos Magni Sigilli, ex mandato Dominae Reginae tunc praesentis dissoluit praesens Parliamentum.*

11th April. RELIEF FOR MAIMED SOLDIERS.

Until the Act of Parliament made for the relief of maimed soldiers can be put into execution the Lords Lieutenant of counties shall give every man weekly the sum of two shillings. For the convenience of those too impotent to come themselves to fetch the money from the Deputy Lieutenant, some trusty person residing near is to be appointed to receive and pay the money. All these maimed soldiers having received conduct money at the rate of 1d. a mile, and to the most lame 2d. a mile, are ordered to return to their own counties where they shall receive relief.

14th April. FALSE REPORTS CONCERNING THE QUEEN'S DEALINGS WITH THE TURKS.

There have of late been set forth in Germany many scandalous libels about her Majesty as if she had invited the Turk to make war against Christendom; and the letters which she sent the Turk published, but falsified and corrupted many things being added. A letter is now sent to the Emperor very strongly denying these calumnies and showing how by the Turk's own confession her Majesty did make peace between him and the King of Poland. This letter also setteth forth the insatiable desire for conquest of the King of Spain, and the troubles which he stirreth up in France and in Scotland.

15th April. THE QUEEN'S DIRECTIONS TO SIR JOHN NORRIS.

Some days since Sir John Norris wrote showing what inconveniences would follow if his troops were withdrawn and to ask for absolute directions whether to stay or return. The Queen now answereth that his doubts appear strange, for she could not have written more plainly or directly to him than she had done; for she had first assured him that not one man would be sent if the King had not in those parts such settled troops as might make head against the enemy; she had also commanded him to take special care not to be so engaged by any siege as to be driven either dishonourably to quit the place, or else to plunge her into the necessity of relieving him; being an action of more charge and hazard than for the town of Pempole or Brehat she meant to be put. Yet if he were not likely to be pressed by the forces of the enemy he might remain a short time; but in referring anything to his judgment as General, it ought not to be used as a reason to complain of want of plain direction; unless he preferred her either to judge certainly of things there which time and distance must make uncertain, or else to leave him no more reputation of his opinion than as a cipher that could judge of nothing.

However understanding his apprehension of the dangers the country will take from his sudden return, she is now content that he shall stay for a short time if he find the enemy retired from him, or can have such intelligence of his approach as not to be overtaken with a siege. If not, he is commanded to retreat to the Islands with the ships already provided.

16th April. THE LIBELS AGAINST STRANGERS.

A certain man hath been arrested on suspicion of being the author of a libel against strangers. He is to be very strictly examined by the Lord Mayor of his meaning and purpose in making that writing and who are in any way privy of that fact; if there be any pregnant matter to argue him to be guilty of writing the placard and he will not by fair means be brought to utter his knowledge, he shall be punished by torture and compelled to reveal it.

17th April. MEASURES AGAINST VAGABONDS.

An order is to be printed and set up in the City that all poor, aged and impotent persons repair to the place where they were born or where they were most conversant during the space of three years, there to be maintained; likewise all others wandering about as beggars, being whole and strong in body and able to get work, having no lands or other means to get their living, shall be taken as rogues and vagabonds. And if any impotent person so provided for wander abroad out of his parish without licence he shall be whipped and returned, but if eftsoons he offend again then to be punished as a rogue. To this end the officers of the City of London and of Westminster shall make inquisition of all beggars to compel them to depart to the places where they were born.

18th April. 'VENUS AND ADONIS' ENTERED.

Venus and Adonis, a poem written by William Shakespeare, is entered, being dedicated to Henry Wriothesley, Earl of Southampton. In this poem is described the hot love of Venus for the youth Adonis who scorneth her love, and leaving her to pursue the boar is by it slain. And she hearing his dismal cry:

As falcon to the lure, away she flies;
The grass stoops not, she treads on it so light;
And in her haste unfortunately spies
The foul boar's conquest on her fair delight;
 Which seen, her eyes, as murder'd with the view,
 Like stars asham'd of day, themselves withdrew:

Or, as the snail, whose tender horns being hit,
Shrinks backward in his shelly cave with pain,
And there, all smother'd up, in shade doth sit,
Long after fearing to creep forth again;
 So, at his bloody view, her eyes are fled
 Into the deep dark cabins of her head:

Where they resign their office and their light
To the disposing of her troubled brain;
Who bids them still consort with ugly night,
And never wound the heart with looks again;
  Who, like a king perplexed in his throne,
  By their suggestion gives a deadly groan,

Whereat each tributary subject quakes;
As when the wind, imprison'd in the ground,
Struggling for passage, earth's foundation shakes,
Which with cold terror doth men's minds confound.
  This mutiny each part doth so surprise
  That from their dark beds once more leap her eyes;

And, being open'd, threw unwilling light
Upon the wide wound that the boar had trench'd
In his soft flank; whose wonted lily white
With purple tears, that his wound wept, was drench'd:
  No flower was nigh, no grass, herb, leaf, or weed,
  But stole his blood and seem'd with him to bleed.

This solemn sympathy poor Venus noteth,
Over one shoulder doth she hang her head,
Dumbly she passions, franticly she doteth;
She thinks he could not die, he is not dead:
  Her voice is stopp'd, her joints forget to bow,
  Her eyes are mad that they have wept till now.

22nd April. THE LIBELS AGAINST STRANGERS.

Dr. Julius Caesar, one of the Masters of Requests, Sir Henry Killigrew, and others are appointed commissioners to examine by secret means the authors of the libels against the strangers, and their favourers and abettors, and to discover their intentions.

THE LIBEL

'Doth not the world see that you, beastly brutes, the Belgians or rather drunken drones, and faint-hearted Flemings; and you, fraudulent fathers, Frenchmen, by your cowardly flight from your own natural countries, have abandoned the same into the hands of your proud, cowardly enemies, and have by a feigned hypocrisy and counterfeit show of religion placed yourselves here in a most fertile soil under a most gracious and merciful Prince; who had been contented, to the great prejudice of her own natural subjects, to suffer you to live here in better case and more freedom than her own people?

'Be it known to all Flemings and Frenchmen, that it is best for them to depart out of the realm of England, between this and 9th of July next. If not, then to take what follows. For there shall be many a sore stripe. Apprentices will rise to the number of 2336. And all prentices and journeymen will down with Flemings and Strangers.'

23rd April. DRAYTON'S 'IDEA.'

The Shepherd's Garland, fashioned in nine Eclogues, Rowland's Sacrifice to the nine Muses, by Michael Drayton, being dedicated to Mr. Robert Dudley, is entered. In the first of these eclogues (founded after the pastoral mode of *The Shepherd's Kalendar*), Rowland malcontent bewaileth the winter of his grief; in the second old Wynken reproveth Motto's unbridled youth, giving him Rowland's example; in the third Perkin rouseth Rowland to song, who praises Beta the Queen of Virgins. Wynklyn in the fourth bewaileth the loss of Elphin (Sir Philip Sidney). In the fifth, Rowland singeth the praises of Idea, his lady; and of Pandora (the Countess of Pembroke) in the sixth, whom he calleth

> Arabian Phoenix, wonder of thy sex,
> Lovely, chaste, holy, miracle admired,
> With spirit from the highest heaven inspired,
> Oh thou alone, whom fame alone respects,
> Nature's chief glory, virtue's paradise;

declaring that

> Ages shall tell such wonders of thy name,
> And thou in death thy due desert shall have,
> And thou shalt be immortal in thy grave,
> Thy virtues adding force unto thy fame,
> So that virtue with thy fame's wings shall fly,
> And by thy fame shall virtue never die.

In the seventh eclogue Dorrill, an aged shepherd swain, rebukes Batto for falling in love.

In the eighth, Gorbo sings of the age of the golden world, ending with a tale of Dowsabel and her shepherd lover.

The book ends with the lament of Rowland that his Idea is unkind to him.

24th April. PLAGUE DEATHS.

The plague is not yet died out of London, 34 persons being reported dead of it during the past week.

29th April. A CHARITABLE GENTLEMAN.

Some years since Mr. Edward Cotton of his charity disbursed the sum of £444 for the redemption of four captives from the Turks, yet hath he hitherto received but £40, though letters were then sent to the Lord Mayor that his charges should be satisfied from the collections ordinarily made about Easter for this charitable purpose. The Council have again written to the Lord Mayor that the money specially collected for the redemption of captives since Maundy Thursday or before at Spittle sermons or other places be now paid to him, that others may be encouraged to the like good and charitable deed upon like occasions.

4th May. THE NUMBERS OF STRANGERS IN LONDON.

The certificates giving the numbers of strangers in London show the total of all strangers living in London with their children and servants born out of the realm to be 4300; 267 being denizens. This scrutiny hath been taken in every ward because of the complaints of English shopkeepers that the strangers are not content with manufactures and warehouses but would keep shops and retail all manner of goods.

5th May. LIBELS AGAINST STRANGERS.

Between eleven and twelve o'clock at night a rhyme was found set up on the walls of the Dutch Churchyard beginning:

> 'You strangers that inhabit in this land,
> Note this same writing, do it understand;
> Conceive it well for safeguard of your lives,
> Your goods, your children and your dearest wives.'

This was taken down and brought to the constable.

10th May. 'PARTHENOPHIL AND PARTHENOPHE.'

Parthenophil and Parthenophe, by Barnabe Barnes, is entered. In this book are contained sonnets, madrigals, elegies and odes setting forth the passion and desire of Parthenophil for Parthenophe, his mistress, his distress at her refusing, and at the last his enjoyment of her love; with sonnets to the Earl of Northumberland, the Earl of Essex, the Earl of Southampton, the Countess of Pembroke, the Lady Strange and the Lady Bridget Manners. The wantonness of some few of the verses in this book much to be noted, especially of that sonnet wherein the poet wisheth himself the wine that his lady drinketh.

11th May. MORE LIBELS AGAINST STRANGERS.

The malicious libels against strangers continuing to be set up and one especially upon the wall of the Dutch Churchyard that excels the rest in lewdness, the special Commissioners are ordered to take extraordinary pains to discover the author and publisher thereof; to make search and apprehend every person suspected, and for that purpose to enter into all houses where they may be staying; and upon their apprehension, to make search in chambers, studies, chests and the like for all manner of writings or papers that might give light for the discovery of the libellers. All that after due examination be suspected and refuse to confess the truth are to be put to the torture in Bridewell, that by its extremity (to be used as often as the Commissioners deem necessary) they shall be drawn to discover their knowledge.

12th May. THOMAS KYD ARRESTED.

Thomas Kyd, that wrote the *Spanish Tragedy* some years since, hath been arrested and carried to Bridewell by the officers of the Lord Mayor searching for the authors of the libels against strangers. When they examined his papers some fragments of a disputation denying the divinity of Jesus Christ were found; these papers Kyd declareth to have been left in his study by Marlowe when they wrote together two years ago.

15th May. CONTEMPT OF THE COUNCIL'S ORDER AT BRISTOL.

Some months since, on earnest complaint of the French Ambassador of the taking of sundry ships belonging to Bayonne and St. Jean de Lurg, by English men-of-wars, some being of Bristol, and the owners subjects of the King of France, the Council instructed the case to be referred to arbitrament. By the award the captors were condemned to restore the hulk in such state as she was at the taking, together with 100,000 fish and the sum of £60. This ought to have been performed in December; yet notwithstanding the Council's earnest letters nothing is yet effected. The Mayor and Council of Bristol are now required to see that the owner of the ship is satisfied; or in default the Council will be constrained to consent to letters of marque being granted to those of Bayonne and St. Jean de Lurg against the City of Bristol, which will turn to no small prejudice of their adventures.

20th May. MARLOWE BEFORE THE COUNCIL.

This day Christopher Marlowe, who was sent for by the Council two days since, hath entered his appearance and is commanded to give his daily attendance until licensed the contrary.

21st May. A PRIEST'S DECLARATION OF HIS MOTIVES.

William Harrington, a priest, that was taken, being charged with treason, and examined, hath set forth his reasons for coming to England in a letter to the Lord Keeper.

He saith that he is a gentleman by birth, a Catholic, and a priest of the Seminary of Rheims. He first left his country, desiring to imitate others of innocent lives and glorious deaths, especially Campion (the Jesuit that was executed in 1580), whom he believed guilty of no treason to the Queen nor the country. He hath always abhorred treachery but is not amazed at being accused as a traitor, nor troubled at the popular outcry, 'Hang him, hang him.' If his cause is good, he suffereth for Justice's sake, and that law is too severe that maketh his function treason; if his cause be bad, death itself is too merciful a punishment. He is compelled by his conscience to discharge his priestly office, but hath refrained from other practices, which he detests. Having so determined, he would make his life of no account. He hath never been made privy to any plot against the Queen or the country or he would have been forced by his oath of allegiance to give notice of it. Since he will not serve his Prince or country by betraying his friends, he hopeth to be excused for not wishing to live with such a spot of infamy. He therefore beggeth life and liberty on such conditions as he may conscientiously observe; if not, he resigns himself to God's disposal.

23rd May. THE PLAGUE IN THE SAVOY.

The Master of the Hospital of the Savoy is to forbear for the time to receive any into the hospital because of the danger that the poor people repairing there daily may be infected with the plague, to the great danger of the inhabitants in general and especially to some of the Council that dwell in those parts and are often occasioned to be at Court and near the Queen. This hospital was founded in former times for poor suitors from the country that are unable to defray the charge of lodging during their abode in the City on their necessary business, but the greater part of those now received are young boys, rogues and vagabonds.

24th May. PENRY CONDEMNED.

John Penry, the Puritan, was arraigned this day. At his trial many seditious and slanderous speeches were urged against him, collected from his papers and writings. He had said that the Queen stands against the Gospel and will not move a finger to help it, nor speak a word to reform it. The magistrates, ministers and people are conspirators against God, murder whole troops of souls, and are godless men. The Council are rebels against God and levy their force against the Gospel. Nor may the people serve God under the Queen but are bond slaves of the man of sin; nor would the Queen have embraced the Gospel if she could have received the crown without it, and only useth it to strengthen her sceptre. If Queen Mary had reigned to this day, the Gospel would have flourished more; without the Gospel, outward peace is nothing.

A REQUEST OF THE CITIZENS OF PARIS.

From Paris it is reported that 500 of the inhabitants went to the lodging of Monsieur de Blyn, and signified to him that they would live and die in the maintenance of the Catholic religion, but if the King would render himself a Catholic they would make a peace with him that would not be in the power either of the Governor or of Monsieur de Mayne to impeach. They prayed him signify so much to Monsieur de Mayne; and if he would have it better confirmed, they would within an hour bring ten thousand persons who would affirm their resolution.

25th May. ABUSES OF THE QUEEN'S SERVICE IN GLOUCESTERSHIRE.

The Justices of the Peace for the county of Gloucester are ordered to inquire into the complaints that the Queen's services are much hindered and neglected by the inferior officers that from time to time have the conducting of the soldiers pressed for service in Normandy and Brittany. These officers have sold, freed or exchanged the most part of those of any suffering and ability before they were delivered over to their captains to be embarked.

26th May. MARLOWE'S BLASPHEMIES.

Information hath been received by the Lord Keeper of the opinions of Christopher Marlowe, and by him laid before the Queen. This Marlowe is accused of many vile and horrible blasphemies concerning Christ and His Mother; affirmeth that Moses was but a juggler and that one Harriott, Sir Walter Ralegh's man, can do more than he. Into every company he cometh he would persuade men to atheism, willing them not to be afeared of bugbears and hobgoblins, and utterly scorning both God and His ministers.

28th May. PRECAUTIONS AGAINST PLAGUE.

Trinity Term is adjourned owing to the great increase of the plague in London, Westminster, and the parts adjoining. But seeing that great prejudice would grow to many in their causes and suits if the term be wholly adjourned, some few days at the beginning and ending of the term shall be held for the better expediting those causes that can be performed in the absence of the parties by their attorneys. No party, save in case of outlawry, is compelled to appear in person.

STRATFORD GOOSE FAIR FORBIDDEN.

At this time of the year there is usually held a 'Goose feast' at Stratford Bow, whither a disordered assembly of all the vagabond and idle persons come from the City; whereat through excess of drinking, divers quarrels and other great inconveniences have fallen out in that place. As an opportunity is offered thereby to the worst sort of apprentices and others ill disposed to resort thither to make their matches and appointments to sundry ill purposes, and also because the infection is more dispersed that way than towards any other villages, the Council have ordered the magistrates to take timely order to prevent this inconvenience. They shall charge the taverners, alehouse keepers and other victuallers to forbear to make extraordinary provision of victuals and to cause a straight watch to be set about the place for better intercepting all that pass to the town without good and lawful occasion.

Mr. Wentworth in the Tower.

Mr. Peter Wentworth, who is very old and subject to continual infirmities, is much impaired in health, by reason of his close imprisonment and especially owing to the great heat of the present season. The Council allow him the liberty of the Tower in company with some trusty servant and also to see his sons, friends, and physicians for his better comfort and recovery of health; but he shall not be permitted to have any conference with them except in the presence of the Governor or his servants.

30th May. Marlowe Slain.

Christopher Marlowe is slain by one Ingram Frizer at the Bull Inn at Deptford.

31st May. The Execution of John Penry.

John Penry, suspected of being the author of the Martinist pamphlets, that was condemned at the King's Bench on the 24th May, was hanged at St. Thomas Watering, with little warning and few spectators, lest he should have raised some tumult, either in going to the gallows or upon the ladder.

Three Suspected Soldiers.

Three soldiers that arrived at Poole without passports and were arrested, are now to be released and dismissed with passports to their homes. It is found on examination that they were abandoned by the rest of the troops at a place called St. Susan's, not far from Laval, and thereby constrained hazardously to adventure the saving of their lives by attempting to recover Caen, whence they have come to England.

1st June. THE INQUEST ON CHRISTOPHER MARLOWE.

At the inquest on the body of Christopher Marlowe, it was testified by those present at the time that Marlowe with three gentlemen, Ingram Frizer, Robert Poley and Nicholas Skeres, met in the house of a certain Eleanor Bull, and there dined. After dinner they walked in the garden until 6 o'clock in the evening, when they returned and supped. Thereafter malicious words passed between Marlowe and Frizer about the payment of the reckoning, until Marlowe, who was lying on a bed, sprang on Frizer, then sitting at the table, and taking Frizer's dagger from his back wounded him twice in the head. Frizer being then put in fear of his life strove to get back his dagger, and in the struggle gave Marlowe a mortal wound over the right eye of which he instantly died.

Frizer is found to have acted in defence of his own life. But though this is the Coroner's verdict, there want not other stories making his end more fearful. He is reported to have been an atheist, a blasphemer, given to the vice of sodomy; which offences with many others of a like nature had been charged against him in a paper sent to the Lord Keeper but three days before his death. It is much noted that he was smitten in the brain where he conceived his blasphemies and by his own hand wherewith he wrote them, and that together with his last breath an oath fled out of his mouth. Some say that the quarrel first arose over a lewd love. He is buried in the churchyard at Deptford.

5th June. PRECAUTIONS AGAINST PLAGUE AT WINDSOR.

Since the Queen will make her residence at Windsor for most part of the summer, the Mayor of Windsor is to order that no citizen of London or other person coming from any place where there is infection do resort to the town or make stay there. Those persons that are obstinately and undutifully refusing to obey the orders of the Mayor, shall be admonished to remove from thence with their families; and if any of them refuse, the Mayor to take bonds of them to appear before the Council to answer their contempt.

7th June. Mr. Cotton's Claims to be satisfied.

Mr. Edward Cotton complaining that the Lord Mayor not only refuseth to pay him any money but will not so much as vouchsafe an answer to the Council's letters, the Council have required the Lord Mayor either to make some reasonable satisfaction or else to send a true and perfect account of the collection for the release of captives of every year from the beginning of 1589 until the end of April last, showing what captives have been released and for what sums of money.

8th June. Relief of Maimed Soldiers.

The Sheriffs and Justices of the Peace throughout the realm are ordered to confer together and consider of the Statute passed this last Parliament for the relief of those hurt or maimed in the service of the Queen. Officers shall be ordained for receipt of the collections, that such as should come with warrant to demand their allowances may receive the benefit without any further trouble to them or occasion ministered to the Queen to think any slack in the performances of their duties.

10th June. Charity for a Prisoner in the hands of the Leaguers.

The Lord Mayor and Aldermen are asked to bestow on Peter Brown, a captive, so much money as will satisfy his ransom from the collections that have been made for this purpose. This Brown, one of the ordinary posts, coming towards England in a voyage from Sir Roger Williams, has lately been taken by the garrison of Rouen. There he remains, and will not be delivered without paying so great a ransom as far exceedeth his ability to pay.

12th June. Rumours of Changes in France.

There is much talk at this time of the likelihood that the King of France has turned Catholic, and of a peace between the King and the League. This detaineth all resolution with the Vidame of Chartres, his ambassador. The Queen stormed at first but it is believed that nothing will come of the matter.

16*th June.* CHUTE'S 'BEAUTY DISHONOURED.'

Beauty Dishonoured: written under the title of Shore's Wife, by Mr. Anthony Chute, is entered, being dedicated to Sir Edward Wingfield.

Even on her dying bed divinely sorry,
Pensive in heart she weeps thus forth her story.

She complaineth that her great beauty caused her to be suspected of immodesty even when she was still bashful and chaste. Being then forced into marriage with an old man that she loathed, she was importuned by many lovers and at first despised them all, but in time, saith she,

My speed from humble, decent, pure and true,
That hid no secrets in a plainly meaning,
To courtlike, wanton, pleasant did ensue;
I left my nature to my follies meaning:
And I by practice learn'd so well
In wanton art the best I could excel.

Her fame was now carried to the King, whose mistress she became. But he dying soon after, she was accused by Richard, Duke of Gloucester, of witchcraft, shamed, and turned out to beg; and so died.

18*th June.* A PROCLAMATION TO RESTRAIN SUITORS AT COURT.

A Proclamation is published to restrain the access of so many suitors to the Court. No persons but such as have cause to come to the Court for their ordinary attendance on the Queen shall repair within two miles upon pain of contempt, and all that attend on the Queen, her Councillors and the Officers of her Chamber and Household, are straightly commanded to see these orders obeyed.

If for any extraordinary cause anyone do come to the Court with matter to be certified to the Queen or to any of the Privy Council, he may not enter within the gates until he be licensed by the Lord Chamberlain or some other of the Council. If he have only letters to deliver, then not to come within the gates but to send in the letters, and when answer is given not to tarry longer on pain of imprisonment.

20th June. CAPTAIN JOHN DAVIS RETURNS TO ENGLAND.

Captain John Davis hath returned with some few of his men to Cornwall on the 16th, being but the poor remainder of the company of seventy-six that had left Plymouth on 26th August, 1591, on board the *Desire* with Mr. Thomas Cavendish's fleet.

After losing sight of Mr. Cavendish, their General, on the night of the 20th May, 1592, they had returned to Port Desire, being now in very miserable case, the shrouds all rotten, without pitch, tar or nails, and living only upon seals and mussels. Here they remained hoping for sight of the General until 6th August, when they made for the Straits of Magellan, and there stayed, in the deep of winter, with but little victual and not enough clothing to defend the extremity of the winter's cold. In these seas they were lamentably driven by storms until on 25th October they came to an island named Penquin Island. There the boat was sent on shore, which returned laden with birds' eggs; and the men said that the penquins were so thick that the ships might be laden with them. The Captain therefore sent some of the men ashore whilst he sailed the ship up a river in the mainland, where she was run aground and made fast to the shore with running ropes moored to stakes. Here nine of their men were slain by savages, but the rest remained feeding on eggs, penquins, young seals, gulls, and other birds. In this place they found a herb called scurvy grass which so purged the blood that it took away all kinds of swelling, of which many had died, and restored them to perfect health of body.

In this harbour they stayed until 22nd December, in which time they had dried 20,000 penquins on the island, of which 14,000 were taken on board, but not being able to fetch the rest by reason of the dangerous tides, they shaped course for Brazil. On 30th January, 1593, they landed at the Isle of Placencia, hoping to surprise the Portugals, but when they came to the houses they were all burnt, so that they thought no man remained on the island. Then the Captain went to the gardens and brought thence fruits and roots for the company, and all laboured to put the water casks in order.

The 5th February at night many of the men dreamed of murder and slaughter, and the Captain likewise having dreamed very strangely himself, gave straight charge that those who went on shore should take weapons with them. All the forenoon they laboured in quietness, but when it was ten o'clock, the heat being now extreme, they came to a rock near the woods' side (for all this country was nothing but thick woods) and there they boiled some cazavi roots and dined. After dinner some slept, some washed themselves in the sea, all being stripped to their shirts, and no man keeping a watch. Suddenly as they were thus sleeping and sporting, having gotten themselves into a corner out of sight of the ship, there came a multitude of Indians and Portugals upon them, and slew them sleeping; only two escaped, one very sorely hurt, one unharmed, who ran to the ship.

With all speed the boat was manned and landed to succour the men, but they found them all slain, and laid naked in a rank, with their faces upward and a cross set by them. Moreover, they saw in the river two very great pinnaces full of men. So the next day, choosing rather to fall into the hands of the Lord than into the hands of men, they cast off in great distress, having only eight tuns of water in bad casks.

And now as they came near to the sun the dried penquins began to corrupt and there bred in them a most loathsome and ugly worm of an inch long, which so mightily increased and devoured the victuals that there was in reason no hope of avoiding famine; for there was nothing they did not devour, only iron, cloths, boots, shoes, hats, shirts, stockings, and for the ship they did so eat the timbers that there was great fear lest they should gnaw through her side. In this woeful case after passing the equinoctial toward the north, the men began to fall sick of a monstrous disease so that their ankles and whole bodies began to swell, and some to grow raging mad, and perished thus in most loathsome and furious pain, so that all but sixteen died, and of these but five were able to move, and upon them only stood the labour of the ship.

Thus as lost wanderers upon the sea, it pleased God that they arrived at Bearhaven in Ireland the 11th of June, and there ran the ship on shore, where the Captain left the master and three or four of the company, and within five days after he and certain others passed in an English fishing boat to Padstow in Cornwall.

25th June. THE COUNCIL'S LICENCE ABUSED.

A certain John Wilson hath been travelling about the realm with a counterfeit licence bearing the seal of the Court of Admiralty and the hands of the Lord Admiral and the Archbishop of Canterbury, pretending that he is a sailor that sustained great losses and captivity with the Spaniards, and thereby hath he collected divers sums of money. This man was imprisoned at York and his licence sent to the Lord Admiral, who declared it counterfeit. As this offence of late years had been very frequent, the man is to be set on the pillory at York with one of his ears nailed, and, if the Lord President sees cause, cut off, with a writing set over his head signifying the cause of his punishment.

26th June. 'A DISCOVERY OF THE CONSPIRACY OF THE SCOTTISH PAPISTS.'

A discovery of the unnatural and traitorous conspiracy of Scottish Papists against God, his Church, their native country, the King's Majesty's person and estate, is entered, being extracted from the confessions and letters of Mr. George Ker, that is still in prison, and David Graham of Fintry, justly executed for his treason the 15th February, 1593, with other letters intercepted. This book was first printed and published in Scotland at the special commandment of the King, and is now again to be printed in London.

29th June. CITY FEASTS TO BE CURTAILED.

Owing to the plague, the customary great feasts made by the City Companies at this time are to be curtailed, and the choice of officers made with as small an assembly as conveniently may be. The charges so saved are to be converted to the relief of those infected; and that this contribution may be made without fraud, the Lord Mayor is required to find out what is usually spent by the heads of companies at their feasts.

There is great negligence in the City in suffering houses and shops to remain open or only to be shut up a few days in places where the plague is well known to have been. The Queen is so greatly offended therewith that, except the Lord Mayor and Aldermen take better regard, she will be moved to seize their liberties and commit the government of her City to some others.

1st July. MR. CAVENDISH'S VOYAGE.

From letters received from Mr. Thomas Cavendish, who sailed from England nearly two years since, it appeareth that he hath passed through the Straits of Magellan into the South Sea, where prizes of great value are sometimes taken. Sir Francis Drake and others are ordered that, if God should bless these ships with any such purchase, and if the ships or prizes taken by them should enter any port, they should immediately go on board and see the hatches nailed down. A just inventory shall be taken of all goods found in the cabins or above hatches lest any disorder be committed by the ship's company to the loss of the owners and adventurers and the prejudice of the Queen's customs.

FAIRS TO BE ABANDONED.

Owing to the dangerous increase of the plague, her Majesty out of her princely care for the preserving of her living subjects, and preferring the same before private benefit, commandeth the fairs usually held in the months of July, August and September to be abandoned. In London, St. Bartholomew's Fair in Smithfield upon 24th August and the Fair in Southwark on 8th September; and near London in July, Uxbridge the 20th, St. James's the 25th, and Brainford the 27th; in September, St. Giles in the Bush the 1st, Ware the 7th, Waltham Abbey the 13th, Croydon and St. Catherine Hill near Guildford the 21st.

6th July. MARLOWE'S 'EDWARD THE SECOND.'

The play of *The Troublesome Reign and Lamentable Death of Edward the Second, King of England, with the tragical fall of proud Mortimer*, written by Christopher Marlowe, and sundry times acted by the Earl of Pembroke's players, is entered for the printing.

9th July. THE PLAGUE.

The Lord Mayor hath written to the Council showing the discommodity which will arise, especially to the clothiers, if Bartholomew Fair be not held. The proclamation forbidding the Fair may now be stayed for a while until it is seen how by God's goodness and the Lord Mayor's careful endeavour the increase of sickness be allayed.

Since the white crosses painted on those houses visited with the plague are wiped away in a short space, red crosses are to be nailed upon the doors and a watch kept to prevent those within from going abroad.

THE COLLECTION OF THE SUBSIDY.

The High Sheriffs are appointed commissioners for the collections of the fifteenths and tenths voted for the Queen's use. They are urged to choose men of sufficient worth for this work. As for the Justices of the Peace, since by the statute none should be admitted unless they hold lands to the value of £20 per annum, so is it expected that none of these shall be assessed at under this rate. The commissioners themselves shall give a notable example in the taxation of themselves so that the rest which are able may be drawn the more willingly to assent to the larger taxation now laid on them.

SPANISH SHIPS OFF THE BRITTANY COAST.

From the Isle of Jersey it is reported that 30 ships of the enemy and 5 galleys have been seen on the coast of Brittany about Conquett. Letters are therefore sent to Sir John Gilbert and Sir Francis Drake to warn the forces of the counties on the sea coast to be ready against any sudden incursion that might be made, and especially to take care for the defence of Plymouth now being begun to be fortified.

BLUNDEVILLE'S 'EXERCISES.'

Master Blundeville, His Exercises, is to be printed, being six treatises; the first, of Arithmetic; the second, of the first principles of Cosmography; the third, a plain and full description of the globes, both celestial and terrestrial, with certain tables for the better finding out of the true place of the sun and moon and of all the rest of the planets on the celestial globe; the fourth, a plain description of the universal map of Petrus Plancius set forth in 1592; the fifth, a plain description of Mr. Blagrave's Astrolabe; the sixth, the first and chiefest principles of navigation, showing how the navigator should use his proper instruments and presage the movements of the celestial bodies.

14th July. SIR THOMAS WILKES SENT TO THE FRENCH KING.

Because of the continual rumours that the French King is turned Catholic, Sir Thomas Wilkes is urgently despatched as a special ambassador to the King. He is instructed, after delivering his letters of credence, to say to the King that her Majesty hath forborne hitherto to inquire what course he meaneth to hold in the present state of his affairs, but now she findeth occasion to delay no longer sending unto him. If either the King hath not fully yielded to his conversion to the Catholic religion, or hath not bound himself by promise to perform it, the ambassador shall say that her Majesty can in no wise allow or think it good before God that for any worldly respect or cunning persuasion he should yield to change his conscience and opinion in religion from the truth wherein he was brought up from his youth, and for the defence whereof he hath continued many years in arms. He shall require that the King not only hear a number of reasons conceived by her Majesty to stay his resolution, but also to permit them to be communicated to his principal Catholic estates.

But if in coming thither Sir Thomas Wilkes shall find that the King hath indeed been converted, nevertheless he shall show the reasons conceived by the Queen to stay his resolution, that he may understand her mind and good will towards him. And though she would be grieved with his conversion, being contrary to her opinion and conscience, and indeed by good policy to be misliked, because he would become thereby subject to the Pope, who is her mortal enemy, and who might enjoin him to keep no amity with her; yet she requireth him to advertise her what she may expect thereof.

First she wisheth to know how and by what means he will be stronger in his estate by his conversion than he was before as well against his rebels, that will not be content with his conversion, as also against the King of Spain. Then shall the ambassador ask how the King meaneth to proceed to acquit Brittany of the Spaniards, telling him that her Majesty thinketh it the principal matter of weight that he hath to take in hand after he shall be established in his crown; and is of such importance that she thinketh it more convenient for the King himself to take the same in hand, and in his own person, than to commit it to others, as hitherto.

Further, the King is to understand that until some port town in Brittany be allowed to her Majesty's forces whither they may repair when sent, or to which they may retire for their relief, she cannot with any honour or the good respect of her natural subjects send any more forces thither to be wasted and spoiled as the former have been for the lack of such a place of retire.

The ambassador is also to know of the King what assurance her Majesty may have of him that he will continue jointly with her in offence and defence against the King of Spain. She doubteth not that he will give her this assurance under his hand and the great seal of France; for without it she will think all her kindness, favours and expenses of her treasure and wasting of her people to be as lost and of no effect. Then the ambassador is to require the King to call to his memory how long she hath aided him both before his title to the crown of France, and since, with money (as yet never repaid according to his bonds), and with her subjects with their lives, and in such number as England never yielded in any age to serve in foreign countries.

16th July. THE PLAGUE INCREASES.

The Council have written to the Lord Mayor and Aldermen saying that the Queen is greatly grieved at the increase of sickness, and although these plagues proceed from the hands of God as a due punishment of our wickedness, yet ought we to use all possible means to prevent their increase. If as good care were used in keeping the orders as had been taken for their making, and especially in restraining the infected from the sound, it would, with the help of God, do great good. In the town of Kingston, upon the first infection, they caused a house to be made in the fields distant from the town where the infected might be kept apart and provided for all things convenient for their sustenance and care; and the same should be done in London.

There was also a little book set forth in the time of the great plague and the last year printed again which contained divers good precepts and orders; this might be recommended by the minister of every parish to all housekeepers.

The Council require the suppression of all those that sell old apparel, a trade greatly used of late, and in no wise to be suffered in time of infection.

17th July. PLAGUE DEATHS.

In London this last week 149 persons are dead of the plague. The crops promise well, but notwithstanding corn is risen in price from £9 to £11 10s. owing to the shortage of corn in Spain and Portugal.

19th July. THE ASSIZES HELD IN ST. GEORGE'S FIELD.

This day the Court of Assize for Surrey was held in St. George's field, a tent being set up for the purpose. Many prisoners were there arraigned, condemned, and had judgment, nineteen being burnt in the hand but none executed. This assize is ended in one day which was thought would have needed three days' work, for the Justices (all duties being paid) make haste away for fear of being infected with the pestilence by the repair of people thither.

PLAGUE DEATHS.

The infection is much increased this past week, for out of 666 deaths in the City of London, 454 are from the plague.

29th July. THE COUNCIL'S LETTERS TO THE UNIVERSITIES OF OXFORD AND CAMBRIDGE.

The Council have written to the Vice-Chancellor of the University of Cambridge showing how the Universities are nurseries to bring up youth in the knowledge of God and in all manner of good learning and virtuous living whereby they may serve their Prince and country in divers callings. For this respect a special care is to be had of these Universities that all means may be used to further the bringing up of the youths that are bestowed there in all good learning, education and honest manners; and like care used that all such things that may allure and entice them to lewdness, folly, and riotous manners, whereunto the nature of man is more inclined, in no wise be used. Understanding therefore that common players ordinarily resort to the University of Cambridge to recite interludes and plays, some of them being full of lewd example, and most of vanity, beside the gathering together of multitudes of people, the Council require the Vice-Chancellor to take special order that no plays or interludes of common players be set forth either in the University or any place within the compass of five miles, and especially in the town of Chesterton. Moreover, as Stourbridge Fair is at hand the Masters and Heads of the College should, because of the great infection, cause the gates of the College to be shut and no scholar permitted to repair thither.

A like letter is to be sent to the Vice-Chancellor of Oxford.

30th July. THE RECRUITS TO BE STAYED.

Upon the new advertisements that are come out of France those soldiers that were to be levied in Hertford and Essex are stayed for a season that the county may not be charged with them. The men nevertheless are to be in readiness upon any new warning, and the armour and furniture provided by the county kept for use as occasion may serve.

3rd August. DR. HARVEY'S 'PIERCE'S SUPEREROGATION.'

Dr. Gabriel Harvey hath answered Nashe's *Strange News* in a book entitled *Pierce's Supererogation or a new praise of the Old Ass.* He saith that if he is an ass, what asses are those courteous friends, excellent and learned men, worshipful and honourable personages that have written him letters of excellent commendation. As for Nashe, he is the son of a mule, a raw grammarian, a babbling sophister, a counterfeit crank, a stale rakehell, a piperly rhymer, a stump-worn railer, a dodkin author whose gayest flourishes are Gascoigne's weeds, or Tarleton's tricks, or Greene's cranks, or Marlowe's bravados; his jests but the dregs of common scurrility, the shreds of the theatre, or the offscouring of new pamphlets; his freshest nippitaty but the froth of stale inventions, long since loathsome to quick tastes. His only art and the vengeable drift of his whole cunning is to mangle the sentences of the *Four Letters*, hack the arguments, chop and change the phrases, wrench the words, and hale every syllable most extremely, even to the disjoining and maiming of his whole meaning.

4th August. THE PLAGUE INCREASES.

The numbers of plague deaths are reported to be much increased, but the Lord Mayor is rebuked because no certificates of those dead or infected have been sent in these last two weeks.

5th August. A BOOK ON ASTRONOMY.

A translation of M. Auger Ferrier's *Learned Astronomical Discourse* (first printed in 1549) made by Thomas Kelway, gentleman, one of her Majesty's Trumpets in Ordinary, is to be printed, being dedicated to the Lord Henry, Earl of Northumberland. In the address to the courteous reader Mr. Kelway requesteth that those who find this work of the judgment of nativities harsh and unpleasant shall not wound it with injurious words, thereby charging themselves with folly; for he that readeth with derision, because he understandeth not, must blame his own insufficiency, and not the book. The *Discourse* is divided in three books, whereof the first treateth of the celestial figure of a nativity, showing the fortunes and infortunes of the planets; the second of the signification of the twelve signs and the twelve houses; the third of revolutions and eclipses.

PLAGUE DEATHS.

The plague is worse than ever this last week and whole households have died. Of 1603 deaths, 1130 are from the plague.

6th August. THE TRUCE IN FRANCE.

The terms for a truce general between the French King and the Leaguers were agreed and by sound of the trumpet proclaimed on the 31st July.

The truce is for three months, during which all persons may return to their houses and estates, and enjoy them, except where garrisons are employed. Every man may freely travel through the realm without constraint of taking of passport. Prisoners of war that have not compounded for their ransom shall be delivered fifteen days after the truce; the common soldiers without ransom; the other men of war, having pay of either side, on procuring one quarter of their pay, except the leaders and chief of horsemen, who together with other gentlemen bearing charge shall be acquitted for the half year's worth of their revenue. All other persons shall be used, as touching their ransom, as courteously as may be, respecting their faculties and calling. Any woman or maid a prisoner to be set at liberty immediately without paying ransom, also children under the age of sixteen and men from sixty and upward not bearing arms.

All men of war of either side are to be put in garrison, not being permitted to range and forage the country. No enterprises shall be made upon any foreign princes who hath assisted either side, but they shall withdraw their forces from the field and not make any re-enter of them during the truce. Those in Brittany to be sent back or separated, and put in garrison in such places as may not give matter of suspect.

Bartholomew Fair.

In answer to the Lord Mayor's reasons against holding the fair on St. Bartholomew's Day in the fields towards Islington, her Majesty hath hardly consented, though she were otherwise disposed to have no manner of fair or assembly at this time, to allow leather, butter, cheese and such like to be sold by gross in Smithfield but not by retail; but to avoid any access of the people no booths may be erected for victuallers. A proclamation is now published for the restraining of Smithfield Fair on Bartholomew's Day.

12th August. Unlawful Spoils.

Complaints have been made to the Council by certain merchant strangers of Holland and Zealand that in November and December three ships were cast away on the Goodwins, laden with wax, linen cloth, sayes, grograms and other merchandise. These goods floated ashore at divers places on the coast, and were seized upon by the inhabitants as spoil, without regard to the misery and affliction of the owners and sailors. They are now ordered to make restitution.

14th August. Plague Deaths.

No exact figures of the mortality were given out for this past week because there is commandment to the contrary, but it is rumoured that within the City and without the number is between 1700 and 1800 in one week.

16th August. Rumours concerning France.

This proceeding of the French King in changing his religion is much wondered at and was not at first believed, but the news being now confirmed, the 1500 men levied for France are stayed and determination taken to recall those in Normandy and Brittany. There is great expectation of the treaty of peace now in hand between the King and the Leaguers, being necessary and grateful to the towns, and their great hindrance being removed by the King's coming within the Catholic Church, so that it is likely that they will embrace the peace upon easier conditions.

19th August. SIR THOMAS WILKES' CONVERSATION WITH THE FRENCH KING.

From St. Denis near Paris, Sir Thomas Wilkes writeth that he arrived there on the 11th of the month, finding the King about to depart on the next morning for Fontainebleau; who granted him a brief audience. He presented the Queen's letters of credence, which the King opened but did not read at that time, alleging the difficulty of the hand. Then the King of his own accord fell into a slight discourse of the reasons of his conversion, promising at the next audience to detail it at large. To which Sir Thomas answered little more than to signify how strange it would appear to the Queen that of so resolute and long continued a Protestant he should so suddenly become a Catholic.

The ambassador saith that the King by his action hath assured his Catholics that were declining from him, and by breaking the neck of the third party hath doubtless gotten a strong party: the poverty of the Dukes of Mayne and Guise, the not performing of the promises of the Pope and the King of Spain, the uncertainty of the people of their faction, who all desire a peace, and the general misery of the country which is pitiful to behold, will drive them all to end their present dissensions.

22nd August. THE FORTIFICATIONS OF PLYMOUTH.

The fortification of Plymouth, which had been in good forwardness, is now slacked because very few of the gentlemen of Devon, except the Earl of Bath, who hath given £100, contribute anything at all.

DISBANDMENT OF THE SOLDIERS FROM FRANCE.

Sir John Hawkins prepareth seven hoys to bring 700 or 800 men from Dieppe. Sir Edward Brook and the muster master are to ascertain and record how many men there are in every company, how armed and weaponed, and from what counties they were sent. The treasurer's deputy shall give every soldier at his discharge some portion of what was due to him to discharge his debts. If any so desire they may be suffered to tarry and serve the French King, and be paid their wages then due, but their armour to be detained and brought into England. Every captain shall see that the armour and weapons of all that return is brought to England and delivered to the Mayor at Dover or Rye by indenture, and to give to each soldier of his band a billet of discharge and licence to pass to his county.

23rd August. SIR THOMAS WILKES' SECOND CONVERSATION WITH THE FRENCH KING.

Sir Thomas Wilkes writeth that the French King hath given him a second private audience whereat he delivered at large the sum of his instructions, acquainting the King with her Majesty's care and desire to have prevented his conversion as tending the good of his soul, and giving a summary of the articles which he had received. These the King took in very grateful part, and did acknowledge that they were no small tokens of the Queen's love to him, but the necessity of his State was such that no verbal reasons could have prevented the mischief whereunto he had fallen if his conversion had not then been performed; which he confessed was precipitated by reason that the dangers came more suddenly on him than he expected, for that the day of his promised conversion was to have been two months after.

To the Ambassador's demand for a place of retreat in Brittany, he desired respite to confer with his Council, and promised that in case he might be so happy as to pacify his estate there, he would not fail with all the force he could make to repair in person to Brittany to remove the Spaniard.

26th August. TWO COUNTERFEITERS SENT TO THE GALLEYS.

By order of the Lord Admiral, two men, Walter Pepper and George Ellis, very lewd and loose fellows that have beforetime been censured in the Star Chamber for counterfeiting the hands of some of the Lords of the Council and are now again apprehended and found culpable of the same offence, are committed to the new galleys to be employed as occasion should serve, and to be fast tied with chains that by no means they be allowed to escape.

8th September. NASHE'S 'CHRIST'S TEARS OVER JERUSALEM.'

Nashe hath written a godly book called *Christ's Tears over Jerusalem, whereunto is annexed a comparative admonition to London*, being dedicated to the Lady Elizabeth Carey, wife of the Knight Marshal. Herein is shown how the Jews after God's great mercies to them refused to listen to Christ when He pitifully reproached them ; and how forty years after our Lord's lifting up into Heaven, when the Jews pretended a weariness of the Roman regiment, Jerusalem was sacked and destroyed. So likewise is this London equally in danger of destruction by reason of the deadly sins committed within her walls, being ambition, avarice, vainglory, atheism, discontent, contention ; disdain between courtier and citizen, merchant and retailer, retailer and craftsman ; gorgeous attire, wherein England is become the ape of all nations' superfluities, the continual masquer in outlandish habitments ; delicacy, gluttony, lechery, and the great abundance of cunning bawds whose trade is such that a great office is not so gainful as the principalship of a College of Courtesans ; sloth and security ; the whole ending with a prayer against the plague.

In the Epistle to the reader Nashe saith that he hath bidden farewell to fantastical satirism, desiring reconciliation even with Dr. Harvey, whose fame and reputation he hath so rashly assailed.

10th September. PLAGUE DEATHS.

There is still no sign of an end to the mortality from plague. About a thousand deaths of plague weekly are now being reported in the City, and outside some five hundred.

15th September. A RESTRAINT OF SUITORS AT WINDSOR.

A Proclamation is published to reform the disorder in the great number of persons who attend the Court at Windsor. In many of the houses are lodged more than are allowed by the officers of the town and the Queen's harbingers, and many of these persons with their wives, children and servants. The Queen's Knight Harbinger is now commanded to make a new search with the assistance of the servants of the Knight Marshal and the Mayor of the town. All owners of houses in Windsor, Eton and the towns adjoining within five miles of the Court are warned that within two days of the publication of the Proclamation from Windsor Cross they exclude all persons not warranted by the harbingers' billets to have lodging, upon pain of fine and having their houses shut up.

17th September. NASHE'S 'UNFORTUNATE TRAVELLER.'

A book called *The Unfortunate Traveller*, or *The Life of Jack Wilton*, written by Nashe, is entered, being dedicated to the Earl of Southampton, wherein this Jack Wilton, that was a page at the Court of King Henry the Eighth, telleth his own tale of what he did at the siege of Tournay, and afterward in his travels how he fared at Rotterdam and Wittenberg, and in Venice, Florence and Rome.

28th September. PLAGUE DEATHS.

It is reported that the plague deaths have abated during these last two weeks by 430; the last week between 1100 and 1200 in all died.

1st October. DR. HARVEY'S NEW LETTER OF NOTABLE CONTENTS.

A New Letter of Notable Contents, together with a *Strange Sonnet entitled Gorgon or the Wonderful Year*, being a letter of Dr. Gabriel Harvey's to Mr. John Wolfe, the printer, is printed. He noteth the strange conversion of Nashe from the *Strange News* to *Christ's Tears*. As for Nashe's protestations of repentance, great penmen and pamphlet merchants play much upon the advantage of the time and care not who be the enemy so long as Term be the friend. He loveth *osculum pacis*, but hateth *osculum Judae*; reverenceth the tears of Christ, but feareth the tears of the crocodile.

8th October. HIGH-HANDED DEALINGS.

The Lady Elizabeth Russell hath petitioned the Council for the punishment of her neighbour, Mr. Lovelace, to whom, saith she, she hath shown every friendship these twenty-six years, but who is guilty of foul riots against her.

On Monday last he came to her house with sixteen or twenty men with halberds and long poles, broke open her porter's lodge and the lock of her stocks, and removed thence two of his men who had behaved very lewdly towards her. If she has offered him or his any wrong, the law is open, and it is not for him, a justice of the peace, to break his oath by so foul a riot.

On Thursday last, he sent a man for the key of the Tower at Windsor, where she had been all the year, having all her stuff there; she refused to leave upon such sudden warning, unless by order of the Lord Admiral, and offered him as much rent as it was worth, but it was refused. Two days since, being Saturday last, he and his men changed the lock of her lodging and commanded that none should undo it.

Now she petitioneth that this spite and injury be punished, and Mr. Lovelace put out of the commission of the peace, otherwise it were better to be a mean justice of the peace than a noble woman that dependeth upon God and her Majesty.

19th October. DANIEL'S 'DELIA AND ROSAMOND' AND 'THE COMPLAINT OF ROSAMOND.'

Mr. Daniel hath augmented his *Delia and Rosamond*, and added thereto *Cleopatra*, some few new sonnets, and *The Complaint of Rosamond*, in which the Ghost of Rosamond complaineth that though Shore's wife is graced, her well-told tale finds no such compassion. She runneth through the story of her sin with King Henry the Second, and her death by poison at the hands of his wronged Queen.

The Tragedy of Cleopatra is dedicated to the Lady Mary, Countess of Pembroke, for that she

> 'Call'd up my spirits from out their low repose,
> To sing of State, and tragic notes to frame.'

He promiseth so to work that posterity may find how much he contendeth to honour her.

> 'Now when so many pens (like Spears) are charg'd,
> To chase away this tyrant of the North,
> Gross Barbarism, whose power grows far enlarged,
> Was lately by thy valiant brother's worth,
> First found, encountered and provoked forth:
> Whose onset made the rest audacious,
> Whereby they likewise so discharg'd,
> Upon that hideous beast incroaching thus.'

This *Tragedy of Cleopatra* is not written for the English stages, but after the manner of the ancients, preserving a unity of the time, though not of place, and between each act a chorus to point the moral of the action. The death of Cleopatra at the end of the play is related by a *Nuntius*, concluding thus:

'This said, she stays and makes a sudden pause
As were to feel whether the poison wrought;
Or rather else the working might be cause
That made her stay, as likewise may be thought,
For in that instant I might well perceive
The drowsy humour in her falling brow:
And how each power, each part oppressed did leave
Their former office, and did senseless grow.
Look how a new-plucked branch against the Sun
Declines his fading leaves in feeble sort,
To her disjoined jointures as undone
Let fall her weak dissolved limbs support.
Yet lo! that face, the wonder of her life,
Retains in death a grace that graceth death,
Colour so lively, cheer so lovely rife,
That none would think such beauty could want breath.'

22nd October. EDWARDS' 'CEPHALUS AND PROCRIS.'

Cephalus and Procris, a poem written by Mr. Thomas Edwards and dedicated to the Right Worshipful Master Thomas Argall, Esquire, together with *Narcissus*, is to be printed. Herein is described how Aurora wantonly loved the hunter Cephalus and would have kept him; but he disdained her, being wan with love for Procris. Aurora then taunting him, he went back to Procris and by force and intreaty won his desire on her. But Procris, thereafter overcome with shame at what she had allowed, fled away, and, hiding in a thicket, was by chance struck with an arrow that Cephalus shot. In *Narcissus* the boy betrayeth his effeminate love for his own reflection, supposing it to be a maiden until he seeks it in the stream.

'This done, amain unto the spring I made,
Where finding beauty culling nakedness,
Sweet love reviving all that heavens decayed,
And once more placing gentle maiden likeness,
Thus sought I favour of my shadowed mistress;
  Embracing sighs, and telling tales to stones,
  Amidst the spring I leapt to ease my moans.'

9th November. THE PLAGUE ABATING.

The plague deaths reported in London this past week amount to 420.

14th November. DICKENSON'S 'ARISBAS.'

Mr. John Dickenson hath written a book called *Arisbas, Euphues amidst his slumbers: or Cupid's journey to Hell. Deciphering a mirror of constancy, a touchstone of tried affection, begun in chaste desire, ended in choice delights. And emblazoning Beauty's Glory, adorned by Nature's bounty; with the triumph of true Love, in the foil of false Fortune.*

This Prince Arisbas, having lost his lady, wandered alone, distracted with moody passions, and coming to one Damon who seemed a shepherd, lamented his hard fate, and told how refusing to wed the lady chosen by the King, his father, he had fallen in love with Timoclea.

Pretending, therefore, that he was a poor man and that Timoclea was his sister, he hired a ship and sailed away but, landing alone on the coast of Arcadia to view the country, a tempest arose; and the next morning the ship was nowhere to be seen.

In reply to his laments Damon telleth him that in the autumn before a youth had been cast on their coasts, so beautiful that he was loved of all shepherds and liked by all lasses. Arisbas, hoping that this might indeed be his Timoclea, asked more, and in reply Damon narrateth the story of Hyalus, taken away from Arcadia by Zephyrus. After some days Damon taketh Arisbas to the festivals in memory of Hyalus at the city, where, as he had hoped, he findeth the beautiful youth that was leader of the choir of boys to be no other than his Timoclea.

Arisbas being now reunited to his beloved Timoclea returneth to Cyprus to his aged sire, where there is great change, for the old King, having despaired of Arisbas' safety, had married his second son to the daughter of the Prince of Lemnos. Now with great joy is celebrated Arisbas' wedding with Timoclea, and, his father having resigned the diadem, he reigneth in Cyprus.

17th November. CHURCHYARD'S VERSES.

The poet Thomas Churchyard, in resentment that the Lord Treasurer refused him what the Queen had granted, hath sent her these verses:

'Madam,

You bid your treasurer on a time,
To give me reason for my rhyme;
But since that time and that season,
He gave me neither rhyme nor reason.'

20th November. A CASE OF PLAGUE AT COURT.

There is much alarm in the Court because a page of the Lady Scroop, one of the ladies of the Queen's bedchamber, is dead of the plague in the keep at Windsor Castle. It is expected that the Queen will remove within a day or two.

28th November. THE ARRAIGNMENT OF RICHARD HESKETH.

This day Richard Hesketh, a Jesuit, was arraigned for having treasonably attempted to persuade Ferdinando Stanley, the new Earl of Derby, to revolt against the Queen.

This man had come from Sir William Stanley and the Catholics abroad, being authorised to offer the Crown of England to the Earl of Derby. He was instructed first to approach the Earl signifying to him in general that he had a message of importance to deliver from special friends of his, and to desire leave to utter it, and his promise of good security that he should incur no danger.

Having received this promise and given mutual promise of fidelity and secrecy, he should declare in general that the message concerned the common good of all Christendom, especially of England, and in particular of the Earl. If the Earl was content to hear, though drily and with small desire, he should name Sir William Stanley as having sent him, adding that there was another greater than he; and to know expressly whether the Earl would hear his message or no.

It he were willing, then Hesketh was to offer him all the endeavour, services and helps that the Catholics could employ if he would accept and agree to the Catholic faith; but to be capable he must be a Catholic, and bind himself to restore, advance and perpetually maintain the Catholic faith in England. Let the Earl signify what help he needed and when, and by God's help it would be provided: 4000 or 5000 men might be sent within seven or eight months. He was not to fear strangers; neither did the King of Spain now seek the Kingdom of England for himself; nor would the Pope or Cardinal Allen agree to it, if there was any other remedy; nor could the King of Spain hold it though he might invade and conquer the realm, for the people of England were most impatient of foreign government. The Pope himself held it better for Christendom to have many Christian Catholic kings than one too great and monarch of all, and the Cardinal was a true Englishman. It was better that he should obtain the crown now before the Queen's death, because he might prevent competition; besides, the Cardinal and Sir William Stanley were now able to assist, the Pope was willing (and perhaps another would not be); the state of France could not hinder but rather further, for now he could have some Spaniards, but not too many; it was like that some other was provided to challenge it after her death; and he had many enemies that were daily seeking his overthrow.

Hesketh delivered his message to the Earl, but was by him denounced and arrested. At his trial he acknowledged all his former confessions to be true so that there needed no further testimony against him. Nevertheless the Attorney General laid open all the plot and course of his treasons for the satisfaction of the standers-by, making collections from his confessions to note that the malice of those fugitive traitors and other enemies of the Queen proceeds from no other ground but that she preferreth the true worship of God and the peaceable government of her subjects above all other things. The Lord Chief Justice also, before passing judgment, used a very grave speech to the comfort of the Queen's subjects by these and the like graces which God hath showed.

29th *November*. A RECUSANT'S CONFESSION.

Edward Pemberton, a recusant, being examined by order of the Archbishop of Canterbury as to the coming and going of Catholic priests from overseas, declareth that those who leave England take shipping either at Portsmouth or Arundel, agree with the ship master to come at night and are away before morning. Those sent to England take shipping at Antwerp or any other place; if the ship is for London they take a boat between Gravesend and London and so escape examining. When they come, if they are caught privily, any justice of the peace will take £10 and let them go, and the tithing men 20s.

30th November. THE QUEEN'S LETTER TO SIR JOHN NORRIS.

The Queen having been earnestly sued to grant Sir John Norris leave to return on his own affairs giveth him licence to repair home at his convenience. But he is put in mind what disaster happened in his last absence. If he is not assured of the troops being in safety and well guided he should not take the benefit of this favour; but if things are in such terms that he dare adventure he may choose his brother to command, who will have due care of her Majesty's honour, of Sir John's, and of his own. In times past when the generals came away they brought with them captains and lieutenants, leaving the people without leaders. He is admonished not to commit any such error, as nothing can be more grievous to her Majesty than by negligence to suffer the poorest soldier in the company to perish.

7th December. GREENE'S 'ORLANDO FURIOSO.'

A play called *Orlando Furioso*, written by Robert Greene, is entered for printing, in which Alleyn played Orlando. This play was performed before the Queen.

11th December. HESTER'S 'PEARL OF PRACTISE.'

The Pearl of Practise, or practiser's pearl for physick and chirurgery, found out by John Hester (a spagerick or distiller), is entered, having since his death been gathered and brought into some method by James Fourestier. This book is dedicated to Sir George Carey and setteth out the methods, cures and prescriptions for many diseases, swellings, wounds, and injuries.

21st December. ANXIETY IN GUERNSEY.

From Sir Thomas Leighton, Governor of Guernsey, it is reported that five thousand or six thousand Spaniards are lately arrived at Blavet in Brittany. He beseecheth that the sum of £500, the remainder of the £1000 promised for the works to be done at the Castle, may be sent speedily.

22nd December. PEPPER FROM THE GREAT CARRACK.

The merchants that lately contracted with the Queen for the pepper taken in the Great Carrack are unable to vend any quantity of it except at very mean prices because of the great quantities still remaining in the realm and being brought in. As they are bound to pay her great sums of money at Christmas and other short periods, the Queen in answer to their petition hath caused restraint to be put on the bringing in of all pepper into the realm from 25th December.

26th December. Playing Resumed.

As the plague is now abated, playing begins again at the Rose Theatre by the Earl of Sussex's men, who played *God Speed the Plough* this day.

29th December. Plays at the Rose.

During these three days past the Earl of Sussex's men played *Huon of Bordeaux*, *George a Green*, *Buckingham*, and *Richard the Confessor*.

31st December. Gentlemen's Sons Overseas.

The Council issue a warrant for inquisition to be made in the counties of Lincoln, Hertford and Essex as to what gentlemen have sons relieved or maintained out of the realm that are sent over under colour to learn languages or for any other respects, and are not notoriously employed in the Queen's martial services or trade or merchandise as apprentices to known merchants. A catalogue is to be made as well of the parents as of the sons so sent over; in what parts they be; and how long they have been absent. Bonds are to be taken of the fathers if any are known recusants or have been evil affected or are but feignedly reformed; and their houses to be searched for seminary priests, Jesuits and other suspected persons, books, letters and writings concerning matter against the State or established religion.

Chapman's Σκιὰ νυκτός.

Σκιὰ νυκτός, or *The Shadow of Night, containing two poetical hymns*, devised by Mr. George Chapman, is entered, being dedicated to Mr. Matthew Roydon, to whom he writeth that it is the exceeding rapture of delight in the deep search of knowledge that maketh men manfully endure the extremes incident to that Herculean labour. But what a supererogation in wit this is, to think Skill so mightily pierced with their loves who read but to curtail a tedious hour that she should prostitutely show them her secrets, when she will scarcely be looked upon by others but with invocation, fasting, watching, yea, not without having drops of their souls like a heavenly familiar. Yet are there those that most profitly entertain learning in themselves to the admirable lustre of their nobility, such as the most ingenious Derby, deep-searching Northumberland, and the skill embracing heir of Hunsdon.

Of the two hymns, the first is dedicated to Night, which the poet calleth the day of deep students,

> Rich taper'd sanctuary of the blest,
> Palace of ruth, made all of tears, and rest,
> To thy black shades and desolation,
> I consecrate my life.

The second hymn he dedicateth to Cynthia, under whom is figured the Queen, in whose sacred state

> The circles of our Hopes are compassed :
> All wisdom, beauty, majesty and dread,
> Wrought in the speaking portrait of thy face ;

yet fearing

> that sable day,
> When interposed earth takes thee away,
> (Our sacred chief and sovereign general),
> As crimson a retreat, and steep a fall,
> We fear to suffer from this peace and height,
> Whose thankless sweet now cloys us with receipt.

PLAGUE DEATHS.

There have died in London and the suburbs during this year 17,893 persons, whereof 10,675 were from the plague.

SOMEWHAT TO READ FOR THEM THAT LIST

Dr. Bancroft's 'Dangerous Positions and Proceedings.'

Dr. Richard Bancroft's *Dangerous positions and proceedings, published and practised within the Island of Britain, under pretence of a Reformation, and for the Presbyterial Discipline.* Herein is shown the history of the Consistorian Puritans from the first preaching of the Gospel by Farellus, Viretus and others at Geneva to the conspiracy of Hacket, Arthington and Coppinger in July 1591.

Giffard's 'Dialogue concerning Witches and Witchcraft.'

A Dialogue concerning Witches, penned by George Giffard, wherein in form of a dialogue between Samuel, and his wife, Daniel, M.B. a schoolmaster, and the goodwife, is shown how craftily the devil deceiveth not only the witches but many others.

In the Epistle Dedicatory to Mr. Robert Clarke, one of the Barons of the Court of Exchequer, Mr. Giffard declareth that the devils are now let loose, and prevail more than ever he hath heard before, so that Satan is now heard speak and believed, speaking through conjurors, sorcerers and witches. But the devils do this by God's special providence, seeking by this means to punish the world. Yet are the witches themselves deceived when they believe that at their request or pleasure their spirits lame and kill men and beasts; and then to spread the opinion among the people, these subtle spirits betray them, and would have the witches openly confess that they do such things, which all the devils at man's request could never do; for if they could, they would not stay to be intreated. The devil worketh by his other sort of witches, whom the people called cunning men and women, to confirm all his matters, by them teaching many remedies that so he may be sought and honoured as a God.

These positions are demonstrated in the dialogue; Daniel holding that Satan can do nothing without God's leave, so that the witches are of themselves powerless to do much harm; and in the end convincing the others.

Their talk being finished, there cometh to them the good wife R., being one of those upbraided as herself a witch for having thrust a hot poker into her cream when the butter would not come, burning a hen or a hog alive and other such devices. To their speeches she answereth, 'Is that witchcraft? Some Scripture men hath told you so. Did the devil teach it? Nay, the good woman at R.H. taught it my husband and she doeth more good in one year than all these Scripture men will do as long as they live.'

LODGE'S 'PHILLIS.'

Mr. Thomas Lodge's *Phillis*, being a collection of Sonnets and Eclogues wherein Damon declareth his love for Phillis and lamenteth her neglect, being followed by an Ode, bitterly complaining of her falseness; to which is annexed *The Complaint of Elstred*, who telleth the story of her life and death. Being widowed of Humber, her husband, who was slain by Locrine, she loved the conqueror. Locrine, by the consultations of his Lords, was betrothed to Gwendolen of Cornwall; but continuing his love to Elstred he made her a labyrinth where they dallied in secret, until he tired of his betrothed wife, and drove her away to put his mistress in her place. Whereupon the Cornishmen rose to aid Gwendolen, and in the ensuing battle Locrine was slain. Elstred pitifully embracing the corpse of her paramour was by robbers taken and brought before Gwendolen, by whose command she and her daughter Sabrina were cast into the Severn and drowned.

LODGE'S 'LIFE AND DEATH OF WILLIAM LONGBEARD.'

Mr. Lodge's *The Life and Death of William Longbeard*, being dedicated to Sir William Webb, the Lord Mayor. This Longbeard was a man of great strength and parts that in the time of King Richard I. became an instigator of sedition and leader of the people. Being called in question by the Hubert, the Archbishop of Canterbury, he and his fellows took refuge in the church, whence, refusing submission, they were driven out by fire and forced to yield themselves. Being arraigned before his judges, Longbeard thus defendeth himself: 'You Lords and honourable Judges, though I know it a hard thing to strive against the obstinate or to extort pity there, where all compassion is extinguished, yet I will speak, using the office of nature to work you although I know I shall not win you. I am here called and indited before you for high treason ; a heinous crime, I confess it ; and worthy of punishment. I deny it not. But may it please you with patience to examine circumstances. I have emboldened the poorer sort to innovation, to fight for liberty to impugn the rich, a matter in the common weals of Greece highly commended ; but here accounted factious, and why ? There subjects made Kings ; here Kings master subjects. And why not, say you ; and why not, think I ? Yet am I faulty under a good precedent, and the ambition which hath intangled me, hath not been without his profit. To offend of obstinate will were brutish ; but under some limits of reason to default, can you, my Lords, but think it pardonable ? I have raised one or two assemblies ; and what of this ? Peace was not broken, only my safety was assured ; and were it not that the law had been injured, might not the righting of a hundred poor men's causes merit pardon for two unlawful assemblies ? But, you will say, I have animated subjects against their prince. I confess it, but under a milder title. I have counselled them to compass liberty, which, if nature might be equal judge between us, I know should not be heinously misconstered.' But the judges condemned him to die a traitor's death, and the next day he was executed.

There are also in this book divers pleasant histories of pirates and others.

NORDEN'S 'SPECULUM BRITANNIAE.'

The first part of Speculum Britanniae, a historical and chorographical description of Middlesex, compiled by the travel and view of John Norden, being consecrated to the Queen by the author, with an epistle of thanks to the Lord Treasurer. After a brief declaration of the titles, inhabitants, divisions and situation of England, the author describeth the history, the limits and bounds, the nature of the soil and fertility, the Ecclesiastical and Civil Government of the shire, its divisions, parks, and ancient highways ; which are followed by an alphabet of the cities, towns, hamlets and villages, including the City of London, and concluding with the principal highways and a list of noblemen and gentlemen having houses within the shire.

SUTCLIFFE'S 'LAWS OF ARMS.'

The Practice, Proceedings and Laws of Arms, described out of the doings of most valiant and expert Captains, and confirmed both by ancient and modern examples and precedents, written by Dr. Matthew Sutcliffe, being printed by the Queen's printer, and dedicated to the Earl of Essex. In the Epistle Dedicatory Dr. Sutcliffe saith that all men's eyes are fixed upon the Earl of Essex, who hath already made his name honourable by his experience in the service of the Low Countries, of Portugal and France, so that the general hope of soldiers is that he who so well understandeth the common disorders of the wars, will one day be a means to correct them. It is not the courage of the Spaniard, nor force of the Dutch, nor bravery of the French that frustrated our late attempts; neither doth force so often overthrow armies in field, as dalliance, irresolution and delay; then, through niggardize and good husbandry, want of pay and necessary furniture; thirdly, presumption and want of strength and sufficient force; and lastly, those abuses which through want have crept into the armies of late times and cannot be corrected; for what conscience could punish those that spoil and wander abroad when otherwise they would starve. For all these things and for the abuses of imprests, false musters and accounts the only remedy is the true discipline of arms.

In the Epistle to the Reader he saith that this discourse is framed because of the general lamentation that in those actions which have of late been attempted publicly the success hath been so slender, the loss of men so great, the charge so burdensome, and the proceedings and effects so contrary to antiquity.

MR. SMITH'S SERMON AGAINST ATHEISTS.

God's Arrow against Atheists, a sermon preached by Mr. Henry Smith, wherein in seven chapters he showeth the reasons for a belief in God; in the first touching on the absurdity of Atheism and irreligion; demanding who made the world, since it had a beginning and it must needs follow that it had an efficient cause or maker. In the second it is shown that the

Christian religion is the only true religion in the world, and wherewith only God is pleased; in the third the Christian religion is defended against the Gentiles and all the infidels of the world; in the fourth that the religion of Mahomet is false and wicked; in the fifth that the Church of Rome is not the true Church of God nor observeth the right religion; and in the last he toucheth on schism and schismatical synagogues.

1594

1st January. A Prognostication.

It is prognosticated in the Almanack for this year that the spring shall be moist and windy but not very cold, the summer indifferent but with many unkind storms, sudden lightnings and thunder-claps; sicknesses not many but passing dangerous, with hot and fervent agues, great distemperature of men's brains, and immoderate heat, whereby many will run frantick. In the autumn there are like to be mighty storms to the great hindrance of those that shall be late in harvest, especially in the north; together with a great pestilence.

4th January. A Mysterious Stranger.

Mr. Thomas Jeffreys, an English merchant at Calais, hath written to Lord Burleigh that a certain man is come to him with a private communication for the Council. He knoweth not the man but hath seen him divers times with Emanuel Andrada: he may do good, as he hath dealings with Count Fuentes and the King of Spain's principal secretary for war, whereby, as he saith, he hath discovered great matters pretended by the enemy which must be seen to with speed. This man's name is Emanuel Louis Tinoco.

5th January. Plays of the Week.

This past week the Earl of Sussex's men at the Rose played *Richard the Confessor*, *Buckingham*, *George a Green*, *Huon of Bordeaux*, *William the Conqueror* and *God Speed the Plough*.

6th January. Court Revels.

Twelfth Night was celebrated at Court by dancing which continued till one o'clock after midnight, the Queen being seated in a high throne, and next to her chair the Earl of Essex with whom she often devised in sweet and favourable manner.

7th January. CATHOLIC STORIES FROM SCOTLAND.

About a month since (7th December) James Maxwell, Earl of Morton, the Scottish King's Lieutenant General, was slain in pursuing the Lord Johnston to arrest him according to the King's warrant, and the Catholics make much note of his death.

Not many years since, the Earl of Morton, though he was a Catholic, had been persuaded to sign the articles expressing conformity and directed against the Catholic religion. But at 12 o'clock that day, being alone in his room, an angel appeared to him in the form of a youth who said, 'My Lord, do not as your kinsmen would persuade you; for if you do you shall lose the hand with which you sign, and your days shall end with shameful death.' Moved by this appeal, the Earl again put on the gold crucifix and an *agnus dei* which he used to wear round his neck, but had taken off when he abandoned his former professions. He then told the principal kinsmen who had persuaded him to sign how remorseful he was for his error, and what the angel had told him; and in order that God's mercy might for ever be remembered by his house, he added to his arms the figure of an angel. He refused also to sign the articles declaring himself an enemy of the ministers.

But after a time he was greatly moved by his kinsmen, and the King himself made him many offers, creating him his Lieutenant General, so that at last he gave way and signed the articles. But shortly afterwards going to arrest the Lord Johnston with 5000 soldiers he met with the end the angel foretold him.

For when he came up the Lord Johnston, taking advantage of the ground, had posted 600 horsemen in three squadrons in a triangle at some little distance from each other. The Earl of Morton's regiment entering into their midst, Lord Johnston and his men who were on one side threw themselves with such fury upon the Earl's men that they broke and fled; and the Lord Johnston, reaching the Earl, at the first blow smote off his right hand, and at the second cut off a leg. Then being thrown from his horse, the Earl was cut into a thousand pieces.

The Catholics also say that the Lord Claud Hamilton, against his conscience and at the persuasion of his wife and her brothers, had also subscribed to please the King and the ministers. At one time he was dining and, as was the custom in some Scottish houses, the gospel was being read at table during the repast. The reader came to the words, 'Whoso denieth me before men, him will I also deny before my Father'; and as he pronounced these words the Lord Claud rose from the table and attempted to cut his wife's throat, crying out that by her persuasion and that of her brothers, he had denied the faith and sacrificed his soul. For several days after this he remained in a state of frenzy so that it was necessary to bind him; nor is he yet entirely recovered.

12th January. PLAYS OF THE WEEK.

The Earl of Sussex's men played this past week *Friar Francis*, *George a Green*, *Abraham and Lot*, *Buckingham*, *Huon of Bordeaux* and *The Fair Maid of Italy*.

15th January. AN ALCHEMIST'S BEQUEST.

Mr. Robert Smith of Great Yarmouth hath brought a letter from one Roloff Peterson of Lubec to the effect that a certain Clement Ouldfield, born in Kent, came to lodge in his house at Lubec in 1587 and continued there until September 1593 when he died. He had studied alchemy night and day, and brought himself to such perfection that, if the Lord had spared his life but six months longer, he believed he would have reaped his heart's desire. The day before he died he secretly informed Peterson that he had at last found out and long kept a secret of such high value, and so far exceeding all other, that none but high and mighty Princes should participate in it; and then delivered to him three glass bodies, containing alchemical preparations, sol, luna, and mercury, explaining the use of these and of sundry others.

Moreover, he declared that he had a most wonderful secret, which in the hands of any man but meanly skilful in this art, would work wonderful things, wishing Peterson to make profit thereby in regard of his kindness; but insomuch as the great and infinite treasures that might be attained by these means rather appertained to the majesty of Kings and Princes than to men of his estate, he bound him by an oath to present the same to the Queen of England, and to await her answer six months before opening the matter to any other, or making profit thereof;

which he might then do, if she refused. After this he yielded up the ghost.

If the Queen will send any skilful man to be further advertised, and to see the things, Peterson promises that he is ready to discharge his trust; but if he shall have had no knowledge within six months, then will he esteem himself free of the covenant, and at liberty to dispose thereof.

ATTEMPTS AGAINST THE QUEEN.

The Portuguese that was sent over from Calais, by name Emanuel Louis Tinoco, being taken to the house of Sir Robert Cecil, hath delivered an advertisement of many things which should be made known to the Queen for the sake of her person. He declareth that he was the servant of Don Antonio from the day when he was proclaimed King until July last, serving him always with zeal, fidelity and love; but seeing him ungrateful, and poor of council and government, he consented with one Stephen Ferrara de Gama to seek liberty for their country, seeing that they had the Duke of Braganza, a young man and well beloved in the Kingdom. They therefore went to the Count Fuentes to seek the favour of the King of Spain, by means of Don Christofer de Moro, and to offer him service.

Upon this the King wrote to Count Fuentes that he should send Tinoco to England and that Stephen Ferrara should leave his wife there, feigning that he hath business in France, and thence go together to Don Antonio who would employ them. For less suspicion Ferrara was to go alone and bring Tinoco orders what to do; he was to try and win Dr. Lopez, the Portugal Jew that is her Majesty's physician, and endeavour to draw a letter from him, promising to do him service; he was to remind Lopez that he had daughters and that they should not want good marriages. They were to take knowledge of all affairs of England, especially of any secret preparations of an army, how many ships the Queen hath at home and abroad, the names of their captains, and to take a good view of the Isle of Wight and the Downs, and to note the forts and weak places.

16th January. ANOTHER DECLARATION BY TINOCO.

Tinoco having been very straightly examined by the Earl of Essex, and in some respects confused, hath again written to Sir

Robert Cecil to clear himself. He declareth that he will show the true intentions of his coming so as to clear all doubts, and that without reward; which shall be reserved until it should be lawful for him to demand recompense. He saith that he has come voluntarily to Court, and gives his word as a gentleman to serve the Queen with all possible diligence and fidelity by giving secret advertisements of all things. He hath served Don Antonio for thirteen years and thereby lost all he had in Portugal, and the best part of his life; for the remainder he would serve the Queen, but knew of nothing that would do her service.

18th January. PLAYS OF THE WEEK.

This last week the Earl of Sussex's men played *Friar Francis*, *George a Green*, *Richard the Confessor*, *Abraham and Lot*, *King Lud*.

23rd January. DR. LOPEZ DEEPLY IMPLICATED.

Emanuel Louis Tinoco the Portuguese hath made further declaration, saying that Andrada had offered him, on behalf of Dr. Lopez, service to the King of Spain, and brought a jewel of great value from the King of Spain to Lopez, which he now hath. Stephen Ferrara de Gama also wrote to Count Fuentes that Dr. Lopez would do the King great service.

24th January. PLAYS OF THE WEEK.

During this past week the Earl of Sussex's men played *Friar Francis*, *The Fair Maid of Italy*, *George a Greene*, and *Titus Andronicus* (for the first time).

DR. LOPEZ EXAMINED.

Dr. Lopez was called before the Lord Treasurer, Sir Robert Cecil, and the Earl of Essex, who are appointed by the Queen to this end. The Earl hath for a long time been sifting out matter against Dr. Lopez but the other two opposed him.

After the first hearing Sir Robert Cecil posted to the Court before the Earl, and related to the Queen that there was no matter of malice, for in the poor man's home were found no kind of writings of intelligences of which he was accused, or otherwise that hold might be taken of him. In the meantime he is committed to the custody of Mr. Gelly Meyrick, the Earl's Steward, at Essex House. Upon my lord coming to the Queen, she, being prepossessed of the matter by the others, took him up, calling him a rash and temerarious youth to enter into a matter against the poor man, which he could not prove and whose innocence she knew well enough; but malice against Dr. Lopez, and no other, hatched all this matter, which displeaseth her much, and more for that her honour is interested therein.

These words of the Queen's so angered the Earl of Essex that he went back to his chamber, with great fury casting open the chamber door before him, and so passed into his cabinet where he kept himself shut in for an hour.

Essex and Lopez

This enmity between the Earl of Essex and Dr. Lopez is of old standing. Some time since, the Earl of Essex, having resolved to make use of intelligencers to do him service, to this end spoke to Dr. Lopez, telling that many did practise treason against her Majesty. The Spaniard hated her; the Papists would do her what hurt they could; she was ancient and childless; and the good of the Kingdom wholly depended on her life. Now for preventing this design it would be best to find someone on whom the Spaniard might repose trust. After some talk with the Queen, Lopez undertook the business, and made offer of his service to some special friends in Spain or Portugal. They to whom he wrote gave him encouragement and promised a good reward.

Here began a mutual intercourse of letters between them; and as soon as ever Lopez received any intelligence, he went instantly to the Queen to acquaint her therewith; and afterwards he went to the Earl of Essex and acquainted him. Then did the Earl of Essex come to the Court and acquaint her with the same: and the Queen knowing it before did but laugh at the Earl of Essex. And so it fell out several times, whereby the Earl saw himself utterly disappointed, for though he had gotten an intelligencer yet he proved not to be his but went in immediately to the Queen. This hath bred very ill blood between the Earl and Lopez.

In the last vacation, Dr. Lopez went to visit Don Antonio and Antonio Perez; and making merry with them, Lopez began to inveigh against the Earl of Essex, telling them some secrecies, how he had cured him, and of what diseases, with some other things that did disparage his honour. But as soon as Lopez was gone, they went instantly to the Earl and, to ingratiate themselves into his favour, acquainted him with all. Whereupon the Earl was so much incensed that he resolved to be revenged.

25th January. A NOTABLE JESUIT TAKEN IN THE NORTH.

From York Topcliffe reporteth that Father Walpole, a very notable priest and Jesuit, was taken on landing at Flamborough, together with his younger brother and one Lingen, both soldiers of Sir William Stanley. After the Lord President of the Council, with the aid of his chaplain, had toiled day and night with the prisoners, he so prevailed with the young Walpole to see his offence, that all the truth, secrets, and matter, even against himself, flowed from him as fast as the questions could be put. He confessed that his brother gave him six small pieces of parchment and twelve letters. When all had been examined, the Lord President sent the Jesuit and Lingen to rest; but to prove young Walpole's honesty, he despatched him to the sea side, well guarded, to see if he could find the place where he said that the letters were buried. The bundle was found, but all wet with rain, and brought to his Lordship who leapt for joy, and after tenderly handling them before a fire twenty-two are unfolded without blemish.

31st January. RUMOURS AT COURT.

Since his rebuke by the Queen the Earl of Essex hath kept to his chamber these two days, opening it to none but the Lord Admiral, who passeth to and fro about atonement which at last is made, and they two go off to London. It is rumoured that on further examination Dr. Lopez is found to be deeply touched in the plot for working the Queen's destruction, and discovered to have been the King of Spain's pensioner these seven years, the ground of which treason is believed to have been discovered by Don Antonio before his recent going over to France. The Queen hath forbidden all access to her, except only of four persons, besides the Council and the ladies of nearest attendance, by which it appeareth that all is not yet discovered.

PLAYS OF THE WEEK.

At the Rose this week are played *Buckingham*, *Titus Andronicus* and *Abraham and Lot.*

1st February. BARNFIELD'S 'GREENE'S FUNERALS.'

Danter hath printed *Greene's Funerals*, by R. B., gentleman, contrary to the author's expectation and wish; wherein Greene's death and works are celebrated in fourteen sonnets of various metres. In the seventh, written in the English hexameter, R. B. protesteth against those

That inveigh against the dead, like deadly maligners,
What if he was a man, as bad or worse than a hell-hound ?
As shall I think that he was as bad or worse than a hell-hound ?
Yet it ill became sweet minds to haunt in Avernus,
Ill became such cutes, to bark at a poor silly carcase,
Some had cause to moan, and mourn, and murmur against him,
Others none at all, yet none at all so against him,
For myself I wish that none had written against him,
But such men which had just cause t'have written against him.

2nd February. THE ALCHEMIST'S BEQUEST.

In the matter of Roloff Peterson's letter concerning the three glasses or bodies in alchemy bequeathed to the Queen by Mr. Ouldfield, Mr. Robert Smith now promiseth Sir Thomas Wilkes, at peril of his head, to bring 40,000 dollars to the Queen's coffers for these glasses without one penny of expense, if it shall please her not to meddle with the receiving of them. Since doubts have been moved as to how the Queen might consider the virtues of these glasses as being without error or deceit, and whether she would accept them or the money, he confirmeth on his allegiance and life the first two particulars, offering to bring Peterson, if he be alive, and the glasses before the Queen to be examined : after which, if she shall refuse them, he will be bound to procure the money at his own charge.

3rd February. BURGLARY AT WINDSOR.

Yesterday four of the gentlemen pensioners of the Court were robbed at Windsor. In their absence at six o'clock at night their chamber door, which is in one of the five towers of the tiltyard, was broken open, and all their trunks likewise, out of which the thieves took in jewels and ready money to the value of £400.

Sir Robert Cecil is reported to be very busy coming and going very often between London and the Queen, so that he appeareth with his hands full of papers and his head full of matter, and so occupied passeth through the presence chamber like a blind man, not looking upon any.

PLAYING PROHIBITED.

Owing to the great multitudes of people who daily resort to the common plays, lately again set up in and about London, the Council fear that the sickness may gain very dangerous increase. The Lord Mayor is required to take straight order that no plays or interludes be exercised by any company within the compass of five miles of the City.

4th February. A PLOT TO KILL THE QUEEN.

A certain Polwhele that came over from Calais to give information to the Lord Treasurer hath declared that one Captain Jacques, a soldier from Sir William Stanley's company, hath a design to kill the Queen. This Jacques, saith he, several times urged him to come to England to murder the Queen, and on his refusing Jacques said that the end of a soldier was but beggary, to be killed with a bullet and thrown into a ditch, and to take such a matter in hand would be glorious before God, the Queen being a wicked creature, and likely to overthrow all Christendom. Jacques directed him how to get to England safely, and what speeches to use to the Lord Treasurer if intercepted, saying that if he himself could go to England, the killing of the Queen would be the first thing he would do. Polwhele also draweth in two men, John Annias and Patrick Collen, an Irish soldier, with having come to England to kill the Queen. Both are already taken and lodged separately in prison.

5th February. LOPEZ SENT TO THE TOWER.

Dr. Lopez for all those that favour him at noon is committed to the Tower, the Earl of Essex having so busied himself with the examinations for several days past that he scarce had leisure even to eat.

THE CARTER'S WORDS.

The remove of the Court from Windsor is still constantly put off. The carter that three times came to Windsor with his cart to carry away some of the stuff of the Queen's wardrobe, when he repaired there for the third time and was told by those of the wardrobe that the remove held not, clapping his hand on his thigh cried out, 'Now I see that the Queen is a woman as well as my wife.' These words being overheard by her Majesty, who then stood at the window, she said, 'What a villain is this!'. and so sends him three angels to stop his mouth.

6th February. A PLOT TO BURN THE TOWER.

John Daniel, an Irishman, hath given Mr. Justice Young to understand of a plot that is pretended for the firing of the Tower. He declareth that there is a vault where brimstone lies and over it gunpowder, and near to it a trapdoor that stands much open. It is purposed that two men like labourers shall come in as though they were workmen in the Tower, and cast certain bales into the vault where the brimstone is so that in a short time it shall take fire and consume all. Further, that there is a device to set the ships at Billingsgate on fire, and the houses also; and then to set the inns and woodstacks on fire in London.

THE ROSE THEATRE CLOSED.

At the Rose this week the Earl of Sussex's men play *The Jew of Malta*, and *Titus Andronicus*, and now cease playing.

'TITUS ANDRONICUS' ENTERED.

The most lamentable Roman Tragedy of Titus Andronicus, sometime played by the servants of the Earl of Derby, the Earl of Pembroke and the Earl of Sussex, is to be printed.

A CONVERSATION BETWEEN SIR ROBERT CECIL AND THE EARL OF ESSEX.

At seven in the morning Dr. Lopez was again examined before the Earl of Essex and Sir Robert Cecil, and confesseth more than enough.

The office of Attorney-General is still vacant, and canvassed by the Earl of Essex for Mr. Francis Bacon, though the Lord Treasurer and Sir Robert Cecil favour Sir Edward Coke. As the Earl of Essex and Sir Robert returned back in a coach together, Sir Robert began to broach the matter of the Attorney-General, saying, 'My lord, the Queen has resolved e'er five days pass without any further delay to make an Attorney-General. I pray your lordship to let me know whom you will favour.'

The Earl answered that he wondered Sir Robert should ask him that question seeing that it could not be unknown to him that he favoured Francis Bacon.

'Good lord,' replied Sir Robert, 'I wonder your Lordship should go about to spend your strength in so unlikely or impossible a manner.'

After further talk passed between them, Sir Robert said, 'If at least your Lordship had spoken of the Solicitorship, that might be of easier digestion to her Majesty.'

Upon this the Earl answereth, 'Digest me no digestions; for the Attorneyship for Francis is that I must have, and in that will I spend all my power, might, authority and annuity, and with tooth and nail defend and procure the same for him against whosoever; and that whosoever getteth this office out of my hand for another, before he have it, it shall cost him the coming by, and of this be you assured of, Sir Robert, for now do I fully declare myself. And for your own part, Sir Robert, I think it strange both of my Lord Treasurer and you that can have the mind to seek the preference of a stranger before so near a kinsman. For if you weigh in a balance the parts every way of his competitor and him, only excepting five poor years of admitting to a house of court before Francis, you shall find in all other respects whatsoever, no comparison between them.'

THE CONFESSION OF PATRICK COLLEN.

Patrick Collen now declareth that Jacques had persuaded him to kill Antonio Perez, formerly the King of Spain's Secretary, which he undertook, whereupon Jacques gave him £30 in gold, for his voyage. He then departed immediately from Brussels for St. Omar, where he found an old priest to whom he confessed. The priest dissuaded him, saying that it was unlawful to commit murder; but next day Jacques took him to Father Holt who said that he might lawfully enterprise anything for the King's service, and, advising him to prepare himself to God, gave him absolution.

8th February. A RUMOUR OF THE QUEEN'S DEATH.

There is a rumour in London that the Queen is dead and hath been carried to Greenwich, but it is being kept very secret in Court.

11th February. CLERKE'S 'TRIAL OF BASTARDY.'

William Clerke's *The Trial of Bastardy* is entered, wherein are shown the civil and ecclesiastical laws of matrimony and legitimate issue, together with the statutes in marriage from the 25th year of Henry VIII.

17th February. PRECAUTIONS AGAINST SUSPICIOUS PERSONS.

Because of the dangers threatened at this time to the Queen's person, these special directions are proposed by the Lord Treasurer. Officers are to be appointed in every port that shall not suffer any person to land until examined as to the cause of his coming, and if the cause do not appear clear, he shall be committed to prison, or kept on board until his examinations have been taken and sent to the Council. It is especially likely that such persons will land at Dover, Sandwich, Rye, Gravesend, Yarmouth and London. Every Irishman in London or about the Court that is neither a known householder, nor a resident in commons, in any house, court or chamber as a servant, nor in service with a householder for five years past, must present himself to one of the Council or to the Lord Mayor to be examined how he lives and why he remains in England.

To restrain the great resort of unnecessary persons lodging near or frequenting the Court, the Lord Chamberlain shall appoint an usher and a quarter-waiter, with one or two clerks of the household, to attend and daily view all persons that offer to come to Court; and the Knight Harbinger and Marshal, with some tipstaffs, and, if need be, with the aid of some of the Yeomen of the Guard, shall twice or thrice a week discover who are lodged within two miles of Court; and if any are found not allowed they shall be examined, and if they cannot give just cause be committed to prison.

18th February. FERRARA DE GAMA'S CONFESSION.

Stephen Ferrara de Gama, being examined before the Earl of Essex, Sir Thomas Wilkes, and Mr. William Waad, hath declared that ten months since he received two letters from Dr. Lopez, written in his house in London to be delivered to Don Christophero de Moro. He wrote the letters from Lopez's lips wherein, though obscurely worded, he promised to do all the King required. He thinks that the Doctor would have poisoned the Queen had he been required. Andrada had said that Lopez was willing to poison both the Queen and Don Antonio; and afterwards Lopez said that Don Antonio should die the first illness that befel him.

20th February. THE ALCHEMIST'S BEQUEST.

Mr. Robert Smith hath received the Queen's reply to the letter from Roloff Peterson of Lubec and is to repair thither, deliver the letter, receive the glass bodies and bring them to the Queen; also to ascertain whether the materials therein were considered by Ouldfield to be brought to full perfection and, if anything be lacking, what it is; also to recover any books or papers of Ouldfield's relating thereto or others which treat of alchemy, also a secret *menstruum* without which the materials could hardly be brought to perfection. All these things are to be brought to the Queen.

21st February. A PROCLAMATION AGAINST VAGABONDS.

A proclamation is published for the suppressing of the multitude of idle vagabonds. On certain days in the week, monthly watchers and privy searchers shall be appointed to attach and imprison these idle vagabonds and to send the lamed into their counties according to the statute.

In the City of London, and about her Majesty, a great multitude repair, whereof some are men of Ireland that of late years have unnaturally served as rebels against her Majesty's forces beyond the seas, and cannot have any good meaning towards her, as is manifestly proved in some already taken. These men have secretly come into the realm, by procurement of the devil and his ministers, the Queen's enemies, to endanger her noble person. Such kind of persons are to be directly taken wheresoever they be found and proceeded withal as traitors. But as for the procurers and authors thereof, that are known to be of sundry conditions, some rebellious subjects, fugitives, some of the order of their priesthood yielding dispensation and shrifts to the intended mischiefs, some others more able by reward to hire the offenders, being persons of high degree in the world; the revenge thereof belonged to Almighty God in Whose hands the Queen had of long time reposed herself.

But seeing that the discovery of Irish traitors can hardly be made when so many other vagrants of that nation haunt about the Court, it is commanded that no person born in Ireland (except he be an householder known in some town, or a menial servant with some nobleman, gentleman or other honest householder, or resides, or is in commons, in any house of court or Chancery, as a student in the laws, or a student in any of the Universities, or sent out of Ireland by her Majesty's Deputy) do remain in this realm but repair without delay into the realm of Ireland to the place of his natural habitation, where he ought to live.

THE CONFESSION OF HUGH CAHILL.

Hugh Cahill, an Irishman, hath voluntarily confessed before Topcliffe that when at Brussels, Father Holt and others said it would be a most blessed thing to kill the Queen, as by it he would win Heaven, and become a saint if he should be killed; he that should do it would be chronicled for ever. He was advised to go to Court, and serve someone about the Queen's privy chamber, and then to waylay her in some progress and kill her with a sword and a dagger at a gate or narrow passage, or as she walked in one of her galleries. They promised him 100 crowns towards his charges, and 2000 more to be paid when he had killed her, and his pension augmented from 15 crowns a month to £30.

25th February. DR. LOPEZ.

There hath been a great consultation at the Lord Treasurer's about the persons apprehended for Dr. Lopez's plot; at which all now appears manifest, as well by the confessions of those taken as by the letters found of the others beyond the seas, whereby it is evident that this practice hath long continued, and that Lopez is no new traitor. Great expedition is being made to bring the affair before the public, but it seemeth that this cannot be done so soon as the Court desire, since the indictment must have many branches and there are many Spanish and other foreign letters to be translated and abstracted.

28th February. DR. LOPEZ ARRAIGNED.

This day Dr. Lopez was arraigned at the Guildhall before the Commission on which sit the Lord Mayor, the Earl of Essex, Lord Charles Howard, the Lord Admiral, Lord Buckhurst, Robert, Lord Rich, Sir Thomas Heneage, Vice-Chamberlain, Sir John Popham, Chief Justice of the Queen's Bench, Sir Robert Cecil, Sir John Fortescue, Chancellor of the Exchequer, and other persons of worth.

The case against Lopez was conducted by the Solicitor-General, Sir Edward Coke, who opened by showing that the grounds of all the plots against the Queen and the realm are not for any offence on her part, but for her constant defence of Christ's cause and His Holy Word against the Pope, and for protecting her dominions against the ambitions of the King of Spain. These were the original causes of the cursed bull of Pius V., and from this root sprung all the rebellions, treasons and devilish practices since attempted. After the 'Invincible Navy,' as they termed it, had been defeated by God and her Majesty's princely care and providence, and by the valiantness of her nobles and true subjects, the King of Spain and his priests, despairing of prevailing by valour, turned to cowardly treachery, and what they could not do by cannon, they attempted by crowns. To achieve this, have they put in practice three devilish attempts: to burn the navy and ships with poisoned fireworks; to seduce some of the nobility to rebellion; and to take the blood of a virgin Queen. To this end many needy and desperate young men are seduced by Jesuits and seminary priests with great rewards and promises to kill the Queen, being persuaded that it is glorious and meritorious, and that if they die in the action, they will inherit Heaven and be canonised as saints.

This Lopez, a perjured murdering traitor and Jewish Doctor, worse than Judas himself, undertook the poisoning, which was a plot more wicked, dangerous, and detestable than all the former. He is her Majesty's sworn servant, graced and advanced with many princely favours, used in special places of credit, permitted often access to her person, and so not suspected, especially by her who never feareth her enemies nor suspecteth her servants. The bargain was made and the price agreed upon, and the fact only deferred until payment of the money was assured. The letters of credit for his assurance were sent, but before they came to his hands, God most wonderfully and miraculously revealed and prevented it. The manner of it is as follows:

Some followers of Don Antonio, hoping to raise themselves by his fortunes, and finding his success not answerable to their expectations, grew discontented, and so became instruments to betray their master to the King of Spain, and practise any treason that could be devised, either against Don Antonio's state or the Queen's person. Lopez, outwardly pretending to favour Don Antonio, was a secret instrument for the King of Spain, and carried his actions therein more covertly under pretext of service for Don Antonio. He continued his secret course of intelligence with the King of Spain for many years by means of Emanuel Andrada, Bernardino Mendoza and others. Andrada wrote to Mendoza that he had won Lopez, but the letter being intercepted, Andrada was apprehended and committed. Lopez practised to have secret speech with Andrada before he was examined, and directed him what answer he was to make, insomuch that Andrada was released. These services were so acceptable to the King of Spain that he sent Lopez a jewel.

After this Andrada dealt with Lopez for poisoning the Queen. They had many conferences when Lopez undertook to do it, and directed them to signify this to Count Fuentes and to Stephen de Ibarra, the King's secretary. Andrada then went to Calais to convey intelligence between Lopez and the King of Spain and his Ministers; he told Ferrara de Gama that he might commit all things to Lopez, who hoped to do one great service to the King, and a remedy for Christendom, which was to poison the Queen, the King paying for it. Lopez and Ferrara afterwards conferred together, and Lopez undertook the poisoning for 50,000 crowns, which Ferrara signified by letters to Count Fuentes and Stephen de Ibarra. Ferrara, with the privity of Lopez, wrote to Christofero de Moro, assuring him of Lopez's affection to the King of Spain. Lopez also sent two packets of letters to Count Fuentes, de Moro and de Ibarra, wherein he promised to do all the King of Spain should command, and, since the King knew the business, as he told Ferrara, he made him write in obscure and covert words.

Lopez often asked if the money and answer were come, and

said he was ready to do the service. The money he was to receive at Antwerp, where he meant to go after the treason had been committed, and to this end he gave directions for a house to be prepared for him, intending afterwards to go and live at Constantinople.

Tinoco, who acted as go-between, was apprehended with the letters from the Count Fuentes and Ibarra, letters of credit for the money being found upon him, and, although Ferrara de Gama was then in prison, and examined long before and Tinoco since, without any conference with each other, both agreed in all things concerning the plotting of the treason. It is also to be observed that in handling of these treasons Lopez was so careful that he never wrote anything himself nor treated directly with Tinoco, but used Ferrara de Gama as a means between them. Nor did he ever discover any part of their proceedings or pretences to her Majesty or to any of the Council.

Being often charged with these treasons by his examiners, Lopez, with blasphemous oaths and horrible execrations, denied that he had ever had speech with any person or any understanding at all of any such matter, but then confessed that he had indeed spoken of it and promised it, but all to cozen the King of Spain. But when he saw that his intent and overt fact were apparent, the vile Jew said he had confessed talking of it, but belied himself only to save himself from racking.

At the bar Lopez said little in his own defence, but cried out that Ferrara and Emanuel were made up of nothing but fraud and lying. He had intended no hurt against the Queen, but abhorred the gifts of a tyrant; he had presented the jewel to the Queen that was sent by the Spaniard; and he had no other design in what he did but to deceive the Spaniard and wipe him of his money.

All these charges being plainly and fully proved by witnesses, by the intercepted letters, and by the confession of Lopez himself to the great satisfaction of the judge, jury and hearers, he is found guilty in the highest degree and judgment passed on him with universal applause.

5th March. 'A LOOKING GLASS FOR LONDON.'

A Looking Glass for London, a play written by Thomas Lodge and Robert Greene some years since, and played by the Lord

Strange's players, is to be printed, wherein is shown the story of the prophet Jonas and the repentance of the Ninevites.

6th March. THE CORONATION OF THE FRENCH KING.

The account of the anointing and crowning of the French King is at hand. The King, having been advised by the Princes of his blood, the Lords of his Council and other notable persons to frame himself to his anointing as other Kings his predecessors always used, would have wished the ceremony to be performed at Rheims; but in as much as the city of Rheims was still in possession of the rebels it was determined to hold the Coronation at the Church of Our Lady at Chartres. From the 17th February when the King entered the town to the day of the Coronation all the preparations were being finished.

Upon the 19th the Holy Vial, preciously preserved in the Abbey of Marmonster, near Tours, was brought to the City of Chartres, being conducted by the Lord of Souure, the Governor and King's Lieutenant-General in the land and Duchy of Tourraine, accompanied by four friars of the Abbey. Being arrived at Chartres, the vial was carried with great ceremony to St. Peter's Abbey, attended on by the clergy and a great number of people, the streets being hanged all the way in honour and reverence of so precious a relic.

Thither was brought the Imperial Close Crown, the Middle Crown, the Royal Sceptre, the Hand of Justice, the Cloak Royal, the Shirt, the Sandals, the Spurs, the Sword, the Tunicle, and the Dalmatic, with all the other ornaments royal, as fair and rich as might be, but they had to be newly made because the rebels had molten and defaced the others which time out of mind had been preserved in the Church of St. Denis.

Upon Saturday the 26th, at eight o'clock at night, the King came to the Church of Our Lady there to do his devotions and to be shriven.

On the 27th, about six in the morning, the King sent four Barons to fetch the Holy Vial from the Abbey of St. Peter's. The King having been escorted to the Church, the different ceremonies of the anointing were performed, after which the Bishop of Chartres, then subrogated for the Archbishop Duke of Rheims, delivered to the King the garments he was to wear above his doublet, that is the tunicle, representing a subdeacon, the dalmatick representing a deacon, and the cloak royal a priest. The King being thus clothed, the Bishop took again the plate whereupon lay the Holy Ointment, and laid some upon the palm of the King's hands, which being thus hallowed he laid them close upon his breast. After this the Bishop put on the Ring wherewith the King married the realm ; and then delivered him the Sceptre Royal and the Hand of Justice.

These things ended, the Lord Chancellor, standing against the Altar, and turning to the King, with a loud voice called the twelve peers according to their dignities, beginning first with the six lay peers. Then the Bishop rose from his chair, and turned to the High Altar from which he took the Close Crown and held it over the King's head, without touching it, whereto immediately all the peers temporal and spiritual set their hands to support it, the Bishop saying '*Coronet te Deus corona gloriae*,' etc. This prayer ended the Bishop set the crown upon the King's head.

All the other ceremonies being ended, Mass was celebrated, after which the King came forth arrayed in his royal garments, being received by the people with great acclamation and signs of joy.

13th March. DR. LOPEZ'S HEALTH.

Dr. Lopez hath kept his bed for the most part since his trial, and it is suspected that he practises by slow poison to prevent his execution. The trial of the other conspirators is fixed for to-morrow but the Lord Chief Justice is ill. It is much feared that if the trial be longer deferred, Lopez may die before his execution, and great dishonour and scandal ensue thereby.

14th March. LOPEZ'S ACCOMPLICES ARRAIGNED.

This day Emanuel Louis Tinoco and Stephen Ferrara de Gama, the Portuguese conspirators with Dr. Lopez, were brought before the Commissioners at the Guildhall to their trial. Tinoco was arraigned upon an indictment from his own confession :

That he had sent secret messages and intelligences to the King of Spain and his ministers of things treated in this realm in order that they might prepare their forces and direct their actions against the Queen ;

That Christoforo de Moro, one of the King's most secret counsellors, wrote letters to de Gama touching his service to the King and that Tinoco brought them to him in London;

That he came from Brussels to London to deliver a message and an embrace from the Count Fuentes, as also a credence from Andrada to Lopez for himself;

That he wrote word to Lopez that Count Fuentes had sent him a message and an embrace, and was glad that he was such a good servant to the King of Spain and that he should be liberally rewarded, requiring Lopez to procure the treaty of peace between the Queen and the King to be renewed as the King desired it; meaning by 'peace' her destruction by poison; which letters he delivered to Lopez;

That under a false name he had written letters to de Gama in obscure words, such as 'the bearer will tell you the price in which your pearls are held,' by which was meant the poisoning of the Queen, and by 'musk and amber' the burning of the Queen's ships.

That Count Fuentes told him on oath of secrecy that he had received order from the King of Spain to give Lopez whatever he required for poisoning the Queen, and that he delivered to de Gama in London several letters written by him in obscure words in the Spanish tongue concerning it, knowing their interests, which letters were found upon him when apprehended.

These matters being declared to him through a Portuguese interpreter he affirmed them from point to point, acknowledged his faults and called for mercy.

Stephen Ferrara de Gama being also indicted pleaded not guilty; but his former confessions and other proofs being produced against him, confessed all to be true; whereupon he also was convicted by judgment of the Court for imagining and compassing the death of the Queen.

26th March. ATHEISTICAL SPEECHES OF SIR WALTER RALEGH.

At Cerne Abbas in Dorsetshire, on the 21st, was held an inquiry by the High Commissioners in Causes Ecclesiastical concerning blasphemous and atheistical speeches made by some in these parts. It is declared by several witnesses that Sir

Walter Ralegh, his brother, Mr. Carew Ralegh, and Mr. Harriott of their household, are much subjected to atheism, also one Allen, Lieutenant of Portland Castle. This Allen tore two leaves out of a Bible to dry tobacco on, and spoke as if he denied the immortality of the soul, saying, on an occasion when he was like to die and one persuaded him to make himself ready to God for his soul, that he would carry his soul up to the top of a hill, and 'Run God, run Devil, fetch it that will have it.'

Of Sir Walter and his brother, one witness, being the parson of Weeke Regis, declareth that some three years past on coming to Blandford his horse was stayed and taken for a post horse by Sir Walter and Mr. Carew Ralegh. When he entreated to have his horse released to ride home to his charge, from whence he had been some time absent, to preach there next day, being Sunday, Mr. Carew Ralegh replied that he might go home when he would but his horse should preach before him.

Some months before, at Sir George Trenchard's table, at which there were also present Sir Ralph Horsey, Lord Lieutenant of the County of Dorset, Sir Walter Ralegh, Mr. Carew Ralegh, Ralph Ironside, minister of Winterbottom, and others, Mr. Carew Ralegh uttered some loose speeches and was rebukèd by Sir Ralph Horsey. Whereupon turning to the minister he demanded what danger he might incur by such speeches.

To which Mr. Ironside answered, 'The wages of sin is death.' Whereunto Mr. Ralegh making light of death as common to all, sinner and righteous, the minister inferred further that 'As life which is the gift of God through Jesus Christ is life eternal, so that death which is properly the wages of sin is death eternal, both of the body and of the soul also.'

'Soul,' quoth Mr. Ralegh, 'what is that ?'

'Better it were,' answered Mr. Ironside, 'that we should be careful how the soul might be saved than to be curious in finding out its essence.'

Sir Walter then requested that the minister would answer the question that had been proposed by his brother ; 'I have been,' quoth he, 'a scholar some time in Oxford, I have answered under a bachelor of art, and had talk with divines, yet hitherunto in this point (to wit, what the reasonable soul of man is) have I not by any been resolved.'

The dispute was then continued until Sir Walter wished that grace might be said; 'for that,' said he, 'is better than this disputation.'

30th March. GREAT STORMS.

This month there have been great storms of wind, that overturn trees, steeples, barns and houses; in Beaulieu forest in Worcestershire, many oaks are uprooted, and on the Thursday before Palm Sunday, more than fifteen hundred in Horton Wood. In the town of Stafford the steeple is thrown down, and a thousand pound's worth of damage done to the roof. In Cankewood more than three thousand trees overthrown, and some fifty other steeples in Staffordshire fallen.

31st March. DEATH OF SIR JOHN BURGH.

Sir John Burgh, that took the great carrack, hath been slain in a duel by Mr. John Gilbert, after various letters had passed between them. Sir John first challenged his adversary to meet him at five o'clock in the morning between Charing Cross and Hyde Park, with dagger and rapier, and accompanied only by one gentleman of good quality, or alone. No treachery would be used; let him not therefore use any boyish excuses or delays as he did the last time he sent to him, or else he would pick out a time to beat him like a boy.

To this Mr. Gilbert replied that he would fight, but that the time, place, and manner of the meeting, and the weapons belonged to the challenged.

4th April. THE QUEEN'S BOUNTY TO MR. WILLIAM CAMDEN.

The Queen, having used the services of Mr. William Camden, schoolmaster, in things wherein he has attained skill and intending to employ him again, desireth him to be settled somewhere near her, and eased of the charge of living. She hath required the Dean of Westminster to admit Mr. Camden to the table of the Dean and prebends, and allow him diet for one service; this to be granted for life. The grant she will have sent to her that she may herself present it to Mr. Camden as a token of her gratitude.

6th April. PLAYS AT THE ROSE THEATRE.

The Queen's men and the Earl of Sussex's men have begun to play together at the Rose Theatre and during this week play *Friar Bacon*, *The Rangers' Comedy*, *The Jew of Malta*, *The Fair Maid of Italy*, *Friar Bacon* and *King Leir*.

9th April. PLAYS AT THE ROSE THEATRE.

Yesterday *The Jew of Malta* and to-day *King Leir* are played at the Rose Theatre.

11th April. A GREAT RAINSTORM.

The rain hath continued very sore for more than twenty-four hours long and withal such a wind from the north as pierces the walls of houses be they never so thick.

16th April. DEATH OF THE EARL OF DERBY.

Ferdinando Stanley, the young Earl of Derby, that hath been sick of some strange sickness these eleven days, is dead at Latham. Outwardly his diseases were vomiting of sour or rusty matter with blood, the yellow jaundice, melting of his fat, swelling and hardness of his spleen, a vehement hiccough, and, for four days before he died, stopping of his water. All these were caused in the opinion of his physicians partly by surfeit, partly by the excessive exercise that he took for four days together in Easter week. In all the time of his sickness, which began on the 5th April and continued until he died, he often took Beza's stone and Unicorn's horn; his pulse was always good but his strength indifferent, the number of his vomits being fifty-two and of his stools twenty-nine. His death is so unaccountable that many begin to suspect that he was bewitched. In the beginning of his sickness he had strange dreams. On the 10th April, Mr. Halsall, one of his gentlemen, found in my lord's chamber about midnight an image of wax with hair in colour like his hair twisted round the belly. This image was spotted and soon after spots appeared also upon the Earl's sides and belly. Mr. Halsall hastily cast the image in the fire before it was viewed by others, thinking that by burning it he should relieve his lord of the witchcraft and burn the witch who so much tormented him; but unhappily it fell out the contrary for after the melting of the image the Earl declined.

A homely woman about the age of fifty years was found mumbling in a corner of his chamber. She seemed often to ease his lordship both of vomiting and hiccough, but it was noted that whenever he was so eased she herself was much troubled in the same way, and the matter which she vomited was like that which passed from him. But at the last, one of the doctors, spying her tempering and blessing the juice of certain herbs tumbled her pot down and rated her from the chamber. The Earl himself cried out in all his sickness that the doctors laboured in vain because he was certainly bewitched. During this last illness the Bishop of Chester and his chaplain, Mr. Lee, were with him.

18th April. LOPEZ EXECUTION POSTPONED.

The execution of Lopez, Ferrara, and Tinoco, that was fixed for to-morrow morning at 9 o'clock is by the Queen's orders stayed, to the great discontent of the commissioners and the people who much expect it.

23rd April. ST. GEORGE'S DAY. FOREIGN ORDERS.

There is great press of the people at Court, though very few Knights of the Garter; the Lord Treasurer being unable to go in the procession because of his foot. The Queen is reported to be very angry with Sir Anthony Shirley and Sir Nicholas Clifford for having accepted the Order of St. Michael from the French King, first because they took it without her privity, and next for that they took the whole oath, one part whereof is to defend the Mass while they live.

GIBBON'S 'PRAISE OF A GOOD NAME.'

Mr. Charles Gibbon hath written *The Praise of a Good Name* in answer to certain slanders made against him, being a collection of apothegms, epigrams, and pithy sayings in praise of a good name, and of brief essays showing the reproach of an ill name.

29th April. LADY BRANCH BURIED.

The Lady Helen Branch, wife first of John Minors, citizen and grocer of London, secondly of Sir John Branch, was buried, having died on the 10th of the month in the ninetieth year of her life. Her funerals were very honourably furnished, and accompanied by the Lord Mayor, many mourners, doctors, gentlemen, and kinsfolk, honourable ladies, servants and poor men. In honour of these ceremonies, an *Epicedium* is printed, being a sequence of twelve sonnets describing her life, wherein the author invoketh our living poets:

You that to shew your wits have taken toil,
In registering the deeds of noble men,
And sought for matter in a foreign soil,
(As worthy subjects of your silver pen)
Whom you have raised from dark oblivion's den;
You that have writ of chaste Lucretia,
Whose death was witness of her spotless life,
Or penned the praise of fair Cornelia,
Whose blameless name hath made her name so rife,
As noble Pompey's most renowned wife,
  Hither unto your home direct your eyes,
  Whereas unthought on much more water lies.

For her obsequies Joshua Sylvester also hath written *Monodia*, an Elegy in commemoration of the virtuous life and godly death of the right worshipful and most religious lady, Dame Helen Branch.

THE GROWTH OF POPERY.

It is said by some that for all the dangers of Catholics and their narrow sifting, infinite numbers run daily into the Church and are reconciled to the Catholic faith. Good men, making no account of losing their lives, hazard themselves to save men's souls; and even in the Court there are as many Masses said daily as in any country abroad.

1st May. SIR JOHN SMYTHE'S 'INSTRUCTIONS, OBSERVATIONS AND ORDERS MILITARY.'

A book called *Instructions, Observations and Orders Military*, written in 1591 by Sir John Smythe, is now printed. Herein is shown the reducing of single bands of horsemen or footmen into their simple or single order of ranks from point to point, and how to draw out many troops into squadrons and battles formed, as well to march into the field as to give battle with most advantages. As for those that allege new or old fashions used by such or such nations in matters military without reasons or allowable experience to fortify and confirm them, these Sir John holdeth for vain and frivolous. To those that think a far greater number of archers are not able to encounter a smaller number of musketeers, he answereth that their opinion proceedeth of nothing else but from their lack of understanding and knowing the wonderful imperfections and failings that belong to muskets and musketeers in the field by reason of the heaviness of their pieces; nor are harquebusiers of greater advantage, being more uncertain of their aim so that if they discharge at ten, eleven, or twelve score paces distant at the archers, it will be found that in ten thousand of their shot they would not hit so many as ten archers.

2nd May. 'THE TAMING OF A SHREW.'

The play of *A Pleasant conceited History called the Taming of a Shrew*, is to be printed, a play that was sundry times acted by the Earl of Pembroke's players.

3rd May. GREAT FLOODS.

Yesterday in Sussex and Surrey there came down great water floods by reason of sudden showers of hail and rain that have fallen, which bare down houses, iron-mills, the provision of coals prepared for the mills, and carried away cattle.

SIR NICHOLAS CLIFFORD AND THE ORDER OF ST. MICHAEL.

Sir Nicholas Clifford, that was imprisoned in the Tower for receiving the order of St. Michael from the French King, finding that his former letters to the Queen are received with displeasure hath now sent her the order to be disposed as she considereth best, and petitioneth for enlargement.

9th May. SHAKESPEARE'S 'THE RAPE OF LUCRECE.'

The Rape of Lucrece, a poem written by William Shakespeare, is entered, and dedicated, as was his *Venus and Adonis*, to the Earl of Southampton. In the dedication the poet toucheth upon the favours which he hath received. 'The warrant I have of your honourable disposition, not the worth of my untutored lines makes it assured of acceptance. What I have done is yours; what I have to do is yours; being part in all I have devoted yours. Were my worth greater my duty would show greater.' This poem telleth of the ravishing of the chaste Lucrece by the tyrant Tarquin, and of his everlasting banishment therefor.

Lucrece's Invocation to Night.

'O comfort-killing Night, image of hell!
Dim register and notary of shame!
Black stage for tragedies and murders fell!
Vast sin-concealing chaos! nurse of blame!
Blind muffled bawd! dark harbour for defame!
Grim cave of death! whispering conspirator
With close-tongu'd treason and the ravisher!

'O hateful, vaporous, and foggy Night!
Since thou art guilty of my cureless crime,
Muster thy mists to meet the eastern light,
Make war against proportion'd course of time;
Or if thou wilt permit the sun to climb
His wonted height, yet ere he go to bed,
Knit poisonous clouds about his golden head.

'With rotten damps ravish the morning air;
Let their exhal'd unwholesome breaths make sick
The life of purity, the supreme fair,
Ere he arrive his weary noontide prick;
And let thy misty vapours march so thick,
That in their smoky ranks his smother'd light
May set at noon and make perpetual night.

'Were Tarquin Night, as he is but Night's child,
The silver-shining queen he would distain;
Her twinkling handmaids too, by him defil'd,
Through Night's black bosom should not peep again;
So should I have co-partners in my pain;
And fellowship in woe doth woe assuage,
As palmers' chat makes short their pilgrimage.

'Where now I have no one to blush with me,
To cross their arms and hang their heads with mine,
To mask their brows and hide their infamy;
But I alone alone must sit and pine,
Seasoning the earth with showers of silver brine,
Mingling my talk with tears, my grief with groans,
Poor wasting monuments of lasting moans.

'O Night! thou furnace of foul-reeking smoke,
Let not the jealous Day behold that face
Which underneath thy black all-hiding cloak
Immodestly lies martyr'd with disgrace:
Keep still possession of thy gloomy place,
  That all the faults which in thy reign are made
  May likewise be sepulchred in thy shade.'

14th May. GREENE'S 'FRIAR BACON.'

The play of *The Honourable History of Friar Bacon and Friar Bungay*, written some years before by Robert Greene and played by the Queen's players, is to be printed, containing the story of the wooing of Margaret, the keeper's daughter of Fressingfield, by Lacy, Earl of Lincoln, and of Friar Bacon's Brazen Head.

16th May. PLAYING RESUMED.

The Admiral's men that were forced to travel through the inhibition on playing during the plague are returned to the Rose where they play *The Jew of Malta*, *The Ranger's Comedy* and *Cutlack*.

17th May. MARLOWE'S 'JEW OF MALTA.'

There is entered for the printing the famous *Tragedy of the rich Jew of Malta*, written some years since by Christopher Marlowe and now being played at the Rose Theatre. To this play the ghost of Machiavel as prologue beginneth:

Albeit the world think Machiavel is dead,
Yet was his soul but flown beyond the Alps,
And now the Guise is dead is come from France
To view this land, and frolic with his friends.
To some perhaps my name is odious,
But such as love me guard me from their tongues,
And let them know that I am Machiavel,
And weigh not men, and therefore not men's words;
Admired I am of those that hate me most.
Though some speak openly against my books,
Yet will they read me and thereby attain
To Peter's chair; and when they cast me off,
Are poisoned by my climbing followers.
I count religion but a childish toy
And hold there is no sin but ignorance.

The Prologue endeth:

I come not, I,
To read a lecture here in Britain,
But to present the tragedy of a Jew,
Who smiles to see how full his bags are cram'd,
Which money was not got without my means.
I crave but this; grace him as he deserves,
And let him not be entertained the worse
Because he favours me.

30th May. DRAYTON'S 'IDEA'S MIRROR.'

Mr. Michael Drayton hath sent to the press his *Idea's Mirror*, containing fifty-one sonnets or amours, being dedicated to the dear child of the Muses, and his ever kind Mecenas, Mr. Anthony Cooke, Esquire.

3rd June. THE DEATH OF THE BISHOP OF LONDON.

This day John Aylmer, Bishop of London, died at Fulham.

THE PLAYERS OF THE LORD ADMIRAL AND THE LORD CHAMBERLAIN UNITE.

The Lord Chamberlain's players have also returned to London and join with the Admiral's men to play together at the little theatre in Newington Butts.

7th June. LOPEZ, TINOCO AND FERRARA EXECUTED.

This day Roderick Lopez, with the two other Portuguese, was executed. They were conveyed from the Tower of London by the Lieutenant to the Old Swan, and thence by water to Westminster, where being brought before the King's Bench Bar, the Lieutenant was called to bring in his prisoners, which he then delivered and was discharged of them.

Then it was declared to them by the Court how they had been charged with high treason against the Queen, had been tried, found guilty, and had received judgment; wherefore it was demanded of them what they could say for themselves that they should not suffer death accordingly. Whereunto one of the Portuguese began in his own language to tell a long tale, but was willed to be short, to which he answered that it could not be done without circumstances. Whereupon he was willed to hold his peace. The second answered by a writing in his own language, which being read by an interpreter, the Attorney General bade stay for it was not true. Lopez in English made his submission, affirming that he never thought harm to her Majesty.

Then the Marshal of the King's Bench was called and charged with the prisoners to convey them to the prison of the King's Bench and there to deliver them to the Sheriffs of London with a writ to see them executed. So they were conveyed by water from Westminster to the Bishop of Winchester's stairs in Southwark, from thence to the King's Bench, there laid upon hurdles and conveyed to the Sheriff of London over the bridge, up to Leadenhall, and so to Tyburn.

At the gallows Lopez declared that he loved the Queen as well as he loved Jesus Christ, which coming from a man of the Jewish profession moved no small laughter in the standers-by.

8th June. PLAYS OF THE WEEK.

The plays at Newington Butts this last week are *Hester and Assuerus*, *The Jew of Malta*, *Titus Andronicus*, *Cutlack*.

15th June. PLAYS OF THE WEEK.

The plays at Newington Butts this past week are *Bellendon* (for the first time), *Hamlet*, *Hester and Assuerus*, *The Taming of the Shrew*, *Titus Andronicus*, *The Jew of Malta*.

18th June. LYLY'S 'MOTHER BOMBY.'

Mother Bomby, a play formerly written by Mr. John Lyly, and sundry times played by the Children of Paul's, is entered for printing.

19th June. 'THE TRUE TRAGEDY OF RICHARD THE THIRD.'

The play of *The True Tragedy of Richard the Third*, that used to be played by the Queen's players, is to be printed; wherein is shown the death of Edward the Fourth, with the smothering of the two young Princes in the Tower; the lamentable end of Shore's wife, an example for all wicked women; and lastly the conjunction and joining of the two noble houses of Lancaster and York.

21st June. THE SPANIARDS AT BREST.

From the west Sir Walter Ralegh hath received trustworthy intelligence of the strength of the Spanish Fleet and its readiness to sail. It seemeth likely that some surprise is intended, for the carpenters and all others about the fleet work on the Sabbath Day, which is confirmed by the hugeness of the ships, that will carry many soldiers, since smaller vessels are far fitter for the coast of Brittany. At Brest, the Spaniards, having received no impediment, have finished the fortification of Old Croyzon, within the port, and, the better to command the haven, have also built a strong place at the very entrance. Now that Blavet and Belle Isle are theirs, there will be no entrance for the Queen's fleet. Their ships are huge, eight being between 800 and 1000 tons, two others of good burden, and divers galleys, full filled with soldiers.

22nd June. THE CHAMBERLAIN'S BREAK WITH THE ADMIRAL'S.

The Chamberlain's men have broken with the Admiral's and go to play at James Burbage's house, the Theatre, in Shoreditch. Their chief players now are Richard Burbage, Will Kemp, the Clown, William Shakespeare, Thomas Pope, John Heminges, Augustine Phillips and George Bryan. The Admiral's, with Edward Alleyn, are returned to the Rose, where they played this week *Bellendon* (twice), *Cutlack*, *The Ranger's Comedy*, *The Massacre at Paris*; with Alleyn go John Singer, Richard Jones, Thomas Towne, Martin Slaughter, Edward Juby, Thomas Dutton and James Dunstan.

26th June. THE FUNERAL OF THE BISHOP OF LONDON.

This day John Aylmer, Bishop of London, was solemnly interred in his cathedral church of St. Paul before St. Thomas' Chapel.

THE CHARACTER OF BISHOP AYLMER.

Bishop Aylmer was a man but mean of stature, yet in his youth very valiant, which he forgot not in his age. No bishop was more persecuted and taunted by the Puritans than he was by libels, by scoffs, by open railing and privy backbiting. The story is well known of what passed between him and one Mr. Madox, a Puritan; for when the bishop had reproved him about some matter and he answered somewhat untowardly and overthwartly, the bishop (as he was ingenious ever) said unto him, 'Thy very name expresseth thy nature, for *Madox* is thy name, and thou art as mad a beast as ever I talked with.' The other not long to seek of an answer, 'By your favour, sir,' said he, 'your deeds answer your name righter than mine; for your name is *Elmar*, and you have *marred* all the *elms* in Fulham by lopping them.'

He used for recreation to bowl in a garden; and Martin Marprelate thence takes this taunting scoff, that the bishop would cry, 'Rub, rub, rub,' to his bowl, and when it was gone too far, say, 'the devil go with it'; and then, saith Martin, the bishop would follow.

When there was talk of dangers and rumours of war and invasion, then he was commonly chosen to preach in the Court, and he would do it in so cheerful a fashion as not only showed he had courage, but would put courage in others. 'Here is much doubt,' saith he, 'of *malum sub Aquilone*, and our coal-prophets have prophesied that *in exaltatione Lunae Leo jungetur Leonae*. The astronomers tell of a watery trigon; that great inundations of water foreshow insurrections of people and downfall of princes; but as long as Virgo is the ascendant with us we need fear of nothing; *Deus nobiscum, quis contra nos?*' And for this the Queen would much commend him; yet would she not remove him. It is noted as an ill fortune of his to have died Bishop of London, which eight before him in one hundred have not done, but been either preferred or deprived.

27th June. PLAYS OF THE WEEK.

The plays at the Rose Theatre this past week are *The Ranger's Comedy*, *The Jew of Malta*, *Cutlack* (twice), *The Massacre at Paris*, *Galiaso*.

5th July. VIOLENCE IN WESTMINSTER.

To-day Mr. Edmund Wilton, was sitting in the parlour of Nicholas Nelson in Westminster, when Mr. George Barton, with a drawn dagger and a curtleaxe assaulted him, furiously throwing the dagger at him. Thereupon Mr. Wilton withdrew himself to a corner of the parlour, but Mr. Barton followed with drawn sword intending to have slain him. But his adversary coming between him and the door, Mr. Wilton turned and defended himself with his sword, and in self-defence gave Mr. Barton a mortal blow of which he instantly died.

6th July. PLAYS OF THE WEEK.

The plays this week at the Rose Theatre are *The Jew of Malta*, *Bellendon* (twice), *The Massacre at Paris*, *Cutlack*, *The Ranger's Comedy*.

12th July. SIDNEY SUSSEX COLLEGE IN CAMBRIDGE FOUNDED.

A licence is granted to the Earl of Kent and Sir John Harington, the executors of Frances, Countess of Sussex, to erect a college, to be called Sidney Sussex College in Cambridge University, to consist of a master, ten fellows, and twenty scholars.

13th July. PLAYS OF THE WEEK.

Plays at the Rose Theatre this week : *The Massacre at Paris*, *Philipo and Hippolito* (twice), *The Jew of Malta*, *Bellendon*, *Galiaso*.

15th July. CRUELTY IN PORTUGAL.

Certain merchants coming from Lisbon report that recently the chief Commander of the galleys invited three score and upwards of the chiefest of the city of Lisbon to a banquet aboard the galleys. After much feasting and triumph, having tricked them to sport down the river, he showed them a commandment he had received from the King to execute them all ; which was immediately carried out. They were all beheaded ; their bodies being taken back to Lisbon and their heads carried with speed to the King of Spain. The cause alleged for this murder is that letters were intercepted wherein they had intelligence with England.

16th July. SOLDIERS FOR BREST.

Three thousand soldiers and 50 pioneers are to be sent into Brittany to seize Brest, where the King of Spain is making fortifications. The pioneers are to be raised by Sir Walter Ralegh in Cornwall and ready to embark at Plymouth on 5th August.

20th July. THE SPANISH PREPARATIONS.

Sir Walter Ralegh reporteth that the recent news of the Spanish preparations seem to be confirmed, for within the last week three great Spanish men-of-war have given chase to an English ship and her two prizes, driving them even to the very mouth of Dartmouth. All the Newfoundland men are like to be taken by them if they be not speedily driven from the coast, for the Newfoundland fleet is expected at the beginning of August, above 100 sail. If these are lost it will be the greatest blow ever given to England.

PLAYS OF THE WEEK.

At the Rose this last week *Cutlack*, *The Massacre at Paris*, *The Ranger's Comedy*, *Philipo and Hippolito*, *The Second Part of Godfrey of Bulloigne*, *Belendon*.

21st July. CAPTAIN DAWTRY'S OFFER TO LEAD AN IRISH REGIMENT.

A certain Captain Dawtry, one on whom an Irish pension has been conferred, hath written to Sir Robert Cecil asking to be entrusted to fetch a regiment of 1500 or 2000 trained soldiers of Irish birth out of Ireland to serve the Queen in the expedition to Brittany, which will bring commodity to her and her whole dominions. She will leave at home, saith he, many of her people of England to reserve their lives until further necessity. She will disarm her ill disposed subjects of Ireland whose unnatural mutinies and rebellions are supported by these trained soldiers. They will win more spoil on the enemy than thrice as many soldiers of any other nation, for there are no better soldiers on earth than they, either for the use of their weapons or the strength of their bodies and minds, being such seasoned men of war that they can endure all fortunes, and keep their health when others with a little extremity will lie by the wall. Lastly, if they live, the Queen is like to be well served by them ; if they die, she will be better served, for it is a pity they should ever go back again into their own country so long as she hath any employment for soldiers. If he may have this charge and lay down his opinion of the Captains, he will answer for their true and faithful behaviour.

25th July. THE EARL OF ESSEX NOT ALLOWED TO GO TO BREST.

The expedition to Brest being finally resolved, the Earl of Essex is eager to go, but the Queen using very gentle words to him says that his desire to be in action and give further proof of his valour and prowess is to be liked and highly commended ;

but she loveth him and her realm too much to hazard his person in any lesser action than that which shall import her crown and state, and therefore willeth him to be content, giving him a warrant for £4000 and saying, 'Look to thyself, good Essex, and be wise to help thyself, without giving thy enemies advantage; and my hand shall be readier to help thee than any other.'

26th July. John Boste, a Jesuit, Executed.

John Boste, a Jesuit, was executed for high treason at Durham on the 24th. When he was taken from prison towards the place of execution, more than three hundred ladies and women of good position, all with black hoods, set out to follow him, and being asked where they were going, they answered, 'To accompany that gentleman, that servant of God, to his death, as the Maries did Christ.' A minister offered to dispute with them by the way, but a horseman came up and pushed him away, crying, 'Begone, knave, Mr. Boste has shown himself a true gentleman and a true man.'

Having come to the scaffold, he kissed the ladder and mounting the first step, said, '*Angelus ad Mariam dixit: Ave gratia plena: Dominus tecum Benedicta tu in mulieribus.*' On the second, '*Verbum caro factum est, et habitavit in nobis,*' at the third, '*Ecce ancilla Domini, fiat mihi secundum verbum tuum.*' Turning to the people, as he began to speak he was told that he came not to preach but to die.

'At least,' quoth he, 'you will allow me to thank these ladies and gentlemen who have done me the honour and kindness to accompany me to-day. Although I am now to be deprived of life, my blood withal and death and innocence shall preach in the hearts of those whom God will call and gather to His Holy Catholic Church. My head and quarters will preach every day on your gates and walls the truth of the Catholic Faith.'

Then he placed himself in prayer for a short while, and, as it were awakening, asked leave to recite the 114th Psalm, '*Dilexi quoniam,*' then returning thanks to God, he ended by saying that God had given him grace to die for the Catholic Roman Church, 'outside of which,' he declared, 'believe me, brethren (for this is not the time to dissemble nor to lie), it is impossible to enter unto the Kingdom of Heaven.'

27th July. DISORDERS AT THE PORT OF IPSWICH.

The officers of the port of Ipswich report that divers woodmongers buy up most of the wood and charcoal in Suffolk and Essex, and, under cover of loading it for London and elsewhere, convey it by themselves and in Flemish hoys into Flanders and Zealand; and in their loading sometimes they cunningly lay under their wood, corn, butter and tallow. When the searcher found this out, they altogether refused to come to the Customs Houses to enter the same.

Divers of them, when the officers rode ten miles out to view their loading, falsely affirmed that they were loaden with her Majesty's wood, and such was their obstinacy that they refused to be brought into order. At Harwich of late the searcher's deputy was cast overboard in performance of his duty.

PLAYS OF THE WEEK.

The plays at the Rose this past week are *The Jew of Malta*, *Galiaso*, *Philipo and Hippolito*, *Godfrey of Bulloigne*, *The Massacre at Paris*.

1st August. A PROCLAMATION CONCERNING PRIZES.

A proclamation is issued against those that disorderly enter with ships brought as prizes into any haven, and secretly buy or convey away the goods before they can be customed and allowed as lawful prizes. For the reformation of this frequent abuse, all who go aboard any prizes, or buy, bargain, or receive any goods from the prizes, or from any of the company, shall not only forfeit his goods, but he and the seller be committed to prison, there to remain until order shall be given from the Lords of the Privy Council for their release. And for the better preventing of these disorders, it is commanded that immediately upon the coming in of any prizes from the seas, some of the officers of the Custom House of the port shall go aboard, and remain aboard quietly without any interruption or resistance of the captain, owner, master or mariners until the ship be discharged.

4th August. PLAYS OF THE WEEK.

The plays at the Rose Theatre this past week: *Cutlack*, *The Merchant of Emden*, *Bellendon*, *The Ranger's Comedy*, *Philipo and Hippolito*, *Galiaso*.

8th August. PLATT'S 'JEWEL HOUSE OF NATURE.'

There is entered for printing *The Jewel House of Art and Nature*, brought together by Mr. Hugh Platt, of Lincoln's Inn. In the first book are set down more than a hundred new and conceited experiments, such as to write a letter secretly, to walk safely upon a high scaffold without any danger of falling, to fetch out any stain, the art of memory, one candle to make as great a light as two or three, to close the chops of green timber, to speak by signs only, to refresh the colours of old oil pictures, and many others. To prevent drunkenness, he adviseth to drink a good large draught of salad oil, for that will float upon the wine which you shall drink and suppress the spirits from ascending into the brain.

The second book entreateth of sundry new sorts of soil or marl for the better manuring of pasture or arable ground; the third containeth divers chemical conclusions concerning the art of distillation; the fourth the art of casting and moulding; the last part is an offer of certain new inventions which the author will be ready to disclose upon reasonable consideration, being a new kind of fire in the form of balls made partly of seacoal; a vessel of wood to brew in; a bolting hutch; a portable pump; a wholesome, lasting and fresh victual for the navy; a speedy way for the inning of any breach; a light garment yet sufficient against all rainy weather; and a new conceit in peter works.

10th August. PLAYS OF THE WEEK.

The plays at the Rose Theatre this past week are *The Jew of Malta* (twice), *The Second Part of Godfrey of Bulloigne*, *Philipo and Hippolito*, *The Massacre at Paris*, *Cutlack*.

17th August. PLAYS OF THE WEEK.

This last week at the Rose the plays are *Bellendon*, *Tasso's Melancholy*, *Galiaso*, *Godfrey of Bulloigne*, *Mahomet*, *Philipo and Hippolito*.

19th August. CAPTAIN GLEMHAM'S EXPLOITS IN THE LEVANT SEAS.

News is published of all that befell Captain Edward Glemham since his departure from London in February 1593, whence he sailed with his ship the *Galleon Constance* to meet the rest of his company at Dartmouth. So many were the storms in the spring of last year that not until the 17th of April did he leave the English coast, being separated three days later from the others who believed him to have been cast away in the Gulf. Thence they made their way to Santa Cruz where, finding many other English ships, they refreshed themselves, and were joined by the *Tiger* and the *Elizabeth of Plymouth*, two of their company.

After meeting with several of the enemy it was concluded at length that they should make for Algiers. Here the King entertained them in the best manner, and to show the General what extraordinary favour he could, he came aboard to see the ship. Whereon the General prepared a sumptuous banquet, for which he would not stay, but taking a small repast of such confections as the General had brought for his store at sea he departed, being presented with a cup of silver, double gilt, a fair quilt of Damask with his arms embroidered and a purse, richly wrought, with fifty double pistolets. All of which the King thankfully received, and at the General's departure gave him under his hand and seal free liberty to sell, exchange, carry over and recarry at his pleasure all such goods as he or any of his should bring for his port, without any manner of let or disturbance.

The company then set sail from Algiers to attempt some prize, but though they fought very valiantly with several of the enemy all escaped them, and at length for lack of victual they were obliged to put back to Algiers where they found that the King had seized the ship *Examiner* of their consort, imprisoning the Captain and owner and the company. Whereupon the General immediately went to the King demanding the cause of this vile dealing with his company; but he subtlely smiling on the General gave him good speeches and mused on his choler, saying that he wondered to hear him speak so rashly and unadvisedly to him being in so great authority. After some further parley, the General seeing he could have no answer of his business to his content, departed in fury without bidding farewell but leaving him to the devil whom they served. The next day the King sent to have the General's sails taken ashore. Upon hearing thereof the General commanded his companies that were ashore to repair on board, caused his ship to be provided, his nettings laced, and his ordnance all out, resolutely determined to sink there. But at length a composition was offered and the Englishmen and Flemings that were in prison were released.

But soon afterward other misfortune befell them. While the men were still in prison one of the chiefest men of the French leaguer who was consul in that place entered the prison where they were and began to abuse in most opprobrious terms the name of the Queen. Thereafter two of the Englishmen chanced to meet this Frenchman, and remembering his words, for lack of a weapon began to beat him with their fists, and the quarrel was taken up by others.

When the French Consul heard of it, he went immediately to the King with his complaint, who sent for the General. But he being advertised of the truth by one of his followers made answer that if the quarrel were such as was reported, he would kill him with his own hands that should not offer with his life to maintain the honour of his Mistress, whose match the world afforded not. After further talk the Consul offered his handkerchief to the General's face who was so moved thereat that he struck him over the face with his fist, and craved of the King to grant him the combat against the Consul. But the King, who had received abundance of gold from the Frenchman would not allow it and dismissed them for that night.

About eight o'clock the next morning the King sent for the General and the men who had begun the brawl, and caused the men to receive the bastinado and the General to be committed prisoner, threatening that if he did not become friends with the Consul, he should lose his hand. The General dreading naught his threats refused, but his company came to him and on their knees besought him to tender both his own estate and theirs, for on his welfare depended all their goods. So likewise his especial friend Mr. Benedick Winter pleaded with him, to whom he yielded. Then being sent for by the King he made friends with the Consul who ever afterward showed wonderful great kindness and pleasure to the General and all his company. And so, after many troubles, on the first of February, 1594 they departed the road towards the bottom of the Straits to seek their better fortunes: and from that time they engaged many times with enemy but without success until the 8th of May, when they met with the London fleet by whom news was brought of Captain Glemham's actions.

20th August. THE LADY BRIDGET MANNERS.

The Queen is much incensed at hearing of the marriage of the Lady Bridget Manners, one of her favourite ladies-in-waiting, that took place in the country without her consent.

Two months since, the Countess of Rutland, the Lady's mother, concluded with the executors of Mr. Tyrwhitt for the wardship of his young son, and in July wrote asking that her Majesty would allow her daughter to visit her, whom she had not seen these five years. The Queen having given her consent, the Lady Bridget returned home to her mother and in a short while after is wedded to Mr. Tyrwhitt.

Now that the marriage is known, the Queen is especially enraged with the Countess, refusing to believe that she could be ignorant of it, for the marriage was in her own house, and by her own chaplain, nor will she believe that the Lady Bridget is so undutiful a daughter to have adventured so great a breach of duty without her mother's acquaintance and consent had first been obtained. Her Majesty has therefore ordered that Mr. Tyrwhitt and his wife be sent to London, the former to be committed to prison, the latter, by her favour, not imprisoned but put in custody of some lady.

A PLOT TO KILL THE QUEEN.

Captain Edmund Yorke, a prisoner, son of Sir Edmund Yorke, under examination hath confessed that he was persuaded by Father Holt to come over on the Queen's pardon, and to live in the Court, having the money due to his uncle sent for his maintenance and an assurance on oath of 40,000 crowns with present payment guaranteed by Stephen de Ibarra the Secretary of the King of Spain if he performed the required service of killing the Queen, by his own agents or by others. At the conference held thereon, Sir William Stanley and others were present; some spoke of a poisoned arrow or rapier, or a dagger as she walked in the garden. He was to serve the Earl of Essex; his fellows, Williams and Young, the Lord Chamberlain. They swore on the Sacrament to do it and were absolved by Father Holt.

He declares that one Moody has come, or soon will, to kill the Queen, when the crown will be offered to the Earl of Derby with the King of Spain's assistance. If their plot should fail they were to move some rebellion in the Earl of Derby's name, though he were not privy to it.

SUITORS AT COURT TO BE RESTRAINED.

A commandment is published by the Council to restrain the inordinate repair of multitudes of suitors coming to the Court with petitions and complaints to the Queen or the Privy Council, which for the most part are either private, unmeet to be preferred to her or for a Council of State to deal in, or such as may be decided in some of the Courts of Justice.

It is now ordered that any suitor, intending to exhibit complaint or petition, shall first acquaint one of the Masters of Requests, if any be in Court; who, with one of the Clerks of the Council, upon view and consideration, shall indorse the substance of the matter with their opinions subscribed with their hands. All suitors whose causes are neither meet to be preferred to the Queen nor heard by the Privy Council nor of any other ordinary Court of Justice or Equity shall depart and not remain about the Court upon pain of imprisonment.

The Master of Requests also to deliver the names of the parties that be rejected to the Porter that he may know whom to exclude.

21st August. A FURTHER CONFESSION OF CAPTAIN YORKE.

Captain Yorke adds to his former confession that when he was first moved to perform the service he was promised 40,000 crowns, and told that many at Court would be glad and were looking for it. Having agreed that if they would give him a resolute man to execute the part, he was promised Richard Williams, cousin to that Throckmorton who was executed in 1585. He had then asked time to consider; they replied that they made him the offer as an honour and bade him not undertake it unless he were resolved. Williams has sworn to kill the Queen, he to aid him. Moody and two others are also coming over to kill her ; and, if the English should fail, a Walloon and a Burgundian are to be employed.

24th August. FURTHER CONFESSIONS OF THE PLOTTERS.

Captain Edmund Yorke adds to his former confessions that he and Williams had often wished the deed were done and they on their horses again, for they were to buy the best they could get. They resolved that when one drew sword, the other would do the same, to do the act if the other were hindered. It was plotted that Sir William Stanley should deny them a passport and that the governor of Burborow should stay them. Then Williams should seem to be in want and he would write for a pardon. Williams prevented his coming over without a passport lest he might damn himself, having taken the Sacrament to kill the Queen, by being taken and forced to confess it.

Henry Young, one of the conspirators, examined at the same time declared that at Calais Yorke said he wondered at any man's wronging his friends for a little torture, and that he was armed for any torture. He said if they were secret they might soon ride in London streets with foot-cloths of cloth of silver. Williams declared that he would die rather than betray his friends, and if he said anything when on the rack would deny all again when freed from it.

PLAYS OF THE WEEK.

The plays at the Rose Theatre this past week are *The Massacre at Paris*, *Tasso's Melancholy*, *Bellendon*, *The Ranger's Comedy*, *Galiaso*, *Cutlack*.

27th August. WILLIAMS' CONFESSION.

Richard Williams being examined hath confessed that he was sent by Father Holt and Sir William Stanley to kill the Queen, with promise of great reward, and that he received the Sacrament thereon. Later he acknowledged his confession before the Earl of Essex, declaring that he will avow it to his death, even before Yorke's face.

28th August. YORKE AND WILLIAMS CONFRONTED.

Yorke and Williams being confronted together before the Commissioners in the Tower, Yorke swears that they took the Sacrament to kill the Queen and that Williams had wished his sword in her belly. Williams denying this, Yorke tells him he denies it on account of his oath, but it was unlawfully taken and therefore may be broken.

An Order at Court.

A very special strait commandment from the Queen is given by the Lord Chamberlain that no man shall come into her presence or attend upon her Majesty wearing any long cloak beneath the knee : which order comes in a good hour for tailors, mercers, and drapers, when all men are now wearing long cloaks.

The Return of the Earl of Cumberland's Ships.

The three ships sent out at the charges of the Earl of Cumberland and his friends, the *Royal Exchange* as Admiral wherein Mr. George Cave was Captain, the *Mayflower* under conduct of William Anthony, and the *Sampson* under Nicholas Downton, have returned to Portsmouth, having set out from Plymouth at the latter end of last year.

They reported that on 13th June they met with a mighty carack of the East Indies called *Las Cinque Llagas*, or *The Five Wounds*. The *Mayflower* was in fight with her before night, and soon after the *Sampson*, never ceasing to ply her with their great ordnance until midnight when the Admiral came up and Captain Cave wished them to stay till morning, when both should give three bouts with their great ordnance and then clap her aboard.

At ten o'clock the next morning the Admiral laid her aboard in the mid-ship, the *Mayflower* coming up in the quarter, as it should seem, to be at the stern of the Admiral on the larboard side ; but her Captain was slain and the ship fell to the stern of the out-licar of the carack which, being a piece of timber, so wounded her foresail that her men said they could come no more to fight. The *Sampson* went aboard on the bow, but not having room enough her quarter lay on the *Exchange's* bow, her bow on the carack's bow. The *Exchange* also at her first coming up had her Captain shot through both legs, so that he was not able to do his office and in his absence had not any that would undertake to lead out her company to enter the carack's side. Captain Downton also had been wounded the night before, but his men were led by Captain Grant ; but his forces being small and not manfully backed by the *Exchange's* men, the enemy became bolder than he would have been, slew six and wounded many more, so that the rest returned on board and would not renew the assault.

The Portugals, thus encouraged by the slack working of our men, had barricades made where they might stand without any danger of our shot, and plied our men with fire so that most of them were burnt in some place or other, and while our men were putting out the fire, they kept on assailing them with small shot or darts. When the *Sampson's* men were not able to enter they plied their great ordnance, mounted as high as they could, and by shooting a piece out of the forecastle, they fired a mat on the carack's keal, which ran from thence to the mat on the bowsprit, and from the mat up to the wood of the bowsprit, and thence to the top sail yard, which made the Portugals to stagger and to make show of parle. But they that had the charge encouraged them that it might easily be put out, so they stood again stiffly to the defence.

Anon the fire grew so strong that Captain Downton seeing it was beyond all help, desired to be off, but had little hope of saving his ship unlit, until by the burning asunder of the sprit sail yard with the ropes and sail, whereby they were fast entangled to the carack, she fell apart. The *Exchange* also being further off from the fire was easier clear and fell off from abaft. Soon the fire crept into the forecastle of the carack where was store of Benjamin and other combustible matter which flamed and ran all over the ship so that the Portugals leapt over in great numbers. Then Captain Downton sent Captain Grant with the boat with leave to use his own discretion in saving of them. So he brought aboard two gentlemen, one an old man called Nuno Velis Pereira, who had been governor of Mocambique and Cefala in 1582; three of the inferior sort were also saved in the boat. The rest which were taken by the other boats were set ashore in the Isles of Flores.

The carack burnt all that day and the night, but next morning her powder which was lowest, being 60 barrels, blew her asunder. Some said she was bigger than the *Madre de Dios*, some that she was less; but though much undermasted and undersailed yet she went well.

On the 30th June after long traversing the seas another mighty carack was sighted which some of the company took to be the *San Philip*, the Admiral of Spain, but next day fetching up with her they found her indeed to be a carack, which after a few shot was summoned to yield, but they stood stoutly to their defence and utterly refused. Whereupon seeing that no good could be done without boarding her, Captain Downton consulted what course should be taken in her boarding, but partly because the chief captains had been slain or wounded in the former conflict, and because of the murmuring of some disordered and cowardly companions, his purpose was crossed, and the carack escaped.

After waiting about Corvo and Flores for some West Indian purchase, but being disappointed of their expectation, and victuals growing short, they returned for England.

29th August. SIR JOHN NORRIS DELAYED.

Sir John Norris who is not yet embarked for Brittany writeth from Portsmouth that his men are continuing to run away. He desires that those counties which have so little care for the furtherance of the Queen's service, as a punishment may be commanded to send as many others in the place of those missing, especially Norfolk and Suffolk. He feareth that the seamen do not well intend the service for the fort by Brest, and asketh that any pinnaces sent after them may have special charge to have greater regard to that service than to anything else, otherwise they will seek the liberty of the sea ; for he hath no authority but by bare advice to let them know what is fit for them to do, which is left to their discretion to follow.

31st August. PLAYS OF THE WEEK.

This past week the plays at the Rose were *Philipo and Hippolito*, *The Venetian Comedy*, *Godfrey of Bouloigne*, *Mahomet*, *The First Part of Tamburlane*, *Bellendon*.

3rd September. 'WILLOBIE HIS AVISA.'

A certain book entitled *Willobie His Avisa* is entered, setting out the triumphs of Avisa, a chaste British dame, over the many suitors who attempted her charity. It is believed that under guise of these suitors certain great ones are attacked, especially a young man, called 'Henrico Willobego,' with his familiar friend 'W. S.,' an old player.

DAVIS'S 'SEAMAN'S SECRETS.'

Captain John Davis hath written a book of navigation called *The Seaman's Secrets,* which he dedicates to the Lord Admiral, defending himself against the charges written by Mr. Richard Cavendish with his dying hand that he was the cause of his overthrow, and ran from him. He declares that his ship *The Desire,* separated by stress of weather and forced to seek a harbour to repair his most miserable wants, being without boats, oars, sails, cables, cordage, victuals, or health of the company sufficient for the attempt to find the North-West Passage, upon which he had set out.

In his searches for the North-West Passages where navigation must be executed in most exquisite sort, he has been enforced to search all possible means required in sailing which are here gathered in his treatise.

His book is divided into two parts; in the first are displayed the terms of the art of navigation, the movement of the moon, the tides, the use of the compass, the cross-staff and the chart; in the second are taught the nature and necessary use of the globe, with the circles, zones, climates and other distinctions, the perfect use of sailing, also the use of the cross-staff, the quadrant, and the astrolabe.

5th September. THE SCOTTISH KING'S SON BAPTISED.

The infant son of the King of Scotland was on 30th August baptised at Stirling, after some delays caused by the lateness of the English Ambassador in coming. The Earl of Cumberland was first chosen for this service, and had prepared himself very richly with an honourable convoy of noblemen and gentlemen of renown, but falling sick, the Earl of Sussex was sent in his place; so it fell out that through the sickness of one nobleman and the hasty preparations of the other, the day for the baptism had constantly to be postponed.

During the time of their stay the King entertained the Ambassadors with banqueting and revelling, and, to make this occasion the more magnificent, he committed the charge of the revels to the Lord of Lendore and Mr. William Fowler, that by reason of their travels were much skilled in such things. Having consented together they concluded that the exercises should be divided into field pastimes, with martial and heroical exploits, and household with rare shows and singular inventions. At the first show, three Christians (presented by the King, the Earl of Mar, and Thomas Erskine, Esquire) were followed by three Turks and then by three Amazons, all having pages riding on their led horses, each bearing his master's *impresa* or device. The King's device was a lion's head with open eyes, which signified fortitude and vigilance. All having solemnly entered, they ran three courses at the ring and glove, and the prize was given to the Duke of Lennox.

When at last all the Ambassadors had reached Stirling the baptism was performed. The Chapel Royal had been richly hung with a royal seat of state for the King, and at his right hand a fair wide chair over which was set the arms of the King of France; next to him sat the Ambassador of England, and after him, and also on the King's left hand, the other Ambassadors. The King having taken his seat, the Ambassadors were led into the presence of the infant Prince who was carried with great ceremony into the Chapel. All being seated, Mr. Patrick Galloway, one of the King's preachers in ordinary, went up to the pulpit, and entreated upon the text of the 21st of Genesis. This done, the Bishop of Aberdeen stood up in his seat and explained the Sacrament of baptism, first in the vulgar tongue, next in Latin, that all might understand. Then the provost and the prebends of the Chapel sang the 21st Psalm. Next the Prince was baptised, being named 'Frederick Henry, Henry Frederick.' When all were again seated the Bishop went up into the pulpit where he delivered in verse a praise and commendation of the Prince, and then, turning the rest of his Latin oration into prose, he addressed the Ambassadors, beginning with the English Ambassador and so to the rest, making mention of the chronology of each of their princes, and reciting the proximity and nearness of blood they had with the King. In conclusion, when the blessing had been given, Lyon King of Arms cried with a loud voice, 'God save Frederick Henry, Henry Frederick, by the Grace of God, Prince of Scotland.'

The Prince was then carried into the King's Hall where he was dubbed Knight by his father, and proclaimed by Lyon King of Arms, Knight and Baron of Renfrew, Lord of the

Isles, Earl of Garrick, Duke of Rosay, Prince and Great Steward of Scotland.

That night was held a very magnificent banquet, at which, after the guests had refreshed themselves at the first service, there entered a blackamoor, very richly attired, drawing as it seemed, a triumphal chariot wherein stood Ceres, Fecundity, Faith, Concord, Liberality, and Perseverance, set round a table richly set out. This chariot should indeed have been drawn by a lion, but because his presence might have brought some fear to the nearest, or the sight of the lights and torches might have moved his tameness, it was thought best to supply the blackamoor in his place.

The chariot being withdrawn, a most sumptuous ship entered, her keel 18ft. long, in breadth 8 foot, and to the top of her highest flag 40 feet, and the motion so artificially devised that none could perceive what brought her in. Neptune sat in the fore-stern, with Thetis and Triton, and round about were all kinds of marine people, such as the sirens, and within, mariners and musicians, besides Arion with his harp. By this device was set forth the King's voyage into Norway to fetch his Queen when he was detained by the devices of witches ; and as Neptune had then brought them safely home, so now he brought them such gifts as the sea affords to adorn this festival.

After these revels were ended the King and the Ambassadors went to another Hall where for the collation a most rare, sumptuous and prince-like dessert of sugar had been prepared, whence, after leave-taking and good-nights, the company departed about three o'clock in the morning.

7th September. PLAYS OF THE WEEK.

The plays this last week at the Rose were *The Jew of Malta*, *Tasso*, *Philipo and Hippolito*, *The Venetian Comedy*, *Cutlack*.

8th September. GILES FLETCHER'S 'LICIA.'

Licia or Poems of Love, in honour of the admirable and singular virtues of his Lady, to the imitation of the best Latin poets, and others, by Mr. Giles Fletcher, is sent to the press, being dedicated to the Lady Mollineux, wife of Sir Richard Mollineux. To her the author writeth in his Epistle Dedicatory that though his thoughts and some reasons draw him rather to deal in causes of greater weight, yet the present jar of this disagreeing age drives him into a fit so melancholy that he has leisure only to grow passionate.

There are some fifty-two sonnets in honour of Licia, and other poems, one being *The Rising to the Crown of Richard the Third*, spoken with his own mouth, and imitated from *Shore's Wife* and *Rosamond*.

9th September. THE COUNTESS OF RUTLAND AND THE LADY BRIDGET.

The Queen is not a little offended, thinking herself undutifully handled, because the Countess of Rutland neither answers nor obeys her command to send the Lady Bridget to London. The Lord Hunsdon hath therefore written in the Queen's name commanding the Lady to be sent up forthwith, and demanding why the order has not been obeyed hitherto.

10th September. NEWS FROM BREST.

Sir John Norris landed with new forces at Pempole on the first of the month, where he received letters from the Marshal D'Aumont and Sir Thomas Baskerville showing in what terms they lay outside Morlaix, expecting every day to be attacked by the Duke Mercury. But when the Duke Mercury heard of the coming of Sir John, he not only refrained from coming to the succour of Morlaix but withdrew his forces further away, so that those in the Castle yielded themselves when they heard of it.

11th September. SIR THOMAS WILKES TO BE SENT TO THE ARCHDUKE ERNEST.

The Queen wisheth to expostulate with the King of Spain for his barbarous action in contriving and furthering the foul and dangerous practices of Lopez and the others, and to force him either to avow it or else to cause him to correct those that were the instruments in these plots, such as Christofero de Moro, the Count Fuentes, and Ibarra. She hath resolved therefore to send Sir Thomas Wilkes, her Secretary, to the Archduke Ernest, Governor in the Low Countries for the King of Spain, to open the matter and the proofs. A special messenger is now sent requiring safe conduct for the Secretary's coming and going.

14*th September*. PLAYS OF THE WEEK.

The plays at the Rose this past week were *Godfrey of Bulloigne*, *Mahomet*, *Galiaso*, *Bellendon*, *Tamburlane*, *Philipo and Hippolito*.

18*th September*. THE WAR IN BRITTANY.

The news from Brittany is that after the taking of Morlaix Sir John Norris stayed ten days while the Marshal raised money to satisfy the men. Then Monsieur de Lyseot with some harquebusiers, aided by Sir Martin Frobisher and 400 men from the English ships, was sent forward to block up the fort of Croyzon by Brest.

The same night the Marshal with 400 French and Sir John with as many English marched to Quimpar-Corantin, and suddenly surprised the suburbs, entering them with small resistance. The town was willing to yield but the garrison would not allow them. So Sir John Norris, being still intent on some exploit against the Spaniards at the fort of Croyzon, left the town invested by the Marshal, and three English regiments; himself with one regiment and his own company of horse marched towards Croyzon and lodged there that night. He is now preparing approaches and platforms for the artillery, but much hindered by the badness of the weather.

A DUTCH MILL.

Two Dutchmen, Jacob Senoy and George Frise of Utrecht in Holland, have lately brought with them a certain mill which they have invented that will in very short time grind a greater quantity of corn than will be believed but by such as see the trial of it. These men are recommended to the Lord Mayor and Aldermen for albeit their mill most properly serveth for a camp or besieged city in time of distress yet it may serve the City of good purpose in times of frost when the mills go not. If the mill may be had at a reasonable rate it will be both a good monument to lay up in the Bridgehouse against time of need and also for use as a pattern whereby to frame others by it.

21*st September*. PLAYS OF THE WEEK.

The plays this past week at the Rose were *The Venetian Comedy*, *The Ranger's Comedy*, *Palamon and Arcite* (for the first time), *Tasso*, *Philipo and Hippolito*, *Godfrey of Bulloigne*.

28th September. PLAYS OF THE WEEK.

The plays this week at the Rose Theatre were *Mohamet*, *The Venetian Comedy* (twice), *Bellendon*, *The Love of an English Lady*, *The Massacre at Paris*, *Cutlack*.

30th September. THE ALCHEMIST'S BEQUEST.

Some months since one Clement Ouldfield made a bequest containing certain secrets of alchemy to Roloff Peterson of Lubec on condition of their being first offered on composition to her Majesty. The Queen now ordereth that the bequest shall be delivered unopened to the deputy of the Merchant Adventurers at Stade for Peterson; or if she is pleased to keep it, he shall receive £500 for it within six months.

THE BAD WEATHER AND THE PRICE OF GRAIN.

This summer, in May, there fell many great showers of rain, but much more in June and July; for it has commonly rained every day or night till St. James' Day. Notwithstanding there followed in August a fair harvest, but in September fell great rains, which raised high waters and bare down bridges at Cambridge, Ware, and other places. The price of grain grows to be such that a bushel of rye is sold for 5s., a bushel of wheat for six, seven and even eight shillings; this dearth according to common opinion, is caused more by means of overmuch transporting by the merchants for their private gain than through the unseasonableness of the weather.

3rd October. INMATES TO BE REMOVED.

Great inconveniences grow daily more and more by the number of inmates, and by the erecting of new tenements within the City of London, Westminster and the suburbs, which are a great cause of infection by reason of the multitude of poor people that inhabit them, many dwelling together in one small house. There was a statute made in the last Parliament for the reformation of these inconveniences and especially for the avoiding of inmates. Now, seeing that the greatest number of those dead of the late infection are out of those houses that were pestered with inmates, the Lord Mayor and the Aldermen are bidden to give order that no new persons shall be admitted to these tenements in the room of those that are deceased.

5*th October.* PLAYS OF THE WEEK.

The plays this past week at the Rose were *Tamburlane*, *Galiaso*, *Doctor Faustus*, *The Ranger's Comedy*, *The Venetian Comedy*, *The Love of a Grecian Lady*.

6*th October.* LE ROY'S 'OF THE INTERCHANGEABLE COURSE OF THINGS.'

Mr. Robert Ashley hath translated into English and dedicated to Sir John Puckering, the Lord Keeper, a book entitled *Of the Interchangeable Course or Variety of Things*, first written in French by Louis le Roy.

Herein are surveyed the variety of tongues and arts, the state of arms, and learning, of religion in former ages compared with the present, concluding in the last chapter that the truth has not yet been thoroughly discovered, neither all knowledge forestalled by our forerunners. The learned therefore should add by their own inventions what is wanting in the sciences, doing for posterity that which Antiquity did for us, to the end that learning be not lost, but day by day receive some increase.

12*th October.* PLAYS OF THE WEEK.

The plays at the Rose this week were *Godfrey of Bulloigne*, *Philipo and Hippolito*, *Tasso*, *Doctor Faustus*, *The Venetian Comedy*.

15*th October.* THE LADY BRIDGET AT COURT.

The Countess of Rutland is come to London with the Lady Bridget. Mr. Tyrwhitt, who has been sick in prison, now begins to sue for liberty and the Lord Chamberlain promises to move the Queen on his behalf.

18*th October.* CAPTAIN ANTHONY WINGFIELD SLAIN.

From Brittany the news is that on the 6th October the enemy assaulted the trenches before Croyzon but were beaten back with the loss of 7 or 8 men, but on our side was killed Captain Anthony Wingfield, the Sergeant-Major General, who was shot by a cannon shot from the garrison, as he stood with his rapier drawn, which was by the shot beaten through his bowels.

Captain Wingfield hath served the Queen with great reputation in the wars of the Low Countries, Portugal and France. It is noted at his last going into Brittany that he so disposed of his estate as if he were never to return, and on the day of his death he took such order for his debts as if he had a presage of his end.

The next day the Marshal D'Aumont and Sir Henry Norris with the rest of the English regiments came up from Quimpar that is now taken and were quartered at Croyzon. Four days were now spent in mounting the artillery and making platforms for them to play. On the 12th the enemy made a sally upon the trenches of the French who not having the leisure to arm themselves lost between 30 and 40 men, and as many wounded; from thence they advanced towards the English trenches but were repulsed with the loss of 10 or 12.

19th October. PLAYS OF THE WEEK.

The plays this past week at the Rose Theatre were *Bellendon*, *Mohamet*, *Tamburlane* (twice), *Palamon and Arcite*, *The French Doctor*.

20th October. THE DISRESPECT OF THE ARCHDUKE ERNEST.

The messenger that was despatched to the Archduke Ernest to require a safe conduct for Sir Thomas Wilkes is returned with a passport in ample style, and a letter from the Archduke that greatly displeaseth her Majesty, for on perusing it she found the style and form far inferior to that which she expected from the Duke, being barely addressed *Royne D'Angleterre*, and omitting all the honours formerly given her in all letters sent by Emperors and Kings. Moreover the Archduke expressed in his letter that he expected to have nothing propounded that might be to the disservice to the King of Spain. She hath determined to deal no more in this way, but in a more public manner to declare to the world how far the King was directly touched by these foul practices.

The messenger is now sent back with the passport and a bare and meagre letter to Monsieur Richardott, one of the Duke's Council, signed by the Lord Treasurer, the Earl of Essex, the Lord Buckhurst, the Vice-Chamberlain and Sir Robert Cecil.

In this letter it is written that at some other time the Queen might have overlooked the style and form but she is too tender of the greatness of her state, being by God an anointed Queen over Kingdoms and countries, to disregard so notorious an omission of her dignities whether made by error or of purpose.

As for the Archduke's expectation to have nothing propounded to him that might be to the disservice to the King of Spain, the matters are in very truth such as, without some extraordinary course taken by the King for his clearing, there will be left upon him a most notorious and foul imputation in the judgment of the whole world. The Queen is resolved to trouble the Duke neither with letter or with message any more, being now rather through his cold and unrespectful manner towards her (which she little expected at his hands) induced to look for small indifference at his hands. She hath reserved to herself a further consideration how the same may be made known, even according to the naked truth confessed and sealed with the blood of the conspirators, without any addition or colouring of anything therein.

25th October. PLAYS OF THE WEEK.

The plays this last week at the Rose were *The Jew of Malta*, *Doctor Faustus*, *A Knack to Know an Honest Man* (for the first time), *Tasso*, *The Love of an English Lady*, *Galiaso*.

NASHE'S 'TERRORS OF THE NIGHT.'

Nashe's book *The Terrors of the Night, or a Discourse of Apparitions*, wherein he describeth the nature of dreams, spirits, prophecies and omens, is entered, being dedicated to Mistress Elizabeth Carey, daughter to the Knight Marshal.

The spirits of fire are by nature ambitious, with a humour of monarchising that maketh them affect rare qualified studies; many atheists are with these spirits inhabited. The spirits of water be dull and phlegmatic; and all rheums, dropsies and gout of their engendering; seafaring men are their chief entertainers, and greedy vintners likewise, who having read no more Scripture than that miracle of Christ's turning water into wine at Canaan, think to do a far stranger miracle than ever He did by turning wine into water. Spirits of the earth do especially infect soldiers, for they delight in nothing but iron and gold. As for the spirits of the air, in truth they be all show and no substance, deluders of the imagination, and nothing else; carpet knights, politic statesmen, women and children they most converse with.

Of conjurors and cunning men, Nashe saith that they ascend by degrees, first raking a dunghill from which to temper up a few ointments and syrups, until as their fame grows, at last they set up a conjuring school, and all malcontents intending evasive violence against their prince and country run headlong to this oracle. As for the interpretation of dreams and the arts of physiognomy and palmistry, this is the sum of all; some subtle humorist to feed fantastic heads with innovations and novelties first invented this childish gloss upon dreams and physiognomy, wherein he strove only to boast himself of a pregnant, probable conceit beyond philosophy or truth.

31st October. SIR JOHN NORRIS'S ATTACK ON THE FORT AT CROYZON.

From Brittany it is reported that an assault on the fort of Croyzon was begun on 23rd October. This place is very strongly defended, defended by water on two parts, and the rest as strong as could be made by art or charge. On the south front of the fort are two exceedingly strong bastions, that on the west having frontage of 17 paces, that on the east 10 paces; the curtain between them 37 ft. thick at top, and within these they have a very large entrenchment. The bastions are well defended on the flanks by the water and great ordnance. Our trenches were within four paces of the counterscarp, the French being on the east side, the English on the west, with the battery between them.

On that day the artillery began to play and fired some 700 shot but did so little harm that scarcely any breach appeared; but as the cannon beat upon the parapet and some of the flankers, some 400 men, commanded by Captain Lister, were sent to view it, and to see if they could hold the counterscarp. Thereupon many of the men and the gallants, thirsty after honour and desirous to achieve something further, having possessed themselves of the enemy's counterscarp, undertook the breach as well, and, notwithstanding the inaccessibleness of the place and the great resistance of the enemy, most of them reached the very top and held it for a time, though afterwards they were repulsed, so that six of the officers were killed and some 16 or 18 soldiers, and twelve other officers were hurt or burned with powder.

This attempt was made by the Englishmen only on the bastion of the west side, for the Frenchmen never attempted anything against their bastion, alleging that it was not assailable.

The next day the Marshal and Sir John seeing the little effect that the artillery wrought, devised to make a mine against the east bastion towards the French trenches.

2nd November. Plays of the Week.

The plays at the Rose Theatre this last week were *Palamon and Arcite*, *The French Doctor*, *A Knack to Know an Honest Man* (twice), *Godfrey of Bulloigne*, *Bellendon*.

3rd November. The Sermon at Paul's Cross.

The sermon at Paul's Cross was this day preached by Dr. John Dove, on the Second Coming of Christ, and the disclosing of Antichrist, taking as his text I. John ii., verse 18. He spoke very strictly of those that buy patronages of Church livings to give them to base, ignorant, and beggarly men, who would easily accept of benefices upon unlawful conditions. In concluding he demonstrated at length that the Bishop of Rome was that Antichrist spoken of in the Revelations.

A Petition against a New Theatre.

Learning that some intend to erect a new theatre on the Bankside the Lord Mayor hath written to the Lord Treasurer begging him rather to suppress all stages than to erect any more. Nor will he allow the defence of these plays alleged by some that the people must have some kind of recreation and that policy requires idle and ill-disposed heads to be directed from worse practise by this kind of exercise. These plays, saith he, are so corrupt, profane, containing nothing else but unchaste fables, lascivious devices, shifts, cozenage, and matter of like sort that only the base and refuse sort of people, or such young gentlemen as have but small regard for credit or conscience, are drawn thither. Hence plays are become the ordinary place of meeting for all vagrant persons and masterless men, that hang about the City, thieves, horse stealers, whoremongers, cozeners, connycatching persons, practisers of treason and such like; there they consort and make their matches. Nor can the City be cleansed of this ungodly sort (the very sink and contagion not only of the City but of the whole realm) so long as plays of resort are by authority permitted.

4th November. THE STATE OF IRELAND.

From Ulster it is reported by Sir Richard Bingham that the great ones are of late more openly showing themselves in nature of a rebellion than at first; and it seems that it will be necessary for the Queen to take up the matter by correcting the offenders, for her subjects there have been promised peace, and by degrees much violence has been committed. But if the Queen and the Council wish the Lord Deputy to do anything against the Ulster men let him be given all due assistance and countenance that he might with less strength and time go through with it. The province of Connaught is generally first.

9th November. PLAYS OF THE WEEK.

The plays at the Rose this last week: *Tamburlane*, *Doctor Faustus*, *Mahomet*, *The Knack to Know an Honest Man*, *Caesar and Pompey* (for the first time), *Palamon and Arcite*.

15th November. THE ASSAULT ON THE FORT AT CROYZON.

It is reported from Brittany that Croyzon is taken. By the 7th November the mine being reasonably well perfected, it was determined to begin the battery again with the resolution that so soon as the mine (which was made against the bulwarks opposite the French trenches) should be blown up, the French should attack that part, the English their bastion; and others with scaling ladders should make attempts in every corner so that the defenders should be assailed on every part. But the Marshal being that day sick sent in the morning to our General, showing him that he had learned that Don John d'Aquila, General of the Spaniards, was marching with his Spaniards to rescue Croyzon and had already reached La-coman, a village within five leagues. He therefore advised our General to defloge to Croyzon, thinking it unfit to hazard any more men with so strong an enemy at hand ready to join battle.

But Sir John, nothing daunted, answered that it would be a dishonour to abandon the siege and that if the fort were taken the enemy would have little purpose in coming any nearer. He so importuned the Marshal that he gave him the ordering of that day's service. The General immediately commanded the cannoneers to begin the battery; and every man was assigned his charge, some to the assault, others with scaling ladders to attempt to make entry. By 12 o'clock he gave order for the mine to be fired which albeit it did not do so much as was expected, yet it gave easy access to the French. On the other bulwark our men led by Captain Lathom, Captain Smith, and Captain John Norris, with other gentlemen, assailed the bulwark and continued the assault until at half past four they made entry, and seized upon three ensigns that were there, putting every man they found to the sword, except a certain Alferez. Some of the Spaniards leapt from the rocks into the water, but the mariners in their small boats met them and slew them. Three or four were taken and their lives spared, for no man was slain in cold blood.

In this fight there were slain four officers, eight gentlemen of the General's own company, besides other gentlemen and some 20 or 30 private soldiers. There are wounded Sir Thomas Baskerville who by his bravery won the admiration of all men, Sir Martin Frobisher, and Captains Norris, Brett and Smith.

Throughout the siege the enemy were worthy of all praise, especially their commander; they never showed themselves daunted, and made sundry sallies, mostly on the French, with great resolution. In the last assault, fifty of them were slain by the cannon, but they never quailed until their commander was killed shortly before the entry of our men. By that time the greater part were slain, the rest, overtired and hurt, were forced to give way before our gallants. There were killed of the Spaniards in this fort nearly 400.

The next day the fort was destroyed and the force moved from Croyzon to join the rest of the army and to wait for what the enemy should attempt; but two days afterwards he withdrew five leagues further off. The day after the fight Don John d'Aquila sent a trumpet to redeem his prisoners, to whom our General answered that their ransoms were already paid and that he was now ready and at leisure to fight with him. The three Spanish ensigns he hath sent into England to be presented to the Queen.

16th November. PLAYS OF THE WEEK.

The plays at the Rose this last week were *The Venetian Comedy*, *Tasso*, *The Grecian Comedy*, *Caesar and Pompey*, *Bellendon*, *Dioclesian* (for the first time).

17th November. MEASURES AGAINST VAGRANTS AND BEGGING POOR.

The Lord Mayor hath written to the Council asking that the measures proposed against vagrants may be approved.

THE QUEEN'S ACCESSION DAY.

This day, on the anniversary of her accession thirty years before, the Queen gave a great banquet. The three flags captured from the Spaniards in Brittany have been presented to her.

19th November. SPENSER'S 'AMORETTI' AND 'EPITHALAMIUM.'

Mr. Edmund Spenser's *Amoretti* together with his *Epithalamium*, written in honour of his own wife that he married in July last, are sent to the press.

THE FIFTY-FOURTH SONNET.

Of this world's theatre in which we stay,
My love like the spectator idly sits
Beholding me that all the pageants play,
Disguising diversely my troubled wits.
Sometimes I joy when glad occasion fits,
And mask in mirth like to a comedy:
Soon after when my joy to sorrow flits,
I wail and make my woes a tragedy.
Yet she beholding me with constant eye,
Delights not in my mirth nor rues my smart:
But when I laugh she mocks, and when I cry
She laughs, and hardens evermore her heart.
  What then can move her? If not mirth nor moan,
  She is no woman but a senseless stone.

20th November. THE USE OF THE CITY GARNERS REFUSED.

When of late Sir Francis Drake and Sir John Hawkins demanded the use of the garners and bakehouses in the Bridgehouse to bake bread for the fleet about to be set forth, the Lord

Mayor refused the same. He allegeth that these garners and bakehouses were built solely for the use of the poor in times of scarcity who would be utterly disappointed if they should be employed for any other use. At the same time he hath petitioned the Lord Treasurer that the corn for the fleet may be bought from Kent or other shires and not in the City. Sir Francis and Sir John purpose to make their provision out of the wheat brought from foreign parts for the benefit of the City, and have already bought some, enforcing the same to a lower price than is usual or can be well afforded; hereby the merchants shall be discouraged from bringing in any more.

23rd November. PLAYS OF THE WEEK.

At the Rose Theatre this past week: *The French Doctor, Doctor Faustus, The Knack to Know an Honest Man, Dioclesian, The Grecian Comedy.*

27th November. THE LADY BRIDGET MANNERS.

The Queen hath caused the Lady Bridget Manners to be set free; Mr. Tyrwhitt was released some days since on the mediation of his friends and in respect of his sickness. Her Majesty now bids the Lord Hunsdon to write to the Countess of Rutland in her name that she imputes the fault more to her than to the young couple, for though the Lady Bridget took the fault on herself to excuse her mother, yet the Queen is well assured that the Lady Bridget would never have married without her mother's consent. There now remains only that the Countess should send for the Lady Bridget from the Countess of Bedford, and the sooner the better, and her husband will come down with her.

30th November. PLAYS OF THE WEEK.

The plays at the Rose this last week were *Caesar and Pompey, The Venetian Comedy, Tamburlane, Warlamchester* (twice), *The Knack to Know an Honest Man.*

A CONFERENCE ABOUT THE SUPPRESSING OF ROGUES.

Since the Council approve the measures proposed against vagrants the Lord Mayor hath summoned the Justices of Middlesex and Surrey to meet with him and with the Lord Chief Justices touching the orders to be put in execution for the apprehending and suppressing of vagrant persons and the begging poor.

It is proposed that precise and strait charge shall be given to every several ward that watch and ward be continued from 9 or 10 of the clock at night till 6 in the morning, and the day watch to begin when the night watch giveth over, and to give over again when the night watch beginneth. For the better furnishing and executing of these watches the constable shall be compelled to execute his office not by deputy but in his own person, as the execution thereof by deputy constables is thought to be an occasion of great negligence and abuse in this service.

The watches shall make continual searches at times convenient in all victualling houses, tippling cellars and other places likely to entertain idle and suspicious persons, men, women and children. Those that shall be found not able to give an account of some dwelling-place and honest faculty to live by but shall appear to be vagabonds, rogues and idle beggars, having able bodies, them shall the watch commit to Bridewell, there to be kept till the morning following; what time the constables with other honest persons of the same watch shall resort thither, there to charge them before those who are farther authorized to proceed against them for their lawful punishment.

The Lord Mayor, sheriffs or justices of the peace shall come to Bridewell or other place appointed where the vagabonds shall be brought before them; for the law doth require the presence of some of them at the least at the convicting of such persons. There shall they determine for their enlargement or punishing or both; and that shall be done in as short a time as possibly may be for the easing of the place whither they shall be committed and of the charges that they shall otherwise be put to by the restraining of them.

For the better and more speedy avoiding of such vagabonds present consideration shall be had of some bodily labour to set them on work, as by beating of hemp, scouring the town ditches, abating the shelves in the river Thames, or such other, wherein no detriment can be done by them, in case they should demean themselves wilfully or negligently; which otherwise in matter of art they might and are likely to do. The young ones that can more easily be reclaimed and enforced shall be appointed to some occupation. Women walkers that be of the City or suburbs shall be forced to abide at their prescribed dwelling-places in some honest labour, making of flax, spinning, or such like.

2nd December. A PROCLAMATION AGAINST FIREARMS.

The great disorders in different parts of the realm, and especially in the City of London and the highways towards it, have caused much terror to all people professing to travel and live peaceably. A proclamation is now published reaffirming the former proclamations against the carrying of dags and longer pieces, such as calivers, in times and places not allowable for service, and against the carrying of small or pocket dags and the wearing of privy coats of armour. Yet is it to be allowed to those who come to the musters to serve as horsemen with dags, and also to any of the Queen's ministers or their servants for their more surety to carry her treasure or bring her revenue to places appointed, provided always that the dags be carried openly and manifestly seen.

DE LA MARCHE'S 'THE RESOLVED GENTLEMAN.'

The Resolved Gentleman, first written in French in 1483 by Oliver de la Marche who served Philip, and his son, Charles, Dukes of Burgundy; hence translated into Spanish verse by Don Hernando de Ancunia, and now with additions Englished by Mr. Lewis Lewkenor is entered, being dedicated to the Lady Hune, Countess of Warwick. In this allegorical fiction the author depicteth those qualities which sustain a man against the misfortunes of life, accident and old age; the evils of a courtly life; the blessings of memory, and the like, ending with a prophecy of the Destinies concerning Queen Elizabeth.

6th December. SIR W. RALEGH'S COMMISSION.

A commission is granted to Sir Walter Ralegh to prepare and arm two ships and two small pinnaces in which to do her Majesty service against the King of Spain and his subjects. As his own ability is not sufficient to furnish out such vessels, and he is driven to use the assistance of friends to adventure with him, the Queen for his satisfaction and their assurance further promises that he and they shall enjoy to their own use all goods and merchandise, treasure, gold, silver, and whatever else may be taken by him or his associates, either by sea or land, from the subjects of the King of Spain, after paying such customs and duties as appertain. He is given full power and authority over all captains, masters, mariners, and others, who are commanded to obey him. Whatever he shall do by virtue of his commission for the furtherance of the service and the enfeebling of the subjects and adherents of the King of Spain, he and all who serve under him shall be clearly acquitted and discharged.

7th December. PLAYS OF THE WEEK.

The plays at the Rose Theatre this last week were *The Grecian Comedy*, *The Wise Man of West Chester* (for the first time, twice) *Tasso*, *Mahommed*.

8th December. THE DEATH OF CARDINAL ALLEN.

It is reported that Cardinal Allen hath died at Rome, whereat the Catholics make great lamentation. He was in the sixty-third year of his age and is buried in the English Church of the Holy Trinity.

William Allen, commonly called the Cardinal of England, was born in the county of Lancashire of honest parents and allied by kindred to some noble families. He was brought up at Oriel College in Oxford, where in Queen Mary's time he was proctor of the University, and afterwards a Canon in the Church of York. When religion changed in England, he departed the land, and professed divinity at the University of Douay in Flanders that was founded two and thirty years since. He procured the seminary for the English to be founded at Douay, and the second seminary at Rheims, the third at Rome, and two others in Spain, for the conservation of the Romish religion in England, for the zeal whereof he cast off both his love for his country and his duty to his Prince, instigating both the King of Spain and the Pope of Rome to the conquest of England. Upon that account he engaged himself in dangerous counsels and designs for which Pope Sixtus V. honoured him with the title of Cardinal of St. Martin in the Mounts.

When the Invincible Armada threatened England he it was that brought into the Low Countries that Bull of Excommunication against the Queen, causing it to be printed in English;

and withal he wrote an admonition to the English to adhere to the Pope and the Spaniard. But being disappointed of his hopes he returned to Rome, there greatly wearied by the dissensions and animosities of English fugitives, as well students as gentlemen.

14th December. REVELS TO BE HELD AT GRAY'S INN.

The gentlemen at Gray's Inn, after many consultations, have now determined to hold revels this Christmastide, and more especially as these pastimes have been discontinued for three or four years. They make choice of Mr. Henry Helmes, a Norfolk gentleman, one accomplished with all good parts, a very proper man of personage, and very active in dancing and revelling, to be elected their 'Prince of Purpool' and to govern the state for the duration of the revels. Privy Councillors and all officers of state, of the Law and of the household are assigned to him, and an invitation in the form of a privy seal dispatched to the Gentlemen of the Inner Temple, bidding them appoint an Ambassador to be a minister of correspondence between the two houses or kingdoms.

PLAYS OF THE WEEK.

The plays this past week at the Rose were *Doctor Faustus*, *The Jew of Malta*, *Caesar and Pompey*, *Warlamchester*, *The Knack to Know an Honest Man*, *The Set at the Maw* (for the first time).

20th December. THE REVELS AT GRAY'S INN.

The revels were begun this night. The Prince of Purpool with all his train marched from his lodging to the great Hall and there was installed on his Throne, under a rich cloth of State, with his councillors and great lords about him and before, the rest of his officers taking their places as belonged to their condition. Then the trumpeters were commanded to sound thrice, which being done, the King at Arms, in a rich surcoat, stood forth before the Prince and proclaimed his style. After this entered the Prince's champion in complete armour, on horseback, and so came riding about the fire and in the midst of the Hall made his challenge and then departed.

King at Arms having next blazoned the Prince's Arms, the Attorney stood up and made a speech of gratulation, wherein he showed what happiness was like to ensue by the election of so noble and virtuous a Prince as then reigned over them. To whom the Prince answered that he did acknowledge himself to be deeply bound to their merits, and in that regard did promise that he would be a gracious and loving Prince to so well deserving subjects. Then the Solicitor, having certain great old books and records before him, made a speech to the Prince showing the names of such homagers or tributaries as held lordships, and the services belonging thereto.

Alfonso de Stapulia and Davillo de Bernardia held the Archdukedoms of Stapulia and Bernardia, being there to right and relieve all wants and wrongs of all ladies, matrons and maids within the said Archduchy.

Marotto Marquarillo de Holborn held the Manors of High and Nether Holborn by Cornage in *capite*, rendering on the day of the Prince's Coronation for every of the Prince's pensioners one milk-white doe.

Lucy Negro, Abbess de Clerkenwell, held the Nunnery of Clerkenwell by night service in *cauda*, and to find a choir of nuns with burning lamps to chant *placebo* to the gentlemen of the Prince's Privy Chamber on the Coronation day.

Cornelius Combaldus de Tottenham held the Grange of Tottenham in free and common soccage by the twenty-fourth part of a night's fee, and by rendering to the Master of the Wardrobe so much conny fur as would serve to line his nightcap and face a pair of mittens.

Bawdwine de Islington held the town of Islington by grand sergeantry, rendering at the Coronation, for every maid in Islington continuing a virgin after the age of fourteen years, one hundred thousand million sterling.

Then was a Parliament summoned, but certain necessary officers being absent, the purpose was frustrated, except that a subsidy was granted by the Commons, and the Prince gave his gracious and free pardon, which was read by the Solicitor, and after a further short speech the Prince called for his Master of Revels, and willed him to pass the time in dancing. So the gentlemen pensioners and attendants, very gallantly appointed, in thirty couples, danced the old measures, and their galliards and others kinds of dances, revelling until it was very late, when it pleased the Prince to take his way to his lodging, with the sound of trumpets and his attendants.

21st December. PLAYS OF THE WEEK.

The plays at the Rose Theatre this last week were *Tamburlane*, *The Second Part of Tamburlane*, *Doctor Faustus*.

24th December. 'A CONFERENCE ABOUT THE NEXT SUCCESSION.'

There are being circulated in England some copies of a book called *A Conference about the next Succession to the Crown of England*, dedicated to the Earl of Essex, which was published abroad and written by one N. Doleman, who is believed to be Parsons the Jesuit.

The alleged occasion of the treatise was a meeting in Amsterdam after the late Parliament of certain gentlemen of divers nations qualities and affections, who, hearing that the question of the succession had not been settled by the Parliament in England, began to debate the matter, and especially two lawyers, who agreed that each should deliver his opinion on the case, the one considering the principles of succession, the other the claims of those who pretend to the succession in England.

The first argueth that government by nearness of blood is not the law of nature nor is it divine law; and being only by human law, might upon just causes be altered, and the King deposed. The second, enumerating those who have claim by birth and family, noteth the King of Scots, whose favourers (of whom there are but few in England) believe him the first and chiefest pretender. In this line also is the Lady Arabella Stuart, whom the Lord Treasurer is supposed to favour.

The Puritans at home are thought to be the most vigorous of the parties in religion, having a great part of the best captains and soldiers on their side; but the Catholics by reason of the persecution of seminarists are also strong. The Earl of Beauchamp and the Earl of Derby have some voices, as also the Earl of Huntingdon.

But whoever shall succeed it is likely that the affair cannot be ended without war at the first. As for the future he conjectureth that if a foreign Prince be admitted, the Infanta of Spain is likest to bear away the prize; if, on the other side, one of the domestical competitors, the second son of the Earl of Hertford, or the issue of the Countess of Derby.

26th December. AN ATTEMPT TO MURDER THE FRENCH KING.

From France it is reported that on 17th December a young man, one John Chastel, seminary of the Jesuit College at Claremont, attempted to murder the French King, piercing his cheek with a poniard, and breaking some of his teeth. This Chastel has been tried and executed by the French Parliament, and their decree is now translated and published in English. He was condemned to go before the principal gate of the chief church in Paris, and there, naked to his shirt, with a burning torch of wax of the weight of two pounds, on his knees to acknowledge and confess that wretchedly and traitorously he had attempted the most inhuman and most abominable parricide, and that with a knife he wounded the King in the face. Also that being falsely instructed and persuaded he had affirmed that it was lawful to kill the King, and that King Henry the Fourth, now reigning, was not in the Church until he had received approbation of the Pope; whereof, and every part whereof, he repented and asked forgiveness of God.

This done he was to be conveyed in a tumbril to the place called the Greve; there to have his arms and his thighs rent with burning pincers, and his right hand holding the knife wherewith he had endeavoured to have committed the parricide to be cut off. Then his body to be drawn in sunder and dismembered by four horses, and his carcase and quarters cast into the fire, and so consumed into ashes; and the said ashes to be scattered in the wind. Before the execution of this sentence he was to be put to the torture ordinary and extraordinary thereby to find out the truth of his confederates.

It was also ordained that all priests and scholars of the College of Claremont, and all others that entitled themselves to the Society of Jesus, as corrupters of youth, disturbers of common quietness, and enemies to the King and the State, should within three days after notice of this decree depart out of all towns and places where their colleges were situate, and within fifteen days more out of the whole realm.

27th December. PLAYS OF THE WEEK.

The plays at the Rose this past week were *The Grecian Comedy*, *The Siege of London*, *Doctor Faustus*.

28th December. THE CHAMBERLAIN'S PLAYERS AT COURT.

The Lord Chamberlain's players acted before the Court at Greenwich on St. Stephen's Day, among them being Richard Burbage, William Kemp, and William Shakespeare.

GRAY'S INN REVELS: A NIGHT OF ERRORS.

This night there was a great presence of Lords, Ladies and Worshipful personages, expecting some notable performance, especially after the common report of that which had gone before, but the multitude of beholders was so great that the inventions and conceits could not be performed. Against these performances the Emperor of the Inner Temple sent his Ambassador who was very graciously welcomed by the Prince.

But when the shows were to begin there arose a disordered tumult and crowd upon the stage whither came so great a throng of worshipful personages that might not be displaced, and gentlewomen whose sex did privilege them from violence that when the Prince and his officers had in vain a good while endeavoured reformation at length there was no hope of redress. The Lord Ambassador and his train thought themselves not so kindly entertained as was before expected, and thereupon would not stay any longer but departed in a sort discontented and displeased.

After their departure the tumults somewhat ceased, though still so much as was able to confound any good inventions. In regard whereof, and especially since the sports were intended for the gracing of the Templarians, it was thought good not to offer anything of account saving dancing and revelling with the gentlewomen. After which a *Comedy of Errors* (much like to the *Menechmus of Plautus*) was played by the players. So the night was begun and continued to the end in nothing but confusion and errors, whereupon it was called 'The Night of Errors.'

30th December. Dr. Fletcher Elected Bishop of London.

Dr. Richard Fletcher, Bishop of Worcester, hath been elected Bishop of London.

Plays at the Rose.

Yesterday at the Rose they played *The Wise Man of West Chester*, and to-day *The First Part of Tamburlane*.

SOMEWHAT TO READ FOR THEM THAT LIST

'THE DISPLAY OF FOLLY.'

The Display of Folly, by one O. B., in which under the form of a dialogue, Huddle and Dunstable, two old men, the one a retired gentleman, the other a middling or new upstart franklin, discourse upon the follies and vices of the time, especially amongst the wanton gentlemen of the City. The dedication is to the Earl of Essex.

BARNFIELD'S 'AFFECTIONATE SHEPHERD.'

The Affectionate Shepherd, by Richard Barnfield, containing the very passionate complaints of Daphnis the shepherd for the boy Ganymede, that he would forsake Queen Gwendolen to be his love; and followed by 'The Shepherd's Content,' or the happiness of a harmless life, written upon occasion of the former subject, which endeth:

Thus have I showed, in my country vein,
The sweet content that shepherds still enjoy,
The mickle pleasure and the little pain,
That ever doth await the shepherd's boy:
His heart is never troubled with annoy;
He is a king for he commands his sheep;
He knows no woe, for he doth seldom weep.

He is a courtier, for he courts his love;
He is a scholar, for he sings sweet ditties;
He is a soldier, for he wounds doth prove;
He is the fame of towns, the shame of cities;
He scorns false fortune, but true virtue pities;
He is a gentleman, because his nature
Is kind and affable to every creature.

Who would not then a simple shepherd be,
Rather than be a mighty monarch made?

Since he enjoys such perfect liberty
As never can decay, nor never fade:
He seldom sits in doleful cypress shade,
But lives in hope, in joy, in peace, in bliss,
Joying all joy with this content of his.

But now good fortune lands my little boat
Upon the shore of his desired rest:
Now must I leave awhile my rural note,
To think on him whom my soul loveth best;
He that can make the most unhappy blest;
In whose sweet lay I'll lay me down to sleep,
And never wake till marble stones shall weep.

BARWICK'S 'BRIEF DISCOURSE.'

A Brief Discourse concerning the force and effect of all manual weapons of fire, written by Humphrey Barwick, Gentleman, Soldier, Captain, in which he contesteth the opinions set forth by Sir John Smythe, and Sir Roger Williams; the former holding that the long bow of England was the only weapon in the world for the obtaining of battles and victories in these days, the latter accepting weapons of shot except the musket.

Captain Barwick showeth from his experiences of the wars (which began at the age of 18 in 1548) the greater worth of weapons of fire, being more certain and more deadly, and urging that there should be more men trained in their use. As for Sir John Smith's saying that harquebusiers could give their volleys but at eight, ten or twelve yards while archers could wound and sometimes kill at nine, ten or eleven score, he would stand at six score yards distant from the best archer, armed but in pistol proof, and let him shoot ten arrows one after another at him, and if he stirred from his place let him be punished.

As for those gentlemen and soldiers that reason from their knowledge and experience in the Low Countries and other Civil Wars, and who hold that the like discipline hath not been seen neither in this age nor in any before, and seem thereby to disgrace some more ancient and of greater experience in service than themselves, their knowledge, saith Captain Barwick, is not so worthy as that got in the greater armies of Princes whose subjects were both rich and loyal.

'THE DEATH OF USURY.'

The Death of Usury, wherein are shown reasons against usurers from the jurists, divine and civil, and the statutes now in force concerning usury, being printed at Cambridge.

GRASSI'S 'TRUE ART OF DEFENCE.'

Giacomo de Grassi His True Art of Defence, being translated from the Italian by I. G., gentleman, and dedicated to the Lord Burgh, governor of the Brille, in an epistle by Thomas Churchyard. Herein is described the manner of single combat with the single rapier or single sword, the rapier and dagger, the sword and buckler, the sword and square target, the sword and round target, the case of rapiers; the two-hand sword, and the weapons of the staff as the bill, the partisan, the halberd, and javelin; together with a treatise of deceit or falsing; and a mean how a man may practise himself to get strength, judgment and activity.

HOOKER'S 'ECCLESIASTICAL POLITY.'

Of the Laws of Ecclesiastical Polity, by Richard Hooker. Dr. Hooker saith that he undertook this book because of the wonderful zeal and fervour wherewith the Puritans withstand the received orders of the Church of England; which led him to a consideration of their claiming that every Christian man standeth bound to enter in with them for the furtherance of the 'Lord's Discipline.' But after with travail and care he had examined the reasons he concludeth to set down this, as his final persuasion is that the present form of Church government which the laws of the land have established is such as no law of God nor reason of man hath hitherto been alleged of force sufficient to prove that they do ill who to the uttermost of their power withstand the alteration thereof. Contrariwise, the other which men are required to accept is only by error and misconceit named the ordinance of Jesus Christ; no one proof is as yet brought forth whereby it might clearly appear so in very deed.

The work is four books, with a long preface to the Puritans wherein Dr. Hooker runneth through the history of the Puritan discipline from the time of Calvin, showing their doctrines which are based upon the Bible only (for they think no other writings in the world should be studied), and in rites and ceremonies professing their hatred of all conformity with Rome. The pretended end of their civil reformation is that Christ may have dominion over all, and the means whereby they allure and retain so great multitudes most effectual. They show a wonderful zeal towards God, a hatred of sin, and a singular love of integrity, which men think to be much more than ordinary in them by reason of the custom which they have to fill the ears of the people with invectives against their authorized guides. They bountifully relieve the broken estates of such needy creatures as are apt to be drawn away; and they show a tender compassion for the miseries of the poorer sort, over whose heads they use to pour down showers of tears in complaining that no respect is had unto them, that their goods are devoured by wicked cormorants, their persons had in contempt, all liberty both temporal and spiritual taken away from them, and that it is high time for God now to hear their groans and send them deliverance.

In the first of the four books that follow are considered laws and their several kinds in general; in the second is answered the position of those who urge reformation, in that Scripture is the only rule of all things which in this life may be done by men; in the third is answered the assertion of those who hold that in Scripture there must be of necessity contained a form of Church polity, the laws whereof may in no wise be altered. The fourth book answereth the assertion that the Church polity of the Established Church is corrupted with papist orders, rites and ceremonies.

LAMBARD'S 'EIRENARCHA.'

A new edition of *Eirenarcha, or of the office of the Justices of Peace*, by William Lambard of Lincoln's Inn, having been gathered in 1579, first published in 1581, and now revised according to the reformed Commission of the Peace.

Eirenarcha is written in four books; the first containing a theoric of the office of the Justices of the Peace; the second, the practique of one Justice of the Peace out of the Sessions; the third the practique of two or more Justices out of the Sessions; the fourth book intreating of the Sessions of the Peace and of things incident or belonging thereunto.

MARLOWE AND NASHE'S 'DIDO, QUEEN OF CARTHAGE.'

The Tragedy of Dido, Queen of Carthage, a play written by Christopher Marlowe and Thomas Nashe, and sometime played by the Children of Her Majesty's Chapel.

'THE ORCHARD AND THE GARDEN.'

The Orchard and the Garden, containing certain necessary, secret and ordinary knowledge in grafting and gardening. Herein the author giveth directions for the preparing of the soil and the divers fashions and ways of grafting. To make cherries grow without stones, pare a little cherry tree of one year old at the stump, and cleave it asunder from the top to the root, which do in May; and make an iron fit to draw the heart or marrow from both sides of the tree; then tie it fast together and anoint it with ox dung or loam; and within a year after, when it is grown and healed, another little tree of the same should be grafted upon it; so shall it bring forth fruit without stones.

'THE BATTLE OF ALCAZAR.'

The Battle of Alcazar, fought in Barbary, between Sebastian, King of Portugal and Abdelmelec, King of Morocco; with the death of Captain Stukeley, a play written by George Peele, and sundry times played by the Lord Admiral's men.

PERCY'S 'SONNETS TO THE FAIREST COELIA.'

Sonnets to the Fairest Coelia, by William Percy, containing twenty sonnets in which he vainly begs his mistress's favour; the last ending:

Receive these writs, my sweet and dearest friend,
The lively patterns of my liveless body,
Where thou shalt find in hebon pictures penn'd,
How I was meek, but thou extremely bloody.
I'll walk forlorn along the willow shades,
Alone complaining of a ruthless dame;
Wherere I pass, the rocks, the hills, the glades,
In piteous yells shall sound her cruel name.
There will I wail the lot which fortune sent me,
And make my moans unto the savage ears,

The remnant of the days which nature lent me,
I'll spend them all, conceal'd, in ceaseless tears.
  Since unkind fates permit me not t'enjoy her,
  No more, burst eyes, I mean for to annoy her.

PRESENT REMEDIES AGAINST THE PLAGUE.'

Present Remedies against the Plague. In this little book the people are advised to keep their houses, streets, yards, backsides, sinks and kennels sweet and clean from all standing puddles, dunghills, and corrupt moistures; and not to let dogs, which be a most apt cattle to take infect of any sickness, to come running into the house. Rooms should be aired with charcoal fires, made in stone pans or chafing dishes, and not in chimneys. Of remedies against the plague a good preservative is to chew the root of angelica, setwall, gentian, valerian or cinnamon: to eat a toast of bread, sprinkled with red rose vinegar, buttered and powdered with cinnamon, and eat fasting; to drink rue, wormwood, and scabias, steeped in ale a whole night and drunk fasting every morning, or the water of *carduus benedictus*, or *angelica*, mixed with *mithridatum*.

'A TRUE REPORT OF SUNDRY HORRIBLE CONSPIRACIES.'

A little book is published entitled *A True Report of sundry Horrible Conspiracies of late time detected to have (by barbarous murders) taken away the life of the Queen's most excellent Majesty.* It manifestly appeareth to the world how unjust and dishonourable the King of Spain and his ministers' actions are against the Queen of England; for contrary to all warlike, princely, manlike and Christian examples in any wars or other contentions he has attempted to take her life not by arms or other warlike actions but by secret murder, hateful to God and man from the beginning of the world. Bernardine Mendoza and other of the King of Spain's ministers are shown participant in the conspiracies of Lopez and his fellows, and Ibarra with Yorke and Williams.

THE ENVOY

I HEAR new news every day, and those ordinary rumours of war, plagues, fires, inundations, thefts, murders, massacres, meteors, comets, spectrums, prodigies, apparitions, of towns taken, cities besieged in *France*, *Germany*, *Turkey*, *Persia*, *Poland*, *&c.* daily musters and preparations, and such like, which these tempestuous times afford, battles fought, so many men slain, monomachies, shipwrecks, piracies, and sea-fights, peace, leagues, stratagems, and fresh alarms. A vast confusion of vows, wishes, actions, edicts, petitions, lawsuits, pleas, laws, proclamations, complaints, grievances, are daily brought to our ears. New books every day, pamphlets, currantoes, stories, whole catalogues of volumes of all sorts, new paradoxes, opinions, schisms, heresies, controversies in philosophy, religion, &c. Now come tidings of weddings, maskings, mummeries, entertainments, jubilees, embassies, tilts and tournaments, trophies, triumphs, revels, sports, plays: then again, as in a new shifted scene, treasons, cheating tricks, robberies, enormous villanies in all kinds, funerals, burials, deaths of Princes, new discoveries, expeditions; now comical then tragical matters. To-day we hear of new Lords and officers created, to-morrow of some great men deposed, and then again of fresh honours conferred; one is let loose, another imprisoned; one purchaseth, another breaketh; he thrives, his neighbour turns bankrupt; now plenty, then again dearth and famine; one runs, another rides, wrangles, laughs, weeps, &c. Thus I daily hear, and such like, both private and publick news.

Democritus Junior. To the Reader.

ABBREVIATIONS

The following abbreviations have been used for authorities which are frequently cited :

A.P.C. *Acts of the Privy Council,* edited by J. R. Dasent, 1900, etc.

A.R. *A Transcript of the Registers of the Company of Stationers of London ;* 1554-1640 A.D. Edited by Edward Arber, 5 vols. 1875-1894.

CAMDEN'S ELIZABETH. *The History of the Most Renowned and Victorious Princess Elizabeth, late Queen of England . . . composed by way of annals.* By William Camden. Translated into English, 1630, etc.

BIRCH'S MEMOIRS. *Memoirs of the Reign of Queen Elizabeth from the year 1581 till her Death . . . from the original papers of his [the Earl of Essex's] intimate friend, Anthony Bacon, Esquire, and other manuscripts never before published.* By Thomas Birch, D.D. 2 vols. 1754.

D'EWES JOURNALS. *A Compleat Journal of the Votes, Speeches and Debates both of the House of Lords and House of Commons throughout the whole Reign of Queen Elizabeth.* Collected by . . . Sir Simonds D'Ewes, Baronet. Published by Paul Bowes, of the Middle Temple, Esq. 1693.

FUGGER NEWS LETTERS (2nd Series). *Fugger News Letters, being a further selection from the Fugger papers especially referring to Queen Elizabeth.* Edited by Victor von Klarwill. Translated by L. S. R. Byrne, 1926.

HAKLUYT. *The Principal Navigations, Voyages, Traffiques and Discoveries of the English Nation.* By Richard Hakluyt. References to the edition in 8 vols. in the Everyman Library, 1907, etc.

HENS. DIARY. *Henslowe's Diary.* Vol. i., The Text ; vol. ii., The Commentary. Edited by W. W. Greg, 1904-7.

MIDDLESEX SESSIONS ROLLS. *Middlesex County Records.* Vol i., *Indictments, Coroner's Inquests post mortem, and recognizances from 3 Edward VI. to the end of the reign of Queen Elizabeth.* Edited by John Cordy Jeaffreson, 1886.

PROCLAMATIONS. *A Book containing all such Proclamations as were published during the Reign of the late Queen Elizabeth. Collected together by the industry of Humphrey Dyson, of the City of London, Publique Notary,* 1618. This is an actual collection, not a printed book : references are to the manuscript pagination of the volume in the British Museum (G. 6463).

RYMER'S FŒDERA. *Fœdera, conventiones, literæ, et cuiuscumque generis Acta Publica inter Reges Angliæ et alios quosuis . . .* ex schedis Thomæ Rymer potissimum edidit Robertus Sanderson, 2nd edition, 1727.

S.P. DOM. *State Papers Domestic.* Abstracted in the *Calendar of State Papers Domestic.*

S.P. FOREIGN. *State Papers Foreign,* There is as yet no Calendar or abstract of this collection in the Record Office.

ABBREVIATIONS

SALISBURY PAPERS. *Historical Manuscripts Commission. Calendar of the Manuscripts of the Marquis of Salisbury preserved at Hatfield House*, 1892.

SIEGE OF ROUEN. *Journal of the Siege of Rouen*, 1591. *By Sir Thomas Coningsby.* Edited by J. G. Nichols. Camden Miscellany, vol. i. 1847.

STOW'S ANNALS. *Annales or a General Chronicle of England.* By John Stow, 1592, etc. As there are several editions both of Stow and Camden, and references are quite easy to find, I have not specified particular editions or pages.

STRYPE, ANNALS. *Annals of the Reformation . . . during Queen Elizabeth's happy reign.* By John Strype, 4 vols. 1731 and 7 vols. 1824. [The later edition marks the pagination of the earlier; my references are therefore to the earlier.]

TOWNSHEND. *Historical Collections, or, An exact account of the Four Last Parliaments of Queen Elizabeth* . . . Faithfully and laboriously collected by Heywood Townshend, Esq., a Member in those Parliaments, 1680.

Apart from a few details, there is nothing in Townshend which is not more fully reported in D'Ewes, but I have thought it best to give references to both.

UNTON CORRESPONDENCE. *Correspondence of Sir Henry Unton, Knt, Ambassador from Queen Elizabeth to Henry IV., King of France, in the years* 1591 and 1592. Edited by Rev. Joseph Stevenson, Roxburgh Club, 1847.

NOTES

1590

A Brief Survey of the Year 1590. Camden's *Elizabeth*. The Catholic League had been formed in 1589 when, on the death of the Duke of Anjou, Henry of Navarre (a Protestant) became heir to Henry III. Civil war followed between Henry III. and the League, whose leaders were the Dukes of Guise and Mayne. Shortly afterwards Henry III. was assassinated, leaving his throne to Henry of Navarre. With the aid of Queen Elizabeth (£22,000 in gold and 4,000 men) he defeated the Leaguers at Arques and invested Paris, but being unable to draw Du Mayne to a pitched battle, he withdrew. The English army having done notable service was disbanded, and a way thereby left open for the Spaniards.

1591

1st January. The Privy Council. *A.P.C.*, xxii. 3, under date 1st October, 1591, where the name of Sir Robert Cecil (sworn 2nd August) is added.

Dr. Sutcliffe's 'Treatise of Ecclesiastical Discipline.' Matthew Sutcliffe, *A Treatise of Ecclesiastical Discipline*, 1591, dated 1st January, 1590[-1], in the Epistle Dedicatory. Entered 3rd July. A good statement of the case of the Church of England against the Presbyterian Discipline.

13th January. Stepney's 'Spanish Schoolmaster.' *A.R.*, ii. 573. William Stepney, *The Spanish Schoolmaster*, 1591. A racy little book, giving the Spanish equivalent of those intimate inquiries which the provident traveller makes on arriving at his inn ; also the necessary dialogue for a brief wooing of the chambermaid.

14th January. The Murder of the Lord Burke. See 25th January.

23rd January. Wright's 'Pilgrimage to Paradise.' *A.R.*, ii. 573. Leonard Wright, *The Pilgrimage to Paradise*, 1591.

25th January. The Trial and Condemnation of Cosby. *The Arraignment, Examination, Confession and Judgment of Arnold Cosbye*, entered on 25th January, the day of the trial. This sensational case inspired two ballads, entered on 26th January, and 6th February, and three pamphlets.

27th January. Cosby Hanged. As for 25th January.

30th January. Sir Edmund Yorke sent to the French King. Rymer, xvi. 89.

1st February. Drayton's 'Harmony of the Church.' *A.R.*, ii. 574. M.D., *The Harmony of the Church*, 1591. The Epistle is dated 10th February. Drayton is a notable exception to the rule *poeta nascitur non fit*.

3rd February. Flesh Prohibited during Lent. *Proclamations*, 289. See Appendix I., p. 395.

A Proclamation against Piracy. *Proclamations*, 288.

9th February. JOB HORTOP'S 'TRAVELS.' Job Hortop, *The Travels of an Englishman*, 1591. Another version came out the same year under the title *The Rare Travels of Job Hortop an Englishman, who was not heard of in three and twenty years space.* Both books were printed for William Wright, but neither has the printer's device; the first book is a more polished effort than the second; the present entry is founded on both.

FRAUNCE'S 'COUNTESS OF PEMBROKE'S IVYCHURCH' AND 'EMANUEL.' *A.R.*, ii. 575. Abraham Fraunce, *The Countess of Pembroke's Ivychurch*, and *The Countess of Pembroke's Emanuel*, 1591. For an account of Fraunce see D.N.B. Jonson's comment to Drummond was 'that Abram Francis in his English Hexameters was a fool'; he was at least a very persevering enthusiast. The Countess of Pembroke was an admirable and justly famous lady, but she was partially responsible for the continuance of the attempt to foist classical metres on to the English tongue.

13th February. A PETITION OF THE SKINNERS. *Salisbury MSS.*, iv. 91.

20th February. THE SCOTTISH KING'S POOR ESTATE. Rymer xvi. 148. Approximate date.

26th February. HARINGTON'S 'ORLANDO FURIOSO.' *A.R.*, ii. 576. The editor of *Nugae Antiquae* received this well-known story from a Mr. Walker, who had it from the Earl of Charlemont. It is clear from some references in *Nugae*, and from the prefatory stanzas in Book xxviii. of the translation, that the story is not without foundation. 'That John Harington's *Ariosto* under all translations was the worst,' said Jonson to Drummond.

11th March. PURITAN DISCONTENTS. *Birch's Memoirs*, i. 62. From a letter written to Anthony Bacon, from London, dated 11th March, 1591.

12th March. RUMOURS. *S.P. Dom. Addenda*, xxxii. 7.

22nd March. TOWN GOSSIP. *S.P. Dom.*, ccxxxviii. 82. (Phellippes.) Thomas Phellippes held a post in the Customs, but was employed by Lord Burghleigh as an expert decipherer of captured papers. He used also to send news-letters to spies abroad. These news-letters are particularly valuable summaries of contemporary gossip, as Phellippes had special opportunities for obtaining information.

25th March. COCKAINE'S 'TREATISE OF HUNTING.' Sir Thomas Cockaine, *A Short Treatise of Hunting*; dated 1591 on title-page; 31st December, 1590, in the preface.

30th March. THE SOLDIER'S PAY. *A.P.C.*, xxi. 15.

31st March. CAPTAIN GLEMHAM'S EXPLOITS. The date is approximate. *The Honourable Actions of E. Glemham, Esquire, against the Spaniards*, 1591. Entered 29th April; a ballad on the same subject was entered on 12th May. After putting into Algiers to refit, Glemham returned to England in 1592, having captured a ship laden with spices on the way. The cargo on arrival in London was claimed by Philippo Corsini, representing the Venetian traders, and a lawsuit followed. I suspect that both pamphlet and ballad were inspired by commercial interests to cover a somewhat shady transaction. See 17th May, 1592, and 19th August, 1594.

3rd April. INSTRUCTIONS FOR SIR R. WILLIAMS. Rymer, xvi. 94.

A FRAY AT LIMEHOUSE. *Middlesex Sessions Rolls*, i. 193.

14th April. A QUARREL IN THE PRESENCE. *A.P.C.*, xxi. 53.

16th April. SENTENCES AT THE SESSIONS. *Middlesex Sessions Rolls*, i. 193. Several other cases of rape committed on children are recorded.

24th April. A PROCLAMATION AGAINST TRADING WITH THE FRENCH REBELS. *Proclamations*, 291.

26th April. A PROCLAMATION AGAINST UNAUTHORISED POSTS. *Proclamations*, 293.

29th April. 'THE SHEPHERD'S STAR.' *A.R.*, ii. 579. Thomas Bradshaw, *The Shepherd's Star*, 1591. A dull work.

30th April. FLORIO'S 'SECOND FRUITS.' John Florio, *Florio's Second Fruits*, 1591; so dated in the Epistle to the reader. Florio is more concerned with wit than utility in his phrases; still the book is a good example of the conversation of bright young men, such as Shakespeare heard at Southampton's house in '93-'94 and transmuted into the *Sonnets*, *Venus and Adonis* and *Love's Labours Lost*. Florio enters Southampton's service shortly afterwards.

2nd May. LODGE'S 'ROBERT, DUKE OF NORMANDY.' Thomas Lodge, *The History of Robert, Second Duke of Normandy*, 1591; dated 2nd May, 1591, in the Epistle Dedicatory. A gruesome yarn but well told.

3rd May. BRETON'S 'BOWER OF DELIGHTS.' *A.R.*, ii. 581. N.B., Gent., *Britton's Bower of Delights*. Modern edition by A. B. Grosart in *The Complete Works of Nicholas Breton*, 1876. See note on 12th April, 1592.

8th May. THE FRENCH KING'S ORDINANCES. *Ordinances set forth by the King, for the rule and government of his Majesty's men of war*, 1591. Entered *S.R.*, 8th May.

CARTWRIGHT THE PURITAN BEFORE THE HIGH COMMISSION. *Lansdowne MSS.*, lxviii.; printed in A. F. Scott Pearson, *Thomas Cartwright and Elizabethan Puritanism*, 1925, p. 458.

12th May. RIPLEY'S 'COMPOUND OF ALCHEMY.' *A.R.*, ii. 582. George Ripley, *The Compound of Alchemy*, 1591. Jonson makes effective play with all this apparatus in the *Alchemist*.

15th May. THE 'CENTURION'S' FIGHT WITH FIVE SPANISH SHIPS, *A.R.*, ii. 582. *The valiant and most laudable fight performed in the Straights, by the 'Centurion' of London against five Spanish Gallies. Who is safely returned this present month of May. Anno. D. 1591.* Entered 15th May; a ballad was entered at the same time.

16th May. AN INVASION EXPECTED. *A.P.C.*, xxi. 133.

19th May. A SEDITIOUS FELLOW. *Middlesex Session Rolls*, i. 195.

21st May. THE QUEEN at THEOBALD'S Nicholls' *Progresses*, vol. ii; Strype's, *Annals*, iv, 77.

RUMOURS. *S.P. Dom.*, ccxxxviii. 159. (Phellippes.) For an account of the trial of the witches see 29th February, 1592.

24th May. DR. GERVASE BABINGTON'S SERMON. Gervase Babington, *A Sermon preached at the Court at Greenwich the xxiiii of May, 1591.* On this occasion no virtue at all in IF!

26th May. SIR R. WILLIAMS COMMENDED. *A.P.C.*, xxi. 167.

THE GALLANT ACTION OF SIR R. WILLIAMS. Antony Colynet, *The True History of the Civil Wars of France*, 1591, p. 532.

31st May. RUMOURS. *S.P. Dom.*, ccxxxviii. 188. (Phellippes.)

1st June. SIDNEY'S 'ASTROPHEL AND STELLA.' Sir Philip Sidney, *Astrophel and Stella*, 1591. Modern editions by A. Feuillerat, 1922, etc. Nashe's preface is included in *The Works of Thomas Nashe*, edited by R. B.

M'Kerrow, 1905, vol. iii. The date here given for the publication of *Astrophel and Stella* is a guess; the evidence, such as it is, being (*a*) a sneer at alchemists in Nashe's preface, possibly a reference to Ripley (see 12th May); (*b*) the publication of Breton's *Bower of Delights* (see 3rd May), evidently written at the time of Sidney's death, suggests a particular revival of interest at this time; (*c*) a second edition of *Astrophel* was issued during 1591, but without Nashe's effusion; the first therefore was presumably issued some little time earlier. *Astrophel and Stella* is the most important volume of poetry published during this year; hereafter for the next five years all the pet poets litter sonnets in Paul's Churchyard.

5th June. THE TAKING OF GUINGCAMP. *The True Report of the service in Brittany. Performed lately by the Honourable Knight Sir John Norris and other Captains and Gentlemen soldiers before Guingcamp,* 1591. Entered 5th June.

6th June. UNLAWFUL GAMES TO BE PUT DOWN. *A.P.C.*, xxi. 174.

23rd June. LEONARD DIGGES' 'TECTONICON.' *A.R.*, ii. 585. *A Book named Tectonicon,* Leonard Digges, 1591.

25th June. THE TERMS OF AGREEMENT FOR THE DESPATCH OF FURTHER TROOPS TO NORMANDY. Rymer, xvi. 102, 127. Newhaven was the Elizabethan name for Le Havre.

1st July. RUMOURS. *S.P. Dom.*, ccxxxix. 70. (Phellippes.)

5th July. THE WAR IN BRITTANY. *A Journal, or brief report of the late service in Britaigne, by the Prince de Dombes, General of the French King's Army in those parts, assisted with Her Majesty's forces at present there under the conduct of Sir John Norris: advertised by letters from the said Prince to the King's ambassador here resident with Her Majesty and confirmed by like advertisements from others, imployed in that service. Published to answer the slanderous bruits raised of late by some evil affected to that and other good actions undertaken against the enemy of God's true Religion.* 1591. Entered 5th July. A piece of Privy Council propaganda; the book was entered in the *Stationers' Register* 'by order of the Council under Master Wilks his hand, one of the clerks to the Council.' The 'slanderous bruits' seem to have been caused by a feeling that the English casualties were not justified by the results obtained.

16th July. A CONSPIRACY FOR PRETENDED REFORMATION. Richard Cosin, *The Conspiracy for Pretended Reformation,* dated on the title-page 30th September, 1591, published 1592; a long and detailed account of the whole affair, from which Camden apparently draws. See also Stow's *Annals*, Camden's *Elizabeth*, *A.P.C.*, etc.

19th July. RUMOURS. *S.P. Dom.*, ccxxxix. 93. (Phellippes.)

24th July. SIR HENRY UNTON MADE AMBASSADOR TO THE FRENCH KING. *Unton Correspondence*, p. 1. It has been pointed out to me that ambassadors' letters and instructions were secret documents and therefore not general gossip; still, seven years later John Chamberlain had a wide knowledge of confidential news. Even during the Great War indiscreet revelations by Cabinet Ministers and political jackals were not unknown.

25th July. A RESTRAINT OF PLAYING. *A.P.C.*, xxi. 324.

26th July. THE TRIAL AND CONDEMNATION OF WILLIAM HACKET. Richard Cosin, *The Conspiracy for Pretended Reformation,* 1592.

28th July. THE EXECUTION OF HACKET. Authorities as for 16th July. There seems to have been a recognised etiquette in quartering. Prisoners who annoyed the crowd, or the authorities, were quartered living; but as a mark of favour those who behaved in a markedly courageous and seemly manner (*e.g.* by praying for the Queen or expressing genuine repentance) were allowed to hang until they were dead or at least insensible.

29th July. COPPINGER DIES IN PRISON. Authorities as for 16th July. For the connection of Hacket and his companions with the Puritan leaders see A. F. Scott Pearson, *Thomas Cartwright and Elizabethan Puritanism*, 1925.

2nd August. SIR ROBERT CECIL A PRIVY COUNCILLOR. *A.P.C.*, xxi. 358.

3rd August. A SUSPECTED PORTUGUESE. *S.P.D.*, ccxxiv. 123. See also 23rd January, 1594.

7th August. AN ASSAULT IN ST. PETER'S, WESTMINSTER. *Middlesex Sessions Rolls*, i. 194.

A BUILDING ALLOWED IN BLACKFRIARS. *A.P.C.*, xxi. 367.

13th August. ANDRADA'S DECLARATIONS. *S.P. Dom.*, ccxxxix. 135. See 24th January, 1594, the case of Dr. Lopez. Don Antonio was the pretender to the throne of Portugal. To carry the war into the enemy's country, Drake and Norris, joined by the Earl of Essex, led a great expedition in 1589 to Portugal. But though the English soldiers showed great valour, the voyage was a signal disaster. The Portuguese lacked enthusiasm; and out of 11,500 men 6000 died, mostly from disease. Since then Don Antonio had remained an unwelcome pensioner in England. See pages 115, 278, 280.

20th August. A QUACK FIGURE CASTER. *A.P.C.*, xxi. 409.

21st August. THE QUEEN ON PROGRESS. *The Honourable Entertainment given to the Queen's Majesty in Progress at Cowdray in Sussex by the Right Honourable the Lord Montacute*, 1591; modern editions in Nichols' *Progresses of Queen Elizabeth*, vol. ii.; and *The Works of John Lyly*, edited by R. W. Bond, 1902, who believes that these entertainments are of Lyly's devising; the evidence does not seem strong. Both this pamphlet and the account of the entertainment at Elvetham (see 24th September) went into further editions.

22nd August. THE BORDEAUX WINE FLEET TO BE STAYED. *A.P.C.*, xxi. 413.

28th August. MR. THOMAS CAVENDISH'S EXPEDITION. Hakluyt, viii. 289.

31st August. RUMOURS. *S.P. Dom.*, ccxxxix. 159.

3rd September. ILLEGAL BUILDING IN LONDON. *A.P.C.*, xxi. 422.

4th September. THE EARL OF ESSEX IN FRANCE. *Siege of Rouen*, p. 13 *et seq.*

6th September. THE QUEEN DISCONTENTED AT THE ILL SUCCESS IN FRANCE. *Unton Correspondence*, 59.

10th September. NEWS FROM FRANCE. *Siege of Rouen*, p. 21 *et seq.*

12th September. MR. WALTER DEVEREUX SLAIN. *Memoirs of Robert Cary*, King's Classics, 1905, p. 14.

12th September. The Bordeaux Wine Ships to Sail in Consort. *A.P.C.*, xxi. 442.

13th September. The Earl of Essex Rebuked. *Unton Correspondence*, p. 72.

16th September. A Proclamation against supplying the King of Spain with Corn. *Proclamations*, 296. The opening words of this proclamation are a good example of the doctrine of 'God's own Englishmen.'

21st September. A Secret Marriage. *S.P. Dom.*, ccxl. 17. This Mr. Thomas Shirley was one of the three famous brothers, and father of the dramatist; Captain Anthony Shirley (see pages 41, 298), who distinguished himself in the French war, was another.

24th September. The Queen, on Progress, Visits Elvetham. *The Honourable Entertainment given to the Queen's Majesty at Elvetham in Hampshire, by the Right Honourable the Earl of Hertford*, 1591; modern editions in Nichols' *Progresses*, vol. ii., also in *The Complete Works of John Lyly*, edited by R. W. Bond, 1902, i. 421. From the tone of the pamphlet, it seems to have been written by one of the household. It was entered on 1st October, and went into three editions the same year. The song, 'With Fragrant Flowers,' is attributed to Thomas Watson in *England's Helicon*, and *Coridon and Phillida* to Breton.

29th September. The Beacon Watches. *A.P.C.*, xxi. 470.

30th September. Dr. Cosin's 'The Conspiracy for Pretended Reformation.' Richard Cosin, *The Conspiracy for Pretended Reformation*, 1592. 30th September is the date given on the title-page.

2nd October. The Capture of Gournay. *Unton Correspondence*, p. 96. Gournay was captured on 26th September.

4th October. Three of Lyly's Plays to be Printed. *A.R.*, ii. 596. John Lyly, *Endymion*, 1591; *Galathea*, 1592; *Midas*, 1592. Modern edition by R. W. Bond in *The Complete Works of John Lyly*, 1902, vols. ii. and iii. The importance of this publication has been generally overlooked. Lyly's plays were written for a courtly audience and not acted on the public stages, and might not therefore be expected to appeal to the usual play-going public. The printer realised that the publication was an experiment, and appealed for support—'I refer it [*Endymion*] to thy indifferent judgment to peruse, whom I would willingly please. And if this may pass with thy good liking, I will then go forward to publish the rest. In the meantime let this have thy good word for my better encouragement.' The printed drama, in short, now becomes literature, and not merely the book of words of a stage play.

7th October. A Case of Sorcery. *Middlesex Sessions Rolls*, i. 197.

10th October. The Bordeaux Wine Fleet. *A.P.C.*, xxii. 17.

16th October. The Earl of Essex takes leave of his Army. *Siege of Rouen*, p. 23.

17th October. The Bordeaux Wine Fleet. *A.P.C.*, xxii. 30.

20th October. The Loss of the 'Revenge.' Sir Walter Ralegh, *The Report of the Truth of the Fight about the Azores*, 1591. Entered 23rd November; reprinted in *Hakluyt's Voyages*. This date is approximate, but Phellippes, writing on 31st October, says the news is now stale. Probably some of the survivors reached London before the main fleet came to Plymouth.

22nd October. AN AFFRAY AT WESTMINSTER. *Middlesex Sessions Rolls*, i. 200.

25th October. PRECAUTIONS AGAINST DISORDER AT THE PORTS. *A.P.C.*, xxii. 37.

27th October. DISORDERS AT DARTMOUTH. *A.P.C.*, xxii. 44.

28th October. THE TRIAL OF BRIAN O'ROURKE. Stow, *Annals*. See page 3 and 3rd November.

31st October. RUMOURS. *S.P. Dom.*, ccxl. 53. (Phellippes.) Sir William Stanley being governor of Deventer had betrayed it to the Spaniards in 1587. They pensioned him with the intention of using his services for the proposed invasion of England.

1st November. FATHER JENNINGS, A NOTABLE JESUIT, TAKEN. *Cath. Rec. Soc.*, v. 206. Topcliffe was in charge of the counter-recusant secret police; he greatly distinguished himself by his success in rounding up the Jesuits who came over with Fr. Campion in 1580, and since then had enjoyed considerable extra-legal power. He was expert in the methods of the 'third degree' and had certain special tortures of his own; see p. 140.

3rd November. THE EARL OF ESSEX IN NORMANDY. *Siege of Rouen*, p. 29.

THE EXECUTION OF O'ROURKE. Stow, *Annals*.

4th November. AN AFFRAY NEAR WHITEHALL. *Middlesex Sessions Rolls*, i. 200.

SPANISH DISASTERS. Walter Ralegh, *The Report of the Truth of the Fight about the Azores*, 1591.

'MEDIUS' PRINTED. William Byrd, *Liber Secundus Sacrarum Cantionum*, 1591.

5th November. A PROCLAMATION AGAINST VAGRANT SOLDIERS. *Proclamations*, 300. In this company are to be found such ex-soldiers as Ancient Pistol (after Agincourt), Brainworm, Peter Skirmish (of the *Puritan Widow*) and other stage worthies.

MEASURES OF RELIEF FOR RETURNED SOLDIERS. *A.P.C.*, xxii. 58.

8th November. SOUTHWELL'S 'MARY MAGDALEN'S FUNERAL TEARS.' *A.R.*, ii. 598. Robert Southwell, *Mary Magdalen's Funeral Tears*, 1591.

15th November. SPANISH LOSSES. Strype, *Annals*, iv. 77.

20th November. THE DEATH OF SIR CHRISTOPHER HATTON. Camden's *Elizabeth*, Stow's *Annals*. See page 152-3.

21st November. THE PROCLAMATION AGAINST JESUITS. *Proclamations*, pp. 298, 301. Strype's *Annals*, iv. 56, 62.

25th November. THE SIEGE OF ROUEN. *Siege of Rouen*, pp. 33-47. Gabriel D'Estrée was Henry's mistress.

26th November. THE QUEEN'S LETTERS TO THE EMPEROR OF RUSSIA. *S.P. Dom.*, ccxl. 70.

ABUSES IN THE CLOTH TRADE. *A.P.C.*, xxii. 89.

THE CHARGES OF THE BORDEAUX FLEET. *A.P.C.*, xxii. 86.

4th December. A PETITION OF THE PURITAN PRISONERS. *Lansdowne MSS.*, lxviii., printed in A. F. Scott Pearson, *Thomas Cartwright and Elizabethan Puritanism*, 1925, p. 470.

ORDERS FOR REFORMING THE ARMY IN NORMANDY. *A.P.C.*, xxii. 98.

5th December. AN UNSUCCESSFUL AMBUSCADE AT ROUEN. *Siege of Rouen*, p. 52.

6th December. GREENE'S 'A MAIDEN'S DREAM.' *A.R.*, ii. 600. Robert Greene, *A Maiden's Dream*, 1591. This professional ululation in form parodies in anticipation some of the most notable English elegies, *Lycidas*, *Adonais*, and *The Vision of Judgement*—Southey's. Modern editions in A. B. Grosart, *The Complete Works of Robert Greene*, 1881; and J. C. Collins, *The Plays and Poems of Robert Greene*, 1905.

10th December. SEVEN CATHOLICS EXECUTED. *The Life and Death of Mr. Edmund Geninges* . . . at S. Omers, 1614. *Cath. Rec. Soc.*, v. 206. See 1st November.

13th December. GREENE'S 'NOTABLE DISCOVERY OF COSNAGE,' AND 'THE SECOND PART OF CONNY-CATCHING.' *A.R.*, ii. 600. Robert Greene, *A Notable Discovery of Cosnage*, 1591, and *The Second Part of Conny-Catching*, 1592. Modern editions by A. B. Grosart in *The Complete Works of Robert Greene*, 1881; and *The Bodley Head Quartos*, vol. i., 1923. Though entered together, the *Notable Discovery* was evidently published some little time before the *Second Part*. Both pamphlets went into second editions in 1592. There were two important results of Greene's conny-catching pamphlets; they turned the attention of the gentleman reader, now beginning to grow weary of *Arcadia* and *Euphues*, to new interests, and they attracted a new kind of reader. Greene's previous works, *The Mourning Garment* and *Never Too Late*, were dedicated to the gentlemen scholars of both Universities; now he successfully appeals to merchants, apprentices, farmers, and plain countrymen. The conny-catching pamphlets are a symptom of the reaction to realism which was the first stage towards the satires and the humour plays at the end of the century.

15th December. THE DEFENCE OF PLYMOUTH. *A.P.C.*, xxii. 121.

A NEGLIGENT COMMISSARY DISMISSED. *A.P.C.*, xxii. 125.

16th December. SIR CHRISTOPHER HATTON'S FUNERAL. Stow, *Annals*.

17th December. MASTERLESS MEN IN THE CITY TO BE TAKEN UP. *A.P.C.*, xxii. 129.

18th December. TWO SUSPECTED RECUSANTS. *A.P.C.*, xxii. 131.

A NOTABLE INSTANCE OF THE CORRUPTION OF THESE WARS. *Siege of Rouen*, page 60.

19th December. FURTHER MEASURES AGAINST RECUSANTS. *A.P.C.*, xxii. 138.

21st December. MASTERLESS MEN TO BE TAKEN UP IN KENT. *A.P.C.*, xxii. 150.

24th December. A HIGH-HANDED ARREST. *A.P.C.*, xxii. 151.

26th December. THE TRIPOLI MERCHANTS RECOMMENDED TO CHARITY. *A.P.C.*, xxii. 158.

BEACON WATCHES. *A.P.C.*, xxii. 160.

29th December. Goods rifled from Prizes in Cornwall and Devon to be restored. *Proclamations*, p. 302.

31st December. The Siege of Rouen. *Siege of Rouen*, page 56.

SOMEWHAT TO READ FOR THEM THAT LIST

Under this heading are grouped some of the more interesting books that appeared during the year, which were not entered in the Stationers' Register *and cannot be more accurately dated.*

Clapham's 'Narcissus.' John Clapham, *Narcissus*, 1591. This is one of several poems, written during these years, wherein the physical attraction of male youth is unduly glorified. See also *Cephalus and Procris* (p. 263), *Arisbas* (p. 264), *The Affectionate Shepherd* (p. 344); Shakespeare's *Sonnets*; Marlowe's *Edward II.*, and *Hero and Leander*; and E. K.'s gloss on Hobbinol in the first month of *The Shepherd's Calendar*.

Cosin's 'Apology for Sundry Proceedings.' Richard Cosin, *An Apology: of and for sundry proceedings by Jurisdiction Ecclesiastical*, 1591. This was Whitgift's reply to Burleigh's criticism of his persecution of the Puritans; see page 16.

Digges' 'Pantometria.' Thomas Digges, *A Geometrical practical treatise named Pantometria*, 1591. A learned and finely printed folio.

Garrard's 'Art of War.' William Garrard, *The Art of War*, 1591, so dated on title-page, dated 1590 in the Epistle to the reader. A complete and important military manual, with many diagrams. Anyone who had studied the elaborate numerical diagrams, illustrating the formation of troops in close order, in this and the other military manuals of the time would realise why Iago called Cassio a 'great arithmetician.'

Gibbon's 'Work worth the Reading.' *A Work worth the Reading*, 1591. The question of the right of parents to enforce a marriage on their children was much discussed at this time, especially after the sensational murder of old Mr. Page of Plymouth by his girl-wife Ulalia in 1590, recorded in ballads, a pamphlet, and afterwards in a play (now lost) by Jonson and Dekker. Deloney in writing a suitable dying speech for the murderer lays the ultimate responsibility for the murder on the girl's parents. See page 246.

Giles Fletcher's 'Of the Russe Commonwealth.' Giles Fletcher, *Of the Russe Commonwealth*, 1591. Reprinted in Hakluyt.

Quercetanus' 'Spageric Preparation of Minerals, Animals, and Vegetables.' Joseph Du Chesne, *A Brief Answer*, etc., and *The True and Perfect Spageric*, 1591.

'The Troublesome Reign of King John.' *The first part* and *the second part of The Troublesome Reign of King John*, 1591. Modern edition in Farmer's Facsimile Reprints, 1911.

Wilmot's 'Tancred and Gismund.' Robert Wilmot, *The Tragedy of Tancred and Gismund*, 1591. Modern edition by W. W. Greg, The Malone Society, 1914.

1592

1st January. SPENSER'S 'DAPHNAIDA.' Edmund Spenser, *Daphnaida*, 1591. Modern edition by J. C. Smith and E. de Selincourt in *The Poetical Works of Edmund Spenser*, 1916; etc.

3rd January. ANOTHER PROCLAMATION AGAINST THE DISORDERS AT PORTS. *Proclamations*, p. 303.

7th January. THE LEVANT COMPANY. *S.P. Dom.*, ccxli. 11.

THE COMMISSION AGAINST JESUITS RENEWED. *A.P.C.*, xxii. 174.

MR. HENRY CAESAR RELEASED. *A.P.C.*, xxii. 174.

9th January. A PROTEST ON BEHALF OF THE PURITANS. Thomas Wright, *Queen Elizabeth and her Times*, ii. 417.

AN ATTORNEY'S UNSEEMLY APPAREL. *A.P.C.*, xxii. 175.

16th January. A CASE OF CONTRABAND GOODS. *A.P.C.*, xxii. 181.

CERTAIN GOODS PROHIBITED TO BE CARRIED TO SPAIN. *A.P.C.*, xxii. 183.

19th January. THE EARL OF ESSEX RETURNS TO COURT. *Unton Correspondence*, pp. 251, 265, 276, 294.

22nd January. A PROCLAMATION TO REFORM ABUSES IN THE CLOTH TRADE. *Proclamations*, p. 304.

28th January. A SPECIAL COMMISSION TO DEAL WITH IMPRISONED RECUSANTS. *A.P.C.*, xxii. 214.

30th January. FLESH PROHIBITED DURING LENT. *A.P.C.*, xxii. 217.

4th February. DANIEL'S 'DELIA.' *A.R.*, ii. 603. *Delia, containing certain sonnets*, by Samuel Daniel, 1592.

6th February. NEWS FROM FRANCE. *Unton Correspondence*, p. 301.

SIR FRANCIS WILLOUGHBY BEFORE THE COUNCIL. *A.P.C.*, xxii. 240. See 24th December, 1591.

7th February. GREENE'S 'THIRD PART OF CONNY-CATCHING.' *A.R.*, ii. 603. Robert Greene, *The third and last part of Conny-Catching*, 1592. Modern editions by A. B. Grosart in *The Complete Works of Robert Greene*, 1881-3; vol. iii. in *The Bodley Head Quartos*, 1923.

12th February. THE QUEEN REFUSES FURTHER AID TO THE FRENCH KING. *Unton Correspondence*, p. 319. The war weariness of the 1590's is sometimes forgotten by those critics who take the hearty patriotism of the history-plays as an expression of the general mood.

14th February. NEWS FROM FRANCE. *Unton Correspondence*, p. 303.

15th February. FLESH PROHIBITED IN LONDON DURING LENT. *Proclamations*, p. 306.

19th February. PLAYING RESUMED. *Hens. Diary*, i. 13 and ii. 151. *The Honourable History of Friar Bacon and Friar Bungay* was written by Robert Greene in 1588 or 1589. The record of plays acted from day to day at the Rose, and recorded in *Henslowe's Diary*, justifies, in my opinion, their inclusion as literary gossip. Unfortunately there is no similar record for the other London Theatres—The Theatre and The Curtain—where, presumably, as many plays were being acted.

THE QUEEN RESOLVES TO SEND SOLDIERS TO FRANCE. *A.P.C.*, xxii. 256.

20th February. NEWS OF ROUEN. *Unton Correspondence*, p. 331.

21st February. THOMAS PORMORT, A JESUIT, EXECUTED. *Catholic Record Society*, v. 209. Topcliffe was a lewd liar.

23rd February. A LITIGIOUS FELLOW. *A.P.C.*, xxii. 247.

SIR R. WILLIAMS IN COMMAND IN NORMANDY. *A.P.C.*, xxii. 248.

24th February. VICTUALS SENT TO NORMANDY. *A.P.C.*, xxii. 273, 279.

25th February. A PETITION AGAINST PLAYS. *Remembrancia*, i. 635, quoted in *Malone Society Collections*, i. 68.

26th February. PLAYS OF THE WEEK. *Hens. Diary*, i. 13 and ii. 152. *Muly Mullocco* is perhaps George Peele's *Battle of Alcazar*. *Orlando Furioso* was written by Greene about 1589. *The Jew of Malta* was written by Christopher Marlowe early in 1589. *The Spanish Comedy* (called also in the *Diary*, *Don Horatio* and *The Comedy of Jeronimo*) was apparently the first part of *The Spanish Tragedy*; it does not survive. *Sir John Maundeville* and *Harry of Cornwall* are also lost.

THE DUKE OF PARMA RETREATS. *Unton Correspondence*, p. 341.

28th February. MAIMED SOLDIERS TO BE EXAMINED. *Proclamations*, p. 307.

29th February. THE SCOTTISH WITCHES. *Newes from Scotland*, 1591[-2]. Modern edition in *The Bodley Head Quartos*, vol. IX. There was excuse for King James's excessive interest in witchcraft; some of the evidence brought out at these trials was afterwards incorporated in *Dæmonology*, first published in 1597.

1st March. MEN TO BE IMPRESTED FOR SERVICE IN FRANCE. *A.P.C.*, xxii. 297.

SIR EDMUND YORK'S INSTRUCTIONS. *A.P.C.*, xxii. 297.

ANOTHER PETITION OF THE PURITAN PRISONERS. *Lansdowne MSS.*, lxix. 45, printed in A. F. Scott Pearson, *Thomas Cartwright and Elizabethan Puritanism*, 1925, p. 477.

2nd March. SIR WALTER RALEGH'S EXPEDITION. *Proclamations*, p. 308.

3rd March. MUSTER ROLLS IN THE COUNTIES. *A.P.C.*, xxii. 301.

THE FISHMONGERS REBUKED FOR NEGLECTING TO SUPERVISE THE BUTCHERS. *A.P.C.*, xxii. 305. See Appendix I., p. 395.

4th March. PLAYS OF THE WEEK. *Hens. Diary*, i. 13, ii. 152. *Harry the Sixth* is probably the first part of the play included in the First Folio as Shakespeare's *Henry VI*. *Cloris and Ergasto*, *Pope Joan*, *Machiavel*, *Bindo and Richardo* have perished.

5th March. RUMOURS OF PEACE. *Unton Correspondence*, p. 352.

7th March. REPORT OF SIR JOHN NORRIS ON THE STATE OF FRANCE. Rymer's *Fœdera*, xvi. 174.

ORDERS AGAINST THOSE WHO AIDED DESERTERS. *A.P.C.*, xxii. 318.

8th March. UNDUTIFUL GENTLEMEN. *A.P.C.*, xxii. 312.

9th March. A SPANISH PRISONER'S ACCOUNT OF THE STATE OF ENGLAND. *Spanish State Papers*, iv. 593. It is not perhaps fair to include this entry; but as such accounts at first hand are rare and valuable, it may be excused. For Don Antonio see note on 13th August, 1591.

11th March. PLAYS OF THE WEEK. *Hens. Diary*, i. 13; ii. 153. *The Four Plays in One* was part of a play dealing with the Seven Deadly Sins; the theatre 'plat' survives in the Alleyn Collection but the text has perished. *A Looking Glass for London* was written by Lodge and Greene. *Zenobia* is lost.

12th March. THE EARL OF BOTHWELL AND THE SCOTTISH BORDER. *A P.C.*, xxii. 331.

18th March. PLAYS OF THE WEEK. *Hens. Diary*, i. 13, ii. 153. *The Spanish Tragedy* (better known at this time as *Jeronimo* or *Hieronimo*), written by Thomas Kyd between 1586 and 1588, was the most popular of all Elizabethan plays.

21st March. HOPEFUL NEWS FROM FRANCE. *Unton Correspondence*, pp. 361, 379, 384.

24th March. VOLUNTEERS TO BE LEVIED IN LONDON. *A.P.C.*, xxii. 361.

25th March. DISTRESS IN ROUEN. *Unton Correspondence*, p. 391.

PLAYS OF THE WEEK. *Hens. Diary*, i. 13, ii. 154. *Constantine* and *Jerusalem* have perished.

COMPLAINTS AGAINST THE GOVERNOR OF OSTEND. *A.P.C.*, xxii. 363.

RECUSANCY IN THE NORTH. *A.P.C.*, xxii. 369.

27th March. THE CASE OF ROBERT PAINE. *A.P.C.*, xxii. 372. See 6th February.

CAPTAIN GLEMHAM'S SHIPS TO BE STAYED. *A.P.C.*, xxii. 373. For other ventures of Captain Glemham see pages 18, 132, 311.

31st March. THE PURITAN PRISONERS RELEASED. Pearson, *Cartwright*, 357, 479. Approximate date.

1st April. PLAYS OF THE WEEK AT THE ROSE. *Hens. Diary*, i. 13.

2nd April. MERCY TO BE SHOWN TO DEBTORS. *A.P.C.*, xxii. 384.

7th April. TWO PRISONERS' RANSOM. *A.P.C.*, xxii. 392. See 30th April.

DISTRESS IN ROUEN. *Unton Correspondence*, p. 408.

8th April. PLAYS OF THE WEEK. *Hens. Diary*, i. 13.

12th April. BRETON'S 'THE PILGRIMAGE TO PARADISE' AND 'THE COUNTESS OF PEMBROKE'S LOVE.' Nicholas Breton, *The Pilgrimage to Paradise, joined with the Countess of Pembroke's Love*, 1592. Modern edition by A. B. Grosart in *The Complete Works of Nicholas Breton*, 1876. Nicholas Breton has not received his due because few of his works are available in any accessible reprint. *The Pilgrimage* is an interesting forecast of Bunyan's

Pilgrim's Progress, The Countess of Pembroke's Love an indication of the respect and admiration felt for this remarkable patroness of letters. Dated 12th April in the Epistle.

15th April. PLAYS OF THE WEEK. *Hens. Diary*, i. 14, ii. 155. *Titus and Vespasian* is perhaps an earlier version of *Titus Andronicus*.

16th April. A FRAY AT FULHAM. *Middlesex Sessions Rolls*, i. 206.

ENGLISH MARINERS FORBIDDEN TO SAIL WITH A STRANGER. *A.P.C.*, xxii. 399.

17th April. THE SIEGE OF ROUEN RAISED. *Unton Correspondence*, p. 413.

21st April. 'THE DEFENCE OF CONNY-CATCHING.' *A.R.*, ii. 609. Cuthbert Connycatcher, *The Defence of Conny-Catching.* Modern editions by A. B. Grosart in *The Complete Works of Robert Greene*, 1881-3; vol. x. of *The Bodley Head Quartos*, 1924.

22nd April. PLAYS OF THE WEEK. *Hens. Diary*, i. 14.

THE ENGHUIZEN SHIP RELEASED. *A.P.C.*, xxii. 402.

27th April. THE FRENCH KING ATTACKS PARMA. *Unton Correspondence*, p. 424.

THE TRIAL OF SIR JOHN PERROT. Cobbett's *State Trials*, vol. i., 1315.

29th April. PLAYS OF THE WEEK. *Hens. Diary*, i. 14.

30th April. THE COUNCIL DECEIVED. *A.P.C.*, xxii. 411. See 7th April.

A CONTEMPTUOUS SEA CAPTAIN. *A.P.C.*, xxii. 371, 396 and 417.

4th May. AN ACCIDENT AT GREENWICH. Stow, *Annals*.

6th May. PLAYS OF THE WEEK. *Hens. Diary*, i. 14. In recording these plays from *Henslowe's Diary* I have throughout followed Dr. Greg's corrections of Henslowe's entries (ii. 325).

7th May. THE DUKE OF PARMA'S CAMP PILLAGED. *Unton Correspondence*, p. 435.

8th May. FURTHER REINFORCEMENTS FOR FRANCE. *A.P.C.*, xxii. 431.

13th May. AN UNLUCKY GAOLER. *A.P.C.*, xxii. 443.

DESERTERS FROM FRANCE AT DOVER. *A.P.C.*, xxii. 448.

PLAYS OF THE WEEK. *Hens. Diary*, i. 14.

17th May. A CLAIM AGAINST CAPTAIN GLEMHAM. *S.P.D.*, ccxlii, 19. For Glemham's adventures see 31st March, 1591.

20th May. PLAYS OF THE WEEK. *Hens. Diary*, i. 14.

21st May. THE WEAKNESS OF THE NORMANDY COMPANIES. *A.P.C.*, xxii. 478.

25th May. A RUMOUR. *S.P. Dom.*, ccxlii. 25.

PUCKERING MADE LORD KEEPER. *A.P.C.*, xxii. 500.

27th May. PLAYS OF THE WEEK. *Hens. Diary*, i. 14.

28th May. SEDITIOUS BOOKS FROM ABROAD. *A.P.C.*, xxii. 486.

31st May. A DISASTER IN BRITTANY RUMOURED. *A.P.C.*, xxii. 502.

MR. JOHN HARINGTON AND THE PRINTER. *A.P.C.*, xxii. 504. This seems to be an interesting and early case of an amateur in letters attempting to run his private press.

1st June. SIR WALTER RALEGH DISGRACED. See W. Stebbing, *Sir Walter Ralegh*, 1899, p. 88. There is no direct contemporary evidence of Ralegh's offence, though Camden briefly records it. It must have caused considerable scandal.

2nd June. FOREIGN ARTISANS IN ENGLAND. *A.P.C.*, xxii. 506.

3rd June. PLAYS OF THE WEEK. *Hens. Diary*, i. 14.

5th June. THE DISASTER IN BRITTANY. *Unton Correspondence*, p. 460. News of the disaster in general terms had reached London by 29th May. Lord Burghleigh answered Unton's letter of the 24th on 6th June.

6th June. LEWDNESS IN A CONDUIT. Thomas Wright, *Court and Times of Queen Elizabeth*, ii. 418. Approximate date.

10th June. PLAYS OF THE WEEK. *Hens. Diary*, i. 15, ii. 156.

12th June. RIOTS IN SOUTHWARK. *Remembrancia*, i. 662. Printed in *Malone Society Collections*, i. 71.

15th June. SOME ENGLISH SAILORS ILL-TREATED. *A.P.C.*, xxii. 532.

DISTRESS AT CANTERBURY. *A.P.C.*, xxii. 534.

17th June. SIR HENRY UNTON RETURNS. *Unton Correspondence*, pp. 470, 471.

PLAYS OF THE WEEK AT THE ROSE. *Hens. Diary*, i. 15.

19th June. RECUSANCY IN WALES. *A.P.C.*, xxii. 543.

21st June. A COZENER PILLORIED. Stow, *Annals*.

22nd June. FATHER SOUTHWELL THE JESUIT. Strype's *Annals*, iv. 132.

23rd June. PLAYING CEASES AT THE ROSE THEATRE. *Hens. Diary*, i. 15.

RUMOURS OF PEACE IN FRANCE. *S.P. Dom.*, ccxlii. 58.

ABUSES IN THE NORTH. *A.P.C.*, xxii. 547; *S.P. Dom.*, ccxl. 138.

RIOTING EXPECTED IN LONDON. *A.P.C.*, xxii. 549. For an account of the Midsummer Watch see Stow's *Survey of London*, edited by C. L. Kingsford, i. 101-3.

26th June. SIR JOHN PERROT CONDEMNED. Cobbett's *State Trials*, i. 1327.

28th June. THE MURDER OF JOHN BREWEN. *The truth of the most wicked and secret murthering of John Brewen*, 1592; modern edition by F. S. Boas in *The Complete Works of Thomas Kyd*, 1904. The book was entered on 28th June (the day of the execution); four ballads were entered in July—a sure sign of the public excitement. Dr. Boas attributes the pamphlet to Kyd on the strength of a signature 'Tho. Kydde' written at the end of the only surviving copy, now in Lambeth Palace Library.

10th July. SIR W. RALEGH'S COMPLAINTS AGAINST THE DEPUTY OF IRELAND. E. Edwards, *Life of Sir Walter Ralegh*, 1868, ii. 48. Approximate date.

18th July. A PROGNOSTICATION. James Carre, *An Almanack and Prognostication for the year of our Redemption*, 1593.

21st July. MILITARY EQUIPMENT IN THE COUNTIES. *A.P.C*, xxiii. 39.

GREENE'S 'QUIP FOR AN UPSTART COURTIER.' *A.R.*, ii. 617. Robert Greene, *A Quip for an Upstart Courtier*, 1592. Modern edition by A. B. Grosart in *The Works of Robert Greene*, 1881-3. The suppressed passage is printed in my *Shakespeare's Fellows*, p. 58. This is the beginning of the famous quarrel between Gabriel Harvey and the Greene-Nashe set; for an excellent account see R. B. M'Kerrow, *The Works of Thomas Nashe*, v. 65. The book was very popular (three editions came out in 1592) and started a new vogue for allegory on social problems, well spiced with personal abuse.

23rd July. A MONOPOLY IN STARCH. *A.P.C.*, xxiii. 45. One of several grants of monopoly.

28th July. ROBERT SOUTHWELL SENT TO THE TOWER. *A.P.C.*, xxiii. 70.

31st July. SIR WALTER RALEGH'S LAMENTABLE COMPLAINT. Quoted in E. Edwards, *Life of Sir Walter Ralegh*, 1868, ii. 51. Approximate date.

6th August. DESERTERS IN HERTFORDSHIRE. *A.P.C.*, xxiii. 94.

7th August. ABLE-BODIED IRISHMEN TO BE DEPORTED. *A.P.C.*, xxiii. 99.

8th August. NASHE'S 'PIERCE PENNILESS.' *A.R.*, ii. 619. Thomas Nashe, *Pierce Penniless*, 1592. A most popular book, and an epitome of the gossip of these years. It went into three editions immediately and was again reprinted in 1595. Its popularity was due to the slashing vituperation of well-known personages. In answer to their protests, Nashe took refuge in the conventional defence of the satirist that he was not attacking individuals, and if antiquaries, for instance, took offence it was not his fault or intention. Still it can scarcely have been coincidence that Stow first produced his laboured *Annals of England* this same year. For an official answer to the defence of plays see page 330. Modern editions by R. B. M'Kerrow in *The Works of Thomas Nashe*, vol. i., 1904; and *The Bodley Head Quartos*, vol. xi., 1925.

11th August. THE COUNT MOMPELGARD IN LONDON. W. B. Rye, *England as seen by Foreigners in the days of Elizabeth and James the First*, 1865.

13th August. THE COUNT MOMPELGARD FEASTS WITH THE FRENCH AMBASSADOR. Rye, p. 9.

15th August. A SCURRILOUS JESUIT PAMPHLET. Andreas Philopater, *Responsio ad Edictum Reginae Angliae*, 1592, and John Philopatris, *An Advertisement written to a Secretarie of My L. Treasurers' of England*, 1592

17th August. THE COUNT MOMPELGARD SUMMONED TO COURT. Rye, p. 11.

18th August. THE COUNT MOMPELGARD AGAIN VISITS THE QUEEN. Rye, p. 12.

20th August. THE COUNT MOMPELGARD AT WINDSOR. Rye, p. 16.

21st August. GREENE'S 'BLACK BOOK'S MESSENGER.' *A.R.*, ii. 619. Robert Greene, *The Black-Book's Messenger*, 1592. Modern editions by A. B. Grosart in *The Works of Robert Greene*, 1881-3; and *The Bodley Head Quartos*, vol. x., 1924.

29th August. SIR ROGER WILLIAMS' COMPLAINTS. *S.P. Foreign, France*, xxix. f. 55. Letter dated 23rd August.

24th August. CONDEMNED CRIMINALS AS SOLDIERS. *A.P.C.*, xxiii. 151.

27th August. A PRIEST'S INFORMATIONS. *S.P. Dom.*, ccxlii. 121.

ANXIETY FOR OSTEND. *A.P.C.*, xxiii. 137.

1st September. AN INVASION EXPECTED ON THE SOUTH COAST. *A.P.C.*, xxiii. 160.

3rd September. THE DEATH OF ROBERT GREENE. *The Repentance of Robert Greene, Master of Arts*, 1592. Modern editions in A. B. Grosart, *The Complete Works of Robert Greene*, 1881-3; and *The Bodley Head Quartos*, vol. vi. 1923.

4th September. THE COUNT MOMPELGARD DEPARTS. Rye, p. 47.

5th September. DR. HARVEY AND ROBERT GREENE. Gabriel Harvey, *Four Letters and Certain Sonnets*, 1592. Modern editions by A. B. Grosart, *The English Works of Gabriel Harvey*, 1884; and vol. ii. of *The Bodley Head Quartos*, 1923. I suspect (but without tangible evidence) that the 'fatal banquet' was held to celebrate the publication of *The Quip* and *Pierce Penniless*, and that Nashe and Greene loudly drank damnation to the Harveys thereat.

6th September. GREAT WINDS. Stow, *Annals*. Birch, *Memories*, i. 86.

THE RETURN OF SIR MARTIN FROBISHER'S FLEET EXPECTED. *A.P.C.*, xxiii. 177.

7th September. THE PLAGUE IN LONDON. *S.P. Dom.*, ccxliii. 5.

10th September. THE TAKING OF THE GREAT CARRACK. *Hakluyt's Voyages*, v. 57. The previous adventures of the company of the *Golden Dragon* before joining Sir John Burgh are recorded in *Hakluyt's Voyages*, vol. vii. p. 148.

THE PLAGUE IN LONDON. *A.P.C.*, xxiii. 183.

TWO RICH SPANISH PRIZES BROUGHT IN. *Hakluyt's Voyages*, v. 55.

14th September. SPANISH HOPES. *S.P. Dom.*, ccxliii. 11.

16th September. THE GREAT CARRACK. *S.P. Dom.*, ccxliii. 14.

17th September. THAME FAIR PUT OFF. *A.P.C.*, xxiii. 195.

19th September. THE SPREAD OF THE PLAGUE. *A.P.C.*, xxiii. 203.

20th September. 'GREENE'S GROAT'S-WORTH OF WIT.' *A.R.*, ii. 620. *Greene's Groat's-worth of Wit.* Modern editions by A. B. Grosart in *The Complete Works of Robert Greene*, 1881-3; and *The Bodley Head Quartos*, vol. vi. There can be little doubt that the 'famous gracer of tragedians' is Marlowe, 'young Juvenal' Nashe, and 'the only Shake-scene' Shakespeare.

22nd September. THE GREAT CARRACK. *S.P. Dom.*, ccxliii. 16. Letter dated 19th September.

THE QUEEN AT OXFORD. *Nicoll's Progresses*, vol. ii.

CONSTABLE'S 'DIANA.' *A.R.*, ii. 620. Henry Constable, *Diana*, 1592. Modern edition by M. F. Crow in *Elizabethan Sonnet Cycles*, 1896. The original edition of Constable's *Diana* is interesting as an example of the pretty pocket volume for ladies, and the vogue of the sonnet during the early 1590's; as poetry fairly smooth, passionless and drowsy.

23rd September. THE QUEEN AT OXFORD. Nicoll's *Progresses*, vol. ii.

A PROCLAMATION ABOUT THE GREAT CARRACK. *Proclamations*, p. 311.

24th September. THE QUEEN AT OXFORD. Nicoll's *Progresses*, vol. ii.

SIR ROBERT CECIL AT DARTMOUTH. *S.P. Dom.*, ccxliii. 17. Letter dated 21st Sept.

25th September. THE COURT AT OXFORD. Nicoll's *Progresses*, vol. ii.

27th September. THE QUEEN AT OXFORD. Nicoll's *Progresses*, vol. ii.

28th September. THE QUEEN LEAVES OXFORD. Nicoll's *Progresses*, vol. ii.

1st October. THE INCREASE OF THE PLAGUE. *A.P.C.*, xxiii. 220.

REINFORCEMENTS FOR BRITTANY. *A.P.C.*, xxiii. 223.

6th October. 'THE REPENTANCE OF ROBERT GREENE.' *A.R.*, ii. 621. *The Repentance of Robert Greene*, 1592. Modern editions by A. B. Grosart, *Complete Works of Robert Greene*, 1881-3 ; and *The Bodley Head Quartos*, vol. vi., 1923.

KYD'S SPANISH TRAGEDY. *A.R.*, ii. 621. Thomas Kyd, *The Spanish Tragedy*. The earliest extant edition is not dated. Modern editions by F. S. Boas in *The Works of Thomas Kyd*, 1901 ; etc.

11th October. CITY FEASTS TO BE FORBORNE. *A.P.C.*, xxiii. 232.

12th October. PRECAUTIONS AGAINST THE PLAGUE. *Proclamations*, p. 312.

18th October. PLAGUE DEATHS. *Fugger News-Letters*, 2nd series, p. 243.

19th October. SIR JOHN NORRIS DELAYED. *S.P. Dom.*, ccxlii. 43.

21st October. A PROCLAMATION CONCERNING THE PLAGUE. *Proclamations*, p. 313.

20th October. THE DEATH OF COUNT MONTAIGNE. Birch's *Memoirs*, i. 87. Approximate date.

THE GREAT CARRACK. *A.P.C.*, xxiii. 246.

22nd October. EDWARD ALLEYN MARRIES. E. K. Chambers, *Elizabethan Stage*, ii. 296.

23rd October. BEACON WATCHES TO BE DISCONTINUED. *A.P.C.*, xxiii. 264.

27th October. THE NORMANDY FORCES TO BE SENT TO BRITTANY. *A.P.C.*, xxiii. 268.

30th October. ABUSES AT HERTFORD. *A.P.C.*, xxiii. 274.

THE LORD MAYOR REBUFFED. *A.P.C.*, xxiii. 276.

4th November. THE DEATH OF SIR JOHN PERROT. *The History of that most eminent statesman Sir John Perrot*, 1728, published from the original manuscript by Richard Rawlinson ; Sir Robert Naunton, *Fragmenta Regalia*, 1649 : reprinted in *The Harleian Miscellany*, vol. ii. ; and *D.N.B.* See Appendix I., p. 393.

HARWARD'S 'SOLACE FOR THE SOLDIER AND SAILOR.' *A.R.*, ii. 622. Simon Harward, *The Solace of the Soldier and the Sailor*, 1592.

13th November. MR. HERRICK'S GOODS. *A.P.C.*, xxiii. 289 ; F. W. Moorman, *Robert Herrick*, 1910, p. 19. This is the father of Robert Herrick the poet, then aged 14 months.

14th November. SIR JOHN NORRIS'S COMPLAINTS. *S.P. Foreign*, xxix. f. 296. Letter dated 8th November.

17th November. CORONATION DAY. *Letters of Philip Gawdy*, p. 67. Roxburgh Club, 1906.

20th November. A FAVOURITE LADY-IN-WAITING. *Hist. MSS. Com., Rutland MSS.*, i. 305. See 20th August, 1594.

'SOLIMAN AND PERSEDA.' *A.R.*, ii. 622. *The Tragedy of Soliman and Perseda.* The earliest quarto is undated. Modern editions by F. S. Boas (who attributes the play to Kyd) in *The Works of Thomas Kyd*, 1901 ; J. S. Farmer, in *Students' Facsimile Texts.*

7th December. UNWILLING CAPTAINS TO BE PUNISHED. *A.P.C.*, xxiii. 348.

8th December. CHETTLE'S 'KINDHEART'S DREAM.' *A.R.*, ii. 623. Henry Chettle, *Kindheart's Dream*, n.d. Modern edition in *The Bodley Head Quartos*, vol. iii., 1923.

16th December. THE FUNERAL OF THE DUKE OF PARMA. *Fugger News-Letters*, 2nd series, p. 244.

18th December. 'ELIOT'S FRUITS FOR THE FRENCH.' *A.R.*, ii. 624. John Eliot, *Ortho-Epia Gallica*, 1593.

30th December. PLAYING RESUMED. *Hens. Diary*, i. 15.

31st December. THE BILLS OF MORTALITY FOR THE YEAR. John Graunt, *Reflections on the Weekly Bills of Mortality*, 1665, p. 3, and *Natural and Political Observations made upon the Bills of Mortality*, 1662, p. 33. I have assumed that the practice in 1592 was similar to that in later years.

COLONNA'S 'HYPNEROTOMACHIA.' Francisco Colonna, *Hypnerotomachia*, translated by R. D., 1592. Modern edition by Andrew Lang, with a short introduction, 1890. Lang draws attention to the many quaintnesses of vocabulary, reminiscent of Keat's *Endymion.* A good example of Renaissance 'lusciousness' but dull reading.

GREENE'S 'DISPUTATION.' Robert Greene, *A Disputation between a He Conny-catcher, and a She Conny-catcher*, 1592. Modern editions by A. B. Grosart in *The Complete Works of Robert Greene*, 1881-3 ; and in *The Bodley Head Quartos*, vol. iii., 1923.

'THE GROUNDWORK OF CONNY-CATCHING. Thomas Harman, *The Groundwork of Conny-catching*, 1592.

JOHNSON'S 'NINE WORTHIES OF LONDON.' Richard Johnson, *The Nine Worthies of London*, 1592. The book went into a second edition this year. Reprinted in *The Harleian Miscellany*, vol. viii., 1746. This is one of the books written for a citizen reader to glorify the tradesman.

1593.

3rd January. RUMOURS. *S.P. Dom.*, ccxliv. 1. The libels presumably were the books summarised under 15th August, 1592.

6th January. PLAYS OF THE WEEK. *Hens. Diary*, i. 15. Fleay, and more recently Dr. Dover Wilson (in *The New Shakespeare*), suggest that the *Jealous Comedy* was the basis of Shakespeare's *Merry Wives of Windsor.* See Appendix I., p. 401.

8th January. THE WAR IN FRANCE. *A.P.C.*, xxiv. 14. *S.P. Foreign*, xxx. f. 7. Letter dated 2nd January.

12th January. NASHE'S 'STRANGE NEWS.' *A.R.*, ii. 624. Thomas Nashe, *Strange News of the Intercepting of Certain Letters*, 1592[-3]. Modern edition by R. B. M'Kerrow in *The Works of Thomas Nashe*, 1904. This piece of abuse made good gossip: two editions are dated 1592, *i.e.* were printed before 25th March, 1593; three are dated 1593.

13th January. PLAYS OF THE WEEK. *Hens. Diary*, i. 15; ii. 156.

18th January. RUMOURS. *S.P. Dom.*, ccxliv. 18.

20th January. PLAYS OF THE WEEK. *Hens. Diary*, i. 15; ii. 157.

21st January. THE PLAGUE AGAIN INCREASES. *A.P.C.*, xxiv. 21.

27th January. PLAYS OF THE WEEK. *Hens. Diary*, i. 15; ii. 157. *The Massacre at Paris* (called in the *Diary* 'the tragedy of the gyves') was printed in an undated quarto with the title, *The Massacre at Paris; with the Death of the Duke of Guise. As it was played by the Right Honourable the Lord High Admiral, his servants. Written by Christopher Marlowe.*

28th January. EVASION OF SERVICE IN PRIVILEGED PLACES. *A.P.C.*, xxiv. 30.

SIR HENRY KNIVETT'S SUBMISSION. *A.P.C.*, xxiv. 33.

PLAYS AND GAMES PROHIBITED BY REASON OF THE PLAGUE. *A.P.C.*, xxiv. 31.

2nd February. PLAYING CEASES. *Hens. Diary*, i. 16.

3rd February. 'GREENE'S NEWS FROM HEAVEN AND HELL.' *A.R.*, ii. 626. B. R., *Green's News from Heaven and Hell*, 1593. Modern edition by R. B. M'Kerrow, 1922.

7th February. LAWLESSNESS ON THE SCOTTISH BORDER. *S.P. Dom. Addenda*, xxxii. 66.

8th February. AN INVASION EXPECTED. *A.P.C.*, xxiv. 53.

11th February. CONTRIBUTIONS EVADED. *A.P.C.*, xxiv. 44.

12th February. RUMOURS: THE GREAT CARRACK. *S.P. Dom.*, ccxliv. 35. The signed award of the Commissioners (*Lansdowne MSS.*, 73, f. 40) gives the following figures: The Earl of Cumberland, £18,000; Sir Walter Ralegh, £15,900; Sir John Hawkins, £2,400; the City of London, £12,000 in goods.

14th February. INSUFFICIENT MEN IMPRESTED AS SOLDIERS. *A.P.C.*, xxiv. 62, 65 and 66. See Appendix I., p. 397.

18th February. REGULATIONS FOR BUTCHERS DURING LENT. *A.P.C.*, xxiv. 71.

19th February. PARLIAMENT ASSEMBLES. D'Ewes' *Journals*, pp. 456, 468. Townshend, p. 32.

20th February. PRECAUTIONS AGAINST DESERTIONS. *A.P.C.*, xxiv. 72.

21st February. THE FRENCH AMBASSADOR ALLOWED MEAT. *A.P.C.*, xxiv. 75.

22nd February. THE SPEAKER PRESENTED. D'Ewes' *Journals*, p. 458. Townshend, p. 34.

PROFESSOR J. E. NEALE pointed out (*Eng. Hist. Rev.* xxxi. 129) that in another version of this speech a member might say 'yea or no' to any Bill 'with some short declaration of his reason therein,' but not to 'speak there of all causes as him listeth.'

24th February. MR. WENTWORTH'S PETITION. D'Ewes' *Journals*, p. 470. Townshend, p. 54.

THE SPEAKER SICK. D'Ewes' *Journals*, p. 470.

SIR ROGER WILLIAMS' COUNSEL. *S.P. Foreign*, xxx. f. 118. Letter dated 18th February.

25th February. MR. WENTWORTH BEFORE THE COUNCIL. D'Ewes' *Journals*, p. 470. Townshend, p. 54.

THE EARL OF ESSEX ADMITTED TO THE COUNCIL. *A.P.C.*, xxiv. 78.

DESERTERS IN GLOUCESTERSHIRE. *A.P.C.*, xxiv. 81.

26th February. A COMMITTEE OF THE HOUSE APPOINTED. D'Ewes' *Journals*, p. 471.

27th February. UNREASONABLE DEMANDS FROM PRISONERS. *A.P.C.*, xxiv. 82.

THE SUBSIDIES. D'Ewes' *Journals*, p. 477.

A BILL AGAINST THE BISHOPS. D'Ewes' *Journals*, p. 474. Townshend, p. 61.

ROGER RIPPON'S CORPSE. Strype, *Annals*, iv. 133.

28th February. THE BILL AGAINST THE BISHOPS. D'Ewes' *Journals*, p. 478. Townshend, p. 61.

FLESH IN LENT. *A.P.C.*, xxiv. 84, 87.

A PLOT TO KILL THE QUEEN. *S.P. Dom.*, ccxliv. 55.

1st March. ROGER RIPPON'S CORPSE. *S.P. Dom.*, ccxliv. 62.

EXTREME TENETS OF THE PURITANS. *Two kinds of schismatics, and the danger of their opinions, either directly or by necessary consequence gathered, to be holden by those who urge a new Church Government.* 'This paper seems to have been drawn up by the Lord Keeper Puckering, to be produced against them in the Star Chamber, after their examinations before him.' Strype, *Annals*, iv. 140.

3rd March. DR. UDALL'S PETITION. *S.P. Dom.*, ccxliv. 64.

THE SUBSIDY. D'Ewes' *Journals*, p. 480.

THE SUBSIDY. D'Ewes' *Journals*, p. 483.

A STRANGER IN THE HOUSE. D'Ewes' *Journals*, p. 486.

4th March. PENRY TO BE ARRESTED. *A.P.C.*, xxiv. 94.

5th March. 'THE GARLAND OF GOODWILL.' *A.R.*, ii. 627. Thomas Deloney, *The Garland of Goodwill*, earliest surviving edition, 1631. Modern edition by F. O. Mann in *The Works of Thomas Deloney*, 1912. It is perhaps doubtful whether the book was issued in 1593. The original entry to Wolfe, dated 5th March, 1593, is crossed out, and 'Edward White the xxvij of August 1596' substituted. As one of the ballads in the third part refers to the attack on Cadiz (1596), it is possible that two parts appeared in 1593, and a third was added in 1596. It is worth noting how the ballad-maker borrows the stories of the gentlemen writers and the dramatists.

6th March. LEGG RELEASED. D'Ewes, *Journals*, p. 491.

THE SUBSIDY. D'Ewes' *Journals*, p. 489.

7th March. MUSTERS TO BE HELD IN THE NORTH. *A.P.C.*, xxiv. 105.

THE SUBSIDY. D'Ewes' *Journals*, p. 491.

9th March. BARROWISTS ARRESTED. Strype, *Annals*, iv. 174.

10th March. THE SUBSIDY AGREED. D'Ewes' *Journals*, p. 495.

11th March. THE BUTCHERS DEFIANT. *A.P.C.*, xxiv. 112.

12th March. A BILL AGAINST RECUSANTS. D'Ewes' *Journals*, p. 498.

MR. DARCY'S UNSEEMLY CONDUCT. *Remembrancia*, i. 651.

13th March. A SPANISH NOBLEMAN SENT HOME. *Spanish State Papers*, iv. 596.

16th March. MEASURES AGAINST THE BUTCHERS. *A.P.C.*, xxiv. 118.

19th March. BUNNY'S 'TRUTH AND FALSEHOOD.' Francis Bunny, *Truth and Falsehood*, 1595. Entered 19th March, 1593, and 13th April, 1593. *The Short Answer* is bound with *Truth and Falsehood*, but has its own title-page.

21st March. KELLWAY'S 'DEFENSATIVE AGAINST THE PLAGUE.' *A.R.*, ii. 629. Simon Kellway, *A Defensative against the Plague*, 1593.

22nd March. BARROW, GREENWOOD AND OTHER PURITANS CONDEMNED. Stow, *Annals*.

23rd March. A DISHONEST CAPTAIN. *A.P.C.*, xxiv. 133. See Appendix I., p. 398.

24th March. GYER'S 'ENGLISH PHLEBOTOMY.' Nicholas Gyer, *The English Phlebotomy*, 1592. Approximate date of publication. From mention of 'this Spring time' on the title-page, and of Penry, Brown and Barrow, it seems likely that the book should be dated 1592-3 rather than 1591-2.

25th March. ABUSES OVER IMPRESSMENTS IN GLOUCESTERSHIRE. *A.P.C.*, xxiv, 136. See Appendix I., page 398.

27th March. A RECUSANT EXECUTED AT WINCHESTER. *Catholic Record Society*, v. 228-232.

31st March. BARROW AND GREENWOOD RESPITED. Stow, *Annals*. See page 222.

1st April. A COUNTERFEIT CAPTAIN. *A.P.C.*, xxiv. 149.

2nd April. MAIMED SOLDIERS TO BE EXAMINED. *A.P.C.*, xxiv. 159.

4th April. A BILL AGAINST THE BROWNISTS. D'Ewes' *Journals*, p. 516. Townshend, page 76

5th April. CHARITABLE CONTRIBUTIONS FOR MAIMED SOLDIERS. D'Ewes' *Journals*, p. 463. Townshend, page 42.

PRECAUTIONS AGAINST PLAGUE. *A.P.C.*, xxiv. 163.

6th April. BARROW AND GREENWOOD HANGED. Stow, *Annals. S.P. Dom.*, ccxlv. 124 (Phellippes).

7th April. SPECIAL WATCH TO BE KEPT FOR TRAITORS. *Hist. MSS. Com. Rye MSS.*, page 105.

8th April. THE DISORDERLY BUTCHERS. *A.P.C.*, xxiv. 166, 170.

9th April. 'CHURCHYARD'S CHALLENGE.' *A.R.*, ii. 629. Thomas Churchyard, *Churchyard's Challenge*, 1593. A very tedious old man.

THE WITCHES OF WARBOYS. *The most strange and admirable discovery of the three Witches of Warboys*, 1593. A very long and detailed description of the whole affair written by an eye-witness (not improbably Dr. Dorrington). The Lady Cromwell was second wife of Oliver Cromwell's grandfather. The pamphlet seems to have caused some excitement when it was entered at Stationers' Hall, as the entry in the *Register* notes that it was 'recommended for matter of truthe by master Judge Ffenner vnder his handwrytinge shewed in a Court or assemblie holden this Daye according to the ordonnances of the company'; 'the note vnder master Justice Ffenners hand is Layd vp in the Wardens cupbord.' *A.R.*, ii. 633.

10th April. THE PARLIAMENT DISSOLVED. D'Ewes' *Journals*, p. 465. Townshend, p. 45. See Appendix I., p. 394.

11th April. RELIEF FOR MAIMED SOLDIERS. *A.P.C.*, xxxiv. 178.

14th April. FALSE REPORTS CONCERNING THE QUEEN'S DEALINGS WITH THE TURKS. Strype, *Annals*, iv. 154.

15th April. THE QUEEN'S DIRECTIONS TO SIR JOHN NORRIS. *S.P. Foreign*, xxx. f. 272.

16th April. THE LIBELS AGAINST STRANGERS. *A.P.C.*, xxiv. 187.

17th April. MEASURES AGAINST VAGABONDS. *A.P.C.*, xxxiv. 193. A copy of this order is included in the volume of *Proclamations* (317a).

18th April. 'VENUS AND ADONIS' ENTERED. *A.R.*, ii. 630. William Shakespeare, *Venus and Adonis*, 1593. Modern edition by C. Knox Pooler in the Arden Shakespeare, 1911: etc.

22nd April. THE LIBELS AGAINST STRANGERS. *A.P.C.*, xxiv. 200; Strype, *Annals*, iv. 167.

23rd April. DRAYTON'S 'IDEA.' *A.R.*, ii. 630. Michael Drayton, *The Shepherd's Garland, fashioned into nine Eclogues*, 1593. An interesting imitation of Spenser, and for the philologist useful for its archaic and rare words. The ballad of Dowsabel is pleasing, otherwise the collection is second-rate, though a considerable advance on *The Harmony of the Church*. Modern edition in Arber's *English Garner*, vol. vi.

24th April. PLAGUE DEATHS. *Fugger News-Letters*, 2nd series, p. 248.

29th April. A CHARITABLE GENTLEMAN. *A.P.C.*, xxiv. 209.

4th May. THE NUMBERS OF STRANGERS IN LONDON. Strype, *Annals*, iv. 167.

5th May. LIBELS AGAINST STRANGERS. Strype, *Annals*, iv. 168.

10th May. 'PARTHENOPHIL AND PARTHENOPHE.' *A.R.*, ii. 631. Barnabe Barnes, *Parthenophil and Parthenophe*, 1593. Modern edition by A. B. Grosart, 1875; and in Arber's *English Garner*, vol. v. Barnes annoyed several of his contemporaries who made the most of the shortcomings of *Parthenophil*; for details see Grosart's Introduction. All the same, though not a Donne, he is trying to explore his own sensations and to get away from the tired conventions of the sonneteers.

11th May. MORE LIBELS AGAINST STRANGERS. *A.P.C.*, xxiv. 222.

12th May. THOMAS KYD ARRESTED. See F. S. Boas, *The Works of Thomas Kyd*, 1901; Introduction, pp. lxx-lxxiii.

15th May. CONTEMPT OF THE COUNCIL'S ORDER AT BRISTOL. *S.P. Dom.*, ccxlv. 25. Approximate date.

20th May. MARLOWE BEFORE THE COUNCIL. *A.P.C.*, xxiv. 244.

21st May. A PRIEST'S DECLARATION OF HIS MOTIVES. *S.P. Dom.*, ccxlv. 66. Approximate date.

23rd May. THE PLAGUE IN THE SAVOY. *A.P.C.*, xxiv. 252.

24th May. PENRY CONDEMNED. *S.P. Dom.*, ccxlv. 21.

A REQUEST OF THE CITIZENS OF PARIS. *S.P. Foreign*, xxxi. f. 60. Letter dated 18th May.

25th May. ABUSES OF THE QUEEN'S SERVICE IN GLOUCESTERSHIRE. *A.P.C.*, xxiv. 257. See Appendix I., p. 398.

26th May. MARLOWE'S BLASPHEMIES. The whole accusation is to be found in *Harleian MSS.*, 6848, f. 155; reprinted (with some omissions) in Dr. Boas' edition of *The Works of Thomas Kyd*, p. cxiv.

28th May. PRECAUTIONS AGAINST PLAGUE. *Proclamations*, 39.

29th May. STRATFORD GOOSE FAIR FORBIDDEN. *A.P.C.*, xxiv. 265.

MR. WENTWORTH IN THE TOWER. *A.P.C.*, xxiv. 269.

30th May. MARLOWE SLAIN. J. L. Hotson, *The Death of Christopher Marlowe*, 1926, p. 31.

31st May. THE EXECUTION OF JOHN PENRY. See W. Pierce, *John Penry*, 1923, p. 480.

THREE SUSPECTED SOLDIERS. *A.P.C.*, xxiv. 278.

1st June. THE INQUEST ON CHRISTOPHER MARLOWE. *The Death of Christopher Marlowe*, by J. Leslie Hotson. Dr. Hotson's discovery of the copy of the Coroner's verdict revealed the 'official' account of the murder; but it is to be noted that the survivor in these numerous fatal quarrels is always the innocent party. The stories are retailed by Thomas Beard in his *Theatre of God's Judgments* (1597), Francis Meres in *Palladis Tamia*, and others; relevant extracts are given in Dr. Hotson's book. The evidence that Marlowe was given to blasphemy and unnatural vice is convincing and, indeed, could be deduced from his writings.

5th June. PRECAUTIONS AGAINST PLAGUE AT WINDSOR. *A.P.C.*, xxiv. 284.

7th June. MR. COTTON'S CLAIMS TO BE SATISFIED. *A.P.C.*, xxiv. 295. See *ante*, 29th April.

8th June. RELIEF OF MAIMED SOLDIERS. *A.P.C.*, xxiv. 298.

10th June. CHARITY FOR A PRISONER IN THE HANDS OF THE LEAGUERS. *A.P.C.*, xxiv. 305.

12th June. RUMOURS OF CHANGES IN FRANCE. *S.P. Dom.*, ccxlv. 30.

16th June. CHUTE'S 'BEAUTY DISHONOURED.' *A.R.*, ii. 632. Anthony Chute, *Beauty Dishonoured*, 1593. The pleading of the lady against the miseries of enforced marriage seems to owe something to Deloney's ballad of *The Lamentation of Mr. Page's Wife.* See page 92. This lament was imitated by Daniel and Giles Fletcher (see pages 262 and 322). The interest in Mistress Shore at this time is worth noting.

18th June. A PROCLAMATION TO RESTRAIN SUITORS AT COURT. *Proclamations*, 318. See 12th October, 1592.

20th June. CAPTAIN JOHN DAVIS RETURNS TO ENGLAND. Hakluyt, viii. 295-312.

25th June. THE COUNCIL'S LICENCE ABUSED. *A.P.C.*, xxiv. 332.

26th June. 'A DISCOVERY OF THE CONSPIRACY OF THE SCOTTISH PAPISTS.' *A.R.*, ii. 633. *A Discovery of the unnatural and traitorous conspiracy of Scottish Papists*, 1593. One of the few pamphlets of news from Scotland.

29th June. CITY FEASTS TO BE CURTAILED. *A.P.C.*, xxiv. 342.

1st July. MR. CAVENDISH'S VOYAGE. *A.P.C.*, xxiv. 346.

FAIRS TO BE ABANDONED. *A.P.C.*, xxv. 347.

6th July. MARLOWE'S 'EDWARD THE SECOND.' *A.R.*, ii. 634. Christopher Marlowe, *Edward the Second*, 1594. Modern editions by C. Tucker Brooke in *The Works of Christopher Marlowe*, 1910; etc.

9th July. THE PLAGUE. *A.P.C.*, xxiv. 373.

THE COLLECTION OF THE SUBSIDY. *A.P.C.*, xxiv. 376.

SPANISH SHIPS OFF THE BRITTANY COAST. *A.P.C.*, xxiv. 406.

BLUNDEVILLE'S 'EXERCISES.' Thomas Blundeville, *His Exercises*, 1594.

14th July. SIR THOMAS WILKES SENT TO THE FRENCH KING. *S.P. Foreign*, xxxi. f. 248.

16th July. THE PLAGUE INCREASES. *A.P.C.*, xxiv. 400. The 'little book' is probably that summarised on page 349, though no copy earlier than 1594 now exists.

17th July. PLAGUE DEATHS. *Fugger News-Letters*, 2nd series, p. 249.

19th July. THE ASSIZES HELD IN ST. GEORGE'S FIELD. Stow, *Annals.*

PLAGUE DEATHS, *Fugger News-Letters*, 2nd series, p. 250.

29th July. THE COUNCIL'S LETTERS TO THE UNIVERSITIES OF OXFORD AND CAMBRIDGE. *A.P.C.*, xxiv. 427. This letter, written in the Council's best literary style, was in answer to a petition from the Vice-Chancellor and heads of Colleges in Cambridge asking for public plays and shows to to be restrained. See Strype's *Annals*, iv. 162.

30th July. THE RECRUITS TO BE STAYED. *Salisbury Papers*, iv. 341.

3rd August. DR. HARVEY'S 'PIERCE'S SUPEREROGATION.' Gabriel Harvey, *Pierce's Supererogation*, 1593. Modern edition by A. B. Grosart in *The Works of Gabriel Harvey*, 1884. Not entered in *S.R.*, but dated in several places varying from 27th April to 3rd August.

4th August. THE PLAGUE INCREASES. *A.P.C.*, xxiv. 443.

5th August. A BOOK ON ASTRONOMY. *A.R.*, ii. 635. Auger Ferrier, *A Learned Astronomical Discourse*, 1593. Kelway's protest is significant of the growth of incredulity in astronomy.

PLAGUE DEATHS. *Henslowe Papers*, edited by W. W. Greg, p. 37. The date is approximate, and as Henslowe's style is none of the clearest his figures are somewhat doubtful, though they agree in general with the other sources.

6th August. THE TRUCE IN FRANCE. *Articles accorded for the Truce General in France*, 1593. Entered 25th August.

BARTHOLOMEW FAIR. *A.P.C.*, xxiv. 448. *Proclamations*, 319.

12th August. UNLAWFUL SPOILS. *A.P.C.*, xxiv. 456.

14th August. PLAGUE DEATHS. *Henslowe Papers*, p. 39.

16th August. RUMOURS CONCERNING FRANCE. *S.P. Dom.*, ccxlv. 79.

19th August. SIR THOMAS WILKES' CONVERSATION WITH THE FRENCH KING. *S.P. Foreign*, xxxii. f. 34. Letter dated 13th August.

22nd August. THE FORTIFICATIONS OF PLYMOUTH. *A.P.C.*, xxiv. 477.

DISBANDMENT OF THE SOLDIERS FROM FRANCE. *S.P. Dom.*, ccxlv. 86.

23rd August. SIR THOMAS WILKES' SECOND CONVERSATION WITH THE FRENCH KING. *S.P. Foreign.*, xxxii. f. 51. Letter dated 17th August.

26th August. TWO COUNTERFEITERS SENT TO THE GALLEYS. *A.P.C.*, xxiv. 486. The original volumes containing the Acts of the Privy Council from 26th August, 1593, to 1st October, 1595, are unfortunately missing.

8th September. NASHE'S 'CHRIST'S TEARS OVER JERUSALEM.' *A.R.*, ii. 635. Thomas Nashe, *Christ's Tears over Jerusalem*, 1593. Modern edition by R. B. M'Kerrow in *The Works of Thomas Nashe*, 1904. When Nashe found that Harvey was suspicious of his offers of friendship (see 1st October) he retracted his apology in a violently abusive preface to the 1594 edition of *Christ's Tears*.

10th September. PLAGUE DEATHS. *Fugger News-Letters*, 2nd series, p. 251.

15th September. A RESTRAINT OF SUITORS AT WINDSOR. *Proclamations*, 320.

17th September. NASHE'S 'UNFORTUNATE TRAVELLER.' *A.R.*, ii. 636. Thomas Nashe, *The Unfortunate Traveller*, 1594. Modern editions by R. B. M'Kerrow in *The Works of Thomas Nashe*, 1904; H. F. Brett Smith in *The Percy Reprints*, 1920.

28th September. PLAGUE DEATHS. *Henslowe Papers*, p. 40.

1st October. DR. HARVEY'S 'NEW LETTER OF NOTABLE CONTENTS.' *A.R.*, ii. 636. Gabriel Harvey, *A New Letter of Notable Contents*, 1593. Modern edition by A. B. Grosart in *The Works of Gabriel Harvey*, 1884.

8th October. HIGH-HANDED DEALINGS. *S.P. Dom.*, ccxlv. 135. The Lady was sister-in-law to Lord Burghley; from the tone of an earlier letter in *S.P. Dom.* (ccxlv. 23) she appears to have been a grasping and cantankerous woman.

19th October. DANIEL'S 'DELIA AND ROSAMOND' AND 'THE COMPLAINT OF ROSAMOND.' *A.R.*, ii. 638. Samuel Daniel, *Delia and Rosamond, augmented with Cleopatra. Rosamond's Complaint*, as Daniel acknowledges in his reference to Shore's wife, is an imitation of Chute's *Beauty Dishonoured* (see 16th June). Daniel is by far the better writer, but Rosamond's pious moralisings savour of the ballad-monger. In his attack on barbarism he is joining forces with Sidney's *Apology for Poetry* (in circulation but not printed for another eighteen months) and Nashe's *Piers Pennilesse*. There can be little doubt that the barbarians at this time were raising the cry of 'Down with poetry, down with plays.' See Appendix I., p. 399.

22nd October. EDWARDS' 'CEPHALUS AND PROCRIS.' *A.R.*, ii. 638. Thomas Edwards, *Cephalus and Procris*, 1595. Only one perfect copy is known, not apparently a first edition. Modern edition by W. E. Buckley, Roxburghe Club, 1882. The envoy to *Narcissus* contains references to various contemporary poets, including the well-known lines beginning '*Adon* deafly masking through'; indeed the influence of *Venus and Adonis* is obvious throughout. See the note on Clapham's *Narcissus*, p. 91.

9th November. THE PLAGUE ABATING. *Fugger News-Letters*, 2nd series, p. 252.

14th November. 'ARISBAS.' *A.R.*, ii. 639. John Dickenson, *Arisbas, Euphues amidst his slumbers*, 1594. A very charming story in the best euphuistic vein; including some interesting and pleasing poems; among them 'The Strife of Love and Beauty'; an English Sapphic, 'Dorylus his Odes'; and an English Elegiac, 'Arisbas his Elegy.' There is an atmosphere of *Twelfth Night* about Timoclea's shipwreck, and strong likeness between Shakespeare's Adonis and Hyalus.

17th November. CHURCHYARD'S VERSES. Birch's *Memoirs*, i. 131.

20th November. A CASE OF PLAGUE AT COURT. Birch's *Memoirs*, i. 133.

28th November. THE ARRAIGNMENT OF RICHARD HESKETH. *Salisbury Papers*, iv. 423 and 461.

29th November. A RECUSANT'S CONFESSION. *S.P. Dom.*, ccxlvi. 18.

30th November. THE QUEEN'S LETTER TO SIR JOHN NORRIS. *S.P. Dom.*, ccxlvi. 22. Approximate date.

7th December. GREENE'S 'ORLANDO FURIOSO.' *A.R.*, ii. 640. Robert Greene, *Orlando Furioso*, 1594. Modern edition by J. Churton Collins in *The Plays and Poems of Robert Greene*, 1905.

11th December. HESTER'S 'PEARL OF PRACTISE.' *A.R.*, ii. 641. J. H., *The Pearl of Practise*, 1594.

21st December. ANXIETY IN GUERNSEY. *Salisbury Papers*, iv. 440.

22nd December. PEPPER FROM THE GREAT CARRACK. *S.P. Dom.*, ccxlvi. 40.

26th December. PLAYING RESUMED. *Hens. Diary*, i. 16; ii. 157. A play of this name was entered on 1st March, 1600, but does not survive.

29th December. PLAYS AT THE ROSE. *Hens. Diary*, i. 16; ii. 158. *Huon of Bordeaux* is lost. Commentators see a connection between Oberon of *A Midsummer Night's Dream* and Oberon of the medieval romance; if so, the link was probably this play. *George a Greene, the pinner of Wakefield*, was entered 1st April, 1595. It is reprinted in the *Malone Society Reprints*. *Buckingham* and *Richard the Confessor* are unknown.

31st December. GENTLEMEN'S SONS OVERSEAS. *Salisbury Papers*, iv. 448.

CHAPMAN'S Σκιὰ νυκτὸς. *A.R.*, ii. 642. George Chapman, Σκιὰ νυκτὸς, 1594. Modern edition by A. C. Swinburne, 1875.

PLAGUE DEATHS. Stow, *Annals*. J. Graunt (*Natural and Political Observations . . . upon the Bills of Mortality*, 1662) gives the figures as 17,844 and 10,662.

DR. BANCROFT'S 'DANGEROUS POSITIONS AND PROCEEDINGS.' Richard Bancroft, *Dangerous Positions and Proceedings*, 1593. An important contemporary account of the Puritan movement.

GIFFARD'S 'DIALOGUE CONCERNING WITCHES AND WITCHCRAFT.' George Giffard, *A Dialogue concerning Witches and Witchcraft*, 1593. There are some illuminating stories imbedded in this 'popular' treatise and good patches of dialogue, especially when the women talk ; but like most of his Puritan brethren, Mr. Giffard allows his logic to be somewhat distorted by his intense respect for the devil.

LODGE'S 'PHILLIS.' Thomas Lodge, *Phillis : honoured with pastoral Sonnets, elegies and amorous delights. Whereto is annexed the tragical complaint of Elstred*, 1593. More than one of these sonnet collections contain a 'lament,' as do Shakespeare's. Modern edition by Edmund Gosse in *The Complete Works of Thomas Lodge*, Hunterian Club, 1880.

LODGE'S 'LIFE AND DEATH OF WILLIAM LONGBEARD.' Thomas Lodge, *The Life and Death of William Longbeard—with many other most pleasant and pretty histories*, 1593. Modern edition by Edmund Gosse in *The Complete Works of Thomas Lodge*, 1875.

NORDEN'S 'SPECULUM BRITANNIAE.' John Norden, *Speculum Britanniae*, 1593. Modern edition by W. B. Gerish, 1903.

SUTCLIFFE'S 'LAWS OF ARMS.' Matthew Sutcliffe, *The Practice, proceedings and laws of arms*, 1593. There is no entry, but the book was written after the peace.

MR. SMITH'S 'SERMON AGAINST ATHEISTS.' Henry Smith, *God's Arrow against Atheists*, 1593.

1594

1st January. A PROGNOSTICATION. Robert Westhawe, *An Almanack and Prognostication serving for the year of Our Lord MDXCIIII.*

4th January. A MYSTERIOUS STRANGER. *S.P. Dom.*, ccxlvi. 39. The letter is dated 31st December.

5th January. PLAYS OF THE WEEK. *Hens. Diary*, i. 16.

6th January. COURT REVELS. Birch's *Memoirs*, i. 146.

7th January. CATHOLIC STORIES FROM SCOTLAND. *Spanish State Papers*, iv. 591. Not dated. For further details of James Maxwell, see *D.N.B.*

12th January. PLAYS OF THE WEEK. *Hens. Diary*, i. 16; ii. 159, *Friar Francis*: 'We learn from Heywood's *Apology for Actors* (1612) that this play . . . contained the story of a woman who, for the sake of a lover. murdered her husband, and was haunted by his ghost.'—(Greg.) Nothing is known of *Abraham and Lot* or *The Fair Maid of Italy.*

15th January. AN ALCHEMIST'S BEQUEST. *S.P. Dom.*, ccxlv. 130. Approximate date. Peterson's letter is dated 20th October, 1593, but it seems not to have been received much earlier than this. See also 2nd February and 30th September, 1594.

ATTEMPTS AGAINST THE QUEEN. *S.P. Dom.*, ccxlvii. 12.

16th January. ANOTHER DECLARATION BY TINOCO. *S.P. Dom.*, ccxlvii. 13.

18th January. PLAYS OF THE WEEK. *Hens. Diary*, i. 16; ii. 159. Nothing is known of *King Lud.*

23rd January. DR. LOPEZ DEEPLY IMPLICATED. *S.P. Dom.*, ccxlvii. 19.

24th January. PLAYS OF THE WEEK. *Hens. Diary*, i. 16; ii. 16. For a long discussion of the origin and history of *Titus Andronicus*, see Dr. Greg's note and E. K. Chambers, *Elizabethan Stage*, ii. 129.

DR. LOPEZ EXAMINED. Birch's *Memoirs*, i. 149, 150. Bishop Godfrey Goodman, *The Court of James I.*, 1839, i. 149.

25th January. A NOTABLE JESUIT TAKEN IN THE NORTH. *S.P. Dom.*, ccxlvii. 21. For an account of Fr. Walpole, see A. Jessop, *One Generation of a Norfolk House*, 1878; and *Cath. Rec. Soc.*, vol. v.

31st January. RUMOURS AT COURT. Birch's *Memoirs*, i. 151.

PLAYS OF THE WEEK. *Hens. Diary*, 8, 16.

1st February. BARNFIELD'S 'GREENE'S FUNERALS.' *A.R.*, ii. 644. R[ichard] B[arnfield], *Greene's Funerals*, 1594. Modern edition by R. B. M'Kerrow, 1922.

2nd February. THE ALCHEMIST'S BEQUEST. *S.P. Dom.*, ccxlvii. 36. See 15th January and 30th September, 1594. There is no mention of the bequest of money in Peterson's letter. Apparently the Queen had the choice either of the glasses or a cash payment.

3rd February. BURGLARY AT WINDSOR. Birch's *Memoirs*, i. 155.

PLAYING PROHIBITED. *Remembrancia*, ii. 6. Quoted in *Malone Society Collections*, i. 73.

4th February. A PLOT TO KILL THE QUEEN. *S.P. Dom.*, ccxlvii. 39. For an account of these very complicated plots see Martin Hume, *Treason and Plot*, 1901.

5th February. LOPEZ SENT TO THE TOWER. Birch's *Memoirs*, i. 152.

THE CARTER'S WORDS. Birch's *Memoirs*, i. 155.

6th February. A PLOT TO BURN THE TOWER. *Salisbury Papers*, iv. 474.

THE ROSE THEATRE CLOSED. *Hens. Diary*, i. 16. The *Jew of Malta* reappears with the Lopez sensation.

SHAKESPEARE'S 'TITUS ANDRONICUS.' *A.R.*, ii. 644. William Shakespeare, *Titus Andronicus*, 1594. Modern edition by H. B. Baildon in the *Arden Shakespeare*, etc.

A CONVERSATION BETWEEN SIR ROBERT CECIL AND THE EARL OF ESSEX. Birch's *Memoirs*, i. 153.

THE CONFESSION OF PATRICK COLLEN. *S.P. Dom.*, ccxlvii. 45. See 4th February. The author of the *Troublesome Raigne of King John* makes heavy play with the anticipatory absolution given to the monk who is about to poison King John.

8th February. A RUMOUR OF THE QUEEN'S DEATH. *S.P. Dom.* ccxlvii. 50.

11th February. CLERKE'S 'TRIAL OF BASTARDY.' *A.R.*, ii. 645. William Clerke, *The Trial of Bastardy*, 1594. A book of some interest to anyone concerned with the marriage laws at this period.

17th February. PRECAUTIONS AGAINST SUSPICIOUS PERSONS. *S.P. Dom.* ccxlvii. 66.

18th February. FERRARA DE GAMA'S CONFESSION. *S.P. Dom.*, ccxlvii. 70.

20th February. THE ALCHEMIST'S BEQUEST. *S.P. Dom.*, ccxlvii. 72.

21st February. A PROCLAMATION AGAINST VAGABONDS. *Proclamations*, 324.

THE CONFESSION OF HUGH CAHILL. *S.P. Dom.*, ccxlvii. 78.

25th February. DR. LOPEZ. Birch's *Memoirs*, i. 158.

28th February. DR. LOPEZ ARRAIGNED. *S.P. Dom.*, ccxlvii. 97, 102, 103. Camden, *Elizabeth.*

5th March. 'A LOOKING GLASS FOR LONDON.' *A.R.*, ii. 645. Thomas Lodge and Robert Greene, *A Looking Glass for London*, 1594. Modern edition by J. Churton Collins in *The Plays and Poems of Robert Greene*, 1905.

6th March. THE CORONATION OF THE FRENCH KING. *The Order of Ceremonies observed in the anointing and Coronation of the most Christian French King, and of Navarre, Henry IV. of that name*, 1594. Entered 23rd April.

13th March. Dr. Lopez's Health. *S.P. Dom.*, ccxlviii. 26.

14th March. Lopez's Accomplices Arraigned. *S.P. Dom.*, ccxlviii. 26.

26th March. Atheistical Speeches of Sir Walter Ralegh. *Harleian MSS.*, 6849, ff. 183-9, printed as an appendix in my edition of *Willobie His Avisa*, Bodley Head Quartos, vol. xv.

30th March. Great Storms. Stow, *Annals.*

31st March. Death of Sir John Burgh. *S.P. Dom.*, ccxlviii. 54. Approximate date. For the inference that Sir John met his death at this time see the *D.N.B.* See Appendix I., page 395.

4th April. The Queen's Bounty to Mr. William Camden. *P.S. Dom.*, ccxlviii. 60.

6th April. Plays at the Rose Theatre. *Hens. Diary*, i. 17. *King Leir and his three daughters* was entered *S.R.* 14th May, 1594; beyond the general outline it bears little resemblance to Shakespeare's tragedy.

9th April. Plays at the Rose Theatre. *Hens. Diary*, i. 17.

11th April. A Great Rainstorm. Stow, *Annals.*

16th April. Death of the Earl of Derby. Stow, *Annals*, where further symptoms are detailed.

18th April. Lopez Execution Postponed. *Salisbury Papers*, iv. 512, 513.

23rd April. St. George's Day. Foreign Orders. *Letters of Philip Gawdy*, p. 81. Roxburghe Club, 1907.

Gibbon's 'Praise of a Good Name.' *A.R.*, ii. 647. C. G., *The Praise of a Good Name*, 1594. The essays at the end of the book in style are not unlike Bacon's, which they anticipate by four years. It is interesting to note that Gibbon's *Work worth the Reading*, was dedicated to Sir Nicholas Bacon, elder brother of Francis.

29th April. Lady Branch Buried. W. Har[?]. *Epicedium. A Funeral Song upon the death of Lady Helen Branch*, 1594. This is the first reference to Shakespeare's *Lucrece*, which was entered 9th May. Joshua Sylvester, *Monodia*, n.d.; it is quite as bad as the *Epicedium.*

The Growth of Popery. *S.P. Dom.*, ccxlviii. 83.

1st May. Sir John Smythe's 'Instructions, Observations and Orders Military.' Sir John Smythe, *Instructions, Observations and Orders Military*, composed in 1591, entered 12th April, 1594; dated 1st May in the preface. See page 345 and note thereon.

2nd May. 'The Taming of a Shrew.' *A.R.*, ii. 648. *The Taming of a Shrew*, 1594. Modern edition by F. S. Boas, 1908. The source play for Shakespeare's *Taming of the Shrew.*

3rd May. Great Floods. Stow, *Annals.*

Sir Nicholas Clifford and the Order of St. Michael. *Salisbury Papers*, iv. 523.

9th May. The Rape of Lucrece. *A.R.*, ii. 648. William Shakespeare, *The Rape of Lucrece*, 1594. Modern edition by C. Knox Pooler, in the *Arden Shakespeare*, 1911; etc.

14th May. GREENE'S 'FRIAR BACON.' *A.R.*, ii. 649. Robert Greene, *The Honourable History of Friar Bacon and Friar Bungay*, 1594. Modern edition by J. Churton Collins, *Plays and Poems of Robert Greene*, 1905; A. W. Ward, *Dr. Faustus* and *Friar Bacon*, 1878; etc.

16th May. PLAYING RESUMED. *Hens. Diary*, i. 17; ii. 163. *Cutlack* has not survived.

17th May. MARLOWE'S 'JEW OF MALTA.' *A.R.*, ii. 631. Christopher Marlowe, *The Jew of Malta*, first surviving edition, 1633; modern editions by C. Tucker Brooke, 1910, etc.

30th May. DRAYTON'S 'IDEA'S MIRROR.' *A.R.*, ii. 648. Michael Drayton, *Idea's Mirror*, 1594. Modern edition by Cyril Brett, 1907. The best of the Idea Sonnets are mostly to be found in the later editions.

3rd June. THE DEATH OF THE BISHOP OF LONDON. Stow, *Annals*.

THE PLAYERS OF THE LORD ADMIRAL AND THE LORD CHAMBERLAIN UNITE. *Hens. Diary*, i. 17.

7th June. LOPEZ, TINOCO AND FERRARA EXECUTED. Stow, *Annals*; Camden, *Elizabeth*.

8th June. PLAYS OF THE WEEK. *Hens. Diary*, i. 17; ii. 163. *Hester and Assuerus* is unknown.

15th June. PLAYS OF THE WEEK. *Hens. Diary*, i. 17; ii. 164. *Bellendon* is probably *Belin Dun*, entered on 24th November, 1595, as 'The time-tragical history of King Rufus the first with the life and death of Belin Dun the first thief that ever was hanged in England.' No copy is known, but the play was one of the Admiral's most successful.

18th June. LYLY'S 'MOTHER BOMBY.' *A.R.*, ii. 654. John Lyly, *Mother Bomby*, 1594. Modern edition by R. W. Bond in *The Complete Works of John Lyly*, 1902.

19th June. THE TRUE TRAGEDY OF RICHARD THE THIRD. *A.R.*, ii. 655. *The True Tragedy of Richard the Third.* Modern edition by W. C. Hazlitt, 1875.

21st June. THE SPANIARDS AT BREST. *Salisbury Papers*, iv. 552.

22nd June. THE CHAMBERLAIN'S BREAK WITH THE ADMIRAL'S. *Hens. Diary*, i. 17. J. Tucker Murray, *English Dramatic Companies*, i. 88 *et seq.* I assume that Shakespeare had now joined them; but see Appendix I, p. 392.

26th June. THE FUNERAL OF THE BISHOP OF LONDON. Stow, *Annals*.

THE CHARACTER OF BISHOP AYLMER. Sir John Harington, *Nugae Antiquae*.

27th June. PLAYS OF THE WEEK. *Hens. Diary*, i. 17; ii. 165. Nothing is known of *Galiaso*.

5th July. VIOLENCE IN WESTMINSTER. *Middlesex Sessions Rolls*, i. 215.

6th July. PLAYS OF THE WEEK. *Hens. Diary*, i. 18.

12th July. SIDNEY SUSSEX COLLEGE IN CAMBRIDGE FOUNDED. *S.P. Dom.*, ccxlix, 26.

13th July. PLAYS OF THE WEEK. *Hens. Diary*, i. 18; ii. 160. Nothing certain is known of *Philipo and Hippolito*.

15th July. CRUELTY IN PORTUGAL. *Salisbury Papers*, iv. 562.

16th July. Soldiers for Brest. *S.P. Dom.*, ccxlix. 29.

20th July. The Spanish Preparations. *Salisbury Papers*, iv. 566.

Plays of the Week. *Hens. Diary*, i. 18; ii. 166. *Godfrey of Bulloigne* probably dealt with the Siege of Jerusalem. See Dr. Greg's note.

21st July. Captain Dawtry's Offer to lead an Irish Regiment. *Salisbury Papers*, iv. 566.

Mr. J. Dawtrey (in *The Falstaff Saga*, 1927) claimed Captain Dawtry as the original of Falstaff. The gallant Captain certainly had many of Falstaff's characteristics; he was moreover 'very large and unwieldy,' and a difficult object to move when wounded.

26th July. John Boste, a Jesuit, Executed. *Cath. Rec. Soc.*, v. p. 286.

25th July. The Earl of Essex not allowed to go to Brest. Birch's *Memoirs*, i. 181.

27th July. Disorders at the Port of Ipswich. *Salisbury Papers*, iv. 570.

Plays of the Week. *Hens. Diary*, i. 18.

1st August. A Proclamation concerning Prizes. *Proclamations*, 326.

4th August. Plays of the Week. *Hens. Diary*, i. 18; ii. 166.

8th August. Platt's 'Jewel House of Nature.' *A.R.*, ii. 656. Hugh Platt, *The Jewel House of Art and Nature*, 1594. For details of Platt's life see *D.N.B.* A most interesting and entertaining book. Some of the receipts belong to the long order of untried experiments, but Platt is a genuine inventor who observed for himself and was not merely content to use the scissors on other men's books.

10th August. Plays of the Week. *Hens. Diary*, i. 18.

17th August. Plays of the Week. *Hens. Diary*, i. 18; ii. 167. *Tasso's Melancholy* is not known.

19th August. Captain Glemham's Exploits in the Levant Seas. *A.R.* ii. 657. Entered 19th August. R. H., *News from the Levant Seas*, 1594.

20th August. The Lady Bridget Manners. *Hist. MSS. Com.*, *Rutland MSS.*, i. 322. See 20th November, 1592.

A Plot to Kill the Queen. *S.P. Dom.*, ccxlix. 98. One of several confessions.

Suitors at Court to be Restrained. *Proclamations*, 327.

21st August. A Further Confession of Captain Yorke. *S.P. Dom.*, ccxlix. 103.

24th August. Further Confessions of the Plotters. *S.P. Dom.*, ccxlix. 114.

Plays of the Week. *Hens. Diary*, i. 18.

27th August. Williams' Confession. *S.P. Dom.*, ccxlix. 117.

28th August. Yorke and Williams Confronted. *S.P. Dom.*, ccxlix. 125.

An Order at Court. *Letters of Philip Gawdy*, p. 90. Roxburgh Club, 1906.

The Return of the Earl of Cumberland's Ships. Hakluyt, v. 69.

29th August. SIR JOHN NORRIS DELAYED. *S.P. Dom.*, ccxlix. 128.

31st August. PLAYS OF THE WEEK. *Hens. Diary*, i. 19; ii. 167. *Mahomet*, probably Greene's *Alphonsus of Aragon*. For the *Venetian Comedy* see Dr. Greg's note (ii. 170).

3rd September. 'WILLOBIE HIS AVISA.' *A.R.*, ii. 659. *Willobie His Avisa*, 1594. For a discussion and a tentative solution of the problem of *Willobie His Avisa* and its connection with Shakespeare, see my essay, appended to the reprint in vol. xv. of *The Bodley Head Quartos*, 1926.

DAVIS'S 'SEAMAN'S SECRETS.' *A.R.*, ii. 659. John Davis, *The Seaman's Secrets*, 1594.

5th September. THE SCOTTISH KING'S SON BAPTISED. *A True Reportarie of the most triumphant and Royal accomplishment of the Baptism of the most Excellent, right High and Mightie Prince, Frederick Henry: by the Grace of God, Prince of Scotland. Solemnized the 30th day of August, 1594. Printed by R. Waldegrave, Printer to his Royal Majesty.* Reprinted in London in 1603 on the accession of King James. See Appendix I., p. 401.

7th September. PLAYS OF THE WEEK. *Hens. Diary*, i. 19.

8th September. GILES FLETCHER'S 'LICIA.' Giles Fletcher, *Licia, or Poems of Love*: dated in the Epistle Dedicatory 4th September, 1594; in the Epistle to the reader 8th September. The sonnets are not above the average, but the reference to the 'jar of this disagreeing age' is an interesting sign of the growth of the melancholic humour which was so prevalent five years later. Modern edition in Arber's *English Garner*, vol. viii.

9th September. THE COUNTESS OF RUTLAND AND THE LADY BRIDGET. *Hist. MSS. Com., Rutland MSS.*, i. 323. See 20th August.

10th September. NEWS FROM BREST. *News from Brest. A diurnal of all that Sir John Norris hath done since his last arrival in Brest*, 1594.

11th September. SIR THOMAS WILKES TO BE SENT TO THE ARCHDUKE ERNEST. *Salisbury Papers*, v. 12, 13.

14th September. PLAYS OF THE WEEK. *Hens. Diary*, i. 19.

18th September. THE WAR IN BRITTANY. *News from Brest.*

A DUTCH MILL. *Remembrancia*, ii. 15.

21st September. PLAYS OF THE WEEK. *Hens. Diary*, i. 19; ii. 168. Nothing is known of *Palamon and Arcite*, but presumably it was founded on Chaucer's *Knight's Tale*.

28th September. PLAYS OF THE WEEK. *Hens. Diary*, i. 19; ii. 160. *The Love of an English Lady* is unknown.

30th September. THE ALCHEMIST'S BEQUEST. *S.P. Dom.*, ccl. 9. See 19th January and 2nd February.

THE BAD WEATHER AND THE PRICE OF GRAIN. Stow, *Annals*. See Appendix I., p. 400.

3rd October. INMATES TO BE REMOVED. *Remembrancia*, ii. No. 17. Inmates are lodgers; in the spacious days men lived as close as in a modern Oriental bazaar, and as squalidly. The original is dated 1593, but as (*a*) it occurs in the middle of a number of letters written in 1594, and (*b*) the infection in the beginning of October 1593 was far from 'late,' I venture to correct what seems an obvious error.

5th October. PLAYS OF THE WEEK. *Hens. Diary*, i. 19; ii. 169. Nothing is certainly known of *The Love of a Grecian Lady.*

6th October. LE ROY'S 'OF THE INTERCHANGEABLE COURSE OF THINGS.' Louis Le Roy, *Of the Interchangeable Course of Things*, 1594. Dated in the Epistle; no entry in *S.R.* The author is very vaguely probing after scientific methods of inquiry.

12th October. PLAYS OF THE WEEK. *Hens. Diary*, i. 19.

15th October. THE LADY BRIDGET AT COURT. *Hist. MSS., Rutland MS.*, i. 324. See 9th September.

18th October. CAPTAIN ANTHONY WINGFIELD SLAIN. *News from Brest.*

19th October. PLAYS OF THE WEEK. *Hens. Diary*, i. 19; ii. 170. For a discussion of *The French Doctor* see Dr. Greg's note.

20th October. THE DISRESPECT OF THE ARCHDUKE ERNEST. *Salisbury Papers*, v. 12, 13. See page 349 and note.

25th October. PLAYS OF THE WEEK. *Hens. Diary*, i. 20; ii. 171. *A Knack to Know an Honest Man.*

NASHE'S 'TERRORS OF THE NIGHT.' Thomas Nashe, *The Terrors of the Night*, 1594. Modern edition by R. B. M'Kerrow in *The Works of Thomas Nashe*, vol. ii. 1904. The book, for some reason, was entered twice, on 30th June, 1593, and again on 25th October, 1594; but the earliest edition is dated 1594, and on internal evidence (for which see Dr. M'Kerrow's notes) was not written before that date. An amusing skit, and, as are all Nashe's books, an admirable gloss on contemporary gossip.

31st October. SIR JOHN NORRIS'S ATTACK ON THE FORT AT CROYZON. *News from Brest*, 1594.

2nd November. PLAYS OF THE WEEK. *Hens. Diary*, i. 20.

3rd November. THE SERMON AT PAUL'S CROSS. John Dove, *A Sermon preached at Paul's Cross the 3rd November*, 1594.

A PETITION AGAINST A NEW THEATRE. *Remembrancia*, ii. 73. Quoted in *Malone Society Collections*, i. 74. It is no small tribute to Nashe that the Lord Mayor should officially condemn the arguments in favour of plays made by Pierce Penilesse (see p. 151).

4th November. THE STATE OF IRELAND. MSS. Harl, 6996, f. ii. 6. Quoted in Thomas Wright, *Queen Elizabeth and her Times*, 1838, ii. 438.

9th November. PLAYS OF THE WEEK. *Hens. Diary*, i. 20; ii. 171. Nothing is known of *Caesar and Pompey.*

15th November. THE ASSAULT ON THE FORT AT CROYZON. *News from Brest*, 1594.

16th November. PLAYS OF THE WEEK. *Hens. Diary*, i. 20; ii. 171. For *Dioclesian*, see Dr. Greg's note.

17th November. MEASURES AGAINST VAGRANTS AND BEGGING POOR. *Remembrancia*, ii. No. 74.

THE QUEEN'S ACCESSION DAY. *Fugger News-letters*, 2nd series, p. 262.

19th November. SPENSER'S 'AMORETTI' AND 'EPITHALAMIUM.' Edmund Spenser, *Amoretti* and *Epithalamium*, 1595. *A.R.*, ii. 655. Modern edition by J. C. Smith and E. de Selincourt, 1912, etc.

20th November. THE USE OF THE CITY GARNERS REFUSED. *Remembrancia*, ii. No. 79.

23rd November. PLAYS OF THE WEEK. *Hens. Diary*, i. 20.

27th November. THE LADY BRIDGET MANNERS. *Hist. MSS. Com. Rutland MSS.*, i. 324. See 15th Oct.

30th November. PLAYS OF THE WEEK. *Hens. Diary*, i. 20; ii. 172. Nothing is known of *Warlamchester*.

A CONFERENCE ABOUT THE SUPPRESSING OF ROGUES. *Remembrancia*, ii. Nos. 75, 76.

2nd December. A PROCLAMATION AGAINST FIREARMS. *Proclamations*, 328.

DE LA MARCHE'S 'THE RESOLVED GENTLEMAN.' Oliver de la Marche, *The Resolved Gentleman*, translated by L. Lewkenor, 1594.

6th December. SIR W. RALEGH'S COMMISSION. *S.P. Dom.*, ccl. 46.

7th December. PLAYS OF THE WEEK. *Hens. Diary*, i. 20; ii. 172. *The Wise Man of West Chester* is Anthony Munday's *John a Kent and John a Cumber* which exists in manuscript. It has been reprinted by the Malone Society.

8th December. THE DEATH OF CARDINAL ALLEN. Camden's *Elizabeth; Salisbury Papers*, v. 27. A racy account of Allen's English college at Rome, and the various squabbles, is given in Anthony Munday's *English Roman Life*, 1582; printed in vol. xii. of *The Bodley Head Quartos*.

14th December. REVELS TO BE HELD AT GRAY'S INN. *Gesta Grayorum*, first printed in 1688. Modern editions in Nichol's *Progresses of Queen Elizabeth*, and the Malone Society's Reprints, 1914.

PLAYS OF THE WEEK. *Hens. Diary*, i. 20; ii. 172. For the *Set at Maw*, see Dr. Greg's note.

20th December. THE REVELS AT GRAY'S INN. *Gesta Grayorum.* See Appendix I., p. 402-3.

21st December. PLAYS OF THE WEEK. *Hens. Diary*, i. 21.

24th December. 'A CONFERENCE ABOUT THE NEXT SUCCESSION.' N. Doleman, *A Conference about the next Succession*, 1594. The date is approximate and possibly too soon.

THE ORCHARD AND THE GARDEN. *The Orchard and the Garden*, 1594.

26th December. AN ATTEMPT TO MURDER THE FRENCH KING. *The Decree of the Court of Parliament against John Chastel*, 1595. Entered 28th December, 1594.

27th December. PLAYS OF THE WEEK. *Hens. Diary*, i. 21.

28th December. THE CHAMBERLAIN'S PLAYERS AT COURT. E. K. Chambers, *Elizabethan Stage*, iv. 164.

GRAY'S INN REVELS: A NIGHT OF ERRORS. *Gesta Grayorum.* For discussions of the Shakespearean allusions, see the commentators and Mrs. C. C. Stopes' *The Third Earl of Southampton*, pp. 71-6.

30th December. DR. FLETCHER ELECTED BISHOP OF LONDON. Stow, *Annals*. He was the father of the dramatist, at this time aged 15.

PLAYS AT THE ROSE. *Hens. Diary*, i. 21.

'THE DISPLAY OF FOLLY.' O. B., *The Display of Folly*, 1594. The book is catalogued thus in the Short Title Catalogue, and in the Catalogue of the British Museum, but its title page reads *Questions of Profitable and Pleasant concernings*; the sub-title of the text is 'The display of Folly' and the running title 'The Display of vain Life.'

BARNFIELD'S 'AFFECTIONATE SHEPHERD.' Richard Barnfield, *The Affectionate Shepherd*, 1594. Modern edition by J. O. Halliwell, Percy Society, 1847.

BARWICK'S 'BRIEF DISCOURSE.' Humphrey Barwick, *A Brief Discourse Concerning the force and effect of all manual weapons of fire*, n.d. See page 299. Sir Roger Williams in *A Brief Discourse of War*, 1590, had claimed that 'a hundred muskets are to be valued unto two hundred calivers or more: the calivers may say they will discharge two shot for one, but cannot deny but one musket shot doth more hurt than two calivers, shot far or near, and better cheap, although the musket spend a pound of powder in eight or twelve shots, and the other smaller shoots twenty and thirty of a pound.'

'THE DEATH OF USURY.' *The Death of Usury*, 1594. An anonymous work, apparently a young law student's notebook.

GRASSI'S 'TRUE ART OF DEFENCE.' *Giacomo di Grassi his true Art of Defence*, translated by I. G., 1594.

HOOKER'S 'ECCLESIASTICAL POLITY.' Richard Hooker, *Of the Laws of Ecclesiastical Polity*, 1594. Entered 29th January, 1593. Modern edition by Ronald Bayne in the *Everyman Library*, 1907, etc.

LAMBARD'S 'EIRENARCHA.' William Lambard, *Eirenarcha*, 1594.

MARLOWE AND NASHE'S 'DIDO, QUEEN OF CARTHAGE.' Christopher Marlowe and Thomas Nashe, *Dido, Queen of Carthage*, 1594. Modern edition by C. F. Tucker Brooke, in *The Works of Christopher Marlowe*, 1910.

'THE BATTLE OF ALCAZAR.' *The Battle of Alcazar*, 1594. Modern edition by W. W. Greg, Malone Society Reprints, 1907. See also Dr. Greg's *Orlando and Alcazar*, in the same series.

PERCY'S 'SONNETS TO THE FAIREST COELIA.' William Percy, *Sonnets to the Fairest Coelia*, 1594. Modern edition by A. B. Grosart, 1877.

'PRESENT REMEDIES AGAINST THE PLAGUE.' *Present Remedies against the Plague*, 1594.

'A TRUE REPORT OF SUNDRY HORRIBLE CONSPIRACIES.' *A True Report of Sundry Horrible Conspiracies*, 1594; propaganda for neutrals, possibly prepared for the edification of the Archduke Ernest's subjects, or else issued after his rebuff (see p. 327). The pamphlet was translated into French.

ADDENDA AND CORRIGENDA

3rd March, 1593. DR. UDALL'S PETITION. Udall died in prison a few days afterwards.

2nd February, 1594. THE ALCHEMIST'S BEQUEST. This note is wrong. From subsequent letters in *Salisbury Papers* it appears that the Queen was to be given first offer of the bodies for £500. Ultimately she decided not to buy.

24th December, 1594. 'A CONFERENCE ABOUT THE NEXT SUCCESSION.' This entry is premature. The book was not generally known in England until late September, 1595 (*Sidney Papers*, i, 350).

APPENDIX I

THE STATIONERS' REGISTER

In theory every book ought to have been entered in the *Stationers' Register* before printing; in practice the Elizabethan printer was as casual over his entries in the *Register* as in his obedience to any other kind of regulation. Many books were never entered at all, some after printing but before publication, some after publication. A few of the entries in the *Register* were intended to establish copyright and thereby to block publication; some were made before the books were even written.

For the four years the total number of new books entered was roughly 138 in 1591, 136 in 1592, 110 in 1593 (the plague year), rising to 162 in 1594. These figures are approximate, as it is not always possible to tell whether a book is new or old, though entered for the first time. In 1591, for instance, the total includes 14 foreign works entered to Wolfe, and 9 classics, all entered together. In 1592, 5 ballads, included in the total, may be old ballads, entered to maintain copyright. A margin of error of at least 10 per cent. should therefore be allowed in all totals.

(1) *Books not entered.* Many books (probably not less than one-fifth) were never entered; but there seems to be no principle governing either entry or omission. Of a total of 36 books written by Greene, 29 were entered. Of his five Conny-catching pamphlets written in 1591 and 1592, the *Notable discouery of Coosenage*, the *Second part of conny-catching* and the *Third part* were entered; *A disputation betweene a hee conny-catcher and a shee conny-catcher* was omitted; *The blacke bookes messenger* was entered. Only 6 out of 16 works by Lodge were entered; whilst of 11 by Nashe, only 3 were left out—two anti-Martinist pamphlets, and *Haue with you to Saffron-walden*, whose omission is not surprising. Hence, of these three authors, 20 books out of a total of 63 were not entered, or rather less than a third.

(2) *Normal entry.* It is rare for the biography of a book to survive. One instance is Simon Forman's *Grounds of Longitude.* Forman noted in his Diary that he sent the book to the press on 6th July, 1591; it was entered on 12th July, and published before the end of the year. Another instance is *The most strange discouerie of the three witches of Warboys*, who were executed on 7th April, 1593 (p. 224 and note). The book was submitted for entry on 30th June, and probably published at the end of November, as a ballad, *The Lamentable Song of the*

Three Witches of Warboys, was entered on 4th December, being presumably founded on the printed book.

Ballads were often published when a sensational book or play came out, and publishers sometimes entered both book and ballad together to secure their double right. Thus on 29th August, 1594, Gosson, Millington, and Dawson entered a pamphlet describing the execution of Thomas Merry for murdering Robert Beeche and his servant, and at the same time a ballad of 'Beche his ghoste, complayninge on ye wofull murder committed on him and Thomas Winchester his Servaunt.' There are several other instances.

(3) *Books entered after printing.* Two instances may be noted. The first is Greene's *Notable discouery of Coosenage*, which was entered as *The Arte of Connye katchinge*, together with the *Second parte of Connye katchinge*, on 13th December, 1591. Greene in his preface to the *Second part* answered certain objections to the style of the *Notable discovery*, which had therefore been published and criticized before the preface to the *Second part* was written.

A second instance is Simon Kellwaye's *Defensative against the plague* (p. 217), which is worth following in detail because the evidence is unusually full. The book was entered on 21st March, 1593. An epistle dedicatory to the Earl of Essex is dated 25th March, 1592 (*i.e.* 1593); the Epistle to the Reader is dated 25th March, 1593; next comes a commendation of the author by George Baker, dated 'from my chamber in Court this 7 of Aprill 1593'; finally, the preliminary matter ends with the 'Author to the Reader,' noting the faults escaped, and dated 8th April, 1593. The text of the book begins with signature B 1, as is usual with first editions, and contains 100 pages of matter, set up mainly in black letter, with many medical prescriptions tabulated in roman and italic, and an index.

The history of the book's publication seems to be that as soon as the text had been set up, Windet took a copy to Stationers' Hall and entered it from the printed title-page, which reads: *A defensative against the Plague: contayning two partes or treatises: the first, showing the meanes how to preserve vs from the dangerous contagion thereof: the Second, how to cure those that are infected therewith.* The entry, except for the words 'showing the meanes,' is word for word the same. Next, a few advance copies were assembled, without the preliminary matter, one of which the author sent to the Earl of Essex, others to his friends. Meanwhile the text was checked by Kellwaye, who on 8th April sent in the preliminary matter, corrections, and index.

If, on the other hand, this interpretation of the dates is wrong and *A defensative against the Plague* was entered before printing, it follows that the whole of the text was set up, proofs read, and an index prepared between 21st March and 8th April, which is quick work.

The title of a book as entered in the *Stationers' Register* sometimes varies considerably from that printed on the title-page, but that at other times quite a long title is quoted word for word, or else the beginning is quoted and the rest cut off by '&c.' The probable explanation (though it cannot be proved definitely) is that when a 'long-tailed title' is accurately transcribed in the *Register*, then the entry was made from a *printed copy*. Thus, on the one hand, Shakespeare's *Merchant of Venice* was entered on 17th July, 1598, as 'a booke of the Marchaunt of Venyce or otherwise called the Jewe of Venyce,' but on the title-page reads 'The most excellent Historie of the Merchant of Venice. With the extreame cruelties of Shylocke the Iewe towards the sayd Merchant, in cutting a iust pound of his flesh: and the obtayning of Portia by the choyse of three chests. As it hath beene diuers times acted by the Lord Chamberlaine his Seruants. Written by William Shakespeare.' On the other hand the *Firste part of the Contention* is entered as 'the firste parte of the Contention of the twoo famous houses of York and Lancaster with the deathe of the good Duke Humfrey and the banishement and Deathe of the Duke of Suffolk and the tragicall ende of the prowd Cardinall of Winchester with the notable rebellion of Iack Cade and the Duke of Yorkes ffirste clayme vnto the Crowne,' which is word for word the same as the title-page except that the *Register* reads 'of the twoo' for 'betwixt the twoo.'

(4) *Blocking entry.* Blocking entries used to prevent the publication of a manuscript against the owner's wishes are usually difficult to establish, because when there is a wide interval between the date of entry and of the first known edition it may be due to the fact that no copy of an earlier issue has survived.

A probable instance of a blocking entry is Thomas Campion's *Observations in the arte of Englishe poesie*, entered on 12th October, 1591. The earliest known edition is that of 1602, which evoked a reply in Daniel's *Defence of Ryme* (1603). On internal evidence the *Observations* was more likely to have been written in 1591, when the use of classical metres in English verse was being widely discussed, but the 1602 edition bears every sign of being the first: it is, moreover, dedicated to the Lord Buckhurst as Lord High Treasurer, an office which in 1591 was held by Lord Burleigh.

Another instance is Sir Philip Sidney's *The defence of poesie*, which was entered on 29th November, 1594. *Astrophel and Stella* had been published without the consent of the family in 1591, and it was apparently to prevent another unauthorized publication that Ponsonby (who was the authorized printer of Sidney's works) entered *The defence*. Some months later (12th April, 1595) Olney entered and printed another version, *An apologie for poetry*, but Ponsonby naturally complained, the entry was cancelled, and the note added, 'This belongeth to master ponsonby by a former entrance And an agrement is made between them whereby Master Ponsonby is to enioy the copie according to the former entrance.' Ponsonby's edition is dated 1595.

(5) *Books entered before they were written.* The evidence for this practice is simply cold chronology. On 25th January, 1591, Captain

Arnold Cosbye was executed forty-eight hours after trial for the murder of the Lord Burke (p. 7); the same day was entered to Edward White *The arraynement and Condemnacon of Arnalt Cosbye for murderinge the lord Burghe.* It is a long semi-official account of the trial and gives a short note of the execution. On the other hand the 'mournful Dyttye' which White produced on the same subject was not entered till 6th February, being forestalled by R. Robinson, who entered the 'sorowfull sighes of a sadd soule' for the untimely loss of Lord Burke on 26th January.

Similarly, on 28th July, 1591, was entered to Robert Bourne *The Life, araynement, Iudgement and Execution of William Hacket,* who was quartered that morning in Cheapside (p. 45). This book, not to be confused with Cosin's *Conspiracy for Pretended Reformation* (p. 59), has perished.

On 28th June, 1592, John Parker and Anne Bruen were executed for poisoning John Bruen, goldsmith (p. 145). The same day was entered to John Kyd, 'the Iudgment and execucon of John Parker, goldsmithe, and Anne Bruen for poysoninge her late husband John Bruen goldsmithe.' John Kyd was an enterprising publisher, who tried to forestall competitors by entering his book early; but the officials of the Company were not entirely satisfied, for there was added a note in the Register, 'Prouided that this booke before yt be printed shalbe drawen into good forme and order and then laufullie allowed to be printed.' The title of the printed book is:

> 'The trueth of the most wicked and secret murthering of Iohn Brewen, Goldsmith of London, committed by his owne wife, through the prouocation of one Iohn Parker whom she loued: for which fact she was burned, and he hanged in Smithfield, on wednesday, the 28 of Iune, 1592, two yeares after the murther was committed.'

The Bruen case inspired several ballads. Jeffs got in with 'The Lamentation of Agnes Bruen' on 1st July: Wolfe followed with 'A ballad of the Burnynge of Anne Bruen' on 10th July, and 'John Parker's lamentacon' on the 11th: finally Jeffs provided another 'lamentacion' for John Parker on the 15th. This last entry from its fullness suggests that the ballad was already in print; it reads: 'The Lamentacion of John Parker whoe for consentinge to the murder of John Bruen was hanged in Smithfeild the 28 of June 2 yeres after the fact was committed to the tune of fortune.' The similarity between this title and the title of the pamphlet is worth noting.

On 22nd August, 1592, occurs an entry, again to John Kyd, which is conclusive: 'Entred for his copie by warrant from master Watkins, a booke, of the true reporte of the poysoninge of Thomas Elliott Tailor of London. Prouided that this booke must be perused by master Watkins before yt be printed.' Clearly Master Watkins had not seen the book.

Finally, on 15th November, 1594, was entered 'a ballad of the triumphes at the tilte and thanksgyvinge the xvii of November 1594 for their maiesties xxxvii yeares Reigne,' that is, two days *before* the event happened.

In all five entries the circumstances are similar; they show that entry in the *Register* was used to stake a claim in a piece of startling news, as well as to prevent an unlawful publication. Unfortunately for the *Elizabethan Journal* most of these pamphlets and ballads have perished.

APPENDIX II

NEWS PAMPHLETS

Of the total of some 546 new books entered in the *Stationers' Register* during the period 1591-4, 129 items are concerned with current news, of which 79 are prose and 46 verse, mostly ballads. These figures again are approximate: it is not always possible to tell whether an entry refers to a prose or a verse work, or whether it is news or fiction. Greene's *Black bookes messenger*, for instance, is entered as 'The Repentance of a Cony catcher with the life and death of Mourton and Ned Browne, twoo notable cony catchers The one latelie executed at Tyborne the other at Aix in ffraunce' (p. 155). At first sight it appears to be a news pamphlet; actually the book, as published, contained only the life and death of Ned Browne, and that a manifest fiction.

The issue of news pamphlets was very erratic, and the list is more remarkable for what it omits than what it includes. Nothing was entered which bears on the Lopez conspiracy,[1] and Hacket's execution was unsung in any ballad; as, however, he died blaspheming, a doleful repentance would have been out of place. The figures for 1591-4 are as follows:

	1591. Prose.	Verse.	1592. P.	V.	1593. P.	V.	1594. P.	V.
Foreign News.								
(*a*) The War in France.	24	2	12	–	3	–	10	2
(*b*) General.	4	–	1	–	2	1	4	3
Naval.	4	2	–	1	–	–	1	–
Home News.	4	4	6	6	2	9	2	17
	36	8	19	7	7	10	17	22

The wars in France account for most of the news pamphlets. Twenty-six publications (including two ballads) were entered between 23rd January and 21st November, 1591, after which there was a break for three months, until 28th February, when their issue began again, and twelve were entered in four and a half months. Then there is a considerable gap, for from 19th July, 1592, to 14th April, 1594, only three entries are recorded. The reason for this is that the war was fluctuating and uncertain. The output of pamphlets rose in 1594 to ten in prose, with two ballads.

[1] There were, however, a number of news pamphlets and ballads which were not entered, e.g. *A true report of sundry horrible conspiracies* (p. 349).

Of these 49 French war pamphlets John Wolfe printed no less than 36. Most of them are founded on official or semi-official sources, such as proclamations or orders issued by the French King, the printed terms of truce with the Leaguers, information supplied by the French ambassador in England, and so forth. Those which describe the actions of the English troops are most interesting. Reverses and disasters, needless to say, were not recorded, nor was there much glorification of the army under the Earl of Essex, which accomplished very little.

Other foreign news takes up some fifteen entries, if indeed one may include under the heading of news certain strange birds seen in Flanders, or a monstrous child born in the Dukedom of Brabant, or such items as 'a booke of newes of Twoo angels that came before the Cytie of Droppa in Slesia' with 'a ballad of the same Twoo angelles.'

Naval events occupy two ballads and four prose works in 1591, one of them being Sir Walter Ralegh's account of the loss of the *Revenge*.

There are 50 entries of home news, of which 36 are ballads, mostly of murders, executions, and marvels, with half a dozen laments and epitaphs. Of the fourteen prose pamphlets, six are accounts of criminal trials and executions, and one is a description of Queen Elizabeth's progress to Elvetham.

These figures are taken from the *Register*; a number of books in each class survive which were never entered. It is worth noting that there is no attempt to record home news of any real importance, nor do affairs in Scotland occupy much space. Two semi-official Scotch pamphlets were entered between 1591 and 1594, the first dealing with the conspiracy of the papists in 1593 (p. 249), the second describing the baptism of Prince Henry in August 1594 (p. 320), which also gave birth to a ballad. No Irish pamphlet was entered.[1]

[1] The conclusions summarised in Appendices II and III are worked out at some length in my paper 'Books and Readers, 1591-4,' printed in the *Library*, vol. viii. p. 273.

INDEX

L

For Product Safety Concerns and Information please contact our EU
representative GPSR@taylorandfrancis.com
Taylor & Francis Verlag GmbH, Kaufingerstraße 24, 80331 München, Germany

www.ingramcontent.com/pod-product-compliance
Lightning Source LLC
Chambersburg PA
CBHW070931100726
47908CB00001B/178

* 9 7 8 0 4 1 5 6 0 5 9 3 9 *